The United States at War
Bunker Hill to Baghdad
The Real Story

by
Donald E. Ross

D1280217

DORRANCE PUBLISHING CO., INC.
PITTSBURGH, PENNSYLVANIA 15222

ISBN # 0-8059-6042-2
Printed in the United States of America

First Printing

For information or to order additional books, please write:
Dorrance Publishing Co., Inc.
701 Smithfield Street
Pittsburgh, Pennsylvania 15222
U.S.A.
1-800-788-7654
Or visit our web site on-line catalog at www.dorrancepublishing.com

This book is dedicated to Ginny, the girl next door and my wife for over fifty years. She has been everything I could have ever wished for as a wife.

Table of Contents

Chapter I
The Ascendancy of Democracy

From 1954 to 1975 the United States made a huge effort to stop the spread of communism to French Indochina. The finest American army ever sent to fight (up to that time) was victorious in every major battle yet was withdrawn, leaving the area to be eventually overcome. The true story of this war has never been adequately described and public understanding is virtually nonexistent. This situation is remedied in one of the last chapters of this work.

As historical accounts of all the U.S. wars describe events, but seldom explain the tactics, strategies, mistakes, and actions that should have been taken, this effort covers other major U.S. encounters, the Revolution, The Civil War, World War I, World War II, Korea, Vietnam, and the war with Iraq. These are the broadest conflicts, all fought primarily for principles beyond self interest. The Mexican War and Spanish–American War were somewhat limited in scope and relate to colonialism to some degree. The War of 1812 was primarily a series of naval battles.

To cover the largest battles in some detail, related accounts of political activities are mentioned only where they affect the course of the wars, and this history is therefore an account of the combat. Realistic descriptions of our losses are admitted, but the net result is a tribute to our fighting men from our first professionals, the Continentals, to the mighty divisions that guard our nation today.

In the Revolution a democracy was created, the first since ancient Greece. In the Civil War slavery was abolished and the Union preserved (fortunately for mankind). In World War I the imperialist Central Powers were defeated in the War to End All Wars.

In World War II the murderous Nazi German war machine was crushed by huge Russian armies and a powerful American-British alliance. In the Pacific Japan's bloody conquests were recovered and their armadas smashed by vast American fleets and armies aided by British and Chinese forces. From 1945 to 1989 communism threatened our way of life, but the malignant spread eastward was stopped in Korea and a communist victory in Indochina was denied until 1975. Communism, stoutly resisted and contained by the United States and our

1

allies, finally died in 1989, and democracy emerged supreme over all other forms of government.

This fortunate result is due in no small measure to the remarkable victories of American fighting men and women, and this story, no matter how factual and realistic, can only serve as a testimony to their achievements and sacrifice. Americans, immersed in day to day problems, probably don't appreciate the victory of democracy over the forces of aristocracy, but they will overcome their economic problems and historians will look back to say that the defeat of communism was the greatest moment in all history, the final victory of democracy.

In 1776, however, Americans were colonists, governed by a king thousands of miles away. There was a strong desire for self government and detachment from a despot whose primary interest was not the welfare of his subjects but the raising of funds from those governed. Fighting started and the colonists, embroiled in conflict, then had to find the means to defeat the finest troops in the world. In order to appreciate the nature of the enemy in this struggle, it is essential to explore the development of the British Army and the source of their pride and skill.

Chapter II
The British

The discipline and professional conduct of British troops can be attributed to a tradition begun under Oliver Cromwell. In the English Civil War pitting Parliament against the King, Cromwell served with the Parliamentary Army. In the first battle, Edgehill, on October 23, 1642, the Royalist Cavalry under Prince Rupert made one charge, went right through the Parliamentary Army causing severe casualties, then ran out of control. Cromwell noted the poor performance of both forces and began to raise and train his own regiment, called "The New Model." Cromwell was made a colonel and by May, 1643, he had a force of 500 cavalry. With other groups and a total force of 1,200 he met a Royalist force of 2,100 in Lincolnshire in May. Here he charged and put the Royalists to rout, killing 100 with the loss of only two of his own. On July 28, Cromwell joined up with Lord Willoughby and attacked the Royalists at Gainsborough with a force of 2,000 men. Cromwell dispersed the Royalist force and their reserves, gathered in his cavalry, and withdrew successfully in the presence of newly arrived and overwhelming Royalist squadrons. On October 10, in combination with Manchester and Fairfax, he put the Royalists to flight again at Winceby. The crucial battle, however, came in 1644.

On July 2 of that year 22,000 Parliamentary troops faced 18,000 Royalists under Prince Rupert on Marston Moor near the city of York. Cromwell commanded 2,500 cavalry on the left flank of the Parliamentary army. Cromwell's charge broke the Royalist cavalry opposite him. Cromwell was wounded and not on the field when Rupert's counterattack went through Cromwell's force only to be stopped by a second line of Scottish cavalry. Cromwell returned and led his cavalry forward again, routing the Royalist right wing. Then, still under control of his force, Cromwell went to the aid of the struggling Parliamentary cavalry on the right flank, routing the Royalists there. By dark the Royalist infantry in the center were destroyed and their army beaten, with 4,000 dead and 1,500 captured. Cromwell, whose troops were almost invincible, became known as "Old Ironsides."

In the winter of 1644–45, the New Model Army was organized with a planned force of 22,000 men and a uniform based on red coats.

On June 14, 1645, Cromwell commanded 6,500 cavalry, part of a 14,000 man Parliamentary army. He was opposed by a Royalist force of 9,000 at a place called Navesby. The Royalist cavalry attacked the Parliamentary cavalry on the left flank and went right through and out of control. These Parliamentary cavalry regrouped and fell upon Royalist infantry in the center. Cromwell, with the other Parliamentary cavalry, attacked Royalist cavalry on his right flank, dispersed them, and also turned on the enemy infantry. The result was the destruction of the major force available to the King.

The King's strongholds eventually fell, one after the other; King Charles I surrendered himself to the Scots on May 5, 1646, and Parliament ruled the country. The King was tried for treason and executed on January 30, 1649.

Parliament eventually became completely corrupt, passing laws that benefited members of Parliament. Cromwell used the army to close Parliament, took over leadership of the country as Lord Protector, and called for the election of a new Parliament. He was a benevolent ruler and is today much respected in England. A professional standing army was established and the official uniform was the red coat. The reason for choosing this particular color was the availability at the time of a cheap red dye.

Cromwell died on August 30, 1658; the country was then turned over to Charles II, the son of the executed King, who ruled (with far less authority) together with Parliament.

It is amazing that one man, with limited military experience, could raise and train an army capable of beating government forces. Obviously the King's army lacked numbers, training, and leadership. For this oversight he paid with his life.

The experiments by the English at this time with government by a monarch, government by a legislature, and a government by executive and legislative bodies provided the background experience used by the American scholars who wrote the Constitution in the next century.

The training, discipline, and uniform dress of the army that started with Cromwell's New Model Regiment remained, and the magnificent performance of British forces in the next major war, The War of the Spanish Succession, was a direct consequence.

Marlborough

In the years prior to 1700, Louis XIV of France was called the Sun King. His country dominated Europe as far east as Austria. These were golden times for France; their armies were huge, experienced, and highly regarded. These were the times of d'Artagnan and the Three Musketeers.

In the year 1700, King Charles XI of Spain died. He had no immediate successor and Louis placed his grandson, Philip, on the Spanish throne. The Dutch, English, and Austrians could not accept this, and the War of the Spanish Succession began in 1701.

France occupied the Spanish Netherlands (Belgium), and in early 1702 a French army of 70,000 men under Marshal Boufflers crossed the Meuse River and moved on Nimwegen in Holland. The Dutch had a good army but they chose an English general, John Churchill (Winston Churchill's antecedent), the Duke of Marlborough, as their general. Marlborough promised to quickly relieve Nimwegen, and he did by taking his Dutch, English, and German army across the Meuse, moving south to cut the French supply line. The French, forced to retreat, were also forced to march directly across the front of Marlborough's drawn up army. An attack by the Allies at this point would have been a French disaster, but the Dutch would not risk losing their army and rejected Marlborough's request for permission to attack. The war became one of maneuver and it wasn't until 1704 that Marlborough, with English, Danish, and German forces, marched to the Danube to join Prince Eugene and the Austrians. At Blenheim on the Danube, the combined armies faced the French under Marshal Tallard. An army of 60,000 French and Bavarians faced 56,000 Allies on the evening of August 12, 1704, in the usual parade ground fashion, but on the morning of August 13, the French awakened to see miles of enemy lines coming at them out of the morning mists. The French took the field and the battle began. English infantry fiercely attacked the village of Blenheim (on the Danube) on their left. Austrians attacked on the right. The French feared the loss of the village and pulled infantry reserves from their center. Then Marlborough struck at the center with line after line of cavalry and infantry. The French cavalry in the center were swept into the Danube, their infantry in Blenheim captured, and the remnants of the army chased from the field. The French, in one day, were thrown out of Germany and back to France.

Their losses were 38,600 wounded, killed, or captured, including Tallard. Allied losses were 12,700. After this battle Louis instructed his generals to avoid battle with Marlborough, but in 1706 Louis changed his mind giving permission to fight and advising the generals to put their best troops opposite the English.

On May 23, 1706, Marlborough met the French again under Marshal Villeroy at Ramilles in Belgium. Sixty-three-thousand French were arranged in an arc on high ground. Sixty-two-thousand Allies occupied a straight ridgeline with a shorter distance between flanks. English infantry attacked on their right flank where the French line of retreat was threatened. Allied cavalry attacked Le Maison du Roc (King's Household Cavalry) on the Allied left flank. With the French heavily engaged on his right, Marlborough took most of the cavalry from the right and joined the Allied cavalry on his left. Now the Allies had a five to three advantage over the French cavalry. This splendid host was overwhelmed and the whole French line crumbled. The French lost 12,000 dead or wounded; 6,000 captured; and 30,000 missing. Life at the Sun King's court was much less sunny after this affair. Much of Belgium was lost to the French, but another battle would be required to bring the war into France.

Marlborough was constantly harried by Dutch ministers who followed his army and demanded he not risk their army in pitched battles. Therefore the war continued interminably until Marlborough, with Prince Eugene and 89,000 men, was able to force a battle. On July 11, 1708, Marlborough caught the French again, under Marshal Vendomme with 100,000 men at Oudenard in Belgium. There both armies were on the march, and as the regiments reached the field they were quickly added to the line.

Marlborough placed a small cavalry group near the river on his right and for some unknown reason the large French force facing them never attacked. Marlborough meanwhile kept extending his line to the left until, by nightfall, the French were virtually surrounded. During the night the French split into small groups and dispersed. They lost 6,000 killed and wounded; 9,000 captured; with 15,000 dispersed all over Belgium. The Allies lost only 3,000 and the road to France was at last open.

On both sides of the border there were numerous fortified cities and the path to Paris was strewn with major obstacles. Fortified cities could not be bypassed, as troops in these places would prevent the delivery of supplies to an army that attempted to avoid them. In 1709, outside Mons, another major battle was fought. In two days of fighting in wooded country where the French fought behind fortifications, the Allies prevailed—but at a tragic loss of 25,000 men. This battle, called Malplaquet, cost the French 15,000. The city of Mons was taken, but the war had become a horror. Marlborough took Tournai in Belgium and Lille, Douai, Bethune, and Bouchain in France by the year 1711. France was in desperate straits and only a few fortified cities lay between the Allies and

Paris, but English patience was exhausted.

England's allies let the war drag on too long. The Dutch were originally proud of victory without casualties whereby they gained land but lost no troops. In 1709 the Tories won the English elections, took over the government, and began talking peace.

Marlborough had acted on Queen Anne's behalf as her adviser on foreign affairs, had supervised her military alliances, managed her entire war effort, and led her armies to victory. Undefeated, he was one of the great generals of all time, probably the finest soldier who ever lived. He, more than any other individual, brought Louis XIV to his knees; yet on the eve of victory in 1711 he was recalled, charged with misuse of the Queen's funds (falsely), and forced to flee the country. Shortly afterward the entire English army was pulled out of the line and out of the war, deserting England's allies. A stalemate resulted and the Treaty of Utrecht was signed in 1713 leaving France intact. Philip remained the popular King of Spain, but France and Spain agreed to cease coordinating their foreign policies (which they had done already). Louis said the English had served him well by removing Marlborough.

English failure to destroy French military capabilities resulted in four more wars with France in the next one hundred years. In one of these England lost her American colonies and her opportunity for world domination. As MacArthur said in 1951, "There is no substitute for victory."

The English Army in this war was magnificent. Led by Marlborough they were victorious in every encounter. How did they behave after the American Revolution? A review of their accomplishments against Napoleon 100 years later will show another superb performance.

Wellington

John Wellsely, the Duke of Wellington, is well known for his victory over Napoleon at Waterloo in 1815, but from 1808 to 1814 he conducted a masterful campaign in the Iberian Peninsula.

In 1808 Napoleon dominated Europe, where he could field an army of up to one million men. In Spain alone he at one time had forces of 300,000. England could not raise an army large enough to land in Europe but had to do something to resist French domination of the continent. It was finally decided to put Wellington ashore in Portugal to see what he could do toward recruiting and assisting Portuguese and Spanish forces. Wellington landed in Portugal on

August 1, 1808, with a force of only 9,000 men. He attacked the French at Rolica on August 17 and defeated them. On August 21 a French army of 13,000 attacked the British, then numbering 17,000, at Vimiero. The French attacked in dense columns (a tactic developed by Napoleon), but they were shattered by British lines which outflanked the columns, eventually firing from front and both flanks. In five days the British under Wellington had twice defeated highly regarded experienced French armies. The French surrendered Portugal and left the country.

Senior officers were then placed in command of the British army, which moved into Spain to assist the Spanish. Napoleon, with 200,000 men, also entered Spain and by January 1809, the British were evacuated from northern Spain.

On April 22, 1809, Wellington returned to Portugal where he took command. He left a force of 12,000 men in central Portugal and moved north with 18,400 men to attack 24,000 French under Marshal Soult. On May 12 he chased the French from Oporto, and by May 18 Soult was back in Spain with the remnants of an army.

Wellington then turned south and east into Spain. At Talavera on July 25 Wellington, with 20,000 British and 35,000 poorly trained and equipped Spaniards, faced 40,000 Frenchmen under Victor. Wellington took defensive positions, kept his forces hidden, and beat off attack after attack by the French. Wherever the French made a penetration, Wellington filled the gap using roads prepared behind his positions just for this purpose. British lines overwhelmed French columns and the French retreated. They suffered 7,000 casualties; British losses were 5,000.

When the French concentrated their armies in Spain, Wellington pulled back into Portugal. On September 27, 1810, the French under Marshal Massena invaded Portugal with 65,000 men. Wellington met them at Busaca with 49,000 troops, half Portuguese, half British. Again the French were repulsed with 4,600 casualties to 1,252 Allied. The French sidestepped and continued into Portugal but could not contest Wellington's defensive lines. With major supply problems Massena withdrew from Portugal in March of 1811.

Wellington followed the French into Spain and defeated Massena at Fuentes de Onoro in May. Marshal Soult was beaten at Albuera by Beresford a week later. The fortress cities of Badajoz and Ciudad de Rodrigo were taken by April, 1812. Wellington, with 60,000 men, had opened Spain for invasion while opposed by four of Napoleon's best generals with forces three to four times those at Wellington's disposal. Wellington attacked Marmont at Salamanca on July 22,

1812. Both armies had 48,000 men, but Wellington caught the French stretched out on the roads. Thirty percent of the French were casualties and 30 percent were dispersed throughout the countryside. After this battle a French general compared Wellington to Frederick the Great.

In 1812 Napoleon invaded Russia, pulling his best generals and troops out of Spain. (Like another dictator 129 years later, Napoleon failed to squash the British mouse before attacking the Russian elephant.) After Salamanca the French concentrated their forces by evacuating southern Spain. Wellington resumed his advance in 1813, north and west of Madrid, forcing the French to evacuate that city in May. On June 21 the French were beaten at Vitoria, losing all their artillery and wagons. By this time Napoleon had retreated from Russia and was back in France. In 1813 he defeated the Prussians and Russians, but Vitoria gave new impetus to his European opponents.

The French attacked in the Pyrenees in July but were beaten back. On July 30 Wellington attacked at Sorauren. The French lost 13,000 men in the Pyrenees and fell back into France. In September the Prussians, Russians, and Austrians began to make headway against Napoleon. Wellington then decided to invade France reaching Toulouse by April 12, 1814, when word came that Napoleon had abdicated.

After Napoleon's return from Elba in 1815, Wellington fought him to a standstill at Waterloo until the arrival of Blucher's Prussians on the French flank in late afternoon decided the day. By this time Wellington had become the foremost soldier among the Allied military powers. His fame lasts primarily because of Waterloo, but his campaign in Portugal and Spain is a classic.

Before and after the American Revolution, British armies were superb and led by Marlborough or Wellington they were invincible. How could American colonists expect to fight such troops? One of Washington's most experienced generals, Charles Lee, said that the patriots could not stand up against British regulars. But they did.

Chapter III
The American Revolution, 1775–1783

Lexington and Concord, 1775

On April 19, 1775, Lt. Colonel Smith and 700 British regulars set out to capture American military supplies at Concord. Their path was obstructed by 38 rebel militia at Lexington. These were dispersed after a warning volley, but the British went out of control and chased them, killing eight and wounding ten. This was the spark that ignited the conflagration.

At Concord the British spread out looking for stores. At the North Bridge a company of 30 British faced an accumulation of 450 militia.

All colonists were required by British law to keep arms and to be available for defense if called upon. Many had, however, formed illegal militia companies in anticipation of a revolution. When the British force left Boston the alarm spread far and wide and these militia forces all headed for Concord.

At the North Bridge the Redcoats opened fire, which was returned. Three British were killed and eight wounded before they retired. The whole British force gathered together and retreated. One mile from Concord they were fired upon from both sides of the road by concealed patriots. It is estimated that up to 2,000 colonists came to fight that day, and it is reasonable to assume that many followed the British to fire at them repeatedly. Some fired from houses, and wherever the militia took cover the British light infantry had to dislodge them to allow passage of the main body. A British relief force of 1,000 men met the retreating Concord force at Lexington, and the combined column retreated to Charlestown. Before reaching safety, however, they were assaulted in the village of Menotomy by 1,800 rebels. Fighting here was vicious and the village was strewn with bodies. When the British reached the haven of Bunker Hill near Charlestown, the fighting was over but they had lost 73 dead and 200 wounded or missing. Forty-nine Americans were dead with 46 wounded or missing.

The British were amazed at the ferocity and perseverance of the Americans. Falling back into Boston they allowed the rebels to build a fortified defensive ring around the city.

Fort Ticonderoga, May 10, 1775

On May 10, 1775, Ethan Allen and his Green Mountain Boys took Ft. Ticonderoga, which contained some sizeable pieces of artillery. Benedict Arnold went with them, and on May 11 they took Crown Point and St. Johns, both small posts. Ticonderoga had a British garrison of 45 but only one sentry. All were surprised and captured.

Bunker Hill, June 17, 1775

In 1775 Boston contained 15000 people. General Gage had a force of 4,000 to 5,000 troops for the purpose of keeping order. In and around Boston the Americans accumulated a force of about 7,500 men, and the number was growing. It has been estimated that as many as 20,000 patriots had joined the rebel force for some period of time. Gage decided to occupy the high ground overlooking Boston Harbor and made plans to occupy Bunker Hill to seal off the narrow entrance to the Charlestown peninsula which lay north of Boston. The patriots learned of this and ordered a force to occupy Bunker Hill. This force, however, moved onto a smaller hill nearer the harbor, Breed's Hill. The British landed 2,250 men to take this hill occupied by 700 Americans and later another 500. Twice the British climbed the hill and twice they were mowed down and thrown back. On the third assault the rebels ran out of ammunition and, having no bayonets, they retreated. The British took the hill but with a terrible loss of 226 dead and 828 wounded. Of the wounded many died a slow death in the British hospital. One-hundred-forty Americans were killed and 271 were wounded.

The British could have landed behind Breed's Hill near Bunker Hill and cut off the rebels. Instead they arrogantly decided upon a frontal attack that destroyed the offensive capabilities of their entire army. This failure encouraged the Americans and may have been the worst British blunder of the war. In addition to General Gage, both Generals Howe and Clinton (Gage's successors) witnessed this disaster, and this may have affected their strategy in every future encounter.

Boston, 1775–1776

George Washington was appointed General of the American Army, arriving in Cambridge on July 2, 1775. He was renowned for his efforts in the French and Indian War, particularly his command of the rear guard during Braddock's retreat from Fort Duquesne (now Pittsburgh). He was known to be brave, a good leader, a good soldier, but lacking in the military sciences by his own admission.

Washington established an officer corps with experienced men such as

Charles Lee and young talent such as Nathanael Greene and Henry Knox. He brought along a contingent of riflemen with a weapon that would prove to be very useful. These rifles were slow loading but had twice the range of British muskets.

The lines around Boston were held into 1776. As enlistments ran out, Washington had a constant concern with replenishing his force. By January 1776, Washington had over 8,000 men enrolled but only 5,582 present and fit for duty. General Gage meanwhile received reinforcements raising his force to 6,000 with 1,400 more hospitalized sick and wounded. On October 11, 1775, he was replaced with General Howe.

Then, late in January, Henry Knox arrived with all the Ticonderoga artillery which he had arranged to be transported by boat and sled down Lake George and across Massachusetts. On March 4, Washington sent 3,000 men onto Dorchester Heights south of Boston and installed the artillery. The British were finished and vacated Boston on March 17, 1776, by ship.

Boston was dominated by the heights of Dorchester and Charlestown. Artillery on these heights made the city untenable. The British retreat from Boston was a military disaster for England. If Breed's Hill had been captured with far less loss, the British might have been able to follow up such a success by dispersing the gathering rebels. The incredible mobilization of the militia on April 19 and after, along with the valiant defense of Breed's Hill affected the confidence of the British and encouraged the colonies from Maine to Georgia.

British strategy had to be occupation of a few key cities on the coast for receipt of supplies and for use as military bases for the purpose of seeking and destroying American armies until such time as the rebels would lose heart and cease to gather.

Canada, 1775–1776

The British had only 800 men to defend Canada; this fact, plus fear of an Indian uprising with British instigation and the hope that Canadians would join them, led the Colonies to invade Canada in the fall of 1775. Twelve hundred men from Fort Ticonderoga under Schuyler and Montgomery took St. Johns after a long siege and moved northward. Ethan Allan, with another force of 300, attacked Montreal in a poorly planned escapade. The force was dispersed and Allen was captured. Montgomery later took Montreal on November 12.

Washington sent Benedict Arnold to Canada from Maine with 1,100 men, including Daniel Morgan and a few rifle companies. On December 3 Arnold and Montgomery combined outside Quebec. On January 1, Montgomery attacked Quebec from one side while Arnold attacked from the other. Montgomery was killed and his force withdrew. Arnold's force of 600 ended up in house to house fighting. This assault was unsuccessful also, but survivors stayed outside the city all winter. In the spring Sullivan came up with American reinforcements, but when British troops from England arrived the Americans were routed.

American forces totaling 5,000 had been committed piecemeal and only 3,000 returned. Their sufferings are legendary. With better trained and managed troops the affair might have been successful. At best the invasion held off trouble from Canada for a while. Perhaps of greater significance, some of Washington's officers gained combat experience. Arnold, Sullivan, Morgan, and others learned more in Canada than they would have sitting in Boston. Morgan was a giant of a man and a superb soldier, one of the outstanding heroes of the Revolution.

North Carolina, 1776

At Moore's Creek on February 27, North Carolina Whigs under Colonel James Moore defeated a Tory force of Scotsmen under Donald McDonald. Casualties were light and the whole Tory force of 850 men was captured.

South Carolina, 1776

Fifty British vessels approached Charleston, South Carolina on May 31 but were turned back by Colonel Moultrie who had fortified Sullivan's Island. General Lee was there also. Colonel Moultrie had 2,300 men available and British General Clinton had 5,000, but an infantry battle never took place.

New York and Long Island, 1776

As expected, on June 29, 100 British ships with 10,000 men anchored off Staten Island. On July 12, 150 more ships with 15,000 men came in. On August 1 the 50 vessels from Charleston arrived to bring the total force to 300 ships and 30,000 men. The might of the British Empire had arrived, and the prospect of resistance to such an armada with so many troops must have seemed grim to the Americans. By mid August Washington's army had grown to 23,000 but many were militia with short enlistment periods. The British had selected New York because of its harbor and defensive qualities and because of its central location on the eastern seaboard, facilitating isolation of the southern colonies from the northern. Control of the waterways from the Hudson River to Lakes George and Champlain and to the Richelieu River into Canada gave New York a special significance and suggested a possibility for isolating New England.

The Americans had fortified a number of places on Manhattan Island, in New Jersey, and in Brooklyn. Their main defense on Long Island was on Brooklyn Heights. On August 22 the British began to land on Long Island near Gravesend. Within five days they had 21,000 men on Long Island under General

Howe, initially opposed by 7,000 under Putnam. Sullivan, with 2,800, defended three of the four passes through the Heights of Guan in front of the main defenses. The fourth pass at Jamaica was watched by only five horsemen. On August 27 with the aid of Tory spies, the five American sentries were captured and 10,000 British poured through Jamaica Pass into Sullivan's rear. Sullivan's left wing, pressed front and rear, fell back to the main defenses with heavy casualties. On Sullivan's right Stirling, with Maryland and Delaware Continentals, stood firm until attacked in front, side, and rear. Stirling, with 250 men, attacked Cornwallis in the American rear near Gowanus Road. Five times the Continentals attacked and only British reinforcements prevented them from breaking through. Washington saw this action and moaned over the loss of such brave men. Some of Stirling's men managed to escape to the Brooklyn Heights defenses.

Washington now had half his army in Brooklyn with a superior force in front and a major river at his back. Without sea power he was in danger of being cut off in Brooklyn. On the night of August 29, he pulled his entire force of 9500 back into New York, including all weapons and gear. He was helped by fog in the dawn hours, but this was a masterful move. The cautious British offense cost them another golden opportunity to crush the rebellion. Washington had lost between 700 and 1,000 men on Long Island and he had now to face the problem of defending the large island of Manhattan.

On September 13 the British crossed the East River between Kips Bay and Turtle Bay. The defenses there consisted of one line of trenches. British ships came in close to shore and peppered the trench line with grape shot. The defenders ran away, and Washington pulled his army back to Harlem Heights after some close calls in lower Manhattan where major forces were almost cut off. A professional corps of engineers no doubt would have helped Washington with defensive works on this occasion. Wellington certainly had such specialists for his defense of Lisbon during Massena' s invasion of Portugal in 1810.

At Harlem Heights a party of 300 British faced 150 Connecticut Rangers. Washington sent some Virginia and Maryland companies in on the British flank and chased them from the field. This little episode did some good for American morale. In August and September Washington's force was about 16,000. Greene had 3,000 at Fort Constitution in New Jersey (Fort Lee). The rest were split between the Harlem lines and Westchester to protect against another landing.

The British landed 4,000 men on Throg's Neck on October 12. These were held up by 30 riflemen later supported by New York and Massachusetts regiments. On the eighteenth the main British force landed but was delayed by Glover with a 1,100 man brigade. Washington meanwhile managed to escape the trap and move back to White Plains. These good positions were occupied on the nineteenth . Forces were left to hold Ft. Washington on the New York side of the Hudson. At White Plains the key position was Chatterton's Hill. The British attacked on October 26, took this hill, and forced Washington to withdraw. The British then marched to the Hudson River at Dobb's Ferry on November 4.

Washington had to anticipate an invasion of New Jersey, and on November 10 he took some of his forces across the Hudson while the British turned to attack Ft. Washington. This fort was defended by 2,900 men placed in extended positions miles apart. Eighth thousand British attacked all the positions on November 14 and chased these forces into the fort itself, which unfortunately was too small for such a mob with inadequate food and water. The fort was immediately surrendered and the American Army suffered a major defeat. Washington had earlier correctly stated that Manhattan Island was probably indefensible, primarily because of the control of the waterways by the British. Even so he had to try, and he had to try to maintain Ft. Washington and Ft. Lee to block British passage up the Hudson. He could not risk losing his army on Manhattan and had hoped in vain that Ft. Washington would be self sufficient.

New Jersey, 1776–1777

On November 29, Lord Cornwallis crossed the Hudson near Dobbs Ferry with 4,000 men. Greene pulled his men from Ft. Lee and marched to Hackensack to join Washington. Ft. Lee was of no use to the Americans after the fall of Ft. Washington as cannon were required on both sides of the river to prevent British ships from sailing up the Hudson. Washington now retreated to Newark, then to New Brunswick with a force of only 3,000 men. Stirling, with 1,000 men, joined Washington at New Brunswick. Washington retreated to Princeton, then to Trenton where his supplies were ferried across the Delaware. Cornwallis slackened his pace, not reaching Trenton until December 8, just as Washington's rear guard left New Jersey. Washington now hoped to save Philadelphia as the British held New York City and all of New Jersey. The remnant of the White Plains force and a group under Gates from Ft. Ticonderoga joined Washington in December bringing his strength up to 7,600. The British and Lord Howe, as was the European custom, went into winter quarters. He sent 6,000 men to Newport, Rhode Island, and distributed 14,000 in small posts from Staten Island to Burlington in southern New Jersey. Howe went back to New York to join his mistress, Elizabeth, wife of his commissary of prisoners, Joshua Loring. Cornwallis was given permission to go on leave to England.

The American enlistments would soon run out and Washington, far from beaten, resolved to do something quickly. On the morning of December 26, before dawn, he crossed the Delaware to New Jersey and attacked the Hessians at Trenton. Overconfident, the Hessians, 1500 strong under Rall, had not fortified Trenton. The Americans attacked and killed or wounded forty before the rest ran away or surrendered. One thousand were captured at a loss of two American dead and three wounded. Cornwallis was ordered to return, and he gathered forces at Princeton, rushing to Trenton with 8,000 men. Arriving on January 3 the British passed through the town to face Washington's force of 5,100. Leaving sentries and campfires behind, Washington dashed to Princeton, where he attacked on

January 4. Personally, heroically directing the fight, only 30 yards from the enemy, his troops shot down 100 British and captured another 300 while losing only 44. His losses, however, included General Mercer and Colonel Hazlet. Washington moved northward into Jersey arriving at Morristown on January 6. The British withdrew from all their Jersey posts except for Brunswick and Amboy. Washington had succeeded in pushing the British out of almost all of New Jersey. In this campaign the British had accomplished nothing. Meanwhile their forces dwindled while Washington at any time could hope for reinforcements. The morale of the Colonies and the Continental Army was given a huge boost.

In June of 1777 Howe finally left his mistress to go back to war, and he marched into Jersey to try to lure Washington into battle. Failing three times he pulled his entire army out of the state back to Staten Island where they had started one year ago. After two years of fighting, the British occupied only New York City and Newport, Rhode Island.

Philadelphia, 1777

After vacating New Jersey Howe planned to take Philadelphia. This had been his earlier goal, but overland supply from New York to Philadelphia had proved impractical. He therefore decided to supply his army in Philadelphia by sea. British armies traditionally brought in supplies to their forces rather than depend upon local means, unlike the French who foraged locally to feed their armies. (British generals would not have invaded Russia without proven means of bringing up supplies, unlike Napoleon who took 600,000 men into Russia, losing 500,000 of them.)

Howe's late start in 1777 allowed Washington to build up his army. Down to only 1,000 men at Morristown, Washington had 16,000 when the British landed below Philadelphia. On August 24, Washington paraded his impressive army through the city on the way to meet the British.

Brandywine Creek near Wilmington was selected as the best place to hold off the invaders, and the battle was fought there on September 11. Armstrong was on the Continental left with Pennsylvania militia; in the center Greene commanded the divisions of Wayne's Pennsylvanians, Weedon's and Muhlenberg's Virginians, and light troops under Maxwell. On the right Sullivan commanded three divisions, two led by Stirling and Stephens, one by Sullivan himself. Some light horse under Colonel Bland patrolled on the extreme right.

The Hessians attacked Maxwell in the morning and were repulsed. Half the British Army under Cornwallis marched around the American right undetected until about three o'clock in the afternoon. Stephens and Stirling were sent to block them, but some of these forces did not have time to form properly. Some fought well, but the line gave way. Greene pulled some of his forces to block Cornwallis long enough to allow the army to escape. Wayne and Maxwell also gave way on the left flank and the whole army was in retreat.

Washington's loss was 1,200 to 1,300 and the British loss was just under 600. As at Long Island, Washington had been outflanked. At Brandywine he had cavalry, but for some reason they were unable to guard the flank. The army as a whole performed rather well, but the British occupied Philadelphia on September 26. On the nineteenth the British surprised Wayne's detached force of 1,500 with a night bayonet attack at Paoli. Wayne lost 150 dead, wounded, and captured.

Once Philadelphia was occupied Howe sent 3,000 men to New Jersey; left 3,000 in the city; and camped at Germantown with 8,000. Washington received some New York, New Jersey, and Maryland militia, and his force rose to 11,000. When Howe sent more troops to the Delaware, Washington decided to attack. Howe's camp, again, was not fortified—deliberately, arrogantly—to show contempt for the rebels. Conway, Wayne, and Sullivan were ordered to attack the British right. Smallwood's Maryland and Forman's New Jersey militia were expected to flank the British right and move into their rear. The Americans marched all night October third and attacked at 5 A.M. on the fourth. Sullivan drove the British out of Germantown and back into their camp, but Wayne's force ran into Stephen's force coming down the wrong road. Both forces opened fire and both fled in panic. The British were driven from their camp, but Sullivan's men ran out of ammunition. These men also fell back and the whole army turned victory into defeat. Washington lost about 1,100 men, the British about half as many. Washington showed his indomitable spirit again. His army, too, showed it could fight, far better than in 1776, but there was also a definite shortage of military skill. The British had, in fact, been surprised and beaten. Their lack of defensive works was incomprehensible.

In order to solidify his position in Philadelphia, Howe had to capture several American forts along the Delaware River to facilitate bringing in supplies up the river. On October 22 Donop and his Hessians attacked Fort Mercer, defended by Rhode Island's Colonel Green and 400 men. The Hessians lost 400 men and Donop, but by November 20 all the forts had been taken.

Saratoga, 1777

John Burgoyne had been in Boston with Howe and Clinton in 1775 but went back to England, where he proposed a plan to invade the Colonies from Canada in 1777. One army under Burgoyne would move south through Lake Champlain and the Hudson River to Albany, while another army moved east along the Mohawk Valley, with a third army moving up the Hudson from New York. One objective was to corner Washington's army, but another strategic objective was to sever New England from the rest of the Colonies. The plan was based on a number of misconceptions, such as there being only one American army and that three armies could start from widely separated points and converge simultaneously at Albany. If Albany was the goal, it was most easily taken from

New York City. The main reason for Burgoyne's proposal was to allow him an independent command, and this was granted.

On June 20, Burgoyne sailed south on Lake Champlain with 8,300 men, some women, and considerable personal baggage. The Americans at Fort Ticonderoga under General St. Clair abandoned that post on July 6, to the dismay of the area commander (General Schuyler), and retreated to Ft. Edward on the Hudson. Burgoyne pursued but stopped at Skenesboro, only 23 miles from Ft. Edward, where he dined in style. The Americans devastated the land and blocked the road to Ft. Edward with every impediment available, including trees, water, and stone. At Ft. Anne they sortied before leaving the fort and took some British casualties. Burgoyne didn't reach the Hudson until July 29.

The Indians with Burgoyne unfortunately killed and scalped a local girl, Jane McCrea, and this episode fired up the population, increasing the number of volunteers. Slowly Schuyler built up an army.

Burgoyne was having difficulties with his supplies and decided to send a force into the Hampshire Grants (now Vermont) to pick up supplies and possibly recruits. He sent Colonel Baume and 600 men to Bennington. Bad luck. John Stark had just finished rounding up a force of 1,500 militia and they were all in Bennington. John Stark was a soldier, a former member of Roger's Rangers in the French and Indian War. Stark met Baume's party and surrounded it. Baume was annihilated. Five hundred fifty reinforcements under Breymann arrived on the sixteenth but ran into Stark's men, reinforced by fresh militia from Manchester under Warner. Breymann fought until he ran out of ammunition, then he retreated. The losses were mostly German mercenaries, but they totaled 207 dead, many wounded, and 700 captured. Burgoyne had blundered into a hornet's nest.

On July 25, St. Leger with 400 men from Canada and 1,000 Iroquois under Joseph Brant moved east from Oneida to join Burgoyne. In their path was Ft. Schuyler at the mouth of the Mohawk River, defended by Col. Gansevoort and 750 men. This was the fort portrayed rather loosely in the movie "Drums along the Mohawk." St. Leger reached the fort on August 3. On August 6, General Herkimer with 800 militia, marched from Ft. Dayton to relieve Ft. Schuyler but was ambushed when only six miles from the besieged fort. Herkimer's big force fought well even though surprised but had to turn back with 150 to 200 casualties. Lt. Col. Willett escaped from the encircled fort on August 8 and reached German Flats 50 miles away to get help.

Help was on the way in the person of Benedict Arnold and 950 Massachusetts Continentals sent by Schuyler. Arnold sent Indian friends into St. Leger's camp to warn the Iroquois of a huge American force approaching. Disillusioned by the fight put up by the Americans, the Iroquois deserted the British and St. Leger retreated back to Canada.

On August 19, Horatio Gates succeeded Schuyler in command of the New York area. This was a political move and should not reflect upon Schuyler's reputation, for he had done a good job of delaying Burgoyne, fighting off St. Leger, and building up the army that was to confront the British.

Gates gave the left wing of his army to Arnold, including Dan Morgan's riflemen. Gates moved north to Bemis Heights with 6,000 men and had the Polish engineer, Colonel Kosciuszko, fortify the place. Burgoyne, now without his Indians, moved blindly to within four miles of the Americans. On the American right near the river were Continentals led by Glover, Patterson, and Nixon, but commanded by Gates himself. The center was commanded by Learned and Livingston. Arnold was in charge on the left with regulars, militia, Morgan's riflemen, and Dearborn's light infantry. Burgoyne finally bumped into the Americans and, on September 19, set out in three columns. Riedesel's Germans would attack the American right. Hamilton, with Burgoyne present, was to attack the center, and the strongest force under Fraser and Breymann would hit the Rebel left and try to push it in toward the river.

Gates wanted to stay behind his fortifications but Arnold wanted to attack. Gates allowed him to do so but only with Morgan and Dearborn's troops. At Freeman's Farm, Morgan's riflemen shot up Burgoyne's advance group, then advanced, running into the central British force. Morgan's men were dispersed but recollected with turkey calls.

Some New Hampshire Continentals joined Arnold; then the British attacked only to be repulsed. The Americans attacked, were checked, then fell back. Arnold, against orders, brought up his whole division. Fraser came up on Burgoyne's right, von Riedesel sent most of his force to join in on Burgoyne's left. Arnold's division now faced the bulk of Burgoyne's army. Gates did not send Learned's brigade until late in the day. The fight was a standoff with 300 American and 600 British casualties. The next morning, September 20, Burgoyne planned to attack Arnold again. Arnold's men were low on ammunition and without more support from Gates this attack would have been fatal, but Burgoyne received a note from Clinton saying that he would move north on about September 22. Burgoyne, his force rapidly shrinking, decided to dig in and await Clinton. Clinton, in no particular hurry, however, did not start out until October 3 and thereby sealed Burgoyne's fate.

By October 3, Burgoyne's supplies were just about gone. Meanwhile Gates' army grew to 11,000. Arnold was relieved of his command and Gates placed the division under his own control. Arnold had fought well, and the shabby treatment given him might have been for not obeying orders, but was also due to the political fight between Gates and Schuyler, Arnold's mentor.

On October 7, Burgoyne brought 1,500 men out of his fortifications. Poor's brigade attacked in front while Morgan hit their right flank. As the British changed front, Dearborn attacked strongly and the British were pushed back. Fraser went down and Burgoyne withdrew to his defensive works. Arnold rushed upon the scene without official command and took individual units, leading them into frenzied attacks eventually seizing a key redoubt, which threatened Burgoyne's defense. Arnold was wounded as the fighting came to a halt. Burgoyne had now lost another 600, the American's only 150. Thoroughly beaten, Burgoyne retreated the next night but only moved about 6 or 7 miles to Saratoga before his retreat was cut off. He surrendered on October 17. When

Clinton heard of Burgoyne's disaster, he went back to New York. The coordination of British forces in this campaign had been essentially non-existent. The British army that surrendered to Gates numbered about 5,300—all that remained of the original 8,000. Burgoyne's lack of drive, perhaps because of contempt for his opponents, had lost an army and dealt British hopes for eventual victory a crushing blow.

This had been Benedict Arnold's finest hour. He was a mad genius, probably too unstable for top command, but he had made the difference at Freeman's Farm. His bitterness at his treatment by Gates was justified but his eventual betrayal of his country has made his name synonymous to traitor. Gates gained more glory than he deserved, but when tested again he was not so lucky.

The Continentals and large militia forces produced by the northern states had accomplished a remarkable feat. The British army was, as in Marlborough's time, a well trained and disciplined force. Such a defeat by untrained Americans is almost unbelievable. A great many men left their homes to beat Burgoyne, and a great many regulars, Continentals, stood toe to toe with the best in the world and proved their mettle.

Valley Forge, Winter 1777–1778

Washington located his army at Valley Forge, 20 miles west of Philadelphia. The hardships suffered there are well known but were due, in part, to an incompetent Quartermaster General, Thomas Mifflin. As soon as he was replaced by Greene, food and supplies became more abundant. French materiel were being received in various ports, but few found their way to Washington. The Commissary Department was given to Jeremiah Wadsworth and he improved the food problem to some extent. The most significant event to occur at Valley Forge that winter, however, was the arrival in February of a Prussian, Baron von Steuben. He was no baron, but he had been on the general staff of Frederick the Great and he knew how to train soldiers. He became Inspector General and instructed Washington's army in the various commands, drills, and movements required of a professional army. Then, on May 1, news arrived that France had recognized the United States as a sovereign nation. Saratoga had done that just as Long Island had discouraged the French earlier.

A treaty with France was signed on February 6, promising aid to the United States. In case of war between France and England, the U.S. would support France until the war was over.

The British had a good time in Philadelphia that winter. They ate well and enjoyed frequent parties and dances. American girls were very friendly. Other colonists sold food to the British rather than the Americans because the prices given were better.

Looking back at 1777, the British could not take much pleasure in their military achievements. They had been pushed around at Germantown, turned back at Ft. Schuyler, and destroyed at Saratoga. They occupied only Newport, New York City, and Philadelphia. Howe asked to be relieved and he was, by Clinton. By May the British had 10,000 men in Philadelphia; 5,000 in New York; and about 7,000 in Rhode Island.

Washington had 11,800, with reinforcements expected that could double his force. Clinton was then ordered to supply 8,000 men for defense of Florida and the Caribbean against the French. It was therefore necessary for the British to evacuate Philadelphia.

Monmouth, June 28, 1778

By noon on June 18, Washington had learned of the British evacuation of Philadelphia and their march into New Jersey toward New York City. Washington ordered his army to follow while he looked for an opportunity to strike.

The British marched with their best troops in the rear. Washington pursued with a 5,000 man advance corps under Charles Lee. (Lee had been captured during the retreat across New Jersey and had recently been exchanged for a British general.) The advance corps was ordered to attack at the first opportunity.

On June 28, the advance corps came upon 1,500 to 2,000 British drawn up to contest the American advance. General Lee may have issued orders for his troops to occupy better ground in their rear, but whatever the order, the result was a disorganized retreat. Washington came up, organized the advance corps forces to meet the British, discharged Lee, and took command of Lee's corps. Clinton threw 4,000 men into an assault. Wayne held the center; Stirling with part of the main body came up on the left; and Greene with the rest of the army came up on the right. The Americans fought off all attacks and advanced on both flanks by nightfall to permit an assault in the morning, but by then the British were gone. Both sides lost about 300 men but Washington, for the first time, had faced major British forces, held his ground, and then advanced. Von Steuben's training most certainly made a difference. This army was willing to fight and now it knew how.

Monmouth earned respect for the American army, but for the British it was more of a rear guard effort. Clinton had accomplished his objective, holding off Washington long enough to permit embarkation to New York.

After Monmouth, Washington planned a combined operation with the French. He sent Sullivan to Newport, Rhode Island, with two divisions—3,000 men. Some 7,000 New England militia joined Sullivan and soon there would be 4,000 French troops to attack 6,600 British. Unfortunately, however, a storm damaged the French fleet, causing their withdrawal to Boston. Many of Sullivan's militia deserted, leaving him dangerously exposed to British attack with insufficient force to resist. Sullivan began a withdrawal, but during the process the British attacked. An all Negro Rhode Island regiment fought an outstanding rear guard action, however, and Sullivan was able to bring his forces off intact.

Clinton was inactive for the balance of 1778 and into 1779 as plans for an offensive in the north had been abandoned. Washington spread his forces out from Connecticut to Virginia to minimize any British excursions into the mainland.

Indian Wars

1777 had been a bloody year on the Virginia frontier, and as a result Colonel George Rogers Clark and 175 men were dispatched in June 1778, to take the British forts supplying the Indians. Clark walked 850 miles and captured a number of British posts, including Fort Kaskaskia and Fort Vincennes. His remarkable feat is well covered by history books and Indian action was, as a result of this effort, much reduced on the Virginia frontier.

In July, 1778, Colonel John Butler, with 100 Tories and 500 Senecas, attacked the Wyoming Valley in Pennsylvania; burned 1,000 homes; wiped out a company of regulars and 200 to 300 militia; and took hundreds of scalps. The Iroquois, led by Joseph Brant, also attacked in the Mohawk Valley. Later Butler struck again, destroying Cherry Valley near Albany.

Congress appealed to General Washington, who sent General Sullivan and 4,000 men to retaliate. Sullivan passed through village after village of the Six Nations, destroying homes and crops. The Tories and Indians tried to ambush Sullivan at Newtown but were spotted, outflanked, blasted by artillery, and assaulted by Continentals. The Indians fled, leaving 12 dead. The Indians were ruined and their later efforts much diminished by this expedition, which destroyed their access to supplies within the Pennsylvania–New York area.

Stony Point, July 15, 1779

Clinton tried to bring Washington to battle in the late spring of 1779, first by occupying Stony Point and Verplanck's Point on both sides of the Hudson just south of West Point and Bear Mountain. This move took away Washington's ferry supply line and forced him to use a much longer supply route. Then Clinton pillaged and burned Connecticut towns, but again Washington remained at West Point. The British raids on Connecticut disturbed Washington and he resolved to take some action, finally deciding to attack Stony Point, defended by over 600 British.

General Anthony Wayne was chosen for the job. He was a highly regarded officer, a fighter, and he was given a picked corps of light infantry. Marching around Bear Mountain, Wayne's men approached the Point after sunset on July 15. The plan called for an assault at midnight in front through fortifications while one division scaled cliffs on the south side and another division scaled cliffs on the north side. Bayonets were fixed and no muskets loaded to prevent an accidental early discharge.

Within 20 minutes of the first alarm, the Americans were inside the fort. Wayne's men remembered Paoli (where the British had killed Americans with a bayonet attack) and Connecticut, and the intent was to kill every British soldier in the fort, but the beaten British pleaded for mercy. Only 63 were killed; 543 were captured. The Americans lost 15 dead and 84 wounded.

On July 18, Light Horse Henry Lee attacked the British post at Powle's Hook near Staten Island. The Stony Point affair, however, was devastating to Clinton. Although Washington vacated the fort as indefensible and Clinton took it back, the deed was done.

The British loss of men in Connecticut and at Stony Point paralyzed their offensive capability and depressed Clinton to the extent that he asked to be allowed to resign from the service. It had become obvious that it was impossible to occupy any significant land area in the northern states so long as Washington's army remained. The next winter Newport, Rhode Island, was abandoned as Clinton concentrated in New York.

Washington camped at Morristown in the winter of 1779 and 1780 and his army suffered severely again. 1780 was, however, quiet in the north.

War in the South

The British accomplished virtually nothing in 5 years of war in the northern colonies. Few Tories rallied to the Crown, and it was hoped that an effort in the south would be different. If Georgia and the Carolinas could be neutralized, if Tories would enlist, then Virginia could be invaded. Loss of the southern colonies with a blockade of northern ports would reduce the flow of men and supplies to Washington and reduce American enthusiasm for the war.

In November 1778, Clinton sent 3,500 men down to Georgia under Lt. Colonel Campbell to join a force from Florida under General Prevost. Campbell was met by American Major General Robert Howe with a force of less than 700. Howe was outflanked leaving 500 dead, wounded, or missing. The two British forces then took Sunbury, Savannah, and Augusta.

General Benjamin Lincoln was made commander of American forces in the south,[7] and he gathered 1,500 men from Charleston, South Carolina, and 3,000 Georgia militia. Lincoln, unfortunately, separated his forces, resulting in the annihilation of one force at Briar Creek on March 3, 1779; 400 were lost, 600 dispersed.

British forces under Provost marched directly towards Charleston, but the Americans concentrated there and held the city. By so doing, however, they had evacuated Georgia. In September and October, Lincoln joined the French for an assault on Prevost at Savannah. The attack was slow developing, leaving Prevost time to concentrate and build defenses. On October 9 the attack was made with horrendous results. The Allies lost 800 dead and wounded while the British lost only 57. The French withdrew, and the Americans settled down in defensive positions at Sheldon.

Once the French fleet left, Clinton sailed for Charleston, South Carolina, in November with 7,600 men. A force of 10,000 British approached Charleston in March, defended by Lincoln with 5,500 men. On April 1, the British fleet shot their way past Sullivan's Island into the bay. The city was soon surrounded except for one means of access up the Cooper River. Here Lincoln had an outpost of 500 cavalry under Huger to keep this route open. One night, however, Colonel Banastre Tarleton's Legion, supported by Major Ferguson's Tories, surprised this force, captured 100 men and 400 horses, dispersed the rest, and sealed Charleston's fate. The city—with 5,000 men was surrendered on May 12, the worst American disaster of the war.

Camden, August 16, 1780

After the fall of Charleston, Clinton moved to pacify South Carolina. One force was sent to the west, one to Augusta, and one, under Lord Cornwallis, to Camden. An American force there, gathering for the relief of Charleston, had dispersed, but 350 Virginians under Buford had moved 150 miles north toward North Carolina. Cornwallis sent the bloodthirsty Englishman, Tarleton, after them with 250 cavalry. The Virginians were overtaken, and after fighting as best they could in poor defensive positions, they tried to surrender. Tarleton's murderous band cut them down, killing 113, capturing 53 and wounding the rest with saber or bayonet in one of the war's most brutal massacres. Clinton, thinking South Carolina subdued, went back to New York to plan the invasion of North Carolina.

But South Carolina was not done. Rebel and Tory bands fought vicious battles. Guerrilla bands were formed by Sumter, Hill, Marion, Davie, Bratton, and others. One of Sumter's bands wiped out a 100 man force from Tarleton's Legion. These bands attacked the British posts and the countryside was aflame.

Horatio Gates, the "Victor of Saratoga," was appointed Commanding General in the south. He arrived at Hillsboro in North Carolina on July 25 to find his army, one division of Maryland Continentals plus a Delaware regiment and 120 cavalry, all under "Baron" de Kalb, with little food and few supplies. Twenty-one-hundred North Carolina militia and 700 Virginia militia joined him, but he let over 400 men go off on another mission while he gathered his remaining force of 3,000 to attack Cornwallis at Camden.

Cornwallis was believed to have only 700 men in Camden, but he quickly gathered a force of over 2,200. Both armies simultaneously moved toward each other, meeting at two A.M. on August 16. The British attacked at dawn, causing most of Gates' militia to run away, many without even discharging loaded weapons. Gates went with them, as did his reputation. Smallwood, with

Maryland and Delaware Continentals, held his ground; these were professionals, Continentals. They fought until both flanks were attacked, then retreated. Several hundred dead (including gallant de Kalb) and wounded were left behind.

Cornwallis then proceeded to invade North Carolina with three columns. Tories under Major Ferguson would move through the back country. Another force would drive up the coast while Cornwallis took the central route to Hillsboro. This was the peak of British success in the South and in the war, although no one at the time could have known. Their fortunes were to fade rapidly.

Kings Mountain. October 7, 1780

The Loyalist force under Major Patrick Ferguson consisted of about 1,100 men.

Ferguson was a dedicated professional. He had produced a number of new rapid firing breech loaded rifles earlier in the war, but Clinton had filed these away. This rifle, if issued to the army, might have changed the course of the war but Clinton, the politician, did not feel that he had been properly consulted about the matter.

Ferguson led his force into North Carolina as far as Cane Creek. Here he heard that 3000 "over the mountain men" had gathered to oppose him. Ferguson then turned back to try linking up with Cornwallis at Charlotte. He requested reinforcements, then took up defensive positions on King's Mountain on the road to Charlotte near the South Carolina border.

The American force actually consisted of five militia groups totaling about 1,300 men. Three of the groups were from North Carolina, one was from South Carolina, and one came from Virginia. One of the militia colonels, William Campbell, was elected temporary commander. Traveling in the rain by night and day, the frontiersmen reached King's Mountain in the afternoon, immediately surrounding the hill. Two assaults were made upon the Tories but were repulsed. The American marksmanship was excellent, however, bringing down the British at a steady rate. The Americans fought as individuals, using the cover of trees, each man firing from covered positions. The third assault carried the crest of the hill. Ferguson went down and his army was compressed into one slope of the hill. In one hour the battle was over. The British surrendered with 157 dead, 163 wounded, and 698 prisoners. The Americans lost 28 killed, 62 wounded.

The frontiersmen took their prisoners north, slaughtered some, disbanded, then went home. Cornwallis no doubt overestimated their force and visualized a major threat to his army. He immediately retreated to Camden, losing more men and supplies in the miserable two weeks of the journey.

Cowpens, January 17, 1781

In the fall of 1780, Nathanael Greene was appointed Commanding General in the south. Like Washington, he was a wise and patient man. He brought with him Light Horse Henry Lee, Baron von Steuben (to train recruits), and Daniel Morgan. Morgan suffered from arthritis, but he had distinguished himself in Canada and especially at Saratoga.

Greene posted Morgan inland near the South Carolina border while he watched Cornwallis. Cornwallis sent Tarleton with 750 men to push Morgan back to prevent a flank attack when Cornwallis advanced.

Morgan was now a Brigadier General in charge of light infantry. His army consisted of four regiments of infantry, a company of riflemen, 70 cavalry, and a growing force of militia. Spies advised Morgan of Tarleton' s approach and a defensive position was taken at Cowpens. Morgan posted his Virginia, Maryland, and Delaware Continentals under Howard near the crest of the sloping ground with some Virginia and Georgia militia. In the first line he placed Virginia, North Carolina, and South Carolina militia under Pickens. In front of these he placed skirmishers. Colonel Washington's cavalry were kept in reserve. Morgan stayed up all night encouraging his men, spending most of his time with the nervous militia.

The British appeared on the field at dawn, quickly formed, and advanced. The skirmishers put up a good fight, then moved back to join Pickens. The militia stood firm, firing numerous volleys, then moving back to join Howard. British dragoons came at the militia during this movement, doing some damage, but Colonel Washington charged and routed the dragoons. The British came on, however, attacking Howard's main line. When the British turned Howard's flank, Morgan came up, ordering Howard to adjust his line. This movement looked like a retreat to the British who rose to attack again. Howard stopped them, ordered fixed bayonets, then charged with his entire force. The British were forced back then routed in great disorder. One-hundred-ten were killed, 702 taken prisoner with all their supplies, and the few survivors including Tarleton were forced to flee for their lives. This was Morgan's finest performance, as precise and complete a victory as Trenton or Stony Point.

Cornwallis, not far away, decided to hit Morgan before he could join Greene. Eliminating all but essential supplies, he moved north with a force of only 2,000 in an exhausting march through the hills and over the rivers of North Carolina. Morgan managed to join Greene at Guilford Court House just south of the Virginia border.

Guilford Court House, March 15, 1781

As Greene approached Virginia, his force was increased until he had 2,600 militia; 1,600 Continentals; and 160 cavalry. Greene decided to fight while he had this large a force. Cornwallis wanted to fight to erase the stigma of British defeats at Kings Mountain and Cowpens. Greene occupied pre-selected positions on a hill in a defensive alignment as was advised by Morgan (who, suffering from arthritis and hemorrhoids, had gone home). The first line was composed of North Carolina militia with riflemen and cavalry on both flanks. The second line consisted of more reliable Virginia militia under Lawson and Stevens. The third line at the crest of the hill was formed with Delaware, Maryland. and Virginia Continentals. Greene asked his militia to fire three times, then fall back to the next line.

Cornwallis appeared in early afternoon with 2,200 men. They attacked the first line, which panicked and ran, certainly not staying to fire three rounds. The British advance was halted, however, by destructive fire from the riflemen on both flanks.

Cornwallis realigned to attack these troops, pushing those on the American left back into the woods, and forcing those on the American right back to the second line. When the British attacked the second line, they were met with destructive fire from positions at the edge of a stand of woods. The second line held until the American right was turned, threatening this position. This line then fell back to the third line, closely followed by the British. Now the American fire stopped the British who were suffering heavy casualties.

A counterattack here, as at Cowpens, would no doubt have destroyed the British, but Greene did not want to risk the only American army in the south. The British concentrated and came on again, causing one American regiment to give way. Another American regiment counterattacked supported by Colonel Washington's cavalry. The British stopped this assault with artillery fired on both friend and foe.

Eventually the British slipped around Greene's flank and he was forced to withdraw his army from the field. Greene had lost not more than 300 killed, wounded, and captured plus about 1,000 militia who just "went home." Cornwallis, however, lost 99 dead, 407 wounded, and 26 missing. His army was destroyed and he could no longer pursue. His supplies were in such poor quantity that he retreated all the way to Wilmington. Greene could have followed Cornwallis, but he would have ended up in a quiet position around Wilmington. Instead he decided to join the irregulars in South Carolina and take all the small posts the British had there.

When Cornwallis learned of Greene's plans, he wrote to Clinton saying that he could be of little assistance in South Carolina, advising his plan to join British forces in Virginia which he deemed the critical theatre. Greene left some militia to watch Cornwallis, and he left Steuben with some troops in Virginia where American reinforcements were expected.

The Recovery of South Carolina, 1781

The British held major forts at Camden and Ninety-six inland and at Georgetown near the sea. Other posts were held at Augusta, Fort Granby, Fort Motte, Orangeburg, and Fort Watson. Georgia and South Carolina forces under Lord Rawdon numbered 8,000, with his largest force of 1,500 men at Camden. Greene had 1,500 Continentals, but he stirred up the South Carolina partisans under Sumter, Pickens, and Marion.

Greene moved toward Camden to pin down Rawdon while the irregulars attacked other British posts. On April 25, 1781, Rawdon attacked Greene near Camden. Greene's Continentals began to overcome the smaller British force until a correction of the American line turned into confusion and then a retreat for a distance of several miles.

While Rawdon was entertained by Greene, Francis Marion, supported by Henry Lee, attacked Fort Watson. Here, Marion built a log tower for riflemen, and this device resulted in the surrender of the fort with 109 men on April 14.

Lee and Marion then moved to attack Fort Motte which fell with the help of pitch balls and fire arrows on May 11. Rawdon abandoned Camden on May 10, as it was too far inland to permit support of the other posts. On May 10, however, Sumter took Orangeburg. Henry Lee took Granby, and on May 29 Marion took Georgetown.

Pickens laid siege to Augusta, eventually joined by Clarke and Lee. On June 4 Augusta fell with the loss of 300 men. Greene and Lee lay siege to Ninety-six, but this post was well constructed and defended. Rawdon received reinforcements by sea and moved to relieve Ninety-six. On June 20, Greene gave up the siege, but on July 3, the British evacuated the post. Rawdon retired to Charleston giving the field command to Lt. Col. Stewart. Greene moved into the hills to rejuvenate his army.

On September 7, Greene—now with 2,200 men, including those of Marion and Pickens—attacked Stewart's force of 2,000 at Eutaw Springs. The Americans came on in two lines, Campbell and Marion in the first. When the first line faltered, the second advanced with fixed bayonets and pushed the British from the field. The British took refuge in a stone house in the center and in woods on both flanks. The Americans, passing through the British camp, became undisciplined and turned to looting. Greene finally gathered his disorganized mob and withdrew at the cost of 400 casualties, but they had reduced the British by almost 900. Stewart was finished, retreating into Charleston.

Greene's brilliant campaign had recovered the South, leaving the British in control of only Charleston and Savannah. The only other ports occupied were Yorktown and New York.

Yorktown, October 18, 1781

In December of 1780, Clinton sent Benedict Arnold and 2,000 men to disrupt American operations in Virginia. When this force was threatened by the possible arrival of a French fleet, Clinton sent Major General Phillips with 3,500 more. With no strategic plan and perhaps a desire to command a considerable force (for a change) in more civilized country, Cornwallis joined them in May of 1781 with another 1,400. Phillips died leaving Cornwallis in command of an army of 7,200 men.

Opposing them were 1,200 Continentals under Lafayette with 1,800 militia. Von Steuben had 500 Continental recruits for training and Wayne was expected with a division of Pennsylvania Continentals.

Cornwallis chased Lafayette north to the Rapidan River, where Wayne and Steuben joined him. Cornwallis retreated to Williamsburg. Clinton, meanwhile, felt threatened in New York (because of captured American dispatches) and ordered Cornwallis to occupy a defensive position and return 2,000 men to New York. Cornwallis moved toward Jamestown but set up a trap for Lafayette. Tarleton's rear guard was closely followed by Wayne with 500 men. On July 6, Wayne attacked Tarleton, who withdrew into a nearby woods. Cornwallis had posted his whole army on the other side of the woods and now came out to face what he hoped would be the entire American Army.

Lafayette sent 300 more Pennsylvanians to Wayne, who now saw himself confronted by the whole British Army. Outnumbered by 6 or 8 to 1 and faced with disaster if he retreated, Wayne attacked with bayonets. The British were checked and Wayne was able to withdraw with only 28 dead, 12 missing, and 99 wounded. One of Wayne's Pennsylvanians wrote about the affair, referring to his commander as "Mad Anthony," a label that has become renowned. Lafayette, however, considered the action to be a fine piece of work.

By this time Cornwallis and Clinton were communicating often but were confused about what to do. On July 20, Clinton finally ordered Cornwallis to take a defensive post at Old Point Comfort or Yorktown, as he wanted to be able to obtain troops from Cornwallis should he need them. Cornwallis chose Yorktown, not too far from the mouth of the York River. This position could not be attacked on three sides because of swamps and the river. On the fourth side Cornwallis ordered the erection of defensive works in two lines, one close to town, the other farther out. Yorktown was on a narrow peninsula, formed by the York and James Rivers. If this peninsula were occupied by a hostile army, all access to the town by land could be prevented.

Meanwhile, in May of 1781, the French from Newport had joined Washington above New York, between Dobbs Ferry and White Plains. This concentration was the one that worried Clinton but the Allied force was too small to attack New York. The Allies expected Count de Grasse, with a fleet and reinforcements, to join then, but on August 14 came word that de Grasse's fleet and 3,500 men were headed for the Chesapeake.

Rochambeau wrote to de Grasse with plans to attack Yorktown. Washington left 2,000 men to amuse Clinton, and the Allied army headed south. On September 2, as this host marched through Philadelphia, the French fleet arrived at Jamestown Island. The French troops were put ashore and joined Lafayette. The combined force of 9,000 lay at Williamsburg, 12 miles from Yorktown, where Cornwallis was now trapped. Dan Morgan returned for one more battle.

The British fleet in the West Indies was superior to any that France had in this hemisphere, but the British did not know that a fleet from France would sail directly to America. The net result was French naval superiority in America for a while. When the French fleet at Newport left for the Chesapeake, a British fleet of 19 ships under Admiral Graves tried to intercept. Graves missed his connection at sea and headed for the Chesapeake where he expected them to arrive on September 5. In the Chesapeake, however, Graves ran into the 24 ship fleet of de Grasse, initiating a naval battle. The British were outgunned and withdrew. When the Newport fleet arrived, the French had 32 ships and were masters of the Chesapeake.

Washington and Rochambeau arrived at Williamsburg on September 14 to find that the French could stay only until the end of October, the probable date of British naval reinforcements. A long siege was out of the question; therefore, Yorktown had to be taken by assault. This was feasible as the combined French and American armies outnumbered the British by at least two to one. For two weeks men and equipment arrived while Allied forces were organized. Finally, on September 28, the Allies moved into positions around Yorktown. The British defensive works consisted of an outer series of redoubts and a continuous line of trenches around the town. On the night of September 29, the British evacuated the outer works. Their reasons must have been that these were too extensive to defend against the superior Allied forces. The French and Americans moved in close to the British second line.

The Allies began the digging of trenches and occupied the first series on October 7. By the ninth all the Allied artillery were in place, much of it provided by Henry Knox, who had arranged delivery by ship. Allied firing commenced on that day and it was destructive: 3,600 rounds in one day from 52 pieces. Allied trenches were extended closer with zigzag access trenches and a second line of trenches was constructed only 360 yards from the British by October 11. The artillery enfiladed the British lines from close range with terrible destructive effect.

In front of their main line the British had two redoubts, one called Number 9, the other Number 10. These were bombarded and on the night of October 14, one was taken by the French and the other by the Americans. Cornwallis warned Clinton not to risk the fleet in an effort to save his army and attempted to escape by boat on the night of October 16.

If Cornwallis could transfer his army across the river at night, he might break through Allied lines on the other side (Gloucester Point) in the morning. While this attempt was being made, a storm came up and blew this last hope away. In the morning the British waved a white flag calling for a truce and a parlay to discuss surrender. On October 19 the surrender was formalized; at two that afternoon the British army marched out and lay down their arms. The peace treaty was not signed until April 19, 1783, but the fighting was over.

French military assistance, beyond the invaluable supplies and funds donated, was rather meager, except on this one occasion. At Yorktown, however, it was absolutely crucial. The United States the French helped to create has, twice in this century, repaid the debt. We haven't overpaid.

Analysis

If the British plans for defense of the Colonies had been based on regular forces commanded by British officers with enlisted Colonists, there might not have been a revolution. The Roman Empire lasted 1,000 years with this military format. By relying upon local militia companies for defense, the British created what quickly became an American army.

Even so, could the British have been successful in putting down the rebellion? With a Marlborough instead of a Gage, it is easy to imagine the colonists on Breed's Hill being cut off by a landing near Bunker Hill in their rear. Capture of this force and quick dispersal of the militia gathering around Boston probably would have stopped the rebellion from spreading.

After retreating from Boston, the British sent an army of 30,000 to New York. This was as large an army as Britain was able to muster in the War of the Spanish Succession or in the Napoleonic Wars. What could the British have done to win with this superb force?

They should have vigorously attacked Washington on Brooklyn Heights before he was able to evacuate. A major defeat might well have discouraged the Colonies from attempting to resist. Washington was obligated to try to defend New York, and he had to place his army at risk in order to do it.

Again at Brandywine, Washington stood between the British and Philadelphia. British tactics here, as in Brooklyn, were to send major forces wide in a flanking maneuver. Thus the American line could be collapsed and forced to retreat. A victory was achieved, but the American army survived. Marlborough attacked frontally, threatening at one point with an aggressive assault, taking losses, then throwing a massive strike at another point, severing the enemy line, and allowing destruction and capture of major portions of the opposing force. It may well have been that Howe and Clinton remembered the horror of Breed's Hill and resolved never again to attack Americans frontally, especially when they held prepared defensive works. (Cornwallis attacked frontally in the south, but his forces were too small for complicated flanking attacks.)

Once the Americans were freed from trying to defend or capture cities (after disasters at Savannah and Charleston), the British could only chase them about the countryside. While significant American forces roamed the woods from Maine to Georgia, the British could do nothing but occupy a few major ports.

They could not hold any number of inland posts or occupy any significant territory.

Supply was a major problem. In order to move inland, the British were tempted to divide their forces to better obtain recruits and supplies. This led to defeats such as Bennington and Kings Mountain. The only possible strategy after failing to crush Washington in New York and Philadelphia was to pursue the American army. If the campaign around Philadelphia had been started earlier in the year, the British could have followed Washington after his retreat from Philadelphia. This retreat had to be along the route where he expected to obtain supplies.

If Burgoyne had been attached to Howe, a coordinated plan might have been developed for a two-pronged attack upon Washington in an attempt to trap the main American army. A plan such as this would certainly have been superior to the disastrous scheme proposed by Burgoyne.

All in all, Howe and Clinton were far too cautious to win the war and just not sufficiently dedicated. Marlborough was determined to win, even at the cost of his life. He led cavalry charges twice (once at Ramilles). Cornwallis was aggressive but not in overall command. He had insufficient force in the south to do all that was expected of him, and in New Jersey the Hessians let him down. He was a good soldier, just not good enough.

Washington and Greene learned quickly; after Brandywine their leadership was faultless. Wayne and Morgan stand out as the best of the fighting generals. Maryland and Delaware Continentals, under Stirling or Smallwood, performed superbly from Long Island to Eutaw Springs. The soldier who was called a Continental was a regular, a professional. Unlike the militia, he could be depended upon to attack or to stand and fight. Continentals were the backbone of American armies, and they fought the best troops in the world with honor and distinction.

The militia came in large numbers but were of dubious value. They couldn't be moved in any direction without causing confusion. On many occasions, when attacked, they would run away. But they had courage to come at all, or to fight as much as they did. They lacked training and discipline, but they helped win the war. Lest there be any false notion that one race or nation makes better soldiers than another, look back at Wellington's experience in Portugal where Portuguese infantry were mixed with British in equal numbers with no loss of efficiency. Americans held their own only when trained, equipped, experienced, and well led. The British had tradition behind them that would not accept failure, and their officers had a pride expected of them by the aristocracy to which they belonged. These things make a difference.

No one has ever called Washington a great soldier in the class of Napoleon or Alexander. He didn't have the experience or the forces to enable a fair comparison. Let it be said only that he was a great man, one of the great men of all time. Who *ever* accomplished more under more trying circumstances?

Chapter IV
The Civil War, 1861–1865

On March 4, 1861, Lincoln was inaugurated as the sixteenth President of the United States. He was opposed to slavery, and Southern statesmen felt that the federal Government would now inevitably move to abolish that institution which many of them needed to maintain their lifestyle. Slavery had been discussed by the writers of the Constitution, but their main concern was to bind the colonies together, and addressing such a violently controversial issue at that time might well have destroyed the United States before they were even functional. The evils of slavery, however, became more and more of an issue with Congressmen and their constituents. By 1861 the issue of slavery had reached the boiling point.

Soon after Lincoln's inauguration, the southern states seceded from the Union—South Carolina, North Carolina, Georgia, Virginia, Alabama, Mississippi, Tennessee, Arkansas, Louisiana, and Texas.

The issue of secession hung in doubt in three of the border states, Missouri, Kentucky, and Maryland. If these states joined the Confederacy, the populations of the North and South would be close to equal (including the Negro population in the South).

In Kentucky and Missouri, the governors were Southern sympathizers but the legislatures were mixed and Union efforts to retain these states had to be made.

Fort Sumter was captured by Rebels, and the war was on. In the North the cause was "Preserve the Union." That was enough of a purpose without the still controversial issue of slavery. In the South, the issue was the defense of homes, families, and states. North and South, men rushed to enlist.

In Maryland riots broke out in Baltimore. A 3,000 man regiment from Boston was sent to Baltimore to restore order. The Maryland legislature asked Federal and Confederate governments to respect property. Lincoln said he would, but General Joe Johnston said the South would respect only its own property. Result: Maryland for the Union.

Jefferson Davis, nominated President of the Confederacy, wanted to defend along the Ohio River and sent troops to Columbus and Louisville in Kentucky.

The Kentucky legislature objected, calling for the Union to protect them. Put Kentucky in the Union column.

Lincoln brilliantly managed the battle for the border states. In Missouri the governor formed a militia of Southern sympathizers. Lincoln gave Francis Blair a letter permitting him to declare martial law. Blair then gave Captain Nat Lyon authority to gather troops. Lyon formed a group of 1,000 Germans, captured the entire Rebel militia while they were drilling, and forced the governor to flee. Missouri stayed in the Union. A Confederate army came into southern Missouri, where they were met by Lyon in August 1861. Lyon and 6,000 men faced 10,000 under McCulloch, and in the battle the Union army was beaten with the loss of Lyon. Union numbers eventually prevailed, however, and Missouri remained under Union control.

In Virginia the delegates to the state legislature from the western mountains refused to vote for secession, returning home to vote for removing West Virginia from the state of Virginia. West Virginia turned the tables, seceding from Virginia. Before the South could send troops into the area, West Virginia asked Ohio for military support.

In Ohio a young former officer named McClelland had written a good book about the Crimean War. He was named General of that state's militia, and by May he had 10,000 men. The Confederacy sent General Garnett with 8,000 men to rebellious West Virginia to put down the revolt. Garnett sent 1,500 to Philippi. McClelland invaded West Virginia, dispersing the force at Philippi, then raced to the southern pass through the Alleghanies where Garnett had left 2,000 men. McClelland dispersed this force also, leaving Colonel Rosecrans to round them up, while he attacked Garnett at the northern pass through the mountains. Garnett was defeated, bringing West Virginia into the Union and putting McClelland's name on every front page in the country, where he was called a young Napoleon.

The best officer in the American army was Robert E. Lee, but Lee resigned to serve his state, reporting to Jeff Davis as an adviser. Command of the Union army forming around Washington was given to the man considered second best, Irvin McDowell.

Winfield Scott, a hero of the Mexican War, was Army Chief of Staff. When asked about manpower, he advised the building of an army of 300,000 to be trained and enlisted for three years. He further recommended the capture and fortification of a number of Mississippi River towns plus the blockade of major southern ports. The newspapers thought all this ridiculous, referring to the idea as Scott's Anaconda, but all his advice was eventually followed. The blockade made it difficult to export cotton and deprived the South of badly needed revenue and war material.

Lincoln no doubt thought Scott to be overly pessimistic and called for the enlistment of 75,000 men to serve for a period of three months. Politicians in the North clamored for action, and a council of war was held to consider this. In spite of Scott's advice, it was decided that an attack should be made soon before enlistments ran out. If Northern troops were green, Southern troops would be no better off, and one quick victory might just end the war.

Bull Run, July, 1861

The first major stream south of the Potomac is Bull Run. A town there, called Manassas, is the railroad junction for lines to Richmond and to the Shenandoah Valley on the west side of the Blue Ridge Mountains. Beauregard had 23,000 men near Manassas, but Joe Johnston had 15,000 more in the Valley. Old Union General Patterson had 22,000 men to oppose Johnston, but McDowell had only 28,000. McDowell was ordered to attack Beauregard, and Patterson was ordered to keep pressure on Johnston to prevent him from taking a train to Manassas.

During the night of July 18–19, McDowell sent major forces across Bull Run north of the Confederate line in a flanking attack. Beauregard concentrated to attack on the southern flank. During the morning of the nineteenth, the Confederate left flank was crushed as half the Union army rolled it up. On a plateau in the center of the Rebel line was the division of Thomas J. Jackson. The Union attack was stopped there, and one Confederate General, Bee, while attempting to rally his men, looked up at the plateau to see Jackson sitting on his horse calmly and motionless. Bee called to his men; "Look, there stands Jackson like a stone wall." Jackson has been known as Stonewall Jackson ever since.

McDowell, no longer in control, attempted to rally small groups to attack again, piecemeal, at various points but with no more success. Then, Joe Johnston's army, in by rail from the Shenandoah, came in on the Union rear. The entire Union army ran like rabbits, except for a few units which fought rear guard actions.

The Confederates, no doubt also disorganized, did not pursue. This disaster must be blamed on Patterson, who failed to keep Johnston occupied in the Valley. The poor conduct of the Union troops, once beaten, was to be expected. Scott had advised no attack until the army was ready. Unfortunately, in this country, politicians feel free to ignore their military specialists.

McClellan was appointed General of the Army and soon had a force of 190,000 men, including cavalry, artillery, and engineers. He drilled and organized, but he would not fight, convinced that Beauregard's successor, Johnston, had 250,000 men. Scott and Lincoln put no stock in this, however, and urged McClelland to advance. McClelland began a personal attack on Scott until the old man decided to retire. Thus did 1861 close with no major action in the eastern theatre.

War in Kentucky, 1861

In Kentucky Albert Sidney Johnston, with 20,000 Confederates, occupied Columbus on the Mississippi, threatening Cairo, Illinois, at the junction of the Mississippi and Ohio Rivers. Albert Johnston was considered to be the best general in the Confederate army and there was no Union general of stature in the area to oppose him.

Ulysses S. Grant had been made a Union general along with twenty others, and he just happened to be in the St. Louis headquarters when the appointment for the Cairo command was being decided. An army friend of Grant's (both veterans of the Mexican War) saw him and recommended he be put in command at Cairo. This was done, and Grant went to work. Taking 3,000 men, he attacked the Confederates at Belmont, Missouri, across the river from Columbus. The Rebels ran, but Polk came across the river with 10,000 and Grant just managed to escape.

As a result of this move, however, Johnston called in troops from the Ohio River and sent them to Island Number 10 on the Mississippi, south of Columbus.

Union strategy in the West called for attack down the Mississippi but inland, using the Tennessee and Cumberland Rivers. On the first move Grant sailed east up the Ohio to take Paducah and Smithland at the mouth of the Cumberland and Tennessee Rivers, breaking Johnston's Ohio River line. Because of Grant's adventure at Belmont, Johnston had weakened his forces along the Ohio resulting in the loss of much of Kentucky.

Grant was a heavy drinker, a cigar smoker, and not much of a conversationalist. Short and stocky, unimpressive to look at, he was a superb general, a tough and cold fighting machine, quick to act, and quick to think in combat. His brain worked best in the heat of battle. His concept of military strategy was excellent.

The Tennessee and Cumberland Rivers extended due south into Tennessee. Johnston established a new defense line from Columbus to new Fort Henry and Fort Donelson on the rivers near Tennessee, to Bowling Green, and finally to Mill Spring in the east. 1861 closed with Grant begging his superior in St. Louis, General Henry Halleck, for permission to attack the forts. Halleck procrastinated, but a naval officer, Flag Officer Foote, obtained seven low draft armor plated gunboats and urged the Navy Department to attack Fort Henry and Fort Donelson before their defenses were made formidable. Grant then obtained permission to combine with Foote in an attack on Fort Henry on the Tennessee River.

Forts Henry and Donelson, February, 1862

On February 6, Grant, with 15,000 men, and Foote moved up the Tennessee River, landing his troops 8 miles above Ft. Henry while Foote moved in to bombard the place. The Navy subdued the fort's guns before Grant could attack and a white flag was raised. Few Confederates were taken in the fort as most had gone over to Fort Donelson, there to be better able to make a stand. Without orders, Grant moved by land over to the Cumberland River while Foote sailed down the Tennessee and up the Cumberland.

Fort Donelson was strong and defended by 21,000 men, but the commanding general was Floyd, a politician of dubious character. The fort overcame the gunboats, which were forced to withdraw. Grant put three divisions around the fort, commanded by Lew Wallace, McClernand, and C.F. Smith. The Rebels made a sortie with 8,000 men against McClernand's division and went right through, turning to roll up the Union line. Wallace brought in reserves and held for a while. Grant rode up, saw some prisoners with knapsacks full of food, and realized the sortie was an effort to escape. Suspecting that the far wall of the fort was weakly defended, he ordered Smith to attack. Smith's attack succeeded and Union forces took possession of a portion of the fort. The high ground taken dominated the rest of the fort which became indefensible. Floyd escaped but the fort was surrendered with 17,000 men. Grant called for unconditional surrender and the nickname for U. S. Grant became Unconditional Surrender Grant.

Over at Mill Springs, a division commander in Buell's Army of the Cumberland, General George H. Thomas, caught a Confederate column coming at him; Thomas attacked, forcing the Confederates to form in line, then delivered an oblique attack, rolling up the line and dispersing the entire force. (The oblique attack was one of the favorite tactics of Frederick the Great.)

Kentucky was lost to the Confederates along with much of central Tennessee. The lone east-west railroad from Memphis to Chattanooga running along the Mississippi-Tennessee border was closely approached by the Tennessee River, and any further Union movement to the south was a serious threat to this line.

General Halleck, in command of the western Union armies, had three armies; the Army of Missouri under John Pope, the Army of the Tennessee under Grant, and the Army of the Cumberland under Don Carlos Buell. Halleck decided to attack Island Number 10 on the Mississippi above Memphis using the Army of Missouri.

Island Number 10, March, 1862

Once Island Number 10 was taken, an attack on Memphis was possible. This would narrow Confederate possession of the Mississippi and prevent the Confederates from massing against Grant who planned to move down the Tennessee. Pope, supported by Foote, made the attack. A canal was dug across a bend in the Mississippi. allowing Pope's army to occupy some better ground on the Missouri shore downstream of Island No. ten. One of Foote's gunboats (Carondolet) passed the island guns at night and knocked out the guns on the Kentucky shore, enabling Pope's army to cross the river to the Kentucky side where there was access to the fort. The Confederates surrendered with 7,000 men.

Shiloh April 6–7 1862

Albert Sidney Johnston, falling hack into Tennessee, correctly anticipated Grant's next move to Pittsburg Landing on the Tennessee, the place where the river turns to the east, the closest approach to the railroad from the river. Johnston collected 50,000 men and waited.

Grant moved to Pittsburg Landing on the west side of the river with 35,000 men. Around the town from the river in the south were the divisions of Prentiss, Sherman, McClernand, Hurlbut, and W. H. L. Wallace. Lew Wallace was several miles up the river at Crump's Landing. Grant had no cavalry, made no defensive preparations, and had only an outpost line of pickets. He sent out no probing patrols and had no idea of Johnston's whereabouts. Buell's army was a day's march away but was expected to join Grant.

On a Sunday morning, the Confederates came on from the south. From the river inland were the divisions of Breckinridge, Bragg, Hardee, and Polk. They hit Prentiss first; hearing the pickets, Prentiss called out his division. Sherman and McClernand were worse off with almost no warning; their divisions were overrun or dispersed. Some of Sherman's men formed around Shiloh Church. Prentiss resisted more effectively. Some of his men held an elevated spot called "The Hornet's Nest." Hurlbut and Wallace brought their divisions up and formed a line along a deep gully north of Sherman's and Prentiss's original positions.

Grant came up, surveyed the situation, and sent urgent messages to Lew Wallace, Buell, and Foote. He ordered artillery set up at Pittsburg Landing, where thousands of retreating troops were gathering. He ordered Sherman and McClernand to go get these men and return them to the line. Prentiss was finally cut off but held out into the afternoon before he surrendered with a few survivors. Near the river, Breckenridge and Bragg, finally past Prentiss, approached the gully where they received devastating artillery fire from gunboats on the river.

Inland the Union line of Wallace and Hurlbut, stiffened with Sherman's and McClernand's men, held the position in the gully. Grant rode up the line; his horse was shot, his hat shot off, his shoulder insignia shot away, and his uniform was ripped by two other balls. Johnston came up on the Rebel side and called for one more charge. A ball hit him in the leg and he bled until too weak to sit on his horse. He fell to the ground, where he died from loss of blood. A tourniquet would have saved him, but in the heat of battle his aides apparently did not realize the extent of his wound.

Beauregard took over, pulled Bragg's division out from under all the artillery and gunboat fire, then moved it inland against W. H. L. Wallace. The Union line began to sag, but darkness came, stopping the Confederate advance. Wallace was dead, and his men lay where they were, in the rain, waiting for morning and more horror.

At midnight Lew Wallace came in with 7,000 Union troops. At 2 A.M. Bull Nelson came in with the first of Buell's divisions. At 2:30 Crittenden arrived with a second Buell division. At 3:00 McCook brought in the third of Buell's divisions. By 4:00 Grant had them all in line and at 5:00 he attacked. The Union army swept the Confederates from the field in a complete rout. There was no last stand. Forty thousand Confederates retreated all the way to Corinth in Mississippi. Each army suffered 10,000 casualties.

Johnston, instead of personally trying to encourage his men in the front line, made the same mistake that Vendomme made at Oudenarde against Marlborough. He became too involved in the fight at too local a point. If he had gathered his generals at headquarters and ordered the transfer of Bragg's division that Bragg did later, he might have broken Grant's line earlier. In any event this was as close to defeat as Grant ever did come and under the worst possible circumstances (surprise) imaginable.

Halleck must be given credit for the overall plan and for combining Buell and Grant. The combined armies were just strong enough to handle Johnston. On Sunday afternoon, before Wallace arrived, Johnston must have had a two to one manpower advantage.

After the war, Sherman said that he would have retreated at Shiloh if he had been in Grant's place. At the time of the battle, in the evening of the first day, all that Grant said to Sherman was, "We'll get them in the morning." No one but Grant could have salvaged the battle of Shiloh.

Grant's lack of patrolling and the fact that he was surprised by Johnston offended his superior, Halleck, who replaced him in charge of the Army of the Tennessee. Numerous politicians and civilian groups complained to Lincoln from time to time about Grant, mainly about his heavy drinking. Lincoln said, "What brand of liquor does he drink? I'd like to send a barrel of it to my other generals."

McClelland's Advance in the Peninsula, Spring, 1862

On January 31, Lincoln ordered McClelland to attack Manassas. McClelland suggested a less obvious strategy, a feint at Manassas with a major move to the Peninsula east of Richmond between the York and James Rivers, with a rapid advance to the city. Thirty days later Lincoln agreed but insisted forces be provided to defend Washington. McClelland had 200,000 men and could have used up to 150,000 in the Peninsula. McClelland believed that Joe Johnston had 120,000 to defend Richmond, but Johnston had only 58,000.

The Washington newspapers printed every detail of the Union plan, and Johnston pulled back to the Rappahannock River, halfway between Washington and Richmond.

McClelland sailed to Fort Monroe on the Peninsula where he landed with 90,000 men. McClelland advanced as far as Yorktown where he was stopped by the fortifications of Yorktown, manned by 13,000 Confederates. McClelland had planned to have McDowell take Yorktown from the other side of the river, but McDowell never arrived. McDowell commanded the corps protecting

Washington, and Lincoln refused to allow this corps to move south.

As a result McClelland settled down for a formal siege of Yorktown while Johnston strolled back to Richmond with 80,000 to prepare for the Yankees. McClelland walked to Seven Pines, only 5 miles from Richmond. Here he placed the corps of Keyes and Heintzelman south of the Chickahominy at Gaines Mill. On May 31, Johnston sent three-fourths of his army in against Keyes. Couch and Casey of Keyes put up a stout defense and when McClelland saw the danger he brought in Sumner's corps and all the army artillery reserve. Longstreet and Huger led the Confederates, who threw back Keyes and Heintzelman then ran into Sumner and the artillery. Johnston was wounded and Longstreet took over.

Union General Phil Kearney picked up some dismounted cavalry and Union stragglers, then charged into the Confederates forcing them to fall back to their original positions. McClelland did well that day, but his whole scheme had failed. He had the whole Confederate Army in front of him and called on Lincoln to send McDowell in on Richmond from the north. Longstreet was then replaced with Robert F. Lee, a more agreeable gentleman. Lee heard about McDowell and knew that defense of Richmond was now a problem. He needed a diversion to hold McDowell in Washington. Jackson was in the Shenandoah with a small force. Lee sent Ewell's division to Jackson, and what followed in the Valley is a textbook lesson in military tactics.

Stonewall Jackson in the Shenandoah Valley

With Ewell's division Jackson had 20,000 men in the southern end of the Shenandoah. Union General Milroy with 15,000 was coming at him from the south and Union General Banks from the north with 13,000. Banks had been weakened to defend Washington, allowing McDowell to move on Richmond with 40,000 men. Jackson put Ewell in front of Banks and moved south to strike Milroy, covering 50 miles in three days. Milroy's advance of 4,000 men was pulverized. Jackson turned back to the north, picked up Ewell, and raced up the east valley while Banks retreated slowly up the west valley. Jackson moved north of Banks, blocking the only escape route. Banks, forced to attack, was beaten and the survivors crossed the Potomac into Maryland.

Lincoln planned a retaliation, but fearing for Washington, he recalled McDowell from above Richmond. Lee's strategy worked just as he had conceived it.

Lincoln sent in Shields from Manassas to close Jackson's northern escape route, but Jackson moved south down the west valley while Shields raced down the east.

Jackson reached the southern passage through the Blue Ridge Mountains at Port Republic just before Shields. Leaving a token force to hold off Shields, Jackson turned west to strike Fremont (also sent by Lincoln), now just 10 miles away. Fremont's force was smashed, then Jackson turned back to wait for

Shields. When Shields attacked what he thought was just a holding force, he ran into Jackson's whole army and was crushed.

Jackson had beaten four armies, occupied 100,000 Union troops, and cancelled the Union northern advance on Richmond. Jackson then moved to Richmond to assist Lee, arriving on June 27.

McClelland in the Peninsula

McClelland's dream of victory in the Peninsula was now gone. Worse, the Confederates organized their cavalry under a man named J. E. B. Stuart. Stuart rode into McClelland's rear, destroyed $7,000,000 worth of supplies, and found out everything Lee needed to know about the Union army positions and strength. Now, Porter's corps of Union troops was north of the Chickahominy and the other corps were south of the river with few bridges between.

Lee put all but 30,000 of his army opposite Porter and ordered Longstreet to attack. Jackson was ordered in on Porter's flank to cut the Union escape route. The Confederates attacked at Gaines Mill, but Porter held with the assistance of massed artillery. Jackson failed to attack until late afternoon for some very strange and unknown reason. McClelland moved his supply point from West Point on the York River to Harrison's Landing on the James. Posting artillery on the Chickahominy, McClelland withdrew south toward the James while Sumner held the rear at Savage Station.

Lee assigned Huger and Magruder to attack Sumner while Jackson came in on Sumner's rear. (This was a hammer and anvil tactic used by the Marines in Vietnam.) Again Jackson delayed. Magruder took heavy losses from Union artillery and Sumner escaped.

The next morning Lee attacked again, at Glendale. Longstreet and A. P. Hill came in from the west, with D. H. Hill and Jackson expected to come in from the east. Longstreet ran into McCall's Pennsylvania division with brigade commanders Meade, Ord, and Reynolds, the best division in the Union army. Longstreet finally broke through at night, but Kearny brought the New Jersey volunteers in on the Confederate flank and broke up the attack. Jackson did not appear. He procrastinated much of the day in some kind of a religious mood.

McClelland safely pulled his army into good defensive positions at Malvern Hill on the James. Lee thought the Federals were discouraged and ordered a general assault that failed with 7,000 men killed.

McClelland had lost 20,000 men in the Peninsula and accomplished nothing except for similar Confederate casualties. After Shiloh and the Peninsula, the bloody cost of the war was now becoming painfully clear to both sides.

McClelland was not beaten on the Peninsula, perhaps because the Peninsula was too narrow for complicated maneuvers, and perhaps because of Jackson's peculiar behavior. The Union army showed considerable skill and power, a significant improvement over Bull Run and 1861.

So far Lee's skill had been sufficient to overcome a huge Union preponderance of manpower. South of the Potomac, Lee had a good knowledge of Union strength and dispositions from spies and cavalry. In addition, he had shorter lines of communication and could more easily add or subtract forces as required. When he ventured north of the Potomac, these advantages shifted to the Army of the Potomac. It was once said that Napoleon's presence on a battlefield was equivalent to 40,000 men. Lee might have been worth a similar number while defending in Virginia.

New Orleans, April, 1862

Admiral Farragut attacked New Orleans on April 18, with 5 frigates, 3 sloops, 9 gunboats, and a fleet of mortars. The Confederate forts, Jackson and St. Phillip, and a Confederate fleet put up a good fight, but Farragut fought through and a Union army of occupation took over. Now Vicksburg and Memphis would be the only Confederate fortresses on the entire Mississippi River.

Memphis, June, 1862

After Shiloh Halleck took the combined western armies and headed for Corinth, Mississippi, on the Memphis-Chattanooga Railroad. Halleck moved cautiously, covering 20 miles in 31 days. His army numbered 100,000 while Beauregard had only 55,000.

Rather than be surrounded, the Confederates evacuated Corinth and the Union army occupied the town, cutting the vital railroad. Halleck then moved towards Memphis.

Memphis was well fortified for a land attack and had a fleet of eight ships to defend against a river borne attack. Most of these had rams and the city looked to be a tough place to capture, but there was one weakness. The population depended on water pipelines into the city for their water supply.

On May 10, a Union fleet with seven ironclads, commanded by Davis (Foote had been wounded) came down to give battle. This day resulted in a draw with both fleets losing several ships. On June 6, the Union fleet came back with three fast rams, and this time the Confederate fleet was destroyed. Without a fleet to protect the water supply, the city was helpless and surrendered the next day. Beauregard was replaced with Bragg and Halleck was called to Washington as Army Chief of Staff. He took Pope with him, the best of the western generals.

Grant took over in the west, located at Jackson, with forces at Memphis, Bolivar. and Corinth. As originally directed by Halleck, Buell was in independent command with orders to move east along the railroad toward Chattanooga with 40,000 men.

Iuka and Corinth, September, 1862

After the surrender of Memphis, Bragg took the bulk of his forces to Chattanooga. Two Confederate armies remained in northern Mississippi. Grant's cavalry spotted one of these armies of 16,000 men under Van Dorn moving toward Holly Springs southwest of Corinth in Mississippi on September 15. The other army of 16,000 under Price was observed moving toward Iuka, east of Corinth. Grant assumed the two armies meant to combine and strike Corinth, so he sent Rosecrans south of Iuka with 9,000 men from Corinth to trap Price while Ord with 8,000 from Bolivar (Tennessee) came down to strike the Confederate rear. A third force was sent to block Van Dorn should he come upon the scene prematurely.

Ord arrived above Iuka on the night of September 18 and waited. Rosecrans attacked the town at dawn, but when Price found he was being attacked from the south, he knew he was in trouble and counterattacked. Ord, unfortunately, did not hear the guns and did not attack until evening, but by that time Price had found a road for escape. Rosecrans should have blocked the road, but still it was a victory. Grant had shown how seriously he made war.

Price and Van Dorn then combined forces with only one suitable target, Corinth. Through a female spy they received a map of Corinth showing the main strongpoint there, Battery Robinett, to be almost undefended. The spy, Aurelia Burton, had been captured several weeks before without Confederate knowledge and the map was a hoax.

McPherson with 5,000 planned to hit the Confederate rear as soon as they attacked; Ord with 7,000 would block their escape route.

The outer Corinth defenses were manned by the divisions of MacArthur (grandfather of Douglas MacArthur), Davies, and Hamilton, with Stanley in reserve. Van Dorn came in from the north and hit the divisions of MacArthur and Davies. Price attacked Hamilton, but the Confederates opposite Davies were thrown back in disorder. Davies counterattacked but left a gap between his and MacArthur's divisions. Two Confederate brigades were thrown into the breech and the whole Union line was forced back. Stanley came up and stabilized the fight until dark. Then the Union army moved back to their inner defenses with Stanley in the strong position of Battery Robinett well armed with artillery.

Hebert of Van Dorn was ordered to attack MacArthur on the west flank, drawing off Union reserves. Price then was expected to attack the supposedly weak Battery Robinett with his whole army. Hebert called in sick, however, and Van Dorn, furious, took over, personally leading an assault on MacArthur that was repulsed with heavy loss. Price assumed the attack to be successful and moved against Battery Robinett. Two of his regiments were decimated within 20 minutes by a heavy artillery barrage. Price rallied his retreating force and came on again with more horrendous loss. Price did get some men into the town, but Hamilton sent a brigade from the east flank and Stanley sent artillery from the other. The Confederates were driven out of town and, as they moved back, McPherson showed up in their rear. Van Dorn took the remnants of his army back to Holly Springs where they were held up by Ord for 6 hours. If Rosecrans had followed he could have caught the whole Confederate army, but he did not pursue until it was too late; the survivors managed to get around Ord, scattering and filtering back to Vicksburg.

Van Dorn was replaced with J. C. Pemberton, who had impressed everyone in Richmond with his ability to discuss military matters. Rosecrans received too much credit for these victories resulting in a disastrous promotion, but the whole campaign had been beautifully planned by Grant.

Bragg's Invasion of Kentucky, Autumn 1862

The Confederacy was being pushed back in western Kentucky and Tennessee and some offensive strategy was needed to reverse that process. It was therefore decided to send Bragg north to threaten Cincinnati. This was certain to draw a Union army into battle, perhaps in a situation more favorable than found in defensive measures. The presence of a Confederate army in Kentucky was also expected to draw recruits. On August 27, Bragg crossed the Cumberland River with 40,000 men, sending Kirby Smith on ahead. At Richmond, Kentucky, Smith met a Union army under Bull Nelson (who had been at Shiloh) with 7,000 raw recruits. Nelson's force was destroyed with few survivors. Nelson was twice wounded but did survive the massacre. The road to Cincinnati was wide open, creating much panic among the civilian population. Buell left Thomas in Nashville and moved north to Mumfordville, Kentucky, south of Louisville, but his force was inferior to that of Bragg. Bragg arrived at Mumfordville before Buell and an attack seemed inevitable. Grant had sent a division to Nashville, however, freeing Thomas who took off for Mumfordville with 20,000 men, arriving the night before Bragg planned to attack. When Bragg found out about the huge Union reinforcements, he called off the attack and moved to Frankfurt, east of Louisville. Thomas had saved the day; in fact, everything Thomas did in this war was outstanding. Somehow his name has not been included with that of Grant, Sherman, Sheridan, Lee, and Jackson; perhaps because his achievements were in the west and not in every eastern newspaper.

Buell marched to Louisville where he picked up more men, raising his force to 58,000. Bragg had picked up few recruits as the people of Kentucky were not very sympathetic to his cause; worse, they were hostile.

Buell decided to attack Bragg with the large force now under his command. A division under Sill approached Frankfurt while Buell's army moved toward Richmond to cut off Bragg's retreat and supply line. Two Union corps under McCook and Gilbert arrived at Perryville on October 7, occupying two prominent hills. A third corps was between the hills but more to the rear. Thomas moved around the rest of the army to take up positions on the Union right flank.

Confederate cavalry had found Union troops in a number of places between Frankfurt and Perryville. Bragg, assuming the Federals to be moving in on a wide front, decided to guard the Kentucky River bridges near Frankfurt while sending four divisions to hit the lone Union corps he expected to find at Perryville. The divisions of Cheatham, Hardee, Buckner, and Anderson—20,000 men—arrived at Perryville on October 8, charging lustily into the whole Union army.

McCook's corps of raw recruits was the first to receive the blow, and this corps dissolved. Next, the Confederates struck the veterans of Sheridan's division of Gilbert's corps. Five times Hardee and Buckner attacked Sheridan, and five times they were thrown back with heavy losses. Gilbert sent Sheridan some cavalry, which the fearless Sheridan led in a charge against Anderson, going right through the Confederate line. The Confederates, now in total disarray, retreated. Buell's only action was to send Crittenden's corps to support Sheridan and this move did not come in time to help. Sadly Buell had missed a chance to destroy four divisions. Bragg returned to Tennessee and Buell returned to Nashville.

Perryville was Sheridan's day, and his valiant use of cavalry was well noted by Grant, who one day would make Sheridan commander of the Potomac Army Cavalry Corps. Buell was demoted, and Secretary of War Stanton wanted Thomas to take command of the Army of the Cumberland but Lincoln wanted Rosecrans, a friend of Governor Morton of Indiana. Rosecrans was given the job, another unfortunate military decision made by Lincoln, who still did not have confidence in his military commanders.

The armies of the Civil War had officers familiar with a troop of 50 cavalry but almost no one experienced in handling armies. After the early battles promotions were based on performance, but many times the battles were decided by events other than superior generalship and the promotions were frequently ill deserved. In every war peacetime generals had to be replaced with combat generals after the former failed to perform. The Civil War, however, was a major war in which it was very difficult, on both sides, to find generals capable of leading an army to victory in battle. This resulted in tremendous casualties on both sides. In World War II the United States was fortunate to have senior officers with useful combat experience in World War I.

Stone River, December, 1862

Murfreesboro is on the Stone River, a subsidiary of the Cumberland. The town lay west of Knoxville, southeast of Nashville. Bragg moved into Murfreesboro in order to satisfy the Confederate hierarchy's desire to do something. Rosecrans, with similar pressure to act, also moved down to the town to face Bragg. By December 30, both armies were in position. Most of Bragg's army was west of Stone River with only Breckenridge's corps on the east bank.

Rosecrans had (from west to east) McCook with three divisions, Thomas with five, and Crittenden with three. Only Crittenden was east of the river. Rosecrans planned to reinforce Crittenden, attack east of the river and trap most of Bragg's army on the other side. Bragg planned to attack west of the river and push the Union army into a bend in the river. Both plans were sound, but the Union attack was planned for after breakfast. Bragg, however, attacked at dawn, sending 20,000 men clear around McCook whose divisions were not in position or ready.

Apparently neither McCook or Rosecrans inspected these divisions. Within 30 minutes two of the divisions were routed, leaving only one to face Hardee, but this was Sheridan's division. Sheridan launched a bayonet attack and brought Hardee to a complete stop. Rosecrans brought up Crittenden and posted him on the Nashville road. Thomas bent his corps at a right angle to meet Crittenden. Now the full force of the Confederate attack was directed at the angle in Thomas's line. Once broken, the Union line could be demolished with enfilading artillery fire followed by infantry attacks. Thomas, however, rode up and down the line, directing the defense at every critical point. By 3:30 the attack on Thomas waned. Sheridan gathered McCook's refugees and a division came over from Crittenden. At 4:30 the Rebels came on again, with no success. At 5:30 Thomas counterattacked, pushing the Rebels back.

That night Rosecrans considered retreat but Thomas and Sheridan talked him out of it. While the Union army waited for more supplies, Bragg decided to attack east of the river where Crittenden had been. There was a hill there that looked down on the whole Union army. Breckinridge made the attack but ran into Van Cleve's division firmly posted on the hill, backed by 58 pieces of artillery. Breckenridge went nowhere, and when Thomas sent two divisions to Van Cleve, the Union army took the offensive. Stanley's cavalry threatened the Confederate rear and Bragg decided to retreat, all the way to Chattanooga. Rosecrans was a victor (because of Thomas and Sheridan), with no thanks to McCook, who failed for the second consecutive time. Both sides lost a quarter of their armies and Rosecrans was in no shape to pursue. At Stone River Rosecrans moved much too slowly and almost lost his army. His luck would run out on another day. The Confederates however lost another piece of Tennessee.

Pope's Virginia Campaign, August, 1862

When Halleck became chief of staff he intended to replace McClelland with Pope; however, McClelland was a very popular Democrat and Lincoln did not want to discharge him. The plan for the summer called for Pope to move south into Virginia gathering the Union remnants from the Shenandoah and pulling forces away from McClelland, now idle on the Peninsula. This move, if done rapidly, might get to Richmond before Lee realized that it wasn't a feint. So long as McClelland had a large army, Lee must keep forces east of Richmond.

Pope picked up Banks's and Sigel's corps at Sperryville. McDowell brought a corps from Washington down to Culpepper, east of Sperryville and north of the Rapidan River. Pope put Buford in charge of cavalry, and Buford went across the Rapidan to Gordonsville. This warned Lee, who sent Jackson with 25,000 north across the Rapidan at top speed. Buford spotted Jackson as he crossed the river, advising Pope who was able to concentrate at Culpepper. Pope planned to hold Jackson in place with two divisions while the rest of the Union army moved into Jackson's rear. An officer was sent to Banks with verbal orders to, "take two divisions and hold Jackson at Cedar Mountain." The officer, a colonel, changed the orders to "attack Jackson." Banks did attack, pushing one of Jackson's divisions back until Jackson's whole army fell on him. Banks was routed and Pope missed a golden opportunity to punish Jackson.

Lincoln's plans were leaked to Lee, who then took his whole army north. Buford's cavalry observed this movement and warned Pope, allowing him to move back into good positions on the Rappahannock. Lee arrived on August 21, but Reno's Union corps and Reynolds Union division arrived that same night to produce a standoff.

Lee then took one of his calculated risks, sending Jackson off on a wide sweep west then north on the west side of the Manassas Mountains. Jackson's western movement was reported to Pope, but no danger was apparent. Pope received two more corps from the Peninsula and now saw a chance to attack Lee. This was the risk that Lee took, that the Union army would attack him before Jackson could execute, but Lee was obviously contemptuous of his opponents.

Jackson, meanwhile, cut through the mountains into Pope's rear, cutting off the Union supply route. If Pope attacked Lee, Jackson could come at him from behind. Pope, now in trouble, decided to attack Jackson. By holding Lee and moving swiftly with the bulk of his army, Pope could smash Jackson, then turn and strike Lee.

Buford was left behind with cavalry to hide Pope's move. There weren't many roads north, and precise detailed orders were necessary to move all the divisions simultaneously on separate routes, all to arrive at Manassas at the same time. The orders were muddled and the regiments marched off on the wrong roads in total confusion. When the first Union divisions arrived at Manassas, Jackson wasn't there, having pulled back two miles to the Bull Run River. King's division of McDowell finally located Jackson, but was soon under heavy attack. King held on and was joined by Reynold's division, Sigel's corps, Heintzelman's corps, and Reno's corps. Pope was not in control as the bulk of his army moved against Jackson. Rickett's division of McDowell was by mere chance blocking the exit through the mountains from Thorofare Gap. Unknown to Pope or any other Union officer, Lee's whole army was pouring through the Gap like a tidal wave. On August 28, the Union army was ready to go against Jackson.

Then, incompetence ran amok through the high command of Pope's army. The same Colonel Roberts who had ordered Banks to attack Jackson showed up at Rickett's headquarters while Lee's whole army pressed in hard. Instead of calling for help, Robert's advised Ricketts to fall back, allowing Lee to come thundering in on the left flank of the Union army. King had a nervous breakdown, advising his division to retreat to Manassas. Pope, unaware of Lee's presence, advised McDowell and Porter to move towards Gainesville. To do so would have required an attack, but the order did not say this. Porter ran into Longstreet's corps of Lee's army and halted without attacking. At the same time, under orders, Sigel and Heintzelman attacked Jackson, losing 8,000 men.

Pope wired Washington that he had won a great victory. On the following day he sent Porter in against Jackson's right flank. Porter went in, only to be decimated by Lee's massed artillery on his left flank. Then Lee attacked with Hood and Longstreet, followed by Jackson's whole army. Reno tried to halt the rout; Heintzelrnan's corps ran; McDowell went out of control as at first Bull Run, but one of Sigel's brigades managed to bravely hold a bridge allowing most of the army to escape. Even so 7,000 were captured. Heintzelman and McDowell were demoted; Pope was court-martialed; and for decades Americans would compare liars to John Pope.

Lee's Maryland Offensive, September, 1862

The Confederate government was not pleased with the results of one year of war. Just as Bragg's invasion of Kentucky was expected to extend Southern influence, an invasion of Maryland by Lee was expected to bring that state into the Confederacy. On September 4, Lee crossed the Potomac at Leesburg with 40,000 men.

Lincoln and Halleck had to rejuvenate the Union army quickly. McClelland had raised the army, formed it, and trained it. There was no other choice, and McClelland was ordered to take command of the Army of the Potomac once again. McClelland moved out of Washington with an army payroll of 86,000 men but with only 60,000 available.

Lee needed Harpers Ferry to bring in supplies, but this river town was defended by 11,000 Union troops. Lee issued orders for Jackson with 20,000 to take Harpers Ferry. D. H. Hill guarded the South Mountain passes while Lee pushed northwest to Hagerstown. A Confederate messenger was ambushed, and at 6:30 P.M. on September 9 McClelland had a copy of Lee's orders but no move was made that night.

McClelland ordered Franklin to go through Crampton's Gap and Reno to break through Turner's Gap. Neither succeeded, but the attacks warned Lee, who turned around and raced south well into the night. Reno was killed in Turner's Gap in attacks that were not successful until Hooker came up. By the time that the Union army could pass through the hills, Lee had arrived at Sharpsburg to take good defensive positions along the steep banks of Antietam Creek.

McClelland took 24 hours to pass the hills, then decided to take a day of planning before making his move. This gave Jackson time to accept the surrender of the Union force in Harpers Ferry then hurry back to join Lee. (If the 11,000 men in Harpers Ferry could have held up Jackson a day longer, the Civil War might have been substantially shorter.)

On the evening of the eleventh, Hooker's Union corps crossed Antietam Creek on the Confederate left, and Lee, pleased to know where the morning attack would come from, moved Jackson and Ewell's corps to this point. At dawn "Fighting Joe" Hooker attacked, right through Jackson, through Ewell, south down Hagerstown Road to Dunker Church. J. E. B. Stuart came up with cavalry and artillery, and by 7:30 A.M., Hooker came to a halt. His corps and Jackson's were used up.

Mansfield's Union corps then attacked on Hooker's right. Lee pulled Hood from the center to strike Mansfield, but Mansfield kept going until Stuart hit one flank and Hill the other. By 9 A.M., Mansfield halted near the church with his corps and Hood's no longer able to take the offensive. Sumner made a third attack against the Confederate center, but both flanks were exposed, and two Longstreet divisions struck Sumner's left flank. By 10 A.M., Sumner was routed and driven back.

McClelland then advanced against the Confederate right with Reno's corps, now commanded by Burnside (for whom sideburns were named). Franklin rallied Sumner's corps to support Burnside, but Burnside did not attack until 3 P.M. Crook of Burnside's corps (later to fight the Sioux) took a bridge across the creek and led the charge through the Rebel line. Lee scraped up every reserve he could find to aid Early and McLaws, and the fight stabilized around a sunken road called "Bloody Lane." Sumner's corps did manage to enter Sharpsburg but could get no farther. Darkness ended the battle with 12,000 Union and 11,000 Confederate casualties. Lee moved back to the Potomac and escaped with no Union pursuit.

Lee's army was too small for the task undertaken. To invade enemy country where the capture of a town defended by 11,000 was necessary in order to obtain supplies is an incredible risk. If McClelland had had his full strength and if he had coordinated his attacks, it is hard to see how Lee could have survived to bring much of his army back to Virginia. McClelland had 26,000 men unavailable, many on leave. Lincoln said, "Giving that man reinforcements is like shoveling flies across a room." McClelland was dismissed and replaced with Burnside, a charming man.

Lee did have the advantage of a straight, shorter defense line, as had Marlborough at Ramilles and, later, Meade at Gettysburg. This allowed greater mobility and enabled 40,000 men to hold off 60,000 used in piecemeal attacks. For all the Union dissatisfaction Antietam was a victory, but it did not destroy Lee's army and the war went on, and on, and on.

Fredericksburg, December, 1862

Burnside's army was 113,000 to Lee's 80,000, and an attack was planned, straight ahead to Warrenton as a feint, with the bulk of the army slipping east to

Fredericksburg, there to cross the Rappahannock. By November 19, Sumner had two corps at Fredericksburg but there was no bridge and the pontoon bridges expected did not arrive for six more days. Disaster again, due to high-level incompetence. If Sumner had had pontoons, Burnside could have safely crossed the river. Union cavalry hid this movement for a while, but Stuart soon found out what was planned. When the pontoons arrived, so did Longstreet.

When Burnside arrived a few days later, Lee came up on the other side of the river. Burnside was now stymied without a plan. While he pondered what to do, Lee fortified Marye's Hill behind the town. The heights were steep and covered with artillery, the worst possible place to attack in the presence of a large defending force. Burnside's final plan was hopeless, but on December 12 the Union army was ordered to attack. The troops knew they would die, and they pinned notes on their uniforms with the address of their next of kin.

Franklin crossed with two corps on the left. Sumner crossed with two corps on the right. Meade's Pennsylvania division of Franklin went right up the hill and broke the Confederate line, but there was no one behind them. Lee fenced Meade in and drove him back with two thirds of his division lost. On the other flank, Sumner tried for two hours to gain the crest but lost 5,000 men. Hooker came in behind him with two more corps and he too took heavy losses. By 4 P.M. the battle was over with 15,000 good Union troops gone, the worst slaughter of the war.

If Lee had counterattacked, he might have destroyed the Union army as it struggled to recross the river. At this time, Lee said, "It is good that war is so terrible, otherwise we might grow too fond of it." It is possible that he was horrified at the damage his army had done to his fellow countrymen and that an element of mercy influenced his decision. He had, after all, been a high ranking officer in the U.S. Army, had to leave the service of his country, and then was forced to kill his former associates. If Lee had stayed with the Union. it is hard to see how the war could have lasted so long. Lee is much respected by all Americans and rightly so.

Seven Failures at Vicksburg. 1862–1863

1. While Grant was fighting at Corinth, Farragut brought up a fleet from New Orleans and Porter brought a fleet down from Memphis for a two pronged attack on Vicksburg. This city was located on a steep bluff where Confederate guns poured accurate fire down upon the ships, forcing them to retire.

2. After Corinth, Grant moved down to the Tallahatchie, a good sized stream with steep-banks. The Tallahatchie was strongly defended, however, and Grant needed more men. He decided to abandon the railroad from Columbia, freeing its defenders to join him. Grant needed approval from Washington, however, in order to be able to receive supplies via the Mississippi from Memphis. Halleck refused permission and Grant was stymied. Halleck said he would get more men

for Grant, but while Grant sat idle, Confederate irregulars, John Morgan and Bedford Forrest ("I git thar fustest with the mostest.") chewed up Union railroads, telegraph lines, and small Union posts. Van Dorn destroyed Grant's supplies at Holly Springs, and Grant retreated to Memphis.

Halleck can't be criticized for not agreeing to abandon the railroads. Granted, Vicksburg could have been taken nine months earlier, but the railroads were needed for troop mobility and supplies. The 1863 crisis at Chattanooga illustrated this point perfectly.

3. Grant sent one of his generals, McClernand, to obtain recruits for the next attack on Vicksburg. McClernand, a high ranking Democrat, raised 30,000 men and obtained a promotion from Lincoln to Grant's rank along with permission to use the troops in an independent command. Grant, unaware of this, sent Sherman to Vicksburg with 16,000 men to make an assault up Chickasaw Bluffs. Sherman was thrown back, then dug in to wait for McClernand's reinforcements. When McClernand arrived he outranked Sherman, took all of Sherman's men, and went off for a private side show at Arkansas Post. Halleck found out about this, complained to Lincoln, then had Grant reinstated in overall command, but another effort had failed.

4. In January 1863, Grant tried to dig a canal through a bend of the Mississippi to get below Vicksburg where the bluffs above the river weren't so formidable. By March 7, one gunboat managed to get through only to run into a Rebel battery at the other end of the canal.

5. Grant then tried another canal digging approach using Lake Providence in Arkansas. Unfortunately the lake was full of stumps, which hit the bottom of Grant's ships. A machine was brought in for cutting underwater stumps and was doing the job until a Rebel sniper put a bullet into the boiler and blew it up.

6. In April Grant dug another canal, sending Porter's gunboats into the Yazoo River. Passage into the Tallahatchie was blocked, and Porter proceeded down the Yazoo to the Yalobusha. Here Fort Pemberton blasted the fleet, ending this effort.

7. Porter then attempted to approach Vicksburg from the Yazoo, north of the city. Passage to the Yazoo would be through Steele's Bayou. This Bayou was too narrow and Porter's gunboats were almost blocked in. Sherman had to send troops to get them out.

Grant's failures to take Vicksburg irked a number of congressmen who urged Lincoln to replace him. Lincoln replied, "I can't spare that man. He fights."

1862 had seen some progress by the Union down the Mississippi, in Kentucky, and in Tennessee, but the first half of 1863 was a virtual statement as the South made good use of natural defensive barriers.

Hooker at Chancellorsville, April, 1863

On January 21, Burnside attempted another mindless frontal assault. Hooker protested and was awarded command of the army, now up to 113,000 men. Sumner and Franklin, bypassed by Hooker's promotion for lack of military ability, retired. The army was being structured with more and more combat proven officers.

A clever plan was developed to attack Lee on the Rappahannock. Lee had only 65,000 men, and Longstreet had been sent off with some of them for an attack on a Union sea coast position. Stoneham, with 11,000 Union cavalry, would ride far into Lee's rear to cut off supplies and Lee's retreat route. Sedgewick would create a diversion at Fredericksburg with one corps while Couch with his corps and Sickles would make a secret move (intended to be observed, however) on Bank's Ford west of Fredericksburg. Meade, Howard, and Slocum, three corps (48,000 men) would follow Stoneham well west of Lee's army and approach Chancellorsville from the west through the Wilderness. Rain prevented Slocum from crossing the river, but the plan started off well anyway. Lee had six big divisions, two of which were left to watch Couch while four were sent to meet Sedgewick.

Hooker took the three corps unopposed into the Wilderness and into Chancellorsville by noon on April 30. Although his force was spotted by Stuart's cavalry, his destination was not. Couch and Slocum joined him, and a marvelous opportunity awaited. Hooker made no more moves that day, waiting for morning to crush Lee. But Lee found out what had happened, left one division at Fredericksburg, and rushed the other three back to Bank's Ford. Hooker did not start his attack until noon, moving east on three roads. Jackson hit Slocum on the south road; McLaws struck Couch on the center road; but Meade was unopposed on the north road. By dark, after heavy fighting, the Union army had been pushed back but held stable positions.

J. E. B. Stuart quickly observed that Howard's right flank was uncovered, informing Lee early that night. Lee then gave Stonewall Jackson 35,000 men and sent them around the Union army to hit Howard's flank and the Union rear. Jackson started out at midnight, but he was spotted and Howard warned. Howard had no idea of the size of Jackson's force, however, and posted only one brigade on the exposed flank. When Jackson struck the brigade, it was routed. Howard's corps was smashed from the flank and routed. On the following day, various units of the Union army filled in the gaps until, by evening, a new line was stabilized. That night as Jackson rode over his lines, he was shot by his own men and Lee's right arm was gone. The Confederates attacked in the morning. Reynolds came up through United States Ford and was in position to strike the Confederate flank as soon as orders were received. No orders ever came; a cannon ball hit the porch roof over Hooker's head, knocking him senseless. The rest of the day was chaos as the Rebels continued to attack. By the end of the third day, the Union army was pressed back to United States Ford.

At Fredericksburg Sedgewick waited two days, then attacked Ewell, going right through. Moving west to help Hooker, Sedgewick ran into Anderson and McLaws, sent to punish him. Sedgewick dug in and fought off all attacks but the whole Union army fell back in retreat.

This was Lee's greatest victory. Outnumbered and surprised, he not only staved off disaster but defeated a huge veteran army. Later Halleck talked to Hooker and found him not up to the task of handling an army. He was a good corps commander but had been given one promotion too many. (The Peter Principle—promote a man to his level of incompetence.) The South won the battle, but Jackson's death dealt their cause a major blow.

These were dark days for Lincoln; the draft was started as volunteers were no longer sufficient. Terrible riots broke out, particularly in New York City.

Gettysburg, July, 1863

By 1863 the South was suffering from severe shortages caused by Scott's Anaconda (the blockade). Something had to be done, and by June Lee had collected 80,000 men. An invasion of the North was the most promising thing the South could do, and this time Lee was much stronger than in 1862 when he had been stopped at Antietam. Lee moved up the Shenandoah, across the Potomac, into Maryland. New Union cavalry leaders (Gregg, Buford, and Kilpatrick) from the plains kept Stuart west of the Blue Ridge Mountains, and Lee could learn nothing about Union army movements. Meade was appointed Commander of the Army of the Potomac, and he moved north, parallel to Lee as the Confederates moved into Pennsylvania. Meade created three new cavalry generals: Farnsworth, Merritt, and Custer. On the first of July, Reynolds' I Corps was ordered to hold an outpost at Gettysburg using Buford's cavalry. Meade ordered the other corps into a number of other towns, all south of Gettysburg. When Lee found out that the Union army was north of the Potomac, he decided to strike before the separate corps could concentrate, then he would be able to take Washington and force the Union to sue for peace. The Confederate army was spread out from Chambersburg, west of Gettysburg, to Harrisburg to the north. Lee decided to concentrate at Gettysburg while Meade planned to fortify a position at Pipe Creek south of Gettysburg.

Reynolds had posted his corps west of Gettysburg on Seminary Ridge. blocking two roads from the west. Heth's division of A. P. Hill's corps came down one of these roads, striking a Union cavalry picket line at 9 A.M. Reynolds climbed a church tower, looked around to see Confederates on every road north and west of Gettysburg, and instantly realized that Confederate control of Gettysburg would separate the Union corps, allowing them to be defeated one after the other. Reynolds also saw, just south of the town, a long ridge, Cemetery Ridge, perfect for defense. He sent notes to Meade, Howard, Slocum, Sykes, and Sickles, urging a speedy concentration at Gettysburg, then turned to hold off Hill.

As the Confederates attacked the Union picket line, a solid line of blue coats in black hats came out of the woods with bayonets fixed upon the Confederate flank. This was the Iron Brigade (19th Indiana, 24th Michigan, the 2nd, 6th, and 7th Wisconsin Regiments, the First Brigade of the First Division). Now Heth knew he faced the Army of the Potomac, but before long two of his divisions were crushed. More of Hill's corps came up and the fighting grew in scope and intensity. Reynolds rode among his men until a sharpshooter brought him down. Reynolds actions on this day may have been the difference between victory and defeat. There is a statue of him on the battlefield to remind all visitors for all time of the mighty deeds done by him and his brigades. Doubleday took over I Corps, but by 11 A.M. he was outnumbered by three to one. Ewell came in from the north with only Buford's horsemen in front of him. At noon, however, Howard's XI Corps came in to block Ewell. Howard's Germans (Deutschmen, or Pennsylvania Dutch) made numerous counterattacks, but at 3:30 P.M. Early arrived on Howard's flank, forcing XI Corps to retreat back through Gettysburg. I Corps received orders to withdraw also, but some fought on (including the magnificent Iron Brigade) until all other units had left the field. I Corps was reduced in one day from 8,200 to 2,450 men. Some 5,000 men of XI and I Corps were captured in the congested streets of Gettysburg.

Meade, as soon as he received Reynold's message, ordered Hancock to take all the reserve artillery and Kilpatrick's cavalry to Cemetery Ridge with II Corps immediately. The army would follow as soon as possible.

Hancock was an inspiring leader and his presence on Cemetery Ridge at 4 P.M. encouraged the retreating Union troops to form for a stand with the support of massed artillery. As Hill and Ewell attacked, they received a firm reply; then Kilpatrick charged into Hill's flank. At 4:30, III Corps and XII Corps came in and the line on Cemetery Ridge was secure.

On July 2, Lee planned to attack both Union flanks. A wide envelopment was not possible because Stuart's cavalry were away on a raid. Without cavalry Lee was blind and vulnerable to Union cavalry attacks on his flanks. Lee, however, had 75,000 men to the Union 80,000 and felt strong enough to cope with Meade's army.

On the morning of July 2 Meade had five corps in place on Culp's Hill, Cemetery Hill, and Cemetery Ridge. The hills were on the northern flank of the position with the ridgeline running straight south from the hills. From north to south, the Union corps were formed in the order of XII, I, XI, II, and III Corps. V and VI Corps had not yet arrived.

Lee had most of his army in the vicinity except for Pickett's division of Longstreet's corps, which had been the rear guard. Lee looked at the Union lines near Cemetery Ridge and ordered Longstreet's corps to envelope the Union left while Ewell's Corps struck the Union right and A. P. Hill attacked the center. Hood's division of Longstreet, with his brigades of Robertson, Law, Anderson, and Benning, was ordered to attack toward Little Round Top, south of the Union positions. McLaws' division of Longstreet, with his brigades of Barksdale,

Kershaw, Wofford, and Semmes, was ordered to attack across the Emmitsburg Road between the peach orchard and Little Round Top. It took the better part of the day for Hood and McLaws to get into position. McLaws was astonished at 3 P.M. to reconnoiter and see Union troops as far as he could see in either direction. Longstreet's corps was not ready to advance until about 4 P.M. Hood had the farthest to march to reach position, and McLaws could not start until Hood had cleared the area as there were too few roads or paths in the vicinity. Ewell did not hear from Longstreet until evening, and his attack was too late to be supportive.

Sickles, commander of III Corps, did not like his position at the edge of the woods at the base of Cemetery Ridge. He noticed that the peach orchard dominated his position, and he moved his corps forward to the higher ground. This movement created a salient, however, as he had to bend his line back to touch Cemetery Ridge. DeTrobriand's brigade of Birney's division was placed left of the orchard with Ward's brigade on the extreme left. Graham's brigade and Humphrey's division were in the orchard along the Emmitsburg Road. This movement was completed about 4 P.M., and it spread III Corps much too thin. It did add depth to the Union position, however, although there wasn't much behind Sickles when the attack started.

McLaws moved forward, but not all brigades moved together. Kershaw, moving south of the peach orchard, was devastated by artillery from the orchard, but he pushed De Trobriand back. Hood, on the south flank, pushed Ward back, with Laws going around Ward and toward Little Round Top, then undefended. Loss of this critical hill would have jeopardized the entire Union army as an attack this far south was not anticipated. Late in the afternoon, however, Meade sent his Engineering Officer, General Warren, to Little Round Top to see what was going on—fortunately.

Warren climbed to the top of the hill and saw elements of Laws' and Robertson's brigades starting up the other side. Warren rushed down at 4:30 P.M., desperately seeking help. Just then elements of V Corps were passing by and Warren took Vincent's brigade up to the top of the hill with 20th Maine on the left and 44th New York on the right, just in time to stop the Confederate advance up the hill. Laws lapped around the left flank of the 20th Maine, but this regiment bent and stretched their line to match. Attack after attack was beaten off by the 20th Maine until they ran out of ammunition. As the Confederates advanced again, the 20th was ordered to fix bayonets and charge. The fighting 20th swept the enemy in front of them off the hill, then turned right and outflanked the Confederates in front of the hill in what has been described as one of the finest regimental achievements in the history of the United States Army. This regiment, commanded by Colonel Joshua L. Chamberlain, lost 136 men out of 386, but their opponents lost 150dead and wounded with 400 prisoners.

Ward and De Trobriand, hard hit by the brigades of Robertson, Anderson, Benning, Semmes, and Kershaw, were pushed from the stony hill back through Devil's Den into the wheat field at the base of Little Round Top. Sickles was wounded in the peach orchard giving way to Birney. Birney rallied De

Trobriand's 17 Maine in the wheat field for a counter-attack but was repulsed. II Corps sent Caldwell's division to the wheat field and they attacked, clearing the field. Just then Wofford burst through the woods behind the peach orchard into the wheat field on Caldwell's flank and he fell back. Caldwell took a good defensive position in the woods at the base of Cemetery Ridge and held until relieved by XII Corps.

In the peach orchard, Graham held off Wofford for a while, but Barksdale went right through Humphrey. North of III Corps, Wilcox, Lang, and Wright of Anderson's division of A. P. Hill's corps attacked. (Heth's and Pender's divisions had been depleted in the attack on I Corps on July 1.)

Barksdale cleared Humphrey's division from the peach orchard and pushed forward, but he was stopped by Union artillery near Cemetery Ridge. North of III Corps, Wilcox broke through a thin Union line, moving up to Cemetery Ridge. Here, however. the Confederates were charged by the First Minnesota Regiment and thrown back. Lang also advanced to the ridge where he was met by II Corps. When Wilcox pulled back, Lang's flank was left open and he too had to retreat. One Minnesota regiment had caused two Confederate brigades to fall back!

Wright's attack displaced an element of II Corps from their position on Cemetery Ridge, but Wright had no support. XII Corps elements from the northern end of the Union line came down to push Wright back and stabilize the line down to the wheat field.

The rest of V Corps stabilized the line from the wheat field to Little Round Top, bringing the attacks by Hill and Longstreet to a halt without a decision.

In the north Ewell had waited until late in the day to learn of Hill's attack, which Ewell was to support. When Ewell finally attacked Culp's Hill at 6 P.M., some of the Union trenches were empty, having been vacated by elements of XII Corps sent to support II and III Corps. This put the Confederates in a good position behind Cemetery Ridge for an early attack on July 3. During the night, however, Meade reorganized, returning the XII Corps brigades to Culp's Hill along with VI Corps elements for support. Meade now had all his forces in line with some of the VI Corps in reserve. The order of the forces from north to south was XII, VI, XI, II, I, III, and V Corps.

Lee planned to attack again on July 3, believing that the northern and southern ends of the Union line had been reinforced from the center which he then expected to be weak. Lee had two fresh divisions: Pickett's of Longstreet and Johnson's of Ewell. While Johnson attacked Culp's Hill, Pickett was ordered to attack the Union center with the support of Hill's divisions of Heth and Pender along with Hill's brigades of Perry and Wilcox. In the absence of cavalry, Longstreet had to use his forces to cover both his front and the Confederate right (southern) flank.

Early on July 3, VI and XII Corps forces attacked Johnson on Culp's Hill retaking most of the ground lost the previous evening. Shortly after noon Confederate artillery opened on Union positions, firing for several hours. At 3 P.M. the Confederate division of Pickett started forward over open fields for a distance of 800 to 1000 yards, heading for the positions occupied by II Corps and the remnants of I Corps. Pickett's lines moved magnificently, continuing even as Union shot and shell made huge holes in the perfect formations.

The Confederate right was opposed by I Corps, the Confederate center by III Division, II Corps, and the Confederate left by II Division II Corps. I Corps hit the Confederate right and it moved north. III Division stymied the Confederate center which also moved north. The survivors joined Pickett's brigades which broke the II Division line. Once over the stone wall, however, the Confederates who had survived massive artillery and musket fire at close range found themselves hemmed in on three sides, shot down, or forced to surrender. Wilcox and Perry brought the rest of the Confederates in on an assault about one half hour later, but their left was hit by the same Vermont regiments of I Corps who had earlier flanked Pickett's right. This attack was repulsed and the Army of Virginia offensive was over. Pickett's losses were horrendous; Garnett's brigade alone had started the day with 1,427 men but finished with only 486.

On July 3, J. E. B. Stuart arrived with Lee's cavalry about three miles east of Gettysburg creating a dangerous threat. The only Union cavalry in the area was Gregg's division including Custer's brigade (1st, 5th, 6th, and 7th Michigan Regiments). Custer attacked first with one regiment, then another, and finally with his entire brigade. Custer's attack was delivered with such ferocity that Stuart probably thought he was being attacked by the entire Union Cavalry Corps. Stuart was stopped, and young Custer became a national hero.

Lee was finished and retreated back to Virginia. His casualties were 20,500 and Union losses were 23,000, but the infantry strength of his army was badly diminished.

During the retreat he was held up at the Potomac by high water for a week, but Meade decided not to attack him. After the slaughter of Gettysburg it is hard to fault Meade, who had done a pretty fair job of managing the battle, but Lincoln was not pleased. He thought Meade should have punished Lee while he tried to cross the river. Perhaps Meade repaid the debt owed to Lee for his lassitude at Fredericksburg. Strong pursuit is a sound military principle, but with such casualties to care for as occurred at Gettysburg, lack of swift pursuit is understandable.

Historians like to speculate that on the night of July 1, if Ewell had attacked Cemetery Hill the Confederates might have won. Ewell obeyed Lee's order to, "Take the hill if practicable," and Ewell, who was there, looked at the rugged hill defended by strong forces and decided that it would be more practical to take the hill east of Cemetery Hill, Culp's Hill; however, his only fresh division, Johnson's, did not arrive until Culp's Hill was strongly posted by fresh Union troops.

Lee made a major strategic error at Gettysburg, allowing his cavalry under Stuart to be used for purposes other than keeping track of the Union army. By losing sight of his opponents, he allowed them to occupy a choice defensive position, short and straight, while his offensive positions were in a huge arc.

Meade could shift forces from one flank to the other as Marlborough did at Ramilles and Lee did at Antietam. Meade had a good road behind his position which he used to advantage like Wellington at Busaco. Lee, without his cavalry until July 3, could not maneuver nor could he keep Union cavalry off both flanks. One year after Antietam, the Army of the Potomac had a Cavalry Corps with three divisions and artillery. No longer would Stuart romp free behind Union lines.

It has been said that Lee was one of the great generals of all time. Perhaps if he had had the support of a wealthy government like Marlborough, or if he had the support of a large populace with martial enthusiasm like Napoleon, he might have been. But he was beaten twice within a year and after Gettysburg, faced with a huge Union army staffed with competent generals, he would win no more battles. Marlborough and Wellington were never beaten. Was Grant one of the great generals of all time? This author thinks he was.

July 4, 1863, was the day the fortunes of war swung to the North. On this day after Gettysburg, Grant took Vicksburg, cutting off the western Confederate states.

Vicksburg, July, 1863,

Grant, frustrated by seven failures to take Vicksburg, contemplated his problem. He could not approach the town and maintain an adequate supply line. He then decided upon the biggest gamble of his career. He would land below Vicksburg and feed his army with local supplies.

On April 30, 1863, Grant landed McClernand's corps—16,000 men—at Bruinsburg, 30 miles south of Vicksburg. Bowen's Confederate division came down from Grand Gulf to meet McClernand at Port Gibson but was repulsed with the loss of 1,000 men. Pemberton remained at Vicksburg, where Sherman still threatened. Pemberton had over 50,000 men but 12,000 were at Jackson, 50 miles inland, training under Joe Johnston. Grant's total force was under 50,000.

Pemberton naturally assumed that Grant would come straight north along the Mississippi to try to reestablish his supply line, but Grant quickly concentrated and moved rapidly inland toward Jackson. Johnston sent a brigade from Jackson to fall on Grant's flank as he moved up the river, but Grant smashed the unfortunate brigade at Raymond on May 12 and poured into Jackson where the remainder of Johnston's force was dispersed.

On May 11, Pemberton learned that Grant was headed inland and decided to move south to cut Grant's supply line. With 42,000 men, he felt confident that he could hold off Grant until the Union Army ran out of supplies. Just outside of Cayuga on May 14, Pemberton learned that Grant was attacking Jackson. Pemberton now turned east to relieve Johnston but ran into Grant on the Jackson-Vicksburg road at Edward's Station. Pemberton occupied Champion's Hill while Grant rushed his divisions into the attack. Grant then received a telegram from

Halleck ordering him to return to Arkansas. Grant replied that that would be difficult under the circumstances.

Grant sent Hovey at the Rebel center hoping to force Pemberton to pull troops from his flanks. Then Grant planned to send McClernand, with four divisions, through the Rebel right and into their rear. Hovey's attack did just what it was intended to do, but McClernand was too slow. Grant then struck the Confederate left with two of McPherson's divisions (Logan and Crocker). This attack succeeded, and Pemberton's army collapsed. Loring's division was cut off with a few stragglers finding their way into Alabama. The rest were pushed back into Vicksburg. Johnston wanted Pemberton to save his army, but Grant attacked with such force and speed that Pemberton was trapped in Vicksburg. In 17 days Grant had marched 130 miles, won five battles, reduced Pemberton's army by 14,000 men, and surrounded Vicksburg with the loss of only 2,000 men. Grant's attack on Champion's Hill strongly resembled Marlborough's at Blenheim; his movements were of a speed and ferocity not unlike Napoleon. Johnston gathered 30,000 for the relief of Vicksburg but Stanton sent Grant reinforcements. Sherman with 40,000 chased Johnston and Vicksburg surrendered on July 4 with the loss of 28,000 men. The South was essentially reduced in size, the greatest Union offensive achievement of the war so far.

Chickamauga, September, 1863

In the summer of 1863, Bragg's army rested in central Tennessee, trying to block Rosecrans with a larger Union army from moving south and east to Chattanooga where Bragg's supplies originated. On June 23, Rosencrans's army moved out in an attempt to outflank Bragg. During the course of the summer, with some deft maneuvers, Rosecrans managed to force Bragg to withdraw to the vicinity of Chattanooga. The Union army, the Army of the Cumberland, showed an uncanny ability to move through difficult country (many were westerners, hardy people). Thomas pushed his Union corps into Chickamauga Valley with the other corps of McCook and Crittenden some distance off in opposite directions. Bragg was suddenly reinforced with Longstreet's division of 12,000 in from Virginia and another 15,000 from Mississippi. Now he had 67,000 men and outnumbered Rosecrans, who had only 56,000. Bragg decided to attack Thomas before the Union army could concentrate and moved into Chickamauga Valley. Thomas delayed the Confederate advance, however, while Crittenden rushed to join him. McCook covered 57 miles in a day and a half to join Thomas on September 17. Bragg then decided to outflank the Union left to cut them off from Chattanooga. He sent two divisions but they ran right into Thomas on the morning of the nineteenth. There was a charge and a countercharge. Union reinforcements came up, and more of Bragg's army was brought in. All day the lines grew longer with heavy fighting but no advantage.

On the next day, the brutal contest continued until noon. In the center of the

Union line were the divisions of Wood, Brannan, and Reynolds. Rosecrans rode behind his line and saw that General Wood's left regiment was not in line with the right regiment of General Brannan. He ordered Major Bond of his staff to, "Tell General Wood to close that gap." Bond wrote:

> To General Wood:
> The general commanding directs that you close up on Reynolds as fast as possible and support him.

This was the famous muddled order of Chickamauga. General Wood must have had considerable reservations, but he obeyed, pulling his division out of the line, marching behind Brannan to join Reynolds a quarter of a mile away. It wasn't long before Longstreet knew about the opportunity, and he threw 30,000 men into the opening, spreading in both directions. The divisions of Brannan and Van Cleve were captured. Davis' division was crushed; Wood and Sheridan's divisions were overrun; the cavalry was destroyed, the artillery captured, and headquarters dispersed. Rosecrans fled with the fugitives all the way to Chattanooga.

Thomas saw the Rebel tidal wave and threw up a line of resistance while he took the bulk of his corps to nearby Horseshoe Ridge. Granger's reserve joined him there with some of the stragglers from the broken army. All afternoon Thomas fought off Longstreet, who attacked again and again. As the day grew dark, the Union defenders ran out of ammunition, then one more Confederate assault was made; this was thrown back with bayonets. One more attack and the Union army was finished, but the Confederates had suffered 23,000 casualties and were exhausted. The next morning Thomas took the survivors into Chattanooga, where the Union army was soon surrounded.

Rosecrans was through and Thomas took over the Army of the Cumberland. He became known as "The Rock of Chickamauga," and many a Union soldier could thank his God for a George Thomas.

Chattanooga, November, 1863

The Army of the Cumberland was surrounded in Chattanooga, too weak to fight its way out. Bragg was not strong enough to take the town so he decided to starve Thomas into surrender.

Staunton sent XI Corps and XII Corps under Joe Hooker to Nashville and ordered Grant to meet him in Louisville. He told Grant to take command of all armies west of the Alleghanies, including Hooker's, and to relieve Chattanooga at once.

Grant wired Thomas to hold out at all costs. He wired Sherman to bring his corps in from Mississippi. Hooker was ordered to Bridgeport, and his engineer. Baldy Smith, was ordered to plan for the resupply of Chattanooga. Grant was a dynamo of energy, and for him every situation yielded to effort properly directed.

On the night of October 27, Thomas sent 1,300 men by boat to take Bragg's outpost at Kelly's Ferry on the Tennessee River. Hooker, waiting, moved up and built a pontoon bridge in one hour, then rushed across. Bragg sent a brigade which quickly returned after receiving massed artillery fire from Hooker's corps artillery. XI and XII Corps crossed the river followed by miles of supply wagons, Baldy Smith's Cracker Line.

On the night of October 28, Bragg sent two divisions (Law and Kershaw) against Hooker. There was a good fight until something startled the Union army mules, who stampeded right through the Confederates. These hardy veterans of Gettysburg thought it was a night cavalry charge and ran for their lives. Chattanooga was now safe.

On November 15, Sherman's corps came in and Grant now had 60,000 men.

Bragg had, unfortunately, allowed Longstreet to go to Knoxville to attack a Union force under Burnside, and he was now outnumbered, but he did have excellent defensive positions on Lookout Mountain and Missionary Ridge.

On November 23, Sherman marched out of town, pretending to go to Knoxville, then swung around to attack the Confederate right on Missionary Ridge. Sherman took a hill but was stopped by a large ravine and stiff resistance. Hooker attacked Lookout Mountain on the Confederate left in the battle above the clouds, where he planted the flag on the crest, visible between the clouds. He pressed forward toward the Confederate left on Missionary Ridge, but the distance was too great and he slowed down. Then Grant sent Thomas against the ridge as a diversion to reduce pressure on Sherman. Thomas' men reached the base of the mountain, only to find themselves terribly exposed to musket fire and cannon fire from above. Sheridan led the way then, straight up the mountain, and the Army of the Cumberland went with him, over two lines of infantry and one of artillery, over the top of the mountain and into the Confederate rear. The left and center of Bragg's army were routed. The right was commanded by Hardee, who fought an organized retreat, allowing the fugitives to escape into Georgia. Chattanooga was relieved, and Bragg's army was gone from Tennessee. Longstreet was turned back at Knoxville, and the Confederacy was reduced to six states. The Confederates would fight now with no hope for victory, only for a desperate chance to survive.

Grant was promoted to Lt. General, the first man to hold that rank since George Washington, in command of all the armies of the United States. Now, however, he must face the master, Robert E. Lee.

That autumn Lee and Meade thrust and parried at each other in Virginia between Bull Run and the Rapidan. The armies were equal at this time, both with strong cavalry corps. Both armies made mistakes, but the fighting was a standoff.

Sherman's Advance into Georgia, Spring, 1864

Sherman had proven himself to Grant, who had no reservations about going to Virginia and giving Sherman an army of 100,000 men; but no one, including Grant, could have anticipated the campaign that was to follow. Joe Johnston took over the Rebel army from Bragg and he, with 70,000 men, felt confident of defending the mountain passes into Georgia. Certainly Sherman would attack along the railroad from Chattanooga to Atlanta.

On May 9, Sherman moved up to the Confederate defenses north of Dalton in the Georgia mountains. McPherson, with the Army of the Tennessee, was sent down another valley through a little known pass into Resaca in Johnston's rear. There was a Confederate cavalry division in Resaca, however, and McPherson hesitated. (He could have taken the town and trapped Johnston.)

Johnston sent two corps to Resaca and assumed that the force still in front of him was weak. He therefore launched a full scale attack on Sherman, only to be thrown back with heavy losses. Unable to accept Union pressure on Resaca, Johnston fell back to that town. At Dalton, the distance to Atlanta was 100 miles, but by retreating to Resaca, 20 miles had been given up.

In Resaca Johnston occupied strong positions west of the Oostanoula River. Sherman readied his army for attack but before he could move, Hood attacked Thomas' left flank. Thomas held and Hooker hit Hood's flank forcing a retreat with loss.

On the Confederate left flank, near the town, there was a bridge over the river—the only escape route for Johnston. Osterhaus' division of McPherson attacked, took the key hills, put guns on them, and shelled the bridge. Dodge's corps of McPherson crossed the river further south and came roaring north with substantial cavalry. Johnston hurriedly vacated Resaca, moving another 20 miles to Adairsville.

Sherman was now through the mountains, and as he moved to Adairsville, Johnston set up a defense with elements forward in hills on both sides of the approach based on information that Sherman was coming in one main column. On May 16, Thomas came right in as expected, but when Johnston found out that McPherson was outside his left flank and Schofield was outside his right, he knew that he was in trouble. There was another rapid retreat of 10 miles, but Johnston had Hardee's corps move down the railroad to Kingston, destroying the railroad as he went while Hood and Polk moved further east to Cassville. Schofield followed Hood and Polk while Sherman followed Hardee with the bulk of the Union army. Johnston planned to turn on Schofield before Sherman could join him, but as he made his move, Hardee came over from Kingston with Sherman right behind him with a completed railroad all the way to Kingston. Sherman had rebuilt the railroad as fast as Hardee destroyed it.

Some one said, "That man Sherman will never go to hell. He'll outflank the devil and get past Peter and all the heavenly hosts." Johnston retreated another 10 miles to Allatoona, now only 40 miles from Atlanta. Allatoona was behind the

Etowah River, a deep gorge, hard to assault. Sherman moved south-west to Dallas, away from the railroad, crossed the Etowah, probing at Confederate defenses along Pumpkin Vine Creek.

Sherman pulled Schofield's dispersed corps out of the lines, sent it north-east to Allatoona, now almost undefended. Schofield took the town and the Eutowah was bypassed. Johnston retreated to a new line, Lost Mountain-Pine Mountain-Brush Mountain, outside of Marietta, 30 miles from Atlanta. Sherman made contact on June 5 and attacked several times before breaking through at Gilgal Church. Johnston moved his left to Mud Creek, 5 miles further, but created a bad angle, a salient in the line (like the peach orchard at Gettysburg). Thomas blasted the trenches at the salient in both directions with artillery forcing the Confederates to pull back again on the seventeenth.

The Rebel positions now extended from Kenesaw Mountain down Noses Creek, just outside Marietta, 20 miles from Atlanta. Here Schofield established a bridgehead across the creek. Hood countered but Cox's division massed reserves and hit Hood after his attack had become disorganized. Cox broke through to Zion Church and Johnston was forced to abandon Marietta on July 2 to take up positions along the Chattahoochee, less than 10 miles from Atlanta.

McPherson went west to Sandtown as a diversion. Cox went east with one division to Roswell. Here there was a dam, lightly defended. Cox rushed men across, chased the Confederates, put up a pontoon bridge, and by evening Schofield's entire corps had crossed. Johnston pulled back again into the Atlanta defenses, but this was his last maneuver. He was removed in favor of the fighter, Hood, who had lost an arm at Gettysburg.

Grant's Advance into Virginia, Spring, 1864

Grant was now commander of all Union armies, but he left Meade in charge of the Army of the Potomac. Grant's instructions to Meade merely set strategy and direction with all the details of execution and tactics to be worked out by Meade and his staff. Early on May 4, as Sherman moved into Georgia, the Army of the Potomac moved into the country west of Fredericksburg, known as the Wilderness. Here, for the first time, Grant and Lee would meet to see if Grant could do any better than his predecessors.

Grant had 120,000 men to Lee's 60,000 and hoped to smash Lee in country south of the Wilderness.

On the west flank of the Union advance, Wilson's cavalry division would cross the Rapidan at Germanna Ford followed by the corps of Warren and Sedgewick. On the east flank, Gregg's cavalry division would cross the Rapidan at Ely's Ford, followed by Hancock's corps and the reserve artillery. Burnside's corps (the army reserve) would bring up the rear.

Lee was well aware of the huge Union advantage in numbers and planned to attack Grant's right flank in the Wilderness where a small army could use the difficult terrain to advantage.

After crossing the Rapidan, there were two major east-west roads, Orange Turnpike and, three miles further south, the Orange Plank Road. A. P. Hill's corps moved east on the Plank Road while Ewell traveled in parallel on the Turnpike. Warren's corps was moving south on the Brock Road approaching the Turnpike when he stopped on the evening of May 4.

Wilson sent 500 cavalry under Hammond west on the Plank Road but failed to send anyone down the Turnpike. Early on May 5, Hammond's cavalry discovered A. P. Hill's advance. Hammond's men, armed with rapid firing breech loaded carbines, fought a very effective delaying action against large forces of infantry. Grant did not find out about the presence of Confederates on this road until 10 A.M.

Warren did not discover Ewell's presence until Ewell's advance ran into pickets from Griffin's division. Ewell's corps started forming into line immediately on both sides of the Turnpike while word went to Warren. Griffin was ordered to send a force out to reconnoiter the enemy. Griffin sent two New York companies that quickly made contact with a large force of Confederates. Grant ordered Meade to attack at once, but Griffin did not comply until much later, fearing for his flanks. Grant's repeat order was to attack and forget about his flanks. (Patton would give similar orders during his breakout at Coutances in World War II.) Warren was ordered to spread out on both sides of the Turnpike with Sedgewick on his right.

Getty's division of Sedgewick was sent to the Plank Road to hold until Hancock could come northwest to fill in on both sides of the Plank Road and make contact with Warren's left. Getty attacked A. P. Hill while Griffin attacked Ewell (division attacks on whole corps). It was critical to stop Lee before he crossed the Brock Road and isolated the Union corps. Both Griffin and Getty moved forward successfully, at first, until overcome on both flanks and forced back with heavy losses. Hill and Ewell took up defensive positions, extending their lines on both sides of the roads, eventually making contact in undergrowth that was almost impenetrable.

Lee soon had two of his three corps in line, but Meade had to feed his divisions in as they came up. Grant's strategy was to attack, as one victory could end the war. Not to attack, at best, meant a long siege, probably around Richmond (if he could get there). Grant's attacks had, prior to this campaign, always brought notable success. On this day, however, every Union attack was repulsed with heavy loss as the Confederates remained behind the thick underbrush, using whatever defensive works they could assemble in the few hours available. Towards the end of the day the lines stabilized with Sedgewick, Warren, and Hancock (from north to south) facing Ewell and Hill. Charges met success only to bring troops into a position with front and flanks exposed. A counterattack would regain lost ground and the only result was terrible losses. Wounded men lay unattended. Forest fires developed, and the sufferings in the Wilderness exceeded any ever seen on the continent.

Lee knew he had to defeat Grant before Grant reached Richmond, only 70 miles away. If trapped in Richmond, Lee knew the war was lost. With a substantial shortage of men, however, he could only attack when he had a chance to win. He could not risk his army in costly attacks that were not decisive. Lee waited for Longstreet to come up before he did anything too aggressive, but this corps did not arrive until the morning of May 6.

Early on May 6, Hancock attacked Hill with a 25,000 to 15,000 man advantage. In just over an hour Hill's front was collapsing on the Plank Road, but at 6:30 A.M. Longstreet came up the road to stabilize this front. At 10 A.M. Longstreet was informed of a covered approach to Hancock's left flank and an attack was launched which rolled up the whole Union II Corps line all the way to the Plank Road.

Hancock's men fell back to the Brock Road, where Hancock managed to get them to man prepared defenses. Longstreet, however, had to reorganize his flanking brigades, and it wasn't until late afternoon that the Confederates attacked again. Forest fires channeled this assault into a narrow front which did breech the Union defenses on the Brock Road but which soon received heavy infantry and artillery fire from both flanks until this attack died out. Longstreet was himself wounded by his own men, to be out of action for some time, a serious loss to the Confederacy.

On the Union north flank, Gordon of Ewell's corps saw that the flank was wide open, but he couldn't get Ewell's permission to attack until evening. Lee's main interest was his southern flank, where a major victory might have been possible. Finally Gordon was given permission to attack, which he did, rolling up some of Sedgewick's brigades.

This attack gave Grant some concern, as he wasn't too sure of either flank when night came on. Part of Gordon's force, however, moved in the wrong direction, and Sedgewick managed to stabilize his line at an angle from its previous position.

This day was Grant's worst. It was Meade's army, not his, and Grant did give orders for the major events but he did not direct the individual units. Information was slow to reach him, and it wasn't until the following day that the situation became clear.

May 7 found both armies exhausted, caring for wounded, burying their dead. Grant had lost 13,948 men (War Department statistics), Lee 11,000—horrible casualties.

Grant sent a message to Lincoln, "There will be no turning back." He issued orders to Meade to prepare for a night march and the Union Army slipped away as quietly as possible, on the road to Fredericksburg to the east. The soldiers thought that Grant was retreating just as all his predecessors had done in Virginia, but when the army reached a fork, the march headed south to Spotsylvania. Then every soldier in the Army of the Potomac knew that they had a general, at last.

The Confederates, including Lee, thought that they had beaten Grant, but Grant knew that he had to advance, knew that he would take casualties, but he would travel this road south just once. This battle was the last in which Lee held the initiative. When a reporter delivered Grant's message to Lincoln, the President kissed him.

Spotsylvania, May 8-21

On the night of May 7 Grant's army marched towards Spotsylvania. It was a race to get there before Lee and occupy the key road junction, cutting off Lee's army and forcing him to make attacks on strong defensive positions. Sheridan's cavalry were expected to hold the town until infantry arrived, but unfortunately his divisions had been given varied assignments and only one division was sent to Spotsylvania . J. E. B. Stuart's cavalry arrived in Spotsylvania in force, however, and the Union cavalry were forced out.

By the morning of May 8, Lee realized where Grant was going. He then sent Hill's corps (now under Anderson) to Spotsylvania hoping to get there before the first Union infantry corps (Warren's).

Fitzhugh Lee's cavalry division of Stuart held the approaches to the town, delaying Warren's advance, occupying Laurel Hill outside the town. As Warren's leading division prepared to attack, Anderson's men came up, reinforcing Lee's dismounted cavalry when the Union line was no more than 60 yards away. This affair was decided by just a few minutes. If Warren could have cleared Laurel Hill and occupied the town, the tragic events that followed would have had a much different twist. The fighting that followed was an indication of what the future World War would be like only 50 years later.

By noon Warren's corps had spent itself in futile attacks. As his brigades came up to strengthen the attack, Anderson's brigades came up to stiffen the defense. Grant wanted desperately to take Laurel Hill before Lee's army could get there and he ordered Meade to throw in Sedgwick's corps. A coordinated attack was never made and every attack was made piecemeal. Only Crawford's division of Warren held a portion of Laurel Hill, and they left at 3 A.M. for lack of support. Both armies were exhausted from 24 hours of fighting and marching with efforts that tested human endurance.

On the ninth Grant ordered an attack on Lee's left by Hancock, but when this effort failed, Hancock was pulled back early on the tenth. The Confederates counterattacked when Hancock pulled back, but were stopped. A coordinated attack on Laurel Hill was planned for the tenth. Lee had occupied a horseshoe shaped set of hills with a sharp angle (a salient) in the center of the front facing the Union army. Three assaults were made by Warren and Hancock, all repulsed with loss, then a massed attack upon the salient was made by Colonel Upton of VI Corps with twelve regiments. Upton broke through but Mott' s division of II Corps was supposed to support Upton. Mott was, however, frightened off by artillery, and no one else had fresh regiments to throw into the breech. Upton was forced back but a similar attack was planned for May 12. On the night of May 11, three divisions of II Corps pulled out of the line and moved into position. Lee thought Grant was moving out and the Confederate artillery was pulled out from some sections of the front *including* the salient. Meade added Mott's division to the attack along with two divisions of VI Corps, 19,000 men in all.

At dawn on the twelfth, the Union horde rushed at the salient; Barlow broke through and turned left. Birney and Mott also broke through and turned right. More Union troops poured in until there was a huge confused mass of leaderless men.

Lee's line was broken and his army in serious danger. He rode to Gordon to bring in his reserve. Gordon's counterattack met Yankees one mile behind the Confederate line and started to push them back. Gordon managed to clear the east side of the salient before his division was spent. Ramseur's North Carolinians struck the Union troops inside the western portion of the salient. Lee sent in more brigades against the bloody angle, where prolonged vicious fighting resulted as the Union penetration was gradually reduced. All the other Union corps were supposed to attack to prevent the Confederates from reinforcing the center, but coordination was poor (if Grant had commanded in place of Meade, Lee's army might have been destroyed this day). A stalemate occurred, and Lee built new breastworks to connect his lines, sealing off the Union penetration, reestablishing a stable defense.

Meanwhile on May 11, Sheridan had taken his whole cavalry corps down to Richmond where he met J. E. B. Stuart in a pitched battle at Yellow Tavern. Stuart was mortally wounded, and from this day on Lee no longer had precise information about Grant's army. This may have been due in part to the loss of Stuart but also to the formation and use of a coordinated Union cavalry corps under a fearless and aggressive leader, Sheridan.

It was May 18 before Grant decided not to continue frontal attacks at Spotsylvania. On May 21, Grant moved south again. Spotsylvania was left behind with 13,601 Union casualties and 12,000 Confederate.

Cold Harbor, May 31–June 12, 1864

Hancock's II Corps crossed the Mattaponi River on the twenty-first, only 30 miles from Richmond. Lee, moving further west, took up positions on the North Anna River, which the Army of the Potomac reached on May 23. Hancock, on the left, crossed successfully, as did Warren, on the right, but Burnside in the center was repulsed. Grant found himself in a position of having two corps across the river with Lee between them. (This was no accident. This was the way Lee fought. He was playing a masterly game of chess.) Warren was attacked by the division of Wilcox before the entire Union corps was across. This dangerous situation was brought under control by timely reinforcements and massed artillery.

Lee was in a position to strike Hancock with two corps, but he never made his move. Sickness brought him down and all the subordinate generals he could count on were either dead or in the hospital (Jackson, Longstreet, etc). Lee did not attack and Grant was therefore inclined to think that the Confederates were much weaker than they actually were. (This affair may have contributed to the disaster about to happen at Cold Harbor.)

Grant concentrated his forces, moving east then moving south again, crossing the Pamunkey River before it split into three streams including the North and South Anna. On May 30, Early's Confederate corps attacked at Bethesda Church but was repulsed with loss. At this place Lee was in danger of being cut off from Richmond on roads leading outward from Cold Harbor, three miles away. Both he and Grant recognized the importance of this town, and both generals called in troops from Petersburg to be sent to Cold Harbor. The race was on as Hoke's division from Beauregard (at Petersburg) and Smith's corps from Butler's Army of the James moved toward the vital road junction. On May 31 Sheridan reached Cold Harbor, but he was hard pressed as Confederate infantry moved against him. Hoke's division arrived and 12,000 infantry threatened Sheridan's 9,500.

On June 1, Wright came up to reinforce Sheridan with over two divisions and Smith arrived the same day to hold the town. Meanwhile the Confederates began to dig in on the road west of Cold Harbor, as both Lee and Grant carefully shifted divisions from Spotsylvania to Cold Harbor. Late on June 1, Smith and Wright attacked, with Wright making a temporary breakthrough. Anderson sent up several brigades to pinch this off and night fell upon the field with no decision. All day on June 2 both armies concentrated, but Grant, determined to attack while he might have an advantage, ordered an assault for June 3.

Three corps moved out at 4:40 A.M. (II, IV, and Smith's XVIII), making a coordinated attack. This first wave was decimated within 10 minutes. At 4:50 A.M. the second wave from all three corps went in and this assault was over by 5:15. Further orders to attack were given, but by this time even senior officers refused to obey.

Finally, at 1:30 P.M., orders were passed down to suspend the offensive. By then there were 1,100 dead and over 4,500 wounded. Grant admitted later that this attack was the only one he ever regretted. He had attacked with no knowledge of enemy strength or defenses, only his own erroneous perception. He expected success but the speed of Confederate marches and entrenchment had finally convinced him that frontal assaults were not going to be anything but costly against Lee's army. In all the Cold Harbor fighting, Lee lost 4,800 men, Grant 10,058.

South to Petersburg

On June 7, Grant sent the bulk of Sheridan's cavalry corps to tear up the railroad in Lee's rear and proceed into the Shenandoah. On June 9, Lee sent Wade Hampton's cavalry out to head off Sheridan. There was a battle on June 11–12 which resulted in Sheridan's return to the Army of the Potomac, but the most significant achievement was the removal of Lee's cavalry at a time when Grant made his next move.

On June 12, Wilson's cavalry crossed the Chickahominy followed by

Warren's corps. To attack Richmond, the Union army would have had to turn west between the Chickahominy and the James, but Grant planned to cross the James and attack Petersburg, south of Richmond, where all Lee's supply roads and railroads passed through on the way to Richmond. Warren and Wilson covered the western flank of the army as it moved to the James. Smith's corps was loaded on ships to be taken by water to Bermuda Hundred. Hancock covered the rear as the Union army was transported by boat across the James. One pontoon bridge served the wagons and equipment.

Lee was convinced that Grant would attack Richmond north of the James and brought his whole army across the Chickahominy to dig in and block Grant's path. Attacks against Wilson and Warren were repulsed so firmly that Lee was convinced the whole Union army was in front of him. After the army was across the James, Warren's corps left the lines and Wilson's cavalry alone held off Lee. The Union cavalry were now armed with rapid firing breech loaded carbines and maintained the illusion of a much larger force. Lee did not know that Grant was south of the James in force until cries of panic came from Petersburg.

On the evening of June 13, Beauregard wired that he was hard pressed at Petersburg (by Smith's XVIII Corps, which, unfortunately, did not press hard enough). The next day, a messenger told Lee that the Petersburg horizon was blue with Federal uniforms, but still Lee could not believe it. On the evening of the fifteenth , Beauregard's chief aid came to see Lee, telling him he had to come at once. That same evening the telegraph line to Petersburg was cut and the railroad to Richmond came under artillery fire. Lee knew then that Grant was south of the James, moving on Petersburg, and he knew then that his worst fear had become reality. He rushed his corps to Petersburg and Richmond, filling the lines just in time. Smith had lost the last and best opportunity to deal the Confederacy a mortal blow. Now the war around Richmond would settle down to a long siege.

In six weeks Grant had moved from the Rapidan to Richmond and Petersburg, pinning Lee inside his lines in a stranglehold that could not be broken. Lee had lost 30,000 men, but Grant had lost over 40,000—a cost so high that Grant was referred to as "Butcher Grant." The casualties were terrible but a price that had to be paid, a fine contrast to the years preceding, where losses had also been awful but nothing had been accomplished. Lee's army would suffer from lack of food and supplies and many would desert, but Lee would hold out for nine more months.

Atlanta, July–August, 1864

Sherman moved on Atlanta in mid July, crossing Peach Tree Creek, swinging McPherson around to the east, and sending in Schofield from the northeast and Thomas from the north. Two of Thomas' divisions became separated from the rest of the army, and Hood seized the opportunity to attack.

Hood's lines on the high ground outside Atlanta were manned by large numbers of militia. Hood retained a striking force of 65,000 men in three corps, under Hardee, Stewart, and Cheatham. On July 19, Hood sent Hardee and Stewart against Thomas' divisions under Howard and Palmer just as they crossed Peach Tree Creek. Thomas brought up a division from Hooker along with his reserve artillery. The outnumbered Union troops fought in circles but held. Then McPherson and Schofield slammed into Atlanta's defenses on the east, and Hood had to weaken his attack on Thomas in order to strengthen his eastern lines. Hood gained nothing but lost 8,000 men.

On July 21, Hood struck again, sending Hardee's corps to strike behind the Union left flank (Blair's corp of McPherson). Blair was in trouble but held, and McPherson brought up Dodge's corps to stop Hardee. Further north, Cheatham came out to attack Logan and Schofield. McPherson brought in fresh regiments to link Dodge and Blair but died in the attempt. Cheatham almost broke through between Blair and Logan, but Sherman rode up with Schofield's artillery and punished Cheatham. Logan counter-attacked followed by other Union corps, and the Battle of Atlanta was over with another 8,000 Confederate casualties.

Sherman now pulled his divisions from the east around the western side of the city. On July 28, Hood sent S. D. Lee's corps (formerly Cheatham's) and Stewart's corps to hit Logan, who was on the move. Howard had replaced McPherson as commander of the Army of the Tennessee, and he helped Logan hold off two-thirds of Hood's army until Blair and Dodge arrived toward evening. The Confederates were driven off with losses seven times the Union losses.

Sherman stretched his lines south, trying to cut the Macon railroad, but Hood extended his defenses to match. A stalemate resulted, and as July turned into August, dissatisfaction with the lack of progress grew in the country and in Congress with each fruitless day. Finally on August 27, the Union army moved out. Hood and all Atlanta thought Sherman was beaten and began to celebrate; but on August 30, the Macon railroad was cut by Union forces at Jonesboro far south of Atlanta. Hood sent Lee and Hardee's corps down to chase the Union force believed responsible. On the thirty-first Lee and Hardee attacked, only to be repulsed by immense fire from a good part of the Union army. Lee was chased back to Atlanta, but Hardee was cut off. Hardee finally escaped but lost 5,000 men in the process. Schofield pushed into Atlanta to find the city deserted.

Sherman had cut himself off from his supply lines to cut Hood's, correctly reasoning that there was food in the countryside and Hood would starve first. When Hood found his last supply line cut, he left Atlanta.

After Atlanta Hood moved into Alabama, refurbished his army, then moved back into Georgia to attack Sherman's supply line. He struck Allatoona but was held in check by a stout defense led by General Corse. Sherman came up the railroad within 24 hours, and Hood retreated, only to strike further north at Resaca. At Resaca Hood was repulsed with heavy casualties. Frustrated, Hood crossed into Tennessee, obviously intending to cut off Sherman's supply source at Nashville.

Sherman could not justify wasting his superb army chasing Hood, and he proposed moving through Georgia to the sea to cut off all supplies to Lee from the Gulf Coast states then moving north to finish off Lee. Grant asked how he would supply his army inside Georgia. Sherman advised he would live off the countryside until reaching the sea, also recommending Thomas to take part of the army to Nashville. Grant agreed and sent Wilson to command Thomas' cavalry. On November 12, Sherman moved south with 60,000 men while Thomas with two corps, 22,000 men, moved north.

Sheridan in the Shenandoah Valley, Autumn 1864

In May of 1864, as Grant moved into the Wilderness, a Union army under Sigel moved into the Shenandoah but was defeated at New Market. Hunter then took 16,000 men down the valley again to Staunton. Lee sent a corps under Early, and Hunter was smashed. Early moved north with 30,000 men, crossing the Potomac on July 5, entering Washington virtually unopposed on July 11. That same day VI Corps under Wright arrived by ship from Petersburg and, supported by XIX Corps (in from the west), chased Early back down the Shenandoah. Wright went back to Grant at Petersburg, but Early came north again, this time marching into Pennsylvania to burn Chambersburg.

Lincoln was enraged, and when Grant came to Washington to talk about Early, Grant promised 50,000 men including a corps of cavalry to clean up the Shenandoah and destroy it as a source of food for Lee. Sheridan was selected to command in this vital theatre. Sheridan's army consisted of: VI Corps, 3 divisions, Wright commanding; XIX Corps, 2 divisions, Emory in command; VIII Corps, 2 divisions, Crook (of Antietam fame) commanding; and the Cavalry Corps, 3 divisions, Torbert commanding with Custer, Merritt, Devlin, and Wilson as subordinates.

Lee sent Longstreet to Early's aid, and the two armies faced each other, waiting for the right moment. Then Grant attacked Petersburg. As soon as Longstreet's men appeared in the Petersburg lines, Grant ordered Sheridan to attack.

Early was at Winchester with a good defensive position, but on the morning of September 10, Sheridan attacked. Wright moved across the stream to hold the front. XIX Corps and Wilson's cavalry would attack on the left flank while VIII Corps attacked on the right. Wright was too slow, however, and Early faced him with his whole army. When XIX Corps could not cross the stream on the left, Sheridan sent them over to the right flank. The Confederates then attacked Wright's flank, causing some concern, but this threat was stopped by artillery. When VIII Corps arrived, Sheridan sent it over to the left flank, where Crook made an attack, taking a dominating piece of terrain. Crook blasted Early's flank with artillery then released Wilson's cavalry. Early met this challenge with his entire cavalry force. Then Torbett attacked on the other flank with the entire

Union cavalry force with Custer in the lead. Both flanks gave way, then, and under the combined weight of three Union infantry corps, the whole Confederate line collapsed. Early, routed, fell back to Strassburg, making Sheridan an instant hero.

Sheridan moved on Strassburg, destroying every source of food in the Valley. Early dug in on Fisher's Hill with a deep ravine in front and mountains on both flanks. Sheridan faced him with VI and XIX Corps, sending Crook and VIII Corps up a narrow path on North Mountain around the Confederate left. At sundown Crook charged into the Confederate left and rear. Cheered on by Sheridan, VI and XIX Corps attacked in front, breaking through the defenses everywhere. Early's army disintegrated again, leaving 1000 prisoners. Sheridan followed the beaten Rebels all the way to Staunton, then moved back into a camp at Cedar Creek on October 18.

Lee could not accept the loss of the Valley and, unknown to Sheridan, sent Longstreet's corps to Early's aid. Before dawn on the nineteenth, the Confederates attacked the unsuspecting Federals. Sheridan was at Winchester, some 15 miles away at the time. VIII Corps was struck first and completely dispersed. XIX Corps tried to form but could not. VI Corps and the cavalry did form but were badly outnumbered. Before the onrushing Confederates struck the Union line, they passed through the Union camp. There the deprived troops stopped to loot the camp and enjoy food—of which they had not seen much. Meanwhile Sheridan had heard the artillery, immediately sensed what had happened, grabbed his horse, and raced back to Cedar Creek. On his way back he met many of the fugitives from the early attacks, turned them around, and by the time he reached the thin Union line at Cedar Creek, he had most of his army intact. The units were completely intermingled, but Custer had 8,000 cavalry on one flank and Torbett and Merritt had more on the other. When all were in position, the infantry charged in one long thick line. The Confederate line, spread too thin, broke in many places, then was inundated by Custer and Merritt's cavalry. The Confederates were crushed and the Valley fell under Union control, this time permanently.

Custer's performance in the Civil War was outstanding. He was absolutely fearless and his accomplishments from Gettysburg to Cedar Creek were spectacular. He was brave but reckless, and a decade later, determined to find the Indians at Little Big Horn, he split his regiment into four groups in the presence of the largest army of Indians this country ever saw, eventually dying with over 200 men.

Sherman's March through Georgia

In the fall of 1864, Grant held Lee inside the lines from Richmond to Petersburg.

Lee lost his food supply source in the Shenandoah Valley and Admiral

Farragut had taken Mobile, Alabama, in May. The only Southern ports open to the sea were Savannah, Georgia, and Charleston, South Carolina. Then in November 1864, Sherman headed for Savannah. For 38 days his army disappeared from northern newspapers, his exact location and fortunes unknown. Meanwhile his army devastated a 60 mile wide path through the heart of Georgia, not only destroying all local food sources that could benefit Lee but severing all wire and railroad communications with the Gulf States. The people of Georgia paid a terrible price for their support of the rebellion, and their hatred of Yankees has never entirely disappeared.

Before Christmas Sherman took Savannah, then headed north to close in on Lee. The Army of Virginia now had only one port and three states from which to obtain supplies (South Carolina, North Carolina, and part of Virginia). Supplies to the Rebel army dwindled steadily and their plight worsened daily.

Nashville, December, 1864

After being repulsed in Georgia, Hood moved into Tennessee with 55,000 men. Thomas, in Nashville, had two corps, 22,000 men, plus a provisional brigade of 9,000 casuals (sick, convalescent, etc.) without officers and organization. Wilson had 12,000 cavalry but only 6,000 horses. A 12,000 man corps was coming from Missouri, but in the meantime, Thomas was in trouble.

Thomas sent Schofield out to delay Hood with Cox and his XXIII Corps and part of the IV Corps under Stanley. Wilson was also with Schofield with one cavalry division.

There were two barriers south of Nashville, the Harpeth River at Franklin, and the Duck River further south at Columbia. Wilson annoyed Hood while Schofield set up a defense south of the Duck with his artillery on a hill north of the river. Wilson guarded the fords along the Duck.

On the night of November 26, Hood brought his artillery into position to fire at Schofield while Bedford Forrest, with Hood's cavalry, struck 8 miles east of Columbia.

Wilson's guard at that ford (Huey's Mills) was overpowered, and although Wilson concentrated, Forrest, with superior numbers, pushed him back toward the Harpeth. Schofield, in danger of being cut off, sent IV Corps back to Spring Hill to hold that town while Cox held the rear until the wagons and artillery could move north.

Hood had ordered Cheatham to take Spring Hill, but Cheatham delayed to visit some lady friends, allowing Stanley to entrench. When Hood found out about Cheatham's failure to take Spring Hill, he flew into a rage, ordering an instant attack. Two divisions under Brown and Cleburne moved out, but just as they attacked, the Union artillery from two corps arrived to decimate Cleburne. Hood stopped to concentrate, giving Schofield time to recover Cox and move his force to Franklin.

Franklin, south of the Harpeth, was defended by the XXIII Corps and part of the IV. The artillery and one division of IV Corps managed to cross to the northern river bank over a hastily reconstructed bridge. Wagner of the XXIII Corps defended a rear guard position south of the town.

Hood reached Franklin at night, ordering an early morning assault. He gave no thought to a flanking movement but threw his army head first into the strength of the Union defense. Wagner was quickly overrun with his troops moving back to the Union lines, Confederates right behind them. Cox rallied Wagner's men, and Stanley brought up the reserves as the Union army gathered tightly around the Confederate penetration. Thrown out of town, the Confederates attacked again, taking murderous fire from the front and deadly enfilading artillery fire from across the river where Schofield had massed his guns on the bank. A dozen Confederate generals and 6,000 men went down before the Confederates pulled back again.

Forrest tried to outflank the town as he had at Columbia, but this time Wilson met his attempted crossing with rapid firing dismounted cavalry. Hood did not reach Nashville until December 2.

In Nashville, the XVI Corps had arrived and Thomas was almost ready. He tried feverishly to round up horses for his cavalry but Grant grew impatient with the delay and urged Thomas to attack. Finally, on December 15, the Union forces made their move.

The plan of attack called for the Provisional Corps to demonstrate against the Confederate right. IV Corps would demonstrate in the center and XXIII Corps, XVI Corps, and the cavalry would attack the Confederate left with overwhelming numbers.

The plan was brilliant, but to add to Hood's problems, Forrest was away on a raid (a very bad habit among Confederate armies, as at Gettysburg and during Grant's move across the James). Wilson struck the Confederate flank joined by two corps against Stewart's corps. When a division from the Confederate center was brought over to help Stewart, Thomas threw the IV Corps at the weakened point. By nightfall, the entire Confederate army was in retreat with a loss of 3,000 men.

Hood could not retreat far with Wilson's cavalry all around him. He occupied a position in hills just two miles from his former defense line. The next day Thomas attacked a Confederate salient but was repulsed. Wilson, however, moved into the Confederate rear and rode all over Cheatham's corps. Hood took men from all three corps to stop Wilson but when the latter informed Thomas of his position in Hood's rear, Thomas ordered a simultaneous attack all along the line. Hood's army was destroyed with 13,000 captured, 19,000 killed or captured by cavalry, and the rest dispersed throughout the South. Barely 9,000 men managed to reach the Tennessee and the South was reduced to one army in Richmond. Grant's decision to send Wilson to Thomas is the kind of decision that great generals make. Thomas' achievements throughout the Civil War were absolutely magnificent from start to finish. His name should be revered equally with Grant, Sherman, and Sheridan.

The Final Round, March–April, 1865

In the fall of 1864, Grant attacked Lee frequently with flanking attacks north of Richmond to the south of Petersburg and every attack was repulsed by Lee with great skill. Fighting slowed during the winter, but with Sherman moving north from Georgia, Lee knew that he had to do something.

Sherman's move into South Carolina was resisted by Joe Johnston with such forces as he could accumulate, some 34,000 men. The land was not friendly to attackers, laced with wide rivers and huge swamps; Johnston used these features to try holding Sherman. Johnston sent Bragg inland to Augusta and Hardee to Charleston on the coast to provide resistance at the two most likely targets of Sherman's advance. Johnston remained at Columbia, in between the other cities so that he could reinforce either. On February 7 Johnston learned that Sherman had crossed 100 miles of swamps and was heading rapidly for Columbia with 60,000 men! One river had fifteen channels and Sherman's horde had built fifteen bridges in one day. Another river was a half mile wide and this was bridged in four hours. Johnston exclaimed, "There has never been such an army since Julius Caesar," and he may have been correct. South Carolina was lost, and by March 11 Sherman took Fayetville, North Carolina, and the last Confederate arsenal in the east. On the nineteenth Johnston made his last stand at Bentonville.

Carlin's division of Slocum's corps met the Rebels first. He formed in line and as his flanks were threatened, Morgan's division came forward on Carlin's right. Buell's division joined the line, but then the whole Confederate army burst upon the Union flank and rear. The Confederates kept coming, but Union islands of resistance held until XX Corps came rushing up to smash the Confederate flank. By nightfall the Confederates were back in their trenches. In the morning Sherman attacked with his whole army and Johnston was forced to retreat, eventually moving eastward to the coast with only 17,000 survivors. He surrendered late in April, after Appomattox.

Lee planned one last desperate gambit. He would strike Grant, create enough confusion to allow a temporary pullout, then concentrate with Johnston to attack Sherman, while Grant mended his lines. If successful, he would come back to deal with Grant. On March 25, Gordon led an assault on Fort Stedman near Petersburg. Gordon took the fort but could not find the next line of defense. The Federals came back from both sides, throwing Gordon back with the loss of 6,000 men.

Grant then sent II Corps and V Corps under Sheridan with 13,000 cavalry to move southwest of Petersburg to Five Forks to cut Lee's supply lines. Lee countered with 15,000 men under Pickett. After much hard fighting, Sheridan struck A. P. Hill. pushing back his southern flank and exposing Pickett's northern flank. On April 1, Sheridan took one V Corps division in a flanking attack on Pickett, rolling the Rebel line back, then struck with his cavalry. Pickett's force was beaten and dispersed, cut off from Lee's army with 2,500 casualties and

4,500 prisoners. Grant now knew that Lee's 37 mile line had to be paper thin. He attacked along the whole front and broke through in numerous places. By April 2, Petersburg was taken and Lee was forced to leave Richmond, retreating westward. V Corps marched parallel to Lee and prevented a turn to the south to join Johnston. On the sixth Ewell was cut off and surrendered with 8,000 men. On the night of April 8, Sheridan cut off Lee's retreat with cavalry, joined during the night by VI Corps. In the morning Lee saw cavalry supported by infantry and artillery in front of him and he knew he was finished. He surrendered to Grant, and all Confederates were allowed to go home, the officers with side arms and horses, enlisted men without arms. The Union was preserved.

Analysis

Could the South have won? It was possible. If Grant had been crushed at Shiloh, if McClelland hadn't obtained a copy of Lee's invasion plans prior to Antietam, if McClelland had been defeated. These were close calls. Lee could have occupied Washington, Baltimore, Philadelphia, perhaps Cincinnati, perhaps demoralizing the North until politicians would sue for peace at any price, even the concept of two nations.

On the other hand, the Union armies, spurred on by Lincoln, may have continued the struggle. A nation can never assume the other side will give up. Without occupying most of the North, beating all their armies and destroying their ability to wage war, the South could not be certain of victory. As they had not the population, manufacturing, or navy to achieve total victory, the South could only hope the North would sue for peace.

The North waged total war and did occupy most of the South, did beat all their Armies, and did eliminate their ability to wage war. Fortunately for the Union, the western armies were superbly led right from the start with Grant, Sherman, Thomas, Sheridan, etc. The western armies never took terrible casualties after Shiloh and Chickamauga and consisted of experienced veteran regiments that would never quit; when in trouble, they fought in small units until help came. (This is the tradition of any fine military force such as the Navy, Marine Corps, and many renowned Army divisions.) In the east the Army of the Potomac initially suffered from poor leadership, taking heavy casualties which decimated some of the better units; this army delivered some good and some poor performances, but under Grant it kept moving forward and won by sheer weight of numbers. The Army of Virginia successfully defended for four years although vastly inferior, and this remarkable achievement is still a source of Southern pride.

Southern invasions of the North in 1862 and 1863 were not in sufficient force to be decisive. The Army of Virginia was too small to occupy any significant amount of territory and still maintain adequate fighting strength. The Union maintained three or more large armies while holding many Southern towns with other occupation troops.

The Civil War was the last major American conflict where human bodies and wooden ships were the main army and navy weapons. No more would Americans march shoulder to shoulder with single shot muskets. During this war rapid firing breech loaded rifles were developed as were steel plated and fabricated steel ships. The Monitor had a steam engine driving a screw propeller and also had a rotating gun turret. All these instruments of war were developed so that they were common by the time of World War I, along with machine guns, tanks, rifled artillery, and airplanes. In the Twentieth Century, technology became more and more significant to the conduct of war.

The American armies, North and South, fought ferociously with great valor on both sides. In spite of this, the Central Powers, when plunging into World War I, gave little or no thought to the American military potential.

Several lessons come out of a conflict such as the Civil War. Certainly one is the appreciation that an effort that does not seek total victory may achieve nothing. Another is that war requires professionals, experienced commissioned and non-commissioned officers and enlisted men, combat proven generals, and the finest in equipment and training. If the Union had had such an army and the South did not, then there might have been no civil war, or if fought, the war would have been settled much sooner with far fewer casualties. As it was, a generation of young men either died (497,000 did) or lived to suffer life without two arms and legs. The Civil War was horrible, but was not the last American war where men died because of lack of preparedness or proper direction.

In looking at the structure of a Union army with its infantry, cavalry, and artillery divisions, one has to be impressed with the similarity to the organization of mid twentieth Century American armies. Much was learned in the Civil War, and a good American performance in World War I may have been due in large measure to this experience.

Chapter V
World War I, 1914–1918

In 1870, Germany, newly organized under Bismarck, fought a war with France, quickly crushing the French, obtaining Alsace and Lorraine. The French, bitter and hungry for revenge, rearmed, building a huge army endowed with a strategic concept, "*Attaque, attaque, toujours l'attaque.*" The Germans, feeling powerful and ambitious, also developed a huge army and a navy large enough to threaten English domination of the seas. European powers looked around the world for more potential colonies and looked at their weaker neighbors for acquisition possibilities. Alliances were formed for assurance of sufficient strength to resist aggressive neighbors. The *WORLD BALANCE OF POWER* was a major concern among the nations of this era. This concept has long been a primary consideration in national survival, particularly after World War II with the democracies lining up against the communist dominated states across the Iron Curtain and elsewhere around the world.

Germany formed an alliance with Austria-Hungary. Russia and France, threatened, also formed an alliance. England, worried about German land and sea power, joined France and Russia to form the Triple Entente. Down in the Balkan powder keg, Serbs had beaten Turks and Bulgarians in earlier fights but were not strong enough to cope with Austria, which had an interest in the Balkans. Serbia formed an alliance with Russia, whose rulers considered the Slavs in Serbia to be brethren.

Every nation was armed to the teeth, and it was only a matter of time until some spark caused the explosion. Then on June 28, 1914, the Austrian Archduke Ferdinand, heir to the throne, was assassinated by Serbian patriots in Sarajevo, the capital of Bosnia. a state recently annexed by Austria and which contained many Serbs. Austria decided to punish Serbia and obtained assurance of German support from the Kaiser. On July 28 Austria declared war on Serbia. Russia mobilized and Germany declared war on Russia on August 1. That same night German troops moved into Luxembourg. Germany declared war on France on August 3. Germany warned Belgium that their troops would be using Belgian territory, and England declared war on August 4. Austria-Hungary and Germany eagerly plunged into the conflict; the other countries joined reluctantly. Germany expected a quick victory, no doubt as in 1870. Four years later an entire generation of European youth were lost. Paris became a paradise for young foreign men after the war, still described in book and song, due in large measure to the absence of young Frenchmen.

Germany had two million men initially, in 87 divisions, between four and five million eventually in 200 divisions. Austria-Hungary had 49 divisions (450,000 men) to start, expanding to 2,700,000 men.

France started with 62 divisions (1,650,000 men) and this force grew to 3,500,000. Russia had 1,400,000 men in 114 divisions at war's outbreak but reached a peak of almost 6,000,000 men. The British originally had only 125,000 in seven divisions, but her colonial world wide army grew to 5,900,000. Belgium had 43,000 men but increased to 186,000 in 7 divisions. Serbia had 185,000 men in eleven divisions. When all these huge armies collided, the slaughter was indescribable.

A former German chief of staff, von Schlieffen, developed a plan of attack in France which called for a minimum strength left flank and a massive right flank which would sweep wide through Holland and Belgium to the west and south of Paris, trapping the entire French army against the Rhine and the Alps. Von Schlieffen also planned a minimum force to check the Russians in East Prussia. Von Schlieffen's successor, von Moltke, was not of von Schlieffen's caliber, however, and he weakened his right wing to strengthen his left and his front in East Prussia. On the western front 78 German divisions faced 62 French, 7 Belgian, and 4 British divisions.

On the night of August 5 and 6, the German 1st Army under von Kluck and the 2nd Army under von Bulow attacked in Belgium but were delayed by the Belgians under Lemans at Liege until August 16. The French attacked the German left wing in Alsace-Lorraine on August 14 but were stopped by August 20.

The Germans in the Ardennes met the French then pushed them back. Von Bulow struck the French Fifth Army under Lanrizac near the Sambre on August 21. The German First Army met 30,000 men from the British Expeditionary Force under Sir John French the same day. Everywhere the shock occurred, the Germans successfully caused the Allies to withdraw. Casualties were enormous. By September 2 the Germans were at the Marne. The French, led by Chief of Staff General Joseph Joffre, counterattacked on September 5 and opened a gap between the German First and Second Armies; von Moltke lost his nerve and ordered a retreat to the Aisne in spite of First Army's continued success. Papa Joffre had saved the day for France and von Moltke was replaced with von Falkenhyne.

The Allies attacked at the Aisne in September but with little success. In October the Germans attacked at Ypres with the same result. From mid October to mid November the Allies counterattacked at Ypres. Continued attempts at flank attacks resulted in the lines being extended from the Alps to the English Channel. Then the lines stabilized with trenches and barbed wire. Any attack was met with artillery and machine gun fire unlike anything seen in war before. By year's end the original BEF were almost all casualties. Belgian casualties were 40 percent; French losses were over half a million. German hopes for a quick victory were gone and the only strategy now was endless slaughter.

Eastern Front, 1914

The Russians attacked in East Prussia with two armies in August. In accordance with von Schlieffen's plan, the Germans concentrated south of the Masurian Lakes to crush one army at Tannenburg, killing or capturing 125,000. Now under Hindenburg and Ludendorff, the Germans concentrated north of the lakes, attacking the second Russian army, causing it to evacuate East Prussia in September.

Against Austria the Russians were successful. By mid September the Austrians were pushed back 135 miles with 350,000 casualties. Austria-Hungary did not yet know it, but the empire was in its death throes.

In mid October the Germans sent an army to aid the Austrians and early successes were neutralized by Russian counterattacks until by years' end the lines stabilized. Many experienced officers were gone and future fighting would be with poorly led masses.

In Serbia the Austrians were at first stymied by tough Serb resistance, but by December 2 Belgrade was taken. Once the Serbs received ammunition they counterattacked, retaking the capital and creating another stalemate at the expense of 100,000 men on each side.

Turkey, threatened by Russia in the north and the British Empire in the south, aided by Germany, joined the Central Powers in October. An Indian division took Basra and the Turks lost most of an army of 150,000 men fighting Russia in the Caucasus.

All in all, 1914 cost each side about one and one half million men and the war had just begun.

At sea German war vessels cruised about the world giving and taking losses. Submarine warfare began but was not yet to reach the deadly peaks of later years.

1915

In the east the Germans reinforced the Austrians and attacked both north and south of the Polish salient. The Russians were defeated with huge losses, Poland was lost, and the Czar took over command of the armies from the Grand Duke Nicholas.

On the western front the two armies lunged at each other in futile attacks, not changing the front by more than three miles in any direction all year. The Allies lost another million and a half men to over 600,000 for the Germans. Sir

John French was replaced by Sir Douglas Haig.

In early 1915 Germany used tear gas against the Russians, and in April chlorine was used by the Germans at Ypres.

Winston Churchill was First Lord of the Admiralty, and he proposed an amphibious landing in Turkey on the Gallipolli Peninsula to cut off contact between Turkey and Europe permitting access to the Black Sea through the Dardanelles. On February 19, a British naval task force tried to fight its way up the Dardanelles but was repulsed with loss. A landing on the Gallipoli Peninsula was made on April 25 by Australians and New Zealanders (Anzacs) primarily. This force, 78,000 men under General Hamilton, moved inland too slowly and was soon stymied by a force of 84,000 Turks under Mustafa Kemal (Attaturk). Both sides massed troops and trench warfare developed, the one thing Churchill had tried to avoid. Both sides lost heavily in futile attacks, but malaria and dysentery took an additional heavy toll of the Allies. By mid January, 1916, all Allied troops were withdrawn. 500,000 troops had been used with 250,000 casualties. The Turk losses were also about half a million. Churchill, War Secretary Kitchener, First Sea Lord Fisher, and General Hamilton, were all either finished or tarnished after this disaster.

Italy entered the war in May on the Allied side and attacked Austria in the northern mountains. Nothing was accomplished except for the loss of 160,000 Italians and 160,000 Austrians.

In September Bulgaria entered the war and attacked Serbia across that nation's eastern border. Germany now planned for the elimination of Serbia from the war. On October 6 Germans and Austrians attacked from the north, Bulgarians from the east. The Serbs were crushed by year's end with 140,000 escaping to the Albanian coast, with 100,000 casualties and 160,000 prisoners. The Allies took three divisions from Gallipoli to Salonika to assist Serbia on October 3 but accomplished nothing.

In the Middle East a small British army advanced north from Basra only to find itself surrounded in Kut. A small Turkish army advanced all the way to the Suez Canal, forcing Great Britain to pour troops into Egypt.

Germany started 1915 with only 27 U-boats (submarines), but this number grew throughout the year. 59,900 tons of Allied ships were lost in February, increasing to 185,500 tons in August. In May the *Lusitania*, carrying ammunition and 1,000 passengers—including 440 women and children—was sunk by a U-boat in the Irish Sea. 115 Americans were lost and much ill feeling grew in the U.S.

1915 was not a good year for the Allies. Russia, in particular, had lost over three million men. Serbia was overrun and the war against Turkey had been unsuccessful. Allied shipping losses to submarines were rising to a critical level.

1916

Germany's chief of staff, Falkenhayn, decided upon an attack strategy at a point critical to France, where huge French forces would have to be committed and where massed German artillery could destroy French defenses and chew up their army. He chose Verdun but was not able to attack until February 21. After massed artillery fire, the German infantry were told, "There won't be anything left living out there." (Americans learned in World War II against Japan that such estimates were usually optimistic.) The artillery was devastating but 437,000 Frenchmen survived and the Germans gained only four miles by the end of February. The French kept possession of the Verdun forts and kept them supplied with one road and two railroads although almost surrounded. Germany tried in vain to subdue Verdun until June, even using phosgene gas (combined chlorine and carbon monoxide) and flame throwers. General Henri Petain commanded the French at Verdun with honor and distinction (honor to be discarded as President of Vichy France in World War II). In the second half of 1916 the French counterattacked at Verdun. Here, in a small segment of the front in one year, France lost 460,000 men and Germany 300,000.

To take pressure off the French, the British attacked along the Somme River on a fifteen mile front with 12 divisions and 5 French divisions in July. Joffre selected the point of attack, no doubt for strategic reasons, but the Germans had developed extensive defenses for the same reasons. The British lost 60,000 men in one day and in five months gained only 5 miles. The British used the tank in September for the first time, but there were only 36 tanks; although they did help to gain a mile or more, their future potential was realized by few. Canadians joined the battle on the Somme in September.

In 1916 France and Great Britain lost 1,200,000 men, Germany 800,000. Falkenhayn, who had fought a war of attrition, had exhausted his own forces. He was replaced with Hindenberg and Ludendorff.

In the east Russia was called upon, as in 1914, to attack and relieve pressure on the Allies in France. Again the Russians attacked without adequate training and planning. The Russian Second Army attacked the Germans at Lake Naroch in March, losing 100,000 men. Austria launched an attack in Italy in May, requiring another Russian offensive. This time, Brusilov attacked the Austrians with his Southwestern Army of fifty divisions in June. Two of four Austrian armies collapsed. Germany pulled troops from France, and Austria took forces from Italy to counter Brusilov. In August and September the Russians were stopped with terrible losses. Brusilov lost 1,000,000 men. the Austrians 600,000. Neither Russia or Austria-Hungary could replace the losses of this awful year, but the Western and Italian fronts did stabilize.

In 1916 Rumania joined the fight, attacking Austria. Austria counterattacked on one front while a German-Bulgarian-Turkish army attacked on another. By the end of the year the Rumanians were finished.

The Allied force in Greece, reinforced by Serbs, attacked Bulgaria to relieve the pressure on Rumania. Some progress was made in mountainous country but Rumania could not be saved.

In Italy the Austrians started the year with an offensive on the Isonzo River, but after pulling out troops to stop the Russians, the Austrians went on the defensive. Italy lost 150,000 men, Austria 100,000. Then the Italians assumed the offensive, recapturing some terrain but with further heavy casualties. Cadorna' s strategy was brutal in his willingness to fight a war of attrition. The Austrians under Conrad had been advised by the Germans not to start the 1916 offensive as their means of supply were not adequate, but on both sides of the front there was death and futility.

In Mesopotamia the British tried to relieve Kut, losing 22,000 men in a fruitless attempt. Kut surrendered with the loss of 10,000 more. On the Suez front four British divisions pushed across the Sinai, aided by Arabs (with Lawrence of Arabia) who revolted against Turkey, and captured Mecca and Taif.

At sea in May the battle of Jutland was fought. The British lost 14 ships. the German High Seas Fleet 11. The Germans cruised towards a decisive battle but were met in column by the British Grand Fleet in line. The British under Jellicoe had "capped the T," placing the Germans at a huge disadvantage. Rather than continue the battle in such a situation, the German fleet under Scheer withdrew, never to sortie again.

Submarine warfare continued to destroy Allied and neutral ships. Total sinkings averaged 192,000 tons a month, 79,000 tons more than in 1915. The slaughter in this war was not confined to land alone. This year was a stalemate overall, which, for the Allies at least, represented some progress.

1917

In 1917 on the western front, Germany with 2,500,000 men was outnumbered by 4,000,000 Allies. The French, commanded by Nivelle, attacked on the Aisne in April gaining ground but losing 120,000 men. The British, under Allenby, also attacked in April at Arras where the Canadians took Vimy Ridge, but the British lost 84,000 men. The French army command was given to Petain, but the army revolted in June, refusing to advance. The revolt was quieted down, but the French were through advancing for the rest of 1917. The British took up the offensive at Ypres in July with some progress. In November the Canadians took Passchendaele Ridge, but the British lost 250,000 to 380,000 men. Rain and mud caused indescribable difficulties increased by the German use of mustard gas. The French gained some ground at Verdun in August and on the Aisne in October. The British attacked with 12 divisions at Cambrai in November with 324 tanks, gaining four miles in one day. Without reserves some of this gain was lost but the mass use of tanks provided valuable experience.

In March the Russian revolution occurred. The Czar and his family were arrested and Kerensky took over as Prime Minister. He ordered one more offensive which made some progress against the Austrians in July but when stiffened by Germans, the Austrians held. On July 19 the Germans and Austrians took the offensive against the Russians one more time, but this time the Russians deserted and the Central Powers advanced unchecked. In November the Bolsheviks took over the Russian government, ending Russian war efforts. For Russia this war was an indescribable horror, but the Allies would have been beaten without the huge effort made by Russia and the same can be said about World War II.

On the Italian front Italy went on the offensive in May and continued until September. Then, after heavy losses, the attack stalled. The Austrians were near collapse, however, a situation the Germans could ill afford. Seven German divisions were added and on October 24 the Austrians resumed the offensive. The Italian 2nd Army was smashed but two other armies fell back in orderly fashion. The retreat extended for seventy miles before the attack slowed from lack of reserves and supplies. The battle of Caporetto cost Italy 300,000 men forcing the British and French to send 12 divisions in December to stabilize the situation.

In Greece the government of King Constantine fell, replaced by a pro-Allied government under Venizelos. Greece declared war on Germany, Turkey, and Bulgaria, adding nine divisions to the Allied cause.

In Palestine the British attacked the Turks in March and April but were repulsed with loss. Sir Edmund Allenby then took command (after commanding the British 3rd Army at Arras). Allenby brought in more troops and attacked in October taking Beersheeba, Gaza, and on December 9, Jerusalem. This advance was aided by Lawrence of Arabia with his Arab irregulars, who operated inland on the British flank and in the Turkish rear.

In Mesopotamia a British army of 250,000 men under Maude advanced against extremely weak Turkish resistance, taking Baghdad on March 11. In cooler weather (November) Maude moved north again to take Ramadi and Tikrit.

The United States Enters the War

The people of the United States generally wanted no part of a European war. In 1916, Woodrow Wilson won reelection with campaign slogans such as "He kept us out of war." In this country, however, propaganda battles went badly for Germany. Germans were associated with numerous atrocities and became known as "Huns" and "Boche."

The execution of a British nurse, Edith Cavell; the invasion of neutral Belgium; the sinking of the *Lusitania;* the Zimmerman note (to Mexico promising U.S. land grants if Mexico would declare war on the U.S.) all affected American sympathies. But the German U-boat attacks on neutral ships tipped the scales. Germany was stymied in France and counted upon such measures as starving England with unrestricted submarine warfare.

The possibility of bringing the U.S. into the war must have been considered by the Germans, but the ability of the U.S. to generate large forces quickly was probably underestimated. The U.S. declared war on April 6, 1917.

The U.S. had 208,000 regulars and 101,000 state guardsmen, 130 pilots, and 55 planes. The Navy was in better shape, but the U.S. was definitely not ready for war. The military academies had, however, provided a nucleus of professional officers. A conscription draft law was passed on May 19 and the Army grew steadily. In June 1917, the 1st Division was sent to France with a Marine Brigade, the Fifth and Sixth Marines (5th and 6th Regiments). Major General John J (Blackjack) Pershing was appointed commander of U.S. forces in France. Pershing was well known for his campaign against Pancho Villa in Mexico a few years before the war. Other divisions followed: the 2nd, 26th (Yankee), and the 42nd (Rainbow) Divisions. The 42nd, from all over the country, had a chief of staff named Douglas MacArthur. This division left Hoboken on October 18, completely armed except for artillery. In France division artillery brigades were trained to use and receive French 75s and 155s. (These barrel sizes correspond to three inches and six inches in diameter.) The 1st Division moved into the front near Nancy in late October. By the end of 1917 50,000 men per month were arriving in France; the Yanks were coming.

The war at sea had reached crisis proportions. It was estimated that 15,500,000 tons of shipping were necessary to sustain the war effort. The Allies had 21,500,000 tons but the Germans had sunk 1,300,000 tons from January through March of 1917 and another 900,000 tons in April. New ships were being built at a rate far too low to make up for such losses. U.S. Admiral Sims worked with the British to find a way to reduce losses and protect troop transports. The plan devised was to form convoys escorted by naval vessels. The first convoy from the U.S. sailed in May, and by December only 11 ships out of 1280 in U.S. to England convoys were lost. By years end sinkings were reduced to 400,000 tons a month, while U.S. and British shipyards combined in a massive ship building campaign. The situation at sea had been improved, but the loss of 400,000 tons a month with many of the crewmen and valuable supplies was still horrendous.

1917 was the year of Russian collapse and the U.S. entry into the war. Could American forces build up in time to counter the transfer of major German armies from the eastern front to the western? Could green American troops stand up to experienced Germans? These questions would be answered in 1918.

1918

In early 1918 the Germans pushed deep into Russia until the stalling peace talks were settled at the March 3 signing of the Brest-Litovsk Peace Treaty. Immediately German divisions were transferred to France requiring similar

Allied shifts from Italy and Palestine. German divisions increased from 160 in December, 1917, to 194 by March 21, 1918, numbering 3,600,000 men. There were only six U.S. divisions in France (big divisions of 28000 men, double the size of other divisions, more than double many a depleted hostile or friendly division), 300,000 men. The ultimate crisis was at hand.

On the Somme, 71 German divisions attacked 26 British divisions along a 40 mile front on March 21. Initially the Germans made rapid progress. Foch was then named Allied Commander-in-Chief; for the first time there was a unified command. By April 5 the German offensive slowed and the Somme front stabilized.

The second blow was struck near Ypres upon the British (the Battle of Lys) in April. Here there was another breakthrough and General Haig ordered his troops to hold at all costs and fight to the last man. Foch sent 7 French divisions and by May the Lys assault was stopped. In six weeks the Allies had lost 350,000 men, the German almost as many.

Then on May 27 the Germans struck the French on the Aisne on a twenty-five mile front with 42 divisions. By June 2 the penetration was 10 miles reaching the Marne at Chateau-Thierry only 56 miles from Paris. The U.S. 2nd and 3rd Divisions and the Marine Brigade were assigned to the French to help meet this crisis. The U.S. 1st Division in the Somme area was used to attack Cantigny at the apex of the Amiens bulge.

On June 1 the Germans still outnumbered the Allies, but this would soon change. Americans were pouring into France at the rate of 300,000 men a month. U.S. divisions in France increased as follows: April–9; May–18; June–25; July–29; August–35; Sept–39; Oct–42. By August there were 1,000,000 Americans in France.

Seicheprey, April 20

The first major combat involving Americans occurred on April 20 when the Germans staged a surprise attack on Seicheprey with 3,200 men. The village, defended by the U.S. National Guard 26th Division, was captured along with 136 Yanks, but a counterattack cleared the village and killed 160 Germans. The affair was called a victory but was an indication of lack of skill overcome by a fighting spirit.

Cantigny, May 27

On May 28, the 28th Regiment of the 1st Division was ordered to take a village on high ground overlooking their positions. The town of Cantigny was taken in 35 minutes, successfully held against counterattacks (with the aid of reinforcements) and by the end of the next day the Germans gave up. This was a victory, but there were 1607 casualties.

Chateau-Thierry, May 30

The German breakthrough from the Aisne threatened Chateau-Thierry on the Marne. On May 30 the U.S. 3rd Division, en route to another destination, was diverted to Chateau-Thierry. Here the division blew a bridge and defended positions on the south bank of the Marne. There was little fighting but a gap was plugged. The French, retreating in this area, were completely dispirited.

Belleau Wood, June 1-25

The whole French 6th Army had collapsed and the French were afraid Paris would fall. But, on June 1 the U.S. 2nd Division under General Bundy and the Marine Brigade under General Harbord marched up the Paris-Metz road to the front. The Germans reached the Marne at Chateau-Thierry, couldn't cross there, then moved west to the vicinity of Belleau Wood. In this area there was a three mile gap in French positions. The 2nd Division formed north of the road, the Marines south of the road facing Belleau Wood. The Americans were ordered to hold the line at all costs but, before the Germans could strike, the Marines attacked on June 6. Two battalions of the 5th Marines and one battalion of the 6th Marines penetrated into the woods but one battalion was caught in the open and took heavy casualties. Progress was slow, but on June 11 the Marines pulled back and pulverized the woods with artillery. Shell bursts in tree tops had the same effect as air bursts (like the VT fuse used in Korea) and took heavy casualties among the Germans in open trenches. As soon as the artillery ceased, the Marines were back, clearing two thirds of the wood and capturing 300 Germans. On June 13 the Germans counterattacked but were mowed down with heavy loss.

By June 14, the Marines were famous around the world for stopping the German drive to Paris and taking the offensive. From June 14 to June 16 two Army regiments relieved the Marines but couldn't finish clearing the wood. On June 25 one battalion of the 5th Marines returned with three machine gun companies and cleared the wood, taking another 500 prisoners.

Fighting in the 2nd Division sector did not develop momentum until July 1, when all the artillery supporting the Marines could be diverted to support an attack. The village of Vaux on the Paris-Metz road was taken in one day. U.S. casualties in this fight were 9,777 including 1,811 dead but 1,687 prisoners were taken and the Marines alone had chewed up four German divisions. The wood was renamed "Bois de la Brigade de Marine."

The Marne Salient

The U.S. Army, the AEF (American Expeditionary Force), now entered the struggle in force. Three corps were formed. II Corps included the 33rd (Illinois), 27th (New York), and 30th (Tennessee) Divisions. The 27th and 30th were National Guard units, originally suspect, but soon proven to be first rate fighting divisions. II Corps was assigned to the British and one day in May General Haig watched the 107th Regiment of the 27th Division marching on parade in excellent fashion when suddenly a low flying plane buzzed the marching men just 25 feet over their heads. Not one man looked up! The General learned something about the quality of these men that day. Their commander, General John Francis O'Ryan, said, "They will perform in combat as well as they do in parade," and he did not exaggerate.

The 33rd Division provided four companies to the Australians and these companies did well in the capture of Le Hamel in the Amiens sector on July 4.

I Corps under U.S. General Liggett was composed of the 3rd, 26th, 2nd, 4th, 28th, and 1st Divisions. Only the 3rd and 26th were at the front, near Chateau-Thierry.

The 42nd (Rainbow Division) commanded by General Menoher (Douglas MacArthur, Chief-of-Staff) had been at the front since February, had made a successful battalion strength attack on the Salient du Feys in March and was a highly regarded division. MacArthur himself went out with his troops several times, winning medals for conduct above that required of a chief-of-staff. Not relying only on his talents, MacArthur left no stone unturned in his successful campaign for promotion, even risking his life.

The 42nd Division was assigned to the French under General Gourard on the Marne. Expecting an attack, Gourard put the 42nd into the main line of resistance with two other defensive lines in front to disperse the Germans and to enable the delivery of precise artillery fire on the first two lines after Allied withdrawal and German occupation.

The German Seventh Army with twenty divisions planned to attack southeast along the Marne between Reims and Epernay. The German First Army, east of Reims, would attack to the south, then west to join with the Seventh Army and cut off the French. On July 15 the offensive began. First Army struck the French and the 42nd Division and was smashed. The 42nd stood firm but took 1,600 casualties.

Berthelots Fifth French Army with the 3rd U.S. Division was stretched out on the banks of the Marne. General Dickman wanted to straighten his defense line on high ground from which to counterattack but he was overruled. The defenses were not as elaborate as in Gourard's sector unfortunately and the Marne itself was only a canal in some sectors, merely 50 yards wide. Seventh Army attacked at night, successfully crossing the Marne in many places. The French 125th Division collapsed exposing four Pennsylvania companies. These units held but were surrounded and either killed or captured when ammunition ran out.

In the 3rd Division the 38th Regiment (Colonel McAlexander) on the right flank was exposed on both flanks but formed a horseshoe defense and held. The 30th Regiment was pushed back two miles; the other two regiments fell back also but all held. Three platoons held outpost positions, fighting to the last man. That same day the Germans in front of the fighting 3rd Division were stopped; in fact the 30th Regiment counterattacked, reaching the Marne after dark. Behind the French 125th Division, the U.S. 28th Division plugged the gap and stopped the German advance there. The Seventh Army advance was limited and the last German offensive of the war was over. From mid July to the end, the Germans would know only defeat, death, and surrender.

Prior to the German Marne offensive, Marshall Foch had planned a counterattack for July 18 using a new army under French General Mangin, the 10th Army. Mangin s XX Corps consisted of the U.S. 1st and 2nd Divisions, the Marine Brigade, and a Moroccan division. These forces gathered west of the German Marne salient and were kept intact in spite of the German attack of July 15. XX Corps attacked early on July 18, striking at the base of the salient, breaking through the German Ninth Army. The Americans continued until July 22 driving seven miles into the German rear.

The U.S. 3rd, 26th, 28th, and 42nd Divisions also attacked the salient near Belleau Wood, but the German positions were jeopardized and they began to pull back. The 1st and 2nd Divisions lost more then 10,000 men but the victorious Americans were developing a momentum which carried over to all the Allied forces.

During this offensive Sgt. Joyce Kilmer (the composer of the song "Trees") was killed while serving with the 42nd Division.

The Germans moved back from the Marne to the Ourcq, under pressure from the 3rd, 28th, and 42nd Divisions. The 3rd was relieved by the 32nd (Michigan-Wisconsin) Division; this fine unit helped break the line on the Ourcq. The 42nd moved forward successfully, and the 32nd broke through again. At this time, two American Corps, I and III, took responsibility for sections of the front, crossing the Vesle on August 6. The Marne salient, 30 miles deep at the longest penetration, was now eliminated, but at a cost of 50,000 American casualties.

The Amiens Offensive

On August 8, the British concentrated near Amiens and attacked to eliminate the Amiens salient. On their right, the French joined in, and in three days the Germans were pushed back a distance of nine miles. Allied casualties were 50,000 but German casualties were 75,000 including 25,000 prisoners. This offensive, on top of German reverses on the Marne, convinced the Germans that they no longer had the capability of winning and that peace was now their wisest objective. German morale, as indicated by the large numbers of prisoners being taken, was beginning to decline.

St. Mihiel

On August 10, Pershing was given command of the U.S. First Army of 19 U.S. Divisions and 6 French. His assignment was to cut off the German salient at St Mihiel. Permission to cross the Moselle River into Germany to capture Metz might have unhinged the whole Hindenberg Line of defensive positions but Foci set a limited objective with plans to transfer the Americans to the Argonne. Sixteen U.S. divisions (1, 2, 3, 4, 26, 28, 42, 33, 78, 80, 82, 5, 35, 89, 90, and 91) were assembled around the entire salient, 665,000 men, including the French. First Army had 3,220 guns; 1,500 planes commanded by Colonel Billy Mitchell; and a tank brigade of 267 tanks commanded by Colonel George S. Patton Jr. The battle plan was developed in part by First Army Chief of Staff George C. Marshall. Mitchell was an American pioneer in the use of air power~ while the names of Patton and Marshall reappear as dominant figures in World War II.

The German defenses were formidable, in place for four years, but German numbers were not sufficient to defend the entire salient against such a force. The Germans began to withdraw on September 10, two days before the assault began, obviously aware of the horde to be launched against them. First Army attacked on September 12, continued attacking night and day, and occupied the whole salient against light resistance in two days, taking 15,000 prisoners. The whole campaign was conducted with speed and earned a great deal of respect for the American Army.

Pershing was certain that a golden opportunity existed to move on Metz and unhinge the Hindenberg defensive barrier. MacArthur personally drove to the outskirts of Metz and confirmed the path wide open. Foch was Supreme Commander, however, and his eyes were fixed elsewhere. There can be little doubt that French plans were quite conservative based on four years of futile experience. Within a week the Germans moved thirty divisions into the area and the Americans were moved to the Meuse-Argonne sector, where there were only five German divisions.

The Meuse–Argonne Offensive

Foch planned a massive attack all along the front for late September. One key objective was the rail junction of Sedan. First Army was ordered to attack to Sedan through the Argonne Forest where the Germans were originally outnumbered eight to one. A quick breakthrough here was expected but the terrain and defenses were very difficult, tough enough to delay any offensive until reinforcements could be brought in. The Americans attacked on September

26 with one million men on an 80 mile front, III Corps on the right, V Corps in the center, and I Corps on the left.

V Corps was stopped at Montfaucon; III Corps broke through the first German line and I Corps advanced to La Forge, but once inside the Argonne Forest, both corps were halted. By October 3, Montfaucon fell, allowing V Corps to advance but soon First Army bogged down in the hills and woods of the Argonne. The weather turned cold and wet while the Germans brought in reinforcements. The U.S. General Staff was severely criticized by French Prime Minister Clemenceau for the slow advance. Certainly there were problems with all the untried divisions and many an unproven officer, but in such a critical sector there can be little doubt that the Germans made a huge effort to hold, and this is the prime reason for the lack of progress. Many a good division would be shot up attacking elaborate defenses manned by desperate Germans.

There was a group of hills called the Cote-de-Chatillon, a key feature on the Hindenberg Line in the Argonne. Once taken, the road to Sedan would be open; once Sedan was captured, supplies to German forces elsewhere in France and Belgium would be severely interrupted. Here the famed 32nd Division had been repulsed with heavy losses; the 91st was also thrown back; the 1st Division made some headway but also lost heavily. The 42nd Division then replaced the 1st Division. MacArthur had spent considerable time in the trenches and had observed that German defenses were frequently strongest at certain central points and weaker on both flanks of these strong points. He concentrated on these flanks and attacked Hill 288 (288 meters, 945 feet high) which fell by nightfall. The following day Hill 282 was overrun. Hill 205 was bypassed and Tuilieres Ferme taken. The last defenses were occupied by flank attacks by two battalions but one battalion of 1,475 men suffered 1,169 casualties. By this time MacArthur was considered the greatest front line general of the war. His victories in World War II were not merely the result of overwhelming power, luck, or enemy weakness. His genius made impossible tasks seem easy because of his remarkable analytical ability and judgment.

Here in the Argonne, Corporal Alvin York was a member of a squad which had captured some Germans. The squad was ambushed by a German machine-gun crew and the whole squad shot down except for York. Corporal York had been a conscientious objector, but he was also an excellent marksman. He picked off the members of the machine-gun crew, fought off an attacking platoon, gunned down more Germans in trenches every time they looked over the top, until eventually a whole company surrendered to the lone American. York returned to his lines with 132 prisoners, one of the most incredible individual achievements in American military history.

By November 1, First Army had cleared the Argonne and occupied the Heights of the Meuse. The Hindenberg Line was broken, and the Americans now moved forward rapidly. A new U.S. Second Army joined the fight, and by November 11 the 42nd Division (now commanded by MacArthur) was in front of Sedan. The Argonne was taken but at a brutal loss of 117,000 men. The Germans lost 100,000 men but also lost their ability to continue the war. Obviously the Germans had had more than five divisions in the Argonne. Certainly 100,000 men was not their total strength.

Elsewhere, the Allies advanced successfully. The 27th Division, with the British on August 30 to September 3, made a series of successful attacks, taking Vierstaat Ridge, Rossignol Wood, Petit Bois, and Plauteau Farm. The 27th and 30th Divisions then moved south to attack the Hindenberg Line along the St Quentin Canal between Cambrai and St. Quentin. On September 27, the 106th Regiment of the 27th Division took the outer defenses near the Canal but were thrown back. On the 29th the entire division attacked and after vicious fighting, occupied and held a key position of the Hindenberg Line. On September 30, the Australians passed through the break and the advance accelerated. The 27th lost 8,000 men, over 1,000 dead in the entire war. This division captured 1,000 Germans in two days of fighting, over 6,000 in the war, one eighth of the total prisoners taken by American forces.

On the western front the Allies advanced more than 50 miles from mid September to the Armistice. The Germans were done and the Armistice ended their agony while still sparing the Fatherland from the ravages of war.

Macedonia

By September 1918, the Allies had accumulated a huge army of 550,000 men under Franchet d'Esperey to oppose 430,000 Bulgarians and a few Germans. A vigorous assault over 7,000 foot mountains succeeded and in four days the Bulgarians were routed. Bulgaria surrendered on the last day of September.

Turkey

The British advanced north along the Tigris River, capturing 7,000 Turks at Sharqaton on October 30, occupying Mosul on November 14. In Palestine Allenby (stymied by transfer of major forces to the western front) received reinforcements and attacked on September 19. With a two to one manpower advantage and with Turks dispersed over a 65 mile front, Allenby concentrated near the coast where he achieved a breakthrough. The Turks were destroyed at Megiddo, surrendered Damascus on September 30 to Lawrence and his Northern Arab Army, surrendered Beirut on October 10, Tripoli on the 14th, and Aleppo on the 28th. Turkish killed and wounded in this campaign were less than 6,000 but 75,000 surrendered. Turkey surrendered on October 30.

Italy

In June 1918, the Austrians launched two offensives, one from the Trentino, one from the Piave. Sixty Austrian divisions faced fifty Italian and six Allied divisions. The Austrian attacks made some headway but were stopped by rapid Italian troop movements.

The Italian Tenth Army attacked along the Piave, commanded by Lord Cavan with two British and two French divisions and one U.S. regiment (32nd from the 83rd Division). The Austrians collapsed and Vittorio Veneto fell on October 30; Trent was taken; Trieste fell on November 4; and half a million prisoners were taken by November 4 when an armistice was arranged.

The Armistice

Early in November Germany was the only nation of the Central Powers still fighting. The Germans had fought the entire world for four long years in a ghastly war of attrition. Running out of manpower, the Central Powers could no longer defend the huge frontiers they had established. Germany had spent her strength in futile war throughout Europe and into Asia and by early November could not stop the Allied offensive anywhere. The Armistice between Germany and the Allies was signed on November 11, and on that day the fighting stopped. Germany had lost in a multi-front war much like Napoleon had one hundred years earlier. The same mistakes would be made by the German government only 23 years later.

Analysis

The Central Powers, with no concept of the type of war they faced, plunged into World War I with incredible arrogance. If they had studied the gruesome type of combat seen in the American Civil War, they might have hesitated. They dominated central and eastern Europe, however, and were hungry for more. The easy German victory in the Franco-Prussian War and the might of their armies gave them too much confidence in themselves and too little respect for their opponents. As a result, 10,000,000 men died and 6,000,000 were crippled for life.

The map of Europe was changed as the old empires were replaced with smaller democratic nations. As a form of government, democracy emerged as the winner in World War I, but a collective form of security was not successfully created. Efforts to form a League of Nations failed when the American Congress would not approve American membership. The League became impotent and the defensive alliances formed were not backed by credible force, leaving the way open for future adventure. The peoples of most of Europe were sick of war and as a result too reluctant to rearm or even to face the possibility of another war. The politicians, particularly in England and France, representing the will of their people, ignored all the warning signs of future trouble coming out of Italy, Germany, and Japan. The United States also reverted back to isolationism and sat idle while another catastrophe fermented.

The United States, protected by the two oceans, was fortunate to be able to stay out of the war until the other combatants were exhausted. Even after declaring war, the United States was fortunate to have a year of grace in which to build up, train, and equip her armies. When the Americans joined the fight in force, the result was decisive.

The performance of U.S. troops was outstanding. They came in full of fight and were given tough assignments. The experience gained by U.S. officers was a key to organizing and leading the armed forces in World War II. MacArthur learned how to concentrate and attack at the enemy's weakest point. Patton learned how to use tanks. Billy Mitchell learned the fundamentals of air warfare. George C. Marshall learned how to organize a large army.

The fine performance of the National Guard preserved that institution. The magnificent conduct of the Marine Brigade was a preview of their later exploits in World War II and Korea. The professional conduct of U.S. citizen soldiers, however, misled the United States into continuing to believe that a large professional army was not necessary.

World War I produced most of the weapons used more effectively in World War II, but the missing element was mobility. Troops on foot, after breaking through a defensive position, could only advance for short distances. In World War II mechanized armies could exploit a breakthrough for major gains. The use of submarines was almost decisive in World War I. Only the use of convoys enabled the Allies to preserve shipping and transport troops safely. The terror and resolution of the submarine menace was repeated in World War II.

The Japanese were the only major World War I combatant not to suffer heavy losses. Their militancy continued unabated between World War I and II.

World War I did not settle much. Soon afterward the most evil and dangerous alliance ever formed came into being.

Chapter VI
World War II, 1939–1945

Japanese Expansion and Aggression in the Pacific

By the Twentieth Century Japan had developed a population too large for the available arable land. The Japanese Islands, poor in natural resources, could not support the people. As a result Japan looked to China, rich in land but poor in technology and military strength. After her successful war with Russia in 1904-1905, Japan occupied part of Manchuria. Cautious until 1928, Japan, in the next five years, occupied all of Manchuria. Starting in 1937, Japan moved into China as follows: July 1937, North China, near Manchuria; November 1937, Shanghai; December 1937, Nanking; and October 1938, Canton Province.

The Japanese atrocities in China, particularly in Nanking, were brutal, a preview of future Japanese behavior. In 1939 Japan clashed with Russia near Outer Mongolia but was beaten by the Russian Siberian Army under Marshal Zhukov.

In 1940 France was overrun by Germany, leaving French colonies weakly defended. Japan obtained permission from Vichy France to station troops in northern Indochina. The following year Japan moved troops to southern Indochina in an act of blatant aggression. Starting in 1940 the U.S. and other nations tried to use diplomatic measures to get the Japanese to leave Indochina. An embargo on scrap iron, steel, and aviation fuel was passed in July 1940. In July 1941, the U.S. Britain, and the Netherlands cut off all their oil supplies to Japan. The Japanese, if they were to consolidate their gains, had no other option than to invade an oil rich land, and the Dutch East Indies was the closest.

The U.S. supported China with small financial grants, then in 1941 with 100 P-40 fighters. Colonel Claire Chenault was appointed Chang Kai-shek's air advisor and permission was granted to recruit U.S. Pilots. The American Volunteer Group (AVG) became known as the Flying Tigers, famed for achieving 10 victories for each defeat.

In the last half of 1941 Prince Konoye tried to negotiate with the U.S. but Japan was not about to give up their acquisitions, and no other concession could satisfy the U.S. The negotiations failed, and Prince Konoye resigned to be replaced by General Hideki Tojo. Japan now prepared for war.

Germany Before the War

The terms of the Treaty of Verailles were harsh, demanding huge payments from Germany, well beyond her ability to pay. Germany lost all of her colonies. Other areas were occupied by the Allies temporarily such as the Saar, Germany's coal mining region. No German armed forces were allowed within 28 miles of the Rhine (the Rhineland). Germany's economy failed and inflation caused enormous hardships. With this disturbed condition Germany fell under the control of Adolf Hitler by 1933.

Hitler immediately began to rebuild Germany's military forces in violation of the Versailles Treaty. The Treaty did permit a plebiscite in the Saar which was held in 1933. The vote heavily favored a return to Germany, and Hitler sent in troops to consolidate the return. Hitler took his first aggressive gamble in 1936 when he occupied the Rhineland. A lack of response by the Allies gave Hitler a measure of Allied lack of resolve and may have been the largest mistake made by the Allies in their pathetic measures to avoid the oncoming conflagration.

In 1938 Hitler made moves to annex Austria but ended up sending in troops in March, again with no Allied resistance.

In May of 1938, Hitler demanded control of the Sudetenland in Czechoslovakia where there were numerous Germans. The Czechs mobilized, and in their Sudetenland fortifications, they were a force with which to be reckoned. Hitler applied pressure, indicating he would take action by October 1. Prime Minister Neville Chamberlain of England met with Hitler and decided to avoid war by giving the Sudetenland to Germany. Chamberlain sold this plan to France and signed the Munich Pact on September 29, giving Hitler the right to occupy the disputed land. Chamberlain claimed he had achieved "peace in our time" but his naïve assertion has become an historic example of the futility of appeasement. Hitler not only occupied the Sudetenland but by March of 1939 he took all of Czechoslovakia.

Hitler, by this time, had the correct measure of his opponents. The U.S. had, in 1935 and again in 1937, passed Neutrality Acts prohibiting involvement in a European war. This gave Hitler assurance that there would be no U.S. resistance to his aggressions. England had too little military strength to be a factor on the continent and France, with a sizeable army, had shown no determination in any of Hitler's earlier moves. From the beginning, if the nations of Europe had united in opposition to Hitler, World War II could have been prevented. Foreign policy must always be exercised by the strongest nations in a forceful and enlightened manner to let aggressors know their transgressions will be dealt with but there also has to be some force to back up the brave speeches.

The Fascist Movement in Italy

After World War I, the Socialists in Italy denounced the war, offending many ex-soldiers who formed a party. These men were called Fascists (blackshirts) and soon were strong enough to take over control of various towns wherever Socialists had undue influence. Headed by Mussolini, they took advantage of a weak government to march on Rome in 1922 where King Victor Emmannuel asked Mussolini to form a government.

Mussolini became absolute dictator and eventually began to look for territorial gain. Italy had already occupied Libya, Eritrea, and Italian Somaliland in Africa. In 1935 Italy invaded Abyssinia and in 1939, Albania. The world was too busy looking at Hitler and generally too weak willed to bother with Mussolini. In May of 1939 Italy and Germany signed an agreement to support each other in the event of war.

Spanish Civil War, 1936–1939

In Spain a weak democracy existed prior to 1936, but there was a wide split in the political parties—on the left, the Popular Front (Anarchists, Socialists, Communists, and Republicans); on the right, the CEDA (a coalition of Catholics) and right wing extremists (the Falange). In the last election the Popular Front won, outlawing the Falange and seizing land. The army feared a communist takeover and started a rebellion in Spanish Morocco, which soon spread to the mainland. Nationalist control over about one fourth of Spain, mainly in the northwest, was quickly established. General Franco and his army were airlifted from Morocco to Cadiz by German aircraft and the Civil War was on. Germany and Italy assisted Franco while Russia assisted the Republicans. There was much sympathy for the Republicans in the west, and many volunteers from England, France, and the United States journeyed to Spain to enlist in the Republican Army. Some of these volunteers thought they were fighting for democracy and some were dedicated communists. Americans formed the Abraham Lincoln Brigade and, even 50 years after the war, some of these Americans still maintained their socialistic ideology.

The war was brutal with massacres common on both sides. Germany and Italy supplied weapons and personnel to Franco, using Spain to test their new weapons and tactics. Russia was the principal source of supplies to the Republicans, but Russian help was not sufficient to prevent Franco from gradually pushing the government forces back. Madrid was occupied by the Nationalists in March of 1939.

By the end of the war, the Republican government was dominated by communists and each army battalion had a commissar to indoctrinate the troops. With Russia as the government's main supporter, the communist flavor of the government should not be too surprising. In the long run, Franco's dictatorship may have been hard for the Spanish people, but he brought stability and prevented the loss of another nation to communism. An important consideration to Americans is the fact that a communist government in Spain would have been a dangerous threat to the delicate world balance of power after World War II when capitalism and communism faced each other in constant belligerence. Spain remained neutral in World War II and probably would have if the Republicans had won. Few realized it at the time but the right side won the Civil War.

September 1, 1939. Germany Invades Poland

As soon as he had digested Czechoslovakia, Hitler turned on the Poles, demanding the return of Danzig and access to East Prussia. Poland refused all demands, but in August Germany and Russia signed a non-aggression pact including provisions for the partition of Poland. England formed an alliance with Poland, but on September 1 Germany invaded Poland. There was a little skit performed by the Germans which they claimed was a Polish intrusion across the German border, but the massed divisions along the border clearly indicated the detailed plans made by the Germans for the assault on Poland. The Germans hit hard and fast with mechanized armies, their lightning war (Blitzkrieg), and by October 6 all Polish resistance ended. Poland was split between Germany and Russia whose troops had entered Poland after the Germans had wiped out the Polish army. England, France, and Canada declared war on Germany but little could be done to help Poland. England was too poorly prepared for war to do much for anybody, including herself.

The Russo-Finnish War, 1939-1940

In October of 1939, having digested half of Poland, Russia turned on Finland, asking for land acquisitions. At the same time Russia moved into Latvia, Lithuania, and Estonia. Finland made no concessions so Russia attacked in November. The Russian army, short of high level officers after Stalin's purge, suffered embarrassing setbacks. Russian divisions stalled in the snow, were surrounded, and annihilated. In January 1940, Marshal Timoshenko took over, beginning an offensive which in two months forced the Finns to surrender. The Finns suffered 25,000 dead, the Russians 200,000! From this war Hitler probably obtained a poor opinion of Russian army capabilities. The Finns, hungry for revenge, turned to Germany.

Invasion of Denmark and Norway, 1940

Although World War II started with the German attack on Poland, Allied efforts against Hitler on the continent of Europe were negligible. In April of 1940 Germany occupied Denmark and invaded Norway. British and French troops landed in three places in central and northern Norway to assist the Norwegians but were never coordinated and could not stop the Germans. All Allied troops were withdrawn when Hitler invaded France. There was considerable naval action during the Norwegian campaign with losses on both sides.

The Fall of France, 1940

In 1940 France had 78 divisions deployed, more than half of them in or behind the Maginot Line (between France and Germany), 22 in reserve, including their three armored divisions, leaving only 15 to 20 to cover the unfortified border with Belgium. Britain had 10 divisions in France, only six on the Belgian border.

The German Army Group A under von Rundstedt would make the crucial attack through the Ardennes with seven panzer, three motorized, and 34 infantry divisions. Here the French had only one army, the weakest part of their defense, because the Ardennes was not considered a likely place for an attack. German Army Group B under von Bock would invade Holland and Belgium with three panzer (armored) divisions, one motorized and 24 infantry divisions. Army Group C faced the Maginot Line with only 17 infantry divisions. German and Allied strengths were about even, but in the crucial front opposite the Ardennes the Allies were totally out manned. Further, although the Allies had as many tanks as the Germans, they were not concentrated in armored divisions.

On May 10, von Bock invaded Holland and Belgium. The Allies on the Belgian border moved forward to meet them. Then, on May 12 von Rundstedt burst through the Ardennes into France up to the river Meuse near Sedan, crossing in two places on the thirteenth.

On May 10 Winston Churchill became Prime Minister of England. Alone in the 1930s, he had warned the English that Germany was preparing for war, but no one heard him. Now, in England's hour of peril, he took hold of a hopeless situation and with unlimited courage and energy he carried his people. Speaking with matchless eloquence, his mellow voice put teeth into the British lion, but he could not help France.

On May 15 the Germans broke through from their bridgeheads at Sedan. That same day Holland surrendered. The Germans, instead of attacking southwest towards Paris as in World War I, turned west and cut a 50 mile wide path. The French 9th Army collapsed. Charles de Gaulle attacked the German flank with his 4th Armored Division but was not strong enough to have much effect. The German spearhead, led by Guderian and Rommel, reached Noyelles at the mouth of the Somme River by May 20 cutting off the British, Belgian, and French 1st Armies. On May 20 the British began to evacuate their troops from Dunkirk. On May 27 Belgium surrendered. By June 3 220,000 British and 120,000 Belgian and French troops had been rescued. Two British divisions and another 120,000 men were, however, trapped in France. On June 6 the Germans crossed the Somme, trapping one British and four French divisions on the coast south of Dunkirk. On June 14 the Germans entered Paris. On the 20th Italy attacked France along the Mediterranean (the infamous "stab in the back"), and on June 22 France surrendered.

French generals had been totally unprepared for modern war. Only a few, like de Gaulle, understood mechanized war, the element missing in World War I, speed and mobility.

The Battle of Britain, Summer, 1940

Germany planned to invade England after the fall of France but first had to establish air superiority. Germany had about 2,500 planes in Belgium and France to only 600 British (of which only 400 were serviceable). Churchill made Lord Beaverbrook Minister of Aircraft Production however, and in three months, aircraft production doubled to 500 per month in July. To achieve air superiority by fall, the Germans would have to destroy 600 British planes a month or 20 every day.

Early attacks in July on ships and docks did not produce the desired results and the Germans began to hit the R.A.F. (Royal Air Force). With this strategy the R.A.F. was unable to replace pilots and planes as fast as they were lost. The English bombed Berlin one night in September, however, and the furious Germans switched their strategy again to bombing English cities, giving the R.A.F. a badly needed respite. On September 15 the Germans lost 58 planes to 26 British, and with 170 English fighters in the air it became apparent to the Germans that they were not gaining air superiority. Germany had lost 1880 planes and 2660 airmen, the British losses being 1020 planes and 537 pilots. The Germans had failed to knock out English radar stations and their fighters had limited range, unable to stay in the combat zone for long. The English had other advantages, able to concentrate on shooting down defenseless bombers, and also able to recover some of their downed pilots. The Germans put off their plans to invade England and this failure eventually required Germany to fight on three continents. Hitler's inability to conquer England was the first major mistake in his plans for world domination. Air raids over England continued, but the invasion fear diminished.

Italian Aggressions, 1940

In August Italy invaded and overran British Somaliland on the Gulf of Aden. In September Italy attacked the British in Egypt. The British, with only two divisions, pulled back to prepared defenses at Mersa Matruh until tanks and reinforcements arrived in late September. On October 28, Italy, already in Albania, invaded Greece. Within one week the Greeks under General Metaxas stopped the Italians and invaded Albania.

In December of 1940 the British counterattacked in Egypt, successfully driving the invaders out and continuing on into Libya, advancing as far as El Agheila (halfway to Tunisia) by February of 1941. Two British divisions had defeated five Italian.

In East Africa the British Empire forces gathered in Aden, Kenya, and the Sudan. Attacking the Italian and British Somalilands and Eritrea simultaneously with over five divisions (two Indian, two African, one South African) in January, the British took all of the Italian possessions by late May with some fighting continuing until November.

In Libya the Italians surrendered in large numbers (120,000) and showed a general reluctance to fight until later when stiffened by Germans. Italians were sympathetic to the West, certainly to the U.S. where so many had friends and relatives.

They had fought well with the Allies in World War I, and Mussolini's ambitions do not appear to have been injected into his troops.

The War at Sea, 1939–1940

Germany did not have the submarine force she had had in World War I (only 30 in July, 1940) and did not have the fleet to fight surface battles, but she had some excellent fast, powerful pocket battleships built in violation of the 1924 Naval Treaty. These were to supplement the submarines in attacks on British shipping. The *Graf Spee* sortied in 1939, did some damage, but was finally cornered in Montevideo by British cruisers and scuttled, although she probably could have shot her way out against the lighter vessels waiting outside the harbor. In late 1940 the *Admiral Scheer*, a pocket battleship, ventured out into the South Atlantic in November 1940, returning to Germany in February, 1941, after sinking 17 ships. The *Admiral Hipper* left port in late 1940, again in February of 1941, sank 7 ships, then returned to port. In February and March the battle cruisers *Scharnhorst* and *Gneisenau* sank 115,000 tons of shipping before returning to Brest. In May the battleship *Bismark* and heavy cruiser *Prince Eugene* left port. *Bismark* sank HMS *Hood* before succumbing to torpedoes from aircraft and a fleet of British battleships.

In September of 1940 the U.S. sent England 50 old destroyers in accordance with the terms of the Lend-Lease Agreement. In September and October over

400,000 tons of British shipping were lost. Losses ranged from 300,000 to 400,000 tons per month until June of 1941.

The British developed a radar capable of detecting surfaced submarines, captured the German submarine code, allowing convoys to avoid subs, and developed a system of convoys protected by escort vessels. In July of 1941, although the Germans had 60 U- boats, ship losses were down to 113,000 tons.

In the Mediterranean the British engaged the Italian fleet on several occasions, causing some damage and forcing the Italians to withdraw, but the Germans eventually committed air power to the area and this was to cause great problems for British shipping.

The Desert Fox in North Africa, 1941

In January 1941, Rommel was assigned to take two German divisions to North Africa, one light and one armored (panzer). Rommel was accompanied at first by only one German division but with elements of five Italian divisions (including one motorized), the Axis forces had sufficient superiority to permit an offensive resulting in the retreat of the two British divisions in March and April. Rommel, a panzer division commander in France, became famous. His lightning flanking attacks gave the British no time or place to stand and hold. The 9th Australian Division stayed in Tobruk but the British 2nd Armored fell back into Egypt.

The Balkans, Spring 1941

After postponing plans to invade England, Hitler planned to attack Russia in 1941 as soon as spring weather permitted. But in March 1941, Yugoslavia suffered a coup by military officers hostile to Germany; Hitler then decided to delay his Russian invasion and pacify Yugoslavia and Greece. Yugoslavia was invaded on April 6, and the country was overrun in two weeks. The Greeks had two armies, the 2nd in the east with four divisions, and the 1st in Albania with a larger force. Four British divisions were gathering south of Salonika. The Germans attacked in central Greece on April 6, capturing Salonika on the 9th, cutting off the Greek 2nd Army which was forced to surrender. Moving fast, the Germans cut off the 1st Greek Army still inside Albania, which surrendered on April 20. The British fought a delaying retreat but were out of Greece by April 28. Three hundred thousand Greeks were captured. Hitler was destroying the whole of Europe, nation by nation, piecemeal. Just imagine the potential resistance if all these nations had been united. The invasion of Russia was postponed from May 15 to June 22, a vital factor in events to come.

In May Hitler invaded Crete with 22,750 troops against 40,000 British and

Greek troops, all of whom were lightly armed. With air superiority it took the Germans 10 days to drive all opposition from the island.

The Invasion of Russia, 1941

Hitler planned to destroy Russia's armies before the winter of 1941–1942 and then finish off England. The Germans planned to attack from Finland and Rumania, but mainly from Poland, with three army groups. Against them the Russians were organized in five districts. The forces can be summarized as follows:

	German Divisions				Russian Divisions		
From	Infantry	Armored	Motorized	From	Infantry	Armored	Motorized
Finland	16 Finn			Leningrad	18		
	8 Ger.			Baltic	19	4	2
North	23	3	3	Western	26	12	6
Center	36	9	5	Kiev	35	16	8
South	33 Ger.	5	3	Odessa	16	4	2
	14 Ruman						
Reserve	24	2					
Subtotal	154	19	11		114	36	18
Total	**184**				**168**		

Hitler's original plan was to occupy the Ukraine (Russia's most fertile farmland) to the Dnieper River in the south, take Leningrad in the north, and use the central force with two panzer armies, Guderian's 2nd and Hoth's 1st to cut off and capture Russians.

The Russians in the west were located close to the border with no defense in depth, but had they been better prepared, they had in the west enough divisions and more armored divisions than the Germans with more forces available throughout Russia. For fear of provoking the Germans, however, they were not ordered to mobilize or dig in. The Russians are believed to have had as many as 200 divisions, 4,500,000 men in just the west, to 3,000,000 Germans. On June 22 the Germans attacked with Army Group North under von Lieb, Army Group Center under von Bock, and Army Group South under von Rundstedt. When they could, the Russians fought hard. Many times they were bypassed and cut off with the surrender of huge groups as follows:

Date	Place	Prisoners	Tanks Lost
July 3	Bialystok	290,000	2500
August 5	Smolensk	310,000	
August 8	Uman	100,000	
August	Miscellaneous	300,000	
September 19	Kiev	600,000	2500
October 14	Bryansk	50,000	
October 19	Vyazma	670,000	1000
Total		**2,320,000**	**6000**

The attacks in the center had done well, but Hitler wanted the northern and southern objectives to be taken, so he diverted armor from Army Group Center on July 19, claiming that Moscow was no longer a primary objective. On September 5 Hitler changed his mind and ordered the panzer divisions to return to Army Group Center to enable capture of Moscow, but the time lost by the weakening of the offensive before Moscow was fatal. Moscow was the center of roads and railroads in central Russia, a major manufacturing town, and a huge morale loss to Russia if captured. Although Napoleon had captured Moscow and accomplished nothing by it, occupation in a mechanized war would have been far more significant. The Germans surrounded Moscow on three sides but were stalled by mud, then snow and terrible cold (for which they were not prepared), and by 80 Russian divisions. The Germans were within 19 miles in the north and 50 miles in the south.

The Germans occupied the Ukraine to the Dnieper, invaded the Crimea, and took all but Sevastapol, advancing as far as Rostov on the Don. In the north the Germans stalled outside of Leningrad.

The Germans in Rostov were overextended with weakly held flanks, and on November 29 the Russians counterattacked, recapturing Rostov. Von Runstedt retreated from Rostov and was immediately fired by Hitler. By December 5 the German juggernaut came to a complete halt. That same day, the Russians, stiffened by arrival of the Siberian armies, began counterattacks that would extend over half the entire front.

In 1941 the Germans lost 150,000 men each month, more than they could replace. There can be no doubt that the Russians were fighting. Also, they had an armada of tanks, although many were old and most were dispersed, not concentrated for massed armored movements. Some of the Russian tanks were the huge HV-1 and HV-2 and T-34 models, new with armor that German weapons could not penetrate. By the end of 1941 the German high command knew that they were in deep trouble in Russia. Even after staggering losses the Russians kept coming and there was no end to them.

The Russians broke through the German 2nd Army on December 13, exposing Guderian's 2nd Panzer Army. The German chief of staff, von

Brauchitsch flew to Russia and ordered Army Group Center to pull back 90 miles. Hitler, furious, fired von Brauchitsch, Guderian, and Hoepner (the latter two were German pioneers in armored warfare). In the north the Russians surrounded 90,000 Germans not permitted to withdraw by Hitler, causing von Leeb to resign. The Germans had come close to destroying Russia in 1941, but without their best generals their chances for future success were diminished. Hitler would not tolerate retreat, even limited withdrawals to shorten the long, twisted defensive front, thereby shortening the life of his armies and eventually the reign of the Third Reich.

North Africa 1941

On May 27, Rommel received his panzer division and advanced into Egypt. On June 15, the British under Wavell counterattacked but were repulsed, costing Wavell his job. The British built up their Egyptian forces, now called Eighth Army under Ritchie. Rommel now had a third German division but in November he ran out of fuel and lost air superiority to the British. In late 1941 Eighth Army attacked, forcing Rommel to retreat all the way back to Tripoli where he had started just one year ago.

Japan Attacks Pearl Harbor, December 7, 1941

Japan had hoped to occupy most of Southeast Asia and most of the Pacific Islands. By joining Germany and Italy in the Axis Pact, she expected the U.S. to realize that military resistance would be fruitless, and in 1941 this certainly seemed to be the case. By basing naval forces and aircraft on far out Pacific islands, it would have been nearly impossible for the U.S. to send and supply forces to Australia, which the Japanese hoped to isolate. First Japan had to cripple the U.S. Pacific Fleet based in Pearl Harbor.

On December 7, 1941, at dawn, 214 Japanese planes took off from six aircraft carriers 200 miles north of Hawaii. These planes attacked air bases on land and the major ships docked in Pearl Harbor, sinking five battleships and two light cruisers. A second wave damaged another battleship and three destroyers, leaving the U.S. fleet without a battleship. Fortunately the two U.S. carriers, *Enterprise* and *Lexington*, were out to sea at the time. 2327 Americans died, murdered by an unprovoked attack in what President Roosevelt called the "day of infamy." 1143 more were wounded, and the Army and Navy air forces were reduced from 481 to about 140 undamaged planes.

The U.S. had broken the Japanese diplomatic code and had had scores of messages and clues pertaining to future hostilities but no absolute information as to where or when. The forces at Pearl Harbor were ordered to be on "war alert," whatever that means, but to me it seems serious enough to have warranted putting the fleet out to sea with combat air patrol, long range air search, and all other possible types of search and reconnaissance. Admiral Kimmel and General Short, in duel command at Pearl Harbor, were held responsible, but no one in high command demanded or followed up to see that such measures were taken. No matter how experienced or skilled the military officers in command, it is very difficult for any human to convert from years of peace to warlike behavior based on mere possibilities. Such things happen again and again throughout history and, just to illustrate, the U.S. forces in the Philippines were also surprised, just as completely on the same day, December 7.

On December 8, the U.S. and Great Britain declared war on Japan. On December 11 Germany and Italy declared war on the U.S. The U.S. had been drafting men for over a year, and in August of 1941, 400,000 U.S. troops participated in maneuvers to practice armored warfare. The attack on Pearl Harbor woke a sleeping giant, stirred the martial spirit of a free people, and brought a furious response, as almost every man, woman, and child joined in what had become a struggle for justice and even existence. President Roosevelt promised that, "this nation, in its righteous might, would achieve the inevitable victory, so help us, God." Roosevelt, in this country, would prove to be a great spiritual leader, as he had been during the depression. He, like Churchill, had that marvelous inspirational speaking ability. The United States Congress had been hostile to foreign involvement or a military buildup, but this country was fortunate to have a triumvirate of brilliant men: President Roosevelt, George Marshall (Army Chief of Staff) and Ernest King (Chief of Naval Operations). These men planned for the production of weapons and forces before the war, and once hostilities began it would not be long before American armed might would make itself felt. For a while, however, there would be losses and hardship. Could the U.S. supply sufficient forces before England or Russia collapsed? Could the U.S. defend in the Pacific before the Japanese occupied crucial outlying islands, cutting off potential supply lines? These questions were in doubt all through 1942.

Japanese Conquests

After Pearl Harbor the Japanese landed in scores of places in Southeast Asia and the Pacific Islands. They, like the Germans, were well prepared and quickly overran their poorly armed opponents. Dates of invasion and final conquest were as follows:

Place	Invasion	Conquest
Tarawa, Makin (Gilbert Islands)	12/9/41	12/9
Malay	12/8	1/31/42
Thailand	12/9	12/14
Guam	12/10	12/10

Luzon (Philippines)	12/10	4/9/42
Borneo	12/16	3/7/42
Hong Kong	12/18	12/25
Lingayen Gulf (Luzon)	12/22	
Wake	12/23	12/23
Celebes	1/11/42	3/7/42
Burma	1/15	5/20
Rabaul, Kavieng (New Ireland)	1/23	1/23
Bouganville (Solomon Islands)	1/23	1/23
Lae, New Guinea	1/25	
Amboina	1/30	3/7
Singapore	2/8	2/15
Sumatra	2/14	3/7
Timor	2/20	3/7
Java	2/28	3/7
Corregidor	5/5	5/10

Malaya and Burma

On December 8, General Yamashita landed on the north coast of Malaya with an army of three divisions. He was attacked on the beachhead by an Indian brigade but managed to hang on until the Indians withdrew. The British had two Indian and one Australian division and four brigades, but were poorly armed with few planes and soon lost control of the sea when, on December 10, the battleship *Prince of Wales* and the heavy cruiser *Repulse* were sunk by Japanese planes. The British tried to hold key positions on major roads and rivers but were always bypassed on land or sea and continuously forced to withdraw. A British division, an Indian brigade, and more Australian troops arrived on January 22 but too late to save Malaya. On January 31, all British forces were withdrawn to the island of Singapore. On February 7, Singapore was invaded and taken by February 15. A huge army of 130,000 British surrendered and the Japanese looked invincible. To postulate that the British in Singapore were poorly coordinated is one way to explain such a disaster. Some of the prisoners were used as slave labor on the Thai-Burma Railroad described loosely in the movie "The Bridge on the River Kwai."

The Japanese were concerned that a British presence in Burma would threaten their position in Southeast Asia. Additionally supplies to China passed through Burma on the Burma Road. The Japanese attacked on January 15 in the Kra Isthmus, then again near Rangoon on January 30. The British had one Indian division, one Burmese division, an Indian brigade, and one armored brigade but again, whichever position they defended was outflanked. Rangoon was abandoned. Two Chinese armies under U.S. General Stilwell came into Burma near Mandalay to help defend the Burma Road and General Bill Slim took over command of the British forces. The Japanese probably never outnumbered their opponents but they moved quickly, retaining the initiative, and with control of sea and air, they could supply their forces wherever they went. The British, dependant upon a long thin supply corridor, had to retreat whenever it was threatened. On March 30, the Chinese south of Mandalay let the Japanese cross the Sittang River, then pulled back much to Stilwell's disgust, thus forcing the British to pull back also. On April 29, the Japanese occupied Lashio and put the Burma Road out of business.

By May 1, the Allies were in full retreat. By May 20, all of Burma was lost to the Japanese. Stilwell had to walk out of Burma to India on foot after a long trek through jungle and mountains. His Chinese troops had performed poorly and few expected otherwise, but Stilwell believed in the Chinese soldier and set up training facilities for them in India. They would return. There was much concern in India about stopping the Japanese. Most of the Indian forces were dispersed around the globe; worse still, British forces had not been able to cope with the Japanese.

The Philippines

General Douglas MacArthur was commander of a 100,000 man Filipino army, but the army had only one U.S. division, was not well equipped, and proved to be no match for the Japanese. On December 7, Japanese aircraft destroyed MacArthur's air force on the ground and the Japanese landed a small force on northern Luzon the following day.

MacArthur, trying to defend all of the island, had divided his forces. Those in northern Luzon fell back under the combined air, land, and sea attack.

On December 22, the main Japanese landing on Lingayen Gulf occurred. A defense was established on the River Agno north of Manila, but the Japanese landed on the east coast of Luzon jeopardizing this defense. On December 24, MacArthur decided to gather his forces on the Bataan peninsula. Eight divisions, 80,000 men, were in position by January 5. This line was held until the twenty-second, when a withdrawal to a second line became necessary. By February 8, Allied casualties were 50 percent but (like the Japanese) many were from disease, and the fighting slowed. The Japanese were outnumbered on Bataan and not strong enough to make an overwhelming attack until April when reinforcements were available. By April 9, short of food and ammunition, the Bataan army surrendered. Seventy-eight thousand men became prisoners to be taken over a 65 mile Bataan Death March where thousands died. Of 12,000 Americans only 4,000 survived the war.

On March 11, MacArthur was ordered to Australia to assume command of all forces in the south-west Pacific. Jonathan Wainwright took over in Bataan, was eventually captured, but did survive imprisonment.

On April 10, the Japanese landed on Cebu Island forcing the U.S. Filipino garrison to take to the hills. Landings were made on Panay and Mindanao as well. Japanese landed on Corregidor where the 4th Marines met them on the beach with success in all but one place, not strongly held. Once the perimeter was pierced the battle became hopeless, and on May 7, 15,000 men became prisoners. The forces in the Philippines had held on for five valuable months while the Arsenal of Democracy built its war machine. MacArthur, upon leaving the Philippines, said, "I shall return," and he did, just two years later. He can not be faulted for the loss of the Philippines as the Japanese onslaught quickly isolated the islands and made U.S. supply and support impossible. Efforts to defend islands in the East Indies later were both costly and futile. Our forces in the Philippines were considered lost and a book called *They Were Expendable* says it all in just the title.

The Defense of Australia

It had been agreed between Churchill and Roosevelt that the bulk of the Allied armed forces should be diverted to Europe. Germany was the major threat as the defeat of either England or Russia would be catastrophic. Japan was not in a position to take a major opponent out of the war. It therefore became very difficult for MacArthur to plan for the defense of Australia, one of the few land masses in the western Pacific not occupied by the Japanese. There were few Americans and almost no Australian troops in the country, only 250,000 Australian militia (mostly old men and boys not qualified for regular service).

Some resistance to the occupation of the Dutch East Indies had been made. An Allied fleet under Dutch Admiral Doorman tried to oppose landings on Java, but was badly beaten in the Java Sea on February 27, and hurt again in Sunda Strait on March 1 with a total loss of two heavy cruisers, three light cruisers, five destroyers, and an airplane tender. The U.S. cruiser *Houston* went down in a valiant raid on the Japanese fleet in Sunda Strait. The Japanese did not lose a ship.

In March 1942, U.S. troops arrived in New Caledonia and the New Hebrides Islands off Australia's east coast to protect the supply line. This same month the Japanese landed at Lae and Salamaua on the north coast of New Guinea. MacArthur then explained his strategy for the defense of Australia to the Aussies. He would attack in New Guinea. In this darkest of hours this fantastic statement gave the Australians a badly needed ray of hope. This, as it turned out, was not mere bravado but a brilliant plan for winning by a man who knew how.

In late March and early April, Admiral Nagumo took a Japanese fleet into the Indian Ocean, sinking a British carrier and two heavy cruisers, again without loss of a ship. On land and sea the Japanese were still unbeaten.

On April 18, Jimmy Doolittle took off from the carrier *Hornet* 700 miles east of Tokyo with 16 B-25 bombers, bombed Tokyo, and crash landed in China, out of fuel.

Little damage to Tokyo was done, but the raid was a shock to the Japanese and a humiliation to the military who had promised the people great victories. This minor raid may have contributed to the Japanese decision to attack Midway and bring on a battle with the U.S. fleet. It also may have weakened attempts to take Port Moresby on the south coast of New Guinea. The total effects of this raid may have been far reaching.

The Battle of The Coral Sea

The Japanese had forces on the northern coast of New Guinea, but the terrible Owen Stanley mountains separated them from the southern coast nearest Australia. They therefore decided to sail east of New Guinea into the Coral Sea and from there to Port Moresby, the main port on the southern coast. This force would consist of twelve troop carrying transports, heavy cruisers, and light carrier *Shoho*. To the east and north of this fleet a carrier striking force would sail to be in position to attack an American fleet should it attempt to do battle. The U.S. knew of this plan and sent a fleet with two carriers, *Yorktown* and *Lexington*. MacArthur sent a fleet of three cruisers and some destroyers under Aussie Rear Admiral Crace. On May 4, *Yorktown* bombed Japanese ships off Tulagi in the Solomons, sinking two minesweepers and some smaller craft while damaging a destroyer. The Japanese now knew that they were dealing with U.S. carriers.

On May 7, the Japanese spotted a U.S. destroyer and fleet oiler and, thinking they were major ships, launched a full carrier air strike, sinking both ships but missing the U.S. carrier fleet.

The Japanese carrier *Shoho* was also spotted on May 7 and promptly sunk by planes from *Lexington* and *Yorktown*. Both U.S. and Japanese strikes were mistakes, each thinking they were attacking the other's main carrier force. But Admiral Inouye decided not to take his transports to Port Moresby without *Shoho*, and he turned back. Admiral Crace was sent to attack Inouye but missed contact because of the Japanese withdrawal.

Late on May 7, the Japanese carriers launched another strike at sunset, missing again, but this time 9 planes were shot down, 6 landed by mistake on the U.S. carriers, and 11 crashed on Japanese carriers after dark.

On May 8, *Yorktown* and *Lexington* under Admiral Fletcher launched 85 planes, finally finding carrier *Shokaku* and hitting her with three bombs. Carrier *Zuikaku* could not be located in bad weather. The Japanese under Admiral Takagi also launched 70 planes, hitting *Yorktown* with one bomb, but hitting *Lexington* with two bombs and two torpedoes. *Lexington* sailed under her own power with three manageable fires until gasoline vapor leaked into the generator room. Internal explosions destroyed the ship and she was sunk by U.S. torpedoes.

Tactically the battle was about a draw as both fleets lost most of their planes.

Yorktown went back to Pearl Harbor for repairs while *Shokaku* went back to Tokyo for the same reason, and *Zuikaku* went back to Truk to take on more planes. The U.S. lost one carrier which might otherwise have been at the oncoming battle at Midway, but two Japanese carriers were deleted from the Midway strike force. The major accomplishment of the Americans in this battle was the turning back of the Port Moresby invasion force; thus by bold and aggressive action, the U.S. Navy, with badly outnumbered forces, had succeeded in turning the Japanese back for the first time in the war.

Carrier attack strategy was to launch three groups, fighters, torpedo planes, and dive bombers, which would fly together to the enemy fleet. Fighters would engage the enemy fighters while dive bombers attacked from high altitude and torpedo planes attacked at sea level. Simultaneous high and low attacks prevented enemy planes and gunners from concentrating on one attack sector. It seldom worked that way, as it took hours to launch all the planes, and some would proceed without waiting for all the others. *Yorktown's* dive bombers reached the target 26 minutes ahead of the slower torpedo planes, and had to wait in the combat zone.

The Japanese abandoned their plans for a sea borne invasion of Port Moresby and were now forced to consider the torturous route over the Owen Stanley Mountains. This effort would take some time and time was what MacArthur needed.

Midway

Admiral Yamamoto planned to bring his massive fleet to Midway to take the island and crush the American fleet if it appeared. Possession of the island would push the Americans much further from Japan, and this objective was much more significant after the Doolittle raid. The attack plan was complex, as were most Japanese attack plans, involving the splitting of forces. There was to be an advance force of 16 submarines, the Pearl Harbor Strike Force of four carriers under Admiral Nagumo, an occupation force of 12 transports, with two battleships, six heavy cruisers, and numerous destroyers. The main body under Yamamoto had three new battleships, four older battleships, and a light carrier. Another force would attack in the Aleutians, bringing Japanese strength to 162 ships. Admiral Nimitz, Commander-in-Chief, Pacific, could spare only 25 ships (3 carriers, 8 cruisers, and 14 destroyers) but he had *Yorktown*, *Hornet*, and *Enterprise*, three big carriers. At Pearl Harbor there was a Naval Intelligence Unit led by Commander Joe Rochefort. This genius had been breaking codes for years, and in 1940 he broke the highest level Japanese naval code. By monitoring Japanese radio traffic Joe had known about Japanese plans for the Coral Sea, and he knew that another major effort was coming up at a place that the Japanese always referred to as AF. A fake message was sent from Midway saying, "Fresh water machinery had broken down." The Japanese repeated the message saying that, "Fresh water machinery had broken down at AF." Then Joe knew that the Japanese planned to attack at Midway. Admiral Nimitz courageously sent the bulk of his limited forces to Midway under Admiral Spruance (Halsey would have been in command but he was in the hospital with a bad skin infection). Spruance set sail with two carriers. When *Yorktown* arrived from the Coral Sea, she needed 30 days for repairs but was given only three days before heading for Midway under Admiral Fletcher.

This was a case of David against Goliath, and the only chance the Americans had was a surprise attack. If the Japanese carriers could be eliminated, the U.S. could then attack the Japanese fleet with air power. There were quite a few planes on Midway itself, 16 Vindicator dive bombers, 21 Buffalo fighters, 7 F4F fighters, 18 SBD dive bombers, 7 B26s with torpedoes, 22 PBY patrol planes, 24 B17 bombers, and 6 TBF torpedo planes.

Plans were made for extensive search missions with the long range patrol planes, the two engine sea planes, the PBYs. These could fly out 700 miles and return. Carrier planes could only fly out 175 miles, attack, and return. Spruance posted his fleet northeast of Midway where he could strike as soon as the Japanese carriers were within range hopefully without being observed. If he were west of Midway there was a strong chance that the Japanese would spot him first. *Hornet* and *Enterprise* could each launch from 33 to 35 dive bombers, 15 torpedo planes, and 10 fighters for attack, with a few scout planes and fighters kept at home for combat air patrol (CAP).

At 9:25 A.M. on June 3, the invasion force of transports was spotted by a PBY.

Nine B-17s bombed this fleet from high altitude but made no hits. PBYs made a night torpedo attack and managed to hit one tanker. At 5:34 A.M. on June 4, a PBY spotted the Japanese carrier striking force and six minutes later another PBY warned of Jap planes heading for Midway; there were 107 planes from four carriers, *Hiryu, Kaga, Akagi*, and *Soryu*.

Most of the Midway-based planes took off before the Japanese could catch them on the ground. Major (USMC) Red Parks took 25 fighters to defend Midway, but most of these were the slow old Buffalos, no match for fast, maneuverable Zeros. The Japanese appeared over Midway at 6:34, and the Marines made one successful pass but then were decimated with only ten fighters returning to Midway. Major Parks did not survive. The Japanese raid was over by 7 A.M., but the flight leader reported that another strike would be necessary.

By 7 A.M. Navy Lt. Fieberling had reached the Japanese carriers with his six land based TBFs. Without waiting for any other planes Fieberling made his attack. Five of six torpedo planes were shot down including Fieberling, mostly by Zeros, and no hits were made. At the same time four B26s attacked, also with torpedoes. Two of the planes were shot down but the best these could do was two near misses of Akagi. At 7:50 Marine Major Henderson attacked with 16 SBD dive bombers using a shallow dive technique (because of inexperienced pilots). Ten planes survived but Major Henderson went down, and again, no hits. At 8:14, 15 B-17s attacked. No planes were lost but no bombs landed. At 8:17 Marine Major Norris arrived with II Vindicators, attacking a battleship unsuccessfully. Five separate uncoordinated attacks had been made on the carriers with not one hit. The Americans attacked with great courage but almost a total lack of skill.

Meanwhile, at 7:28, a Japanese patrol plane spotted the U.S. fleet but did not identify the type of ships. At 8:20, however, the patrol plane reported one U.S. carrier. Then the Japanese knew the U.S. had naval air and another Coral Sea type of attack could be expected. At 8:30 more U.S. ships were reported. Nagumo had planes in the air waiting to land, planes on carrier decks armed with bombs (that needed to be rearmed with torpedoes) and he had torpedo planes below decks. At 8:37 the circling planes started landing; this would take half an hour; by 11:00 the whole air fleet could be prepared to attack the American fleet.

The *Enterprise* and *Hornet* launchings began at 7:00 A.M. Over the *Enterprise*, Lt. Commander McClusky circled with Dive Bomber Squadron 6 and Scouting 6, waiting for the fighters and torpedo planes. These were delayed, and McCluskey was ordered to go without them at 7:45. Over the *Hornet*, Dive Bomber Squadron 8 and Fighter 8 climbed to 19000 feet, waiting for the torpedo planes. When Lt. Commander Waldron took off with Torpedo Squadron 8, Bomber 8 and Fighter 8 missed him and traveled in another direction. *Enterprise* Fighter Squadron 6 was supposed to protect Torpedo 6 but by mistake flew over *Hornet's* Torpedo 8.

Waldron guessed the Jap fleet was further north than calculated, and he guessed right. He found the carriers and took his squadron straight in at sea level at 9:20 A.M. Zeros and ships guns shot down all 15 planes of Torpedo 8. Gray's Fighter 6 lost contact and was of no help to Waldron. Then, at 9:38, Lindsey's Torpedo 6 attacked. Ten planes were lost including Lindsey's and by 10 A.M. the second torpedo attack was over with no hits. Thus far seven separate attacks had been hurled at the carriers with not one hit by bomb or torpedo.

Commander Ring with *Hornets* Bomber 8 and Fighter 8 went in the wrong direction and missed the Japanese completely, some returning to the *Hornet*, some to Midway. McClusky, with *Enterprise* Bomber 6 and Scouting 6, also missed the Japanese, but he kept looking.

Meanwhile on the *Yorktown*, Massey's Torpedo 3 (12 planes), Thach's Fighter 3 (6 planes), and Leslie's Bomber 3 (17 planes) circled and moved out together at about 9 A.M. Torpedo planes flew at 1,500 feet, fighters above, and bombers at 16,000 feet. These were veterans of the Coral Sea. At 10:15, as they attacked, Zeros engulfed Fighter 3 and were all over Torpedo 3. 10 of 12 torpedo planes were lost, including Massey's. By now, all the Zeros and ships guns were at sea level. At 10:20, the Japanese carriers, still unharmed after surviving an endless series of piecemeal attacks, were about to launch 93 planes at the American fleet within 10 minutes. Then came the dive bombers.

By 10:20 McClusky found the carriers. He took Gallaher's Scouting 6 in a diving attack at one carrier (*Kaga*). Lt. Best took Bombing 6 at a second carrier but most of his planes followed McClusky. Twenty-five dive bombers hurtled straight down on *Kaga* and so many bombs hit her that the explosions could not be counted. Dick Best attacked *Akagi* with only five planes but three bombs landed. Both carriers were crowded with planes armed with bombs and torpedoes while being refilled with gasoline and the bombs set off numerous explosions as two carriers quickly became hopeless shambles.

At 10:23 *Yorktown's* Bombing 3 arrived over the third carrier (*Soryu*) and attacked, hitting the ship many times. Some of the planes saw the sorry state of *Soryu* and shifted attacks to a destroyer and a battleship. The surviving planes returned, leaving three Japanese carriers in their death throes. The fourth carrier, *Hiryu*, was still untouched and did manage to launch its remaining planes, 18 dive bombers and 6 fighters. These were on their way by 10:58, arriving near the *Yorktown* at noon. *Yorktown's* Combat Air Patrol quickly shot down all but seven planes. These dived, three hitting *Yorktown*. Five dive bombers and one fighter survived.

At 1:31 P.M. *Hiryu* launched another attack, ten torpedo planes with six fighters. By 1:50 the *Yorktown* had put the fires out and was firing boilers, making headway. At 2:32 the Japanese torpedo planes came in. The Japanese had finally learned that there were 3 American carriers, and the torpedo planes were ordered to attack the two not damaged, but *Yorktown* did not look damaged and was hit again. Two torpedoes hit *Yorktown* and this tough ship listed but kept sailing. *Yorktown* was sent back to Pearl Harbor, but on the way, two days later, a Japanese submarine hit her, ending her glorious campaign.

Now it was the American turn to attack. Twenty-four planes from *Enterprise* took off at 3:30, joined by 16 from *Hornet* at 4 P.M. On the *Hiryu* the Japanese thought they had hit two carriers and had only one to deal with as they prepared their last nine planes for launching.

At 5:03 the U.S. planes from the *Enterprise* (including some from *Yorktown*) struck *Hiryu*. Three bombs hit and the carrier burned like a torch. Another wave of dive bombers from *Hornet* attacked the fleet at 5:30 along with ten B-17s from Midway.

At 7:13 P.M. the *Soryu* sank; at 7:25 the *Kaga* went down; at 8 P.M. the *Akagi* was abandoned, to be scuttled the next day; at 5:10 A.M. the *Hiryu* was torpedoed by a Japanese destroyer, sinking at 9:10. At 6:30 P.M. on June 3, Nagumo received a message saying that there were four U.S. carriers. Any thought of continued battle vaporized and Nagumo turned his carrier strike force (minus carriers) around. The rest of Yamamoto's fleet eventually did the same.

During the night two Japanese cruisers collided, one losing its bow. In the morning U.S. Marine planes attacked the cruisers. Captain Fleming flew his injured plane into the turret of the healthy cruiser which converted it into an invalid. All day and all night on the 5th Spruance pursued the retiring Japanese with *Hornet* and *Enterprise*. On the morning of June 6, 80 planes were launched. One heavy cruiser was sunk; the second, with two destroyers, all badly damaged, managed to escape. Spruance then wisely turned back before Yamamoto could hit back with another carrier or land based planes. The job was done. In one of the most decisive naval battles in all history, the great Japanese armada had been smashed and forced to run home without their priceless carriers and their best pilots. Their mighty navy still existed but without carrier domination no fleet would be safe. The Japanese naval move south had been stopped at the Coral Sea and their attack to the east had been thrown back at Midway. Up until this battle the Japanese may have thought that they were having a picnic. Now they must have suspected that they were up against the big boys and in trouble.

Every American who ever reads the story of Midway should stop to reflect with sorrow, yes, but with absolute admiration for the courageous torpedo pilots who gave their lives at Midway in unskilled, hopeless attacks with slow planes and slower torpedoes on an overwhelming veteran Japanese force. This sacrifice opened the way for the dive bombers that did the job. If any one man alone made the difference, it was Joe Rochefort. Without his disclosure of Japanese attack plans, a victory at Midway could not have been achieved. The Americans were not ready or able to fight the Japanese, yet somehow they did. The American crisis was however not over yet. 1942 would be a very hard year.

New Guinea, 1942

In June 1942, MacArthur gathered two battalions at Port Moresby, one Australian, one Papuan. This group, called Maroubra Force, moved halfway across the Owen Stanley Mountains over the Kokoda Trail to Kokoda by July 15. On the twenty-first, 2,000 Japanese landed at Gona on the north coast. After two weeks of fighting the Maroubra Force pulled back.

Port Moresby, the key Allied base on the south coast of New Guinea, already had some Allied aircraft. Numbers of U.S. P-40 fighters had been shipped to Australia and these were manned by U.S. and Aussie pilots. Using techniques developed by the Flying Tigers in Burma, the Allies held their own against the superior Japanese Zeros.

On August 8 the Australian 7th Division arrived in New Guinea from the Middle East. Two brigades went to Port Moresby and one brigade went to Milne Bay on the eastern tip of the island. There a defensive perimeter was established at Milne Bay while American engineers built an airstrip. As soon as the strip was ready an Australian squadron of P 40s landed to provide support.

On August 16 one Aussie brigade moved out from Port Moresby to support the Maroubra Force, but on August 18 the Japanese landed 11,500 men at Buna. These troops moved up the Kokoda Trail pushing the Australians back to the last mountain barrier above Port Moresby by September 15.

On August 26, the Japanese landed troops at Milne Bay, but their attacks were repulsed. Inferior in numbers the Japanese at Milne Bay began to fall back. Australian P-40s destroyed the Jap landing barges, ruining their amphibious flanking capabilities, and they were withdrawn on September 6.

On September 15 a regiment of the U.S. 32nd Division landed at Port Moresby, and these troops moved out on the Kapa Kapa Trail east of the Kokoda on October 6. That same day another regiment of the 32nd Division landed at Pongani, only 30 miles south of Buna, by sea and air. In late October another 7th

Division regiment moved up the Kokoda Trail to reinforce the first regiment. MacArthur's move, putting a green American regiment on the north coast near the Japanese base was remarkably risky, but you can imagine the effect it had on the Japanese.

By November 18, the U.S. Australian forces reached the Japanese defenses in the Buna-Gona area. MacArthur eventually used five divisions, 55,000 men, including the Australian 6th and 7th and the U.S. 32nd and 41st. By December 10, the Australians took Gona; Buna was evacuated on December 14, but resistance in the area did not cease until January 22. In this campaign the Allies lost 8,500 men, the Japanese 12,000. Terrain, climate, and disease on New Guinea were as bad as any place on earth and with tenacious Japanese resistance progress had been painstaking, but by 1943 the Allies occupied the eastern section of New Guinea, 250 miles long from Milne Bay west to Gona. The Australians, veteran troops, did most of the heavy fighting under General Blaney. The Americans were commanded by General Eichelberger.

With a firm grip on New Guinea, many competing strategies were proposed, but MacArthur insisted on taking New Guinea, than moving north to the Philippines and to Japan. The U.S. Navy wanted to move west across the Pacific from island to island. Either strategy would have simplified the Japanese defense, but the strategy finally accepted was to do both, let MacArthur follow his plan and let the Navy follow their plan. This would require the Japanese to defend every island in the Pacific with no way of knowing where the next strike would be.

MacArthur's moves in the early stages of the New Guinea campaign were incredible. He invaded New Guinea with two battalions, 2,000 men, on a huge land mass with an unknown number of Japanese already on the island. Was this insane, or was it genius, knowing the difficulties the enemy faced in doing something about his moves? When a man has the confidence and will to do what other men would not dare to do, does it repeatedly, always with success, we call it genius. Actually such a man may be human, just superior to all other humans. MacArthur then came into possession of one division, the Australian 7th, and he put the whole division on New Guinea, one regiment on Milne bay, one on the Kokoda Trail, with one in reserve. He could have reinforced at Milne Bay or on the Kokoda Trail, but not both. More courage. Perhaps MacArthur knew there were more troops coming, perhaps he didn't, but to defend Australia, he had no choice but to fight on New Guinea with whatever forces he could obtain. This situation was all too common to war in the Pacific in 1942. The Japanese defended Buna and Gona with grim determination.

From this area land-based aircraft on the north coast of New Guinea threatened the flank of Japanese positions in the Solomons, and with the Allies on the north coast, a land attack on the Japanese base at Lau, less than 200 miles away, was inevitable. If the Japanese were not successful in New Guinea in 1942, the reason may have been the drain on their air, land, and naval forces during the Guadalcanal campaign.

Guadalcanal, 1942

Guadalcanal was on the southern end of the Solomon Island chain, and Japanese aircraft there would have dominated the Coral Sea, leaving New Caledonia and the New Hebrides vulnerable. The loss of these would have isolated Australia from shipping from the U.S. When 2,000 Japanese landed on Guadalcanal on July 5, 1942, to build an airstrip, the U.S. was forced to move even though adequate forces were not yet available.

Starting on August 7, elements of the First Marine Division were landed on Guadalcanal and other small islands around the sea approaches, 19,000 men in 31 transports surrounded by 60 warships. The division and attached elements had four objectives.

The First and Fifth Marines (regiments) would land near the center of the 90 mile long northern coast of Guadalcanal.

The First Marine Raider Battalion and a battalion of the Second Marines (from the Second Division) would land on Tulagi, 20 miles to the north.

Another battalion of the Second Marines would land on Florida. The First Marine Parachute Battalion would land on Guvutu-Tanambogo.

The First Division normally included the Seventh Marines but this regiment had assignments elsewhere. Artillery elements from the Eleventh Marines (the First Division artillery regiment) supported the division.

The Fifth Marines had served in the Marine Brigade in France. This regiment has a tradition unlike any other. Most of the Marines were recent additions, but there were veterans, officers and non commissioned officers with combat experience in France, China, Central America, and elsewhere. Men who join the Marines, in most cases, want to fight and want to fight with the best. This spirit combined with the tradition brings out the best in a man. The Marines in World War I were described by one author as the most aggressive troops in France. Certainly the Germans thought so. The performance of Marines in World War I might have been exceptional with an unusually effective group, but throughout this century the Marines have been magnificent in every war. This is no doubt the reason why they are the "first to fight" (from "The Marine Hymn"), the first to be sent to troubled lands.

Warfare as conducted by the Marines includes the coordinated use of rifles, machine guns, grenades, flame throwers, tanks, artillery, close air support, and naval gunfire, all by men trained in their use. They do not rely on massed human bodies but on maximum fire and steel. They are professionals, not supermen, and they are led by combat proven officers and non-commissioned officers.

In the war against Japan, as of August 7, no one had beaten Japanese infantry. On Guadalcanal the Japanese would be confronted by the United States Marine Corps and the long series of Japanese Army conquests would come to a sudden and frightful end.

On August 7 Edson's Raiders and the Second Marine battalion landed on Tulagi where the defense was tenacious. There was even a *banzai* attack by the fanatical defenders, anxious to die for the Emperor, but by the evening of August 8 Tulagi was secure. Florida Island was not defended and was occupied without a shot fired. Resistance was fierce on Guvutu-Tanambogo where there were no beaches and much trouble landing plus numerous caves filled with defenders, but these islands were taken by August 9.

On Guadalcanal there was no resistance, and the First Division moved inland to secure a perimeter around the airfield three miles wide and five miles long. A perimeter this long necessarily results in a thin line of defense, but some units are always kept in reserve to check any breakthroughs. Total casualties ran up to 800 for the Japanese, mostly dead, to 144 U.S. dead and 194 wounded.

The Japanese reacted immediately to the landings and put forth a major effort on land, sea, and in the air, in a brutal struggle. Their experienced navy came down the "slot," the sea passage between the two rows of islands in the Solomon chain, and an inexperienced U.S. Navy, outnumbered in every category, threw their ships against the foe in gallant but costly battles. The price of victory at Guadalcanal was much higher than is generally known.

On August 8, Jap planes sank a U.S. transport but took heavy plane losses from U.S. carrier planes. On August 9, a Japanese naval force came into Ironbottom Sound between Savo Island and Guadalcanal at night and sank 4 U.S. cruisers and one destroyer. The U.S. Navy was forced to leave the area, leaving the Marines stranded on the islands. Fortunately the Japanese fleet withdrew after the battle. Ships with supplies for the Marines would come in occasionally but could not stay.

By August 15, Henderson Field was ready, and on August 20, U.S. aircraft came in, 19 Wildcat fighters and 12 Douglas Dauntless dive bombers. This added a new dimension to the U.S. defense. If the Japanese had landed in force before the twentieth, their chances for success would have been greatest. Now the U.S. controlled the area by day and the Japanese only by night with sea power.

On the night of August 18, 1,000 Japanese troops were landed east of Henderson Field to attack the 3,000 Marines they expected to find. On August 21, the Ichiki detachment threw themselves at the First Marines and ran into a fire storm that left 815 Ichikis dead. The Marines lost 34 men, and the Allied world began to breathe a little easier.

On August 24, the Japanese approached Guadalcanal with 2 carriers, one light carrier, 2 battleships, and 3 heavy cruisers. A U.S. fleet with three carriers, *Wasp, Saratoga*, and *Enterprise* came up to meet them. In the Battle of the Eastern Solomons, Japanese carrier aircraft put 3 bombs into *Enterprise* but U.S. planes sank the Japanese light carrier. The U.S. fleet withdrew and that night the Japs stayed to shell Henderson Field and Marine defenses. (This became a nightly ritual.)

On August 25, a fleet with transports tried to land 5000 Japanese troops. Marine planes damaged a Japanese cruiser and transport while B-17s sank a Japanese destroyer. The Japanese fleet turned back, dumping the troops in the

Shortlands.

The U.S. carrier *Saratoga* was torpedoed by a Japanese sub on August 31, but survived. On September 5 two U.S. destroyer transports were sunk.

On August 30, Marine Major Smith shot down four Zeros bringing the Marine total to 200 planes, but by September 11 the Marines were down to only 11 planes. That day, however, 24 Navy fighters arrived.

The Japanese eventually did manage to land the 5,000 troops under General Kawaguchi, thinking these would be sufficient to drive the Marines off the island. On September 8, Edson and his Raiders landed at dawn near Tasimboko, took the village, and destroyed Japanese supplies (very embarrassing to General Kawaguchi). On the tenth General Vandegrift sensed the Japanese would attack and ordered Edson's battalion to occupy a long ridge south of Henderson Field. Here, on the night of September 12, General Kawaguchi did attack, broke through in numerous places, forcing the Raiders to fight in small groups, outnumbered 4,000 to 400. The next night the Japanese attacked again. More groups were isolated, but the Marines fought back to retake lost positions.

Edson was everywhere. Artillery from the 11th Marines planted a sheet of fire 200 yards in front of Edson. By midnight the Kawaguchis were finished. The Japanese also attacked along the Tenaru and Matanikau Rivers but were repulsed in both places. Edson's ridge would soon be called Bloody Ridge and the battle The Battle of Bloody Ridge. It was strange that the Japanese could attack in one place with 4,000 men and be thrown back by "thousands" of Marines who were also strong in two other places. Eventually it must have occurred to the Japanese that Marine strength on Guadalcanal was a bit higher than original estimates.

On September 15, the carrier *Wasp* and a destroyer were torpedoed by submarines. The *Wasp* went down and the destroyer sank later.

On September 18, the Seventh Marines arrived (4,000 men) to complete the structure of the division. At about this time General Hyakutate began to land his Sendai Division, 20,000 men, which would surely be enough to crush the Marines.

On September 23, the Marines made an offensive sweep over part of the island, but ran into trouble and took some casualties. On October 7, Vandergrift decided to attack again before the Japanese could strike him. At the same time Lt. General Maruyama decided to attack with the Fourth Regiment of the Sendai Division. These men, new on the island, had heard horror stories from the survivors of earlier landings, but would soon be able to add their own.

Edson took five battalions from the Fifth Marines (which he now commanded) west to the Matanikau with Whaling's Scouts. The Japanese were pummeled by Marine Air on October 6. Three companies ran into a battalion of Marines supported by the Raiders (now under Lew Walt) on October 7, and were wiped out. Chesty Puller (Marines should not drink milk or eat ice cream) took his First Battalion, Seventh Marines, out on a reconnaissance on October 9, and spotted some of Maruyama's troops in a ravine. The Marines dropped mortar shells on them, called in air strikes and artillery when they tried to climb the hill to their rear or stayed where they were, then shot them down when they tried to attack. Seven hundred Sendai died that day. The Marines attacked, killing 200 more, and the Fourth Sendai Regiment ceased to be an effective force. That day Captain Joe Foss and 20 Marine Wildcat fighters came in.

On the night of October 11, the Japanese brought more troops in 2 seaplane tenders and 6 destroyers, with 3 heavy cruisers and 2 destroyers. Admiral Scott ambushed them with 2 heavy and 2 light cruisers and 5 destroyers. Scott crossed their Tee (his ships in line, all firing as each enemy ship came up in column). Scott sank one cruiser, one destroyer, and damaged several others, the first U.S. success in fleet to fleet combat. The Japanese did manage to land troops, however, which had been their primary objective. Later in the pre-dawn hours of October 12, Marine planes sank two Japanese destroyers.

On October 13, one Army regiment from the Americal Division arrived to reinforce the Marines.

On October 13, the Japanese opened up on Henderson Field with long range artillery (Pistol Pete). That night Japanese battleships pounded the field and Marine defenses. Of 38 bombers, only four survived in flying condition. These took off however and sank a transport. On the fourteenth, more bombers were repaired and six more flew in. That night cruisers shelled the field, leaving only three bombers. The Japanese now expected the American aircraft to be non operational, and in broad daylight on the fifteenth six transports could be seen unloading the Sendai Division supplies. Somehow the mechanics at Henderson Field managed to put 20 Wildcats, Dauntlesses, Avengers, P 39s, and P 40s into the air. B-17s came from Espiritu Santo and a PBY (The Blue Goose) with torpedoes also attacked. Three transports were sunk with much of Maruyama's artillery shells, food, and medical supplies. There were 20,000 Japanese ashore now. That night the airfield was shelled again but the next day 26 more planes came in along with Lt. Col. Joe Bauer who shot down four Jap planes on an almost empty gas tank just before landing. This was rugged duty, but these were rugged people.

On October 15, Admiral William (Bull) Halsey took over command of the South Pacific Theatre. There was serious concern that the Navy could not provide the necessary support to the forces on Guadalcanal, but Halsey promised Vandergrift to give everything he (Halsey) had, and this he did. Halsey was the tonic needed at this hour, and MacArthur later stated that Halsey was one of America's greatest naval commanders (and MacArthur was not generous with his complements).

On October 17 General Hyakutate landed on Guadalcanal to review Maruyama's plan of attack. Colonel Oka would take a force down the west bank of the Matanikau and cross to outflank the Marines on the east bank at night. The 4th Regiment with 11 tanks would strike over the sandbar at the mouth of the river the same night. Maruyama would also cut a 35 mile road through the jungle to bring the bulk of his forces, a complete division in on the Marines weak southern line where a captured map showed numerous gaps (The map was a fake, actually a copy of a Japanese map showing Japanese defensive positions before the August American landing.)

The Japanese Navy pressured Hyakutake to attack before he was ready. As a result the Fourth Regiment and its tanks attacked after sundown on October 23 and were crushed in two hours.

On the night of October 23, Maruyama's Sendai Division came upon the Marine lines, not a gap but a strong point defended by Chesty Puller's battalion (bad luck). The Marines here were badly outnumbered but this night belonged to men like John Basilone (Manila John), who rushed back and forth from machine gun to machine gun, firing guns left unattended by dead marines, returning jammed guns to working order. In one and one-half hours the Japanese had been thrown back. A battalion of the Americal Division came up to reinforce Puller, and soon afterward the Sendai attacked again, but by dawn this final attack was over.

That day three Japanese destroyers came in to shell the island but were hit with Marine five inch guns and forced to withdraw. Then Jap planes came in. Joe Foss shot down four to bring his score to 15 in 16 days of action. He had to land his own crippled plane and switch planes to go up again for the last two kills.

That night the Sendai attacked once more only to be pulverized by mortars and artillery. Colonel Oka's men finally came down the east bank of the Matanikau through a "gap" only to run into a Marine battalion. After bitter fighting Oka's force was thrown back. The Sendai Division was finished.

From the nineteenth to the twenty-sixth of October, Japanese troops attacked major segments of the American perimeter but were repulsed. The army troops did well in this affair. Five thousand Japanese died.

On October 26, a Japanese fleet sailed into the Santa Cruz Islands to support the land attack on Guadalcanal with 4 carriers, 5 battleships, 14 cruisers, and 44 destroyers.

Admiral Halsey ordered Admiral Kincaid with one battleship, two carriers (*Hornet* and *Enterprise*), two cruisers, and 8 destroyers to "Attack—Repeat—Attack." In the carrier strikes *Hornet* was devastated and sunk. *Enterprise* took three bomb hits but stayed afloat. One Japanese light carrier sank and one, *Shokaku*, took three hits which laid her up for nine months. The Japanese lost 100 planes and many irreplaceable pilots. (The battleship *South Dakota* was very effective against aircraft.) The U.S. had only two carriers left, *Saratoga* and *Enterprise*, both damaged, but the Japanese had again left the area.

Early in November the Japanese landed troops from 65 destroyers and 2 cruisers until they, for the first time, outnumbered U.S. land forces.

On November 2, the Fifth Marines caught 200 Japanese west of the Matanikau and killed them. That same day a regiment of the Japanese Nagoya Division was put ashore east of the Tenaru. Vandergrift sent three battalions and the Americal Regiment at them from the east, west, and south. On November 10, the Americans attacked, killing 350. Most escaped, however, but had to take a huge detour through the jungle to rejoin their forces west of Henderson Field. Carlson's Second Raider Battalion followed, ambushing their rear guard and any troops that came to help on twelve separate occasions. During this bloody retreat,

500 more Japanese were killed.

The Naval Battle of Guadalcanal, November 12–14

On November 11, Admirals Scott and Turner brought in U.S. reinforcements, but on the 12th a Japanese air attack was made which was fought off with no ships sunk and many Japanese planes downed.

That night, however, the "Tokyo Express" was coming in again with 2 battleships, 1 cruiser, and 14 destroyers. Admirals Scott and Callaghan, with only 5 cruisers and 8 destroyers, had to prevent the Japanese from destroying Henderson Field, and on the night of November 12 they valiantly attacked. Their tactics were questionable perhaps, with the loss of both brave admirals, two cruisers, and four destroyers, including the cruiser *Juneau* with the five Sullivan brothers, but they sank two Japanese destroyers and damaged many other ships, including the battleship *Hiei* which was hard hit. Heavy was the U.S. loss in this desperate affair, but great was the reward as the Japanese turned back without blasting Henderson Field. Scott and Callaghan had thrown some light metal and many khaki shirts between the enemy and the Marines, and they achieved their objective in an action of incredible courage.

At this time, after three months of ghastly naval actions, the combatants losses were as follows:

	Carriers	Battleships	Cruisers	Destroyers	Transports
U.S.	2	0	6	8	2
Japan	1	0	1	4	3

The numbers tell the story. The U.S. Navy hung on by its fingernails, but then the tide turned. Halsey had ordered Kincaid's carrier task force, which now included Admiral "Chink" Lee with battleships *South Dakota* and *Washington*, to proceed to Guadalcanal as rapidly as possible.

On the thirteenth, planes from Henderson and *Enterprise* sank the battleship *Hiei*. On November 14, they sank heavy cruiser *Kinugasa* and ten transports, many loaded with troops. On the night of November 13, Japanese ships shelled Henderson Field, but were chased by six PT boats which hit one cruiser with a torpedo.

On the night of November 14, Admiral Kondo came back with a battleship, two heavy cruisers, two light cruisers, and numerous destroyers. Lee raced to meet him with two battleships and four destroyers. Lee sank the Japanese battleship and chased Kondo. Two U.S. destroyers were lost, but the Japanese main thrust on land and sea was over.

Final Victory on Guadalcanal

On November 30 the Navy intercepted Japanese destroyers headed for Guadalcanal, and in the Battle of Tassafaronga 3 U.S. cruisers were hit by the fine Japanese long lance torpedoes, one cruiser sinking. Only one enemy destroyer was sunk, as the Japanese again retired without unloading. On December 9 and 12 U.S. PT boats sank a Japanese submarine and destroyer, but by then the Japanese were beaten. On December 13, the First Marine Division was relieved by the Americal Division and the Second Marine Division, which was to get some experience. The Marines were exhausted, but they had won a huge victory and had smashed the myth of Japanese invincibility.

On January 10, the U.S. lost a PT boat; on January 11, the Japanese lost a destroyer, and on January 30, the U.S. lost a cruiser. In early February the Japanese removed their surviving troops, and by February 9, U.S. troops secured the island. U.S. losses on Guadalcanal were 1,600 killed and 4,000 wounded. The Japanese lost 24,000 killed or dead of disease. The total naval score:

	Carriers	Battleships	Cruisers	Destroyers	Transports	Other
Japan	1	2	2	9	13	1
U.S.	2	0	8	9	3	1

In addition to the ships sunk, there were many damaged. In the air the Japanese had lost 600 planes. The losses at Guadalcanal were terrible, but this was not just a fight for an island. This was six months of brutal war at the outermost reaches of the Japanese Empire.

It is unbelievable that the U.S. was able to win with so few carriers, no battleships (until late), out manned, and outgunned. The entire effort was however the most heroic episode in U.S. Navy history. Admirals Nimitz and Halsey had great courage to suffer the losses they did and still persevere until final victory was achieved.

Analysis

At first the Japanese had planned to concentrate their efforts in New Guinea, but as the campaign for Guadalcanal became more crucial, the main effort was diverted. The Japanese soldier fought bravely, actually fanatically, willing to die if necessary, but General Hyakutake's tactics in Guadalcanal were inadequate. He badly underestimated American strength and committed his forces piecemeal in widely separated portions of the island where they could not be controlled or coordinated. To overcome one Marine division he needed control of the air and sea and 75,000 men. He could not at any time acquire that many troops as the Japanese Army was spread out all over China, Southeast Asia, and the Pacific Islands. They might have controlled the air and sea except for the deadly effectiveness of the Cactus Air Force from Henderson Field, Army, Navy, and Marine. These skilled and fearless pilots took on overwhelming numbers of Japanese planes and shot them down with an extremely high kill ratio, using slower, less maneuverable aircraft. In bombing ships they showed uncanny skill. The battles for Guadalcanal were won with limited resources and many a brave pilot, seaman, and marine. Vandergrift and Halsey were superb; in this department the Japanese were overmatched.

If the U.S. public had known the extent of our naval losses at Guadalcanal, there is a question regarding the extent of public support for the war effort. The naval power imbalance was so severe that one can't help but feel that it was best the public didn't know. Our forces were sent in as soon as they became available, and in many cases they arrived almost miraculously just at the moment they were needed. The arrival of new battleships in November was the first use of the big ships in the area after the loss of so many at Pearl Harbor.

North Africa, 1942

In January 1942, Rommel had been pushed back to El Agheila. He had three German and seven Italian divisions but few tanks. When new tanks arrived, bringing his total to 228, he decided to attack. Facing him was one armored division with 150 tanks and one infantry division. Rommel moved fast, hitting the British First Armored Division and destroying half their tanks on January 22. By February 4, both forces were back at Tobruk where the British had prepared defenses. Supplies for Rommel were held back as the Germans used all available air power in an attempt to neutralize the island of Malta which dominated the Mediterranean between Sicily and Libya. By May, however, Rommel had 637 tanks and 497 planes to the British 563 tanks and 190 planes. The British also had 276 infantry tanks but these were dispersed. Rommel could not be stopped as he punched through the British defenses and captured Tobruk with its 33,000 defenders (including one South African division) on June 21. By June 30, Rommel was at El Alamein, just 60 miles from Alexandria. In July Rommel's weakened attacks were repulsed but British counterattacks failed. El Alamein was the best place to defend Egypt as the Qattara Depression was not passable with tanks and it came closest to the sea (30 miles) at El Alamein.

Churchill, in Washington when Tobruk fell, received Roosevelt's sympathy and an offer of aid. Churchill asked for tanks, and 300 new Shermans slated for U.S. armored divisions were put on the fastest ships available with 100 self-propelled guns. The engines were on a ship which was sunk by a submarine, but a new set of engines was placed on another ship scheduled to catch the tank convoy.

On August 13, General Sir Bernard Law Montgomery took over command of the Eighth Army. From this day on, the Eighth Army would never again retreat or be defeated. Montgomery became the top British field general in Europe.

On August 30, Rommel attacked at El Alamein but by September 2 he had failed to gain ground. Rather than rush to counterattack, Montgomery paused to train, reorganize, and resupply. Rommel pleaded for more supplies but received few as Hitler considered North Africa to be of secondary importance. By September Montgomery had ten divisions, three of them armored, from all over the British Empire. On October 23, Montgomery attacked but until November 1 his progress was limited. A renewed offensive was made on November 2, this time with success. Rommel's tanks were running out of gas and he began another long retreat that put him back at El Agheila by November 24. On January 23, 1943, Montgomery occupied Tripoli and Rommel fell back into Tunisia.

Russia, 1942

No discussion of World War II can be made without discussing the German extermination of the European Jewish population. Six million Jews were put to death and an uncounted number of others considered unfriendly to Germany were disposed of as well. In this century, when civilization is so far advanced, the sober realization of German atrocities warns us that people will never change, that a nation which permits its most perverse and brutal segments to rule can expect similar results. During and after World War I, Turkey exterminated over 1,000,000 Armenians and 1,000,000 Greeks. In Russia millions were allowed to starve after the Bolshevik takeover. In Cambodia after the American withdrawal from Vietnam and the takeover by communists in Indochina in 1975, two to three million people suspected of being unsympathetic to the new rulers were killed by the Khmer Rouge (communists). When the Germans invaded Russia they were welcomed as liberators, but after a brief occupation their behavior was so brutal that the Russians, as in many other European countries, formed underground resistance groups.

After the successful Russian counterattacks of the 1941–1942 winter Germany planned another offensive, but not across the entire front. With a horde of Russians massed before Moscow the Germans planned to remain on defense in this sector. Attacks in the north would be made to take Leningrad and establish contact with the Finns. In the south a major push would be made to take the Ukraine, the Crimea, and the Caucasus where Russian farming, manufacturing, and oil production were the prizes. Hitler never seemed to realize that the farther he pushed, the longer and more vulnerable his supply lines became. Also his front lines became longer and the forces to hold them became thinner. Perhaps he believed that one more campaign similar to 1941 would finish the Russian army and force a surrender. The Russian government however was determined to resist so long as soldiers could be enlisted, no matter how terrible their losses (as were the North Vietnamese during the war in Vietnam). Assumptions that the enemy might surrender are often naïve.

On May 12, the Russians attacked south of Kharkov before the German offensive could be launched. The Russian attack was not well coordinated, however, and German attacks from north and south pinched off the Russian salient trapping the whole Russian army of 214,000 men. In the Crimea, the Germans took Kerch and by July 3, Sevastapol, with 90,000 more prisoners.

East of Kharkov the Germans broke through by the end of June and the whole front from Kursk to the Sea of Azov became fluid. By July 5, von Bock's Army Group B reached the Don River, taking Voronezh on the 7th. That same day, further south, List's Army Group A crossed the Donets. In order to trap Russian armies between the Donets and the Don, both army groups attacked to the southeast. Most of Army Group B's panzers were ordered to assist List while Paulus and his Sixth Army were ordered to cross the Don and take Stalingrad on the Volga. On July 23 Hitler replaced the slow moving von Bock with von Weichs and ordered Hoth's Fourth Panzer Army to rejoin Army Group B. Now von Weichs was attacking east and List was attacking south, each unable to support the other.

By this time the Russians had learned to retreat and save forces that were bypassed. Normally, in defensive positions, every unit is asked to hold in order to limit the width of a breakthrough. In Russia, where continuous fortified lines of defense frequently did not exist, keeping units in place in 1941 had been disastrous. In 1942, if the Germans expected to destroy and capture Russian forces as they had in 1941, they were disappointed. Worse, in August, the Germans suffered 250,000 casualties.

On July 23, List took Rostov and broke through into the Caucasus region. By August 23 the Germans were on Mt Elbrus and at Ordhonikdze, deep into the Caucasus, but here they stalled. Paulus attempted to cross the Don on July 25, but was repulsed. He waited for Hoth but managed to cross the Don on August 10 without him. On August 23 Paulus reached the Volga north of Stalingrad, and on September 3 he was joined by Hoth.

By this time the Russians had decided to defend Stalingrad. Zhukov was put in command and his forces were placed in the heart of the city in a strip four miles wide and ten miles long. German attacks on the city became extremely slow and costly in bitter fighting from one shattered building to another. By September 20, Paulus called for reinforcements and all during October he made little progress.

In September, as the German offensive slowed to a halt, the Russians saw opportunities to strike at the German flanks. When they had time, the Russians were able to gather forces and this they did, north and south of Stalingrad where the defenses were manned by second line troops, Rumanians.

On November 11, Paulus attacked again, and the Russians inside Stalingrad were struggling to hang on. Then on November 19, the Russians attacked the Rumanians north and south of Stalingrad, breaking through. By November 23, the bridge over the Don at Kalach was captured, north and south attacks were linked and the Germans inside Stalingrad surrounded. The Russian flood spread over a huge zone between the Chir, Don, and Volga Rivers at distances from 40 to 150 miles into the German rear. 330,000 Germans were trapped, all of Sixth Army, and part of the Fourth Panzer Army.

Hitler asked Goering if German air could supply Paulus the 750 tons of supplies a day that were required to support the forces at Stalingrad. Goering said yes, and Hitler ordered Paulus to hold. On November 27, Hitler ordered von Mannstein to relieve Paulus and Hoth was chosen to lead the task force. Because of Russian attacks elsewhere, Hoth could not attack until December 12, but the attack, from the southwest along the railroad to Stalingrad, did make progress, reducing the distance to Sixth Army from 75 to 30 miles; however, by December 19 Hoth was stopped along the Myshkova River. On the twenty-third von Mannstein asked Paulus to break out, but Paulus dutifully refused. On the twenty-fourth the Russians threatened Hoth's rear, and the task force was forced to withdraw. The Germans pulled back 125 miles from Stalingrad and Sixth Army was doomed. Goering never supplied more than 250 tons of supplies per day and by the end of January the Germans in Stalingrad were reduced to two small pockets. The last pocket surrendered on February 2. Only 91,000 lived to surrender, and only 5,000 ever saw their homes again. Stalingrad was a crushing blow to Germany, the turning point in the war against Hitler. Up until Stalingrad, the survival of Russia had been a grave concern. With Russia out of the war, it might never have been possible to invade continental Europe and the only hope for Allied victory would have rested on development of the atomic bomb before the Germans. The world was perilously close to a disaster in 1941 and 1942, which would have dealt the cause of human freedom a fatal blow.

The North Atlantic, 1942

When the U.S. entered the war, all commercial shipping was almost totally unprotected, and German submarines had unlimited targets. Losses were as follows:

Month	Number of Ships Sunk
February, 1942	71
March	86
April	69
May	111
June	121

The British had broken the German U-Boat code and generally knew where to expect the attacks, but the Allies were unable to provide enough air cover or escort vessels to protect the convoys. An underwater sound system (Sonar) for detection of submarines had been available since 1918, but without escort vessels not much could be done. Shipping losses were reduced somewhat in the second half of 1942, still amounting to as much as 315,000 tons as late as February of 1943, however. The loss of ships was terrible as every ship that went down took seamen with it. Such brutal events occur to nations pulled into a war for which they are not prepared. Once escort vessels became available the Navy would demonstrate just how effective they could be.

The war against German submarines was not the only crisis in the North Atlantic. The Allies, much concerned about Russia's ability to survive the German invasion, determined to send supplies to Russia; one of the main routes was the Arctic route to Murmansk. This route, unfortunately, was subject to attack by German aircraft, submarines, and surface vessels from Norway. Three convoys in the spring of 1942 lost two cruisers and 15 merchant vessels. In May one convoy lost six ships but look at the statistics:

Convoy Number	Month	Ships Lost
PQ 13	March	
PQ 14	April	17
PQ15	May	
PQ16	May	6
PQ 17	June/July	23
PQ 18	September	15

Convoy PQ 17, consisting of 34 merchant vessels plus 21 escorts, was attacked by subs, planes and surface vessels. The battle fleet escorts required to fight off German battle cruisers did not arrive in time to help and the convoy was ordered to scatter. Only ten ships got through; 23 vessels were sunk, 10 by sub, 13 by aircraft. In December, two convoys, heavily escorted, were sent on parallel routes, both getting through successfully. One convoy was attacked by surface vessels but these were fought off by British destroyers and cruisers. In 1942, the Allies paid dearly for every task they attempted to perform.

Allied Invasion of North Africa, November 1942

Russia, near collapse in 1942, needed all the help the Allies could give. It was essential for the U.S. and England to fight on land somewhere to tie down as many German divisions as possible to lighten the force of their attacks on Russia. The Allies considered the various options available to them in '42. Churchill recommended an invasion of "the soft under belly of Europe." The U.S. wanted to fight in France where the objective would be the heart of Germany, but the Allies were not strong enough to fight in France. An invasion along the Mediterranean coast had little appeal. It would be feasible to get ashore, but the road to Germany over the vast mountains in the south of Europe was not very appealing. The only place to fight with any prospect for gain was

North Africa. There, the Axis had Rommel's army, 10 divisions. Destroying this army would have been an accomplishment. Freeing the Mediterranean from Axis air bases in Africa was another. Additionally, the threat to the Suez Canal would be eliminated, and bases for future invasions of Europe could be established. This would force Hitler to keep more troops in the Mediterranean. The most likely target in Africa was Tunisia, to trap Rommel, but Tunisia was French (Vichy France) and resistance could be expected. Tunis was too far east, in range of Axis air bases. Algiers was the obvious place, but in case of stiff French resistance, other ports were required; there was also concern about getting supplies through the narrow Straight of Gibraltar. It was therefore decided to land at three Atlantic ports in Morocco (U.S. General Patton) and two places in Algeria, Oran (U.S. General Fredendall), and Algiers (U.S. General Ryder). Most troops would be American (53,000 in Morocco, 50,000 at Oran, and 10,000 at Algiers) except for a British force of 15,000 at Algiers. U.S. General Dwight D. Eisenhower was in overall command.

The landings took place on November 8 and the French did resist. Marshal Petain eventually secretly ordered Admiral Darlan in Algiers to cease fighting, and this occurred on November 10. Meanwhile Vichy Prime Minister Laval gave the Germans permission to send troops to Tunisia where flights began to land on November 9. Then it became a race to see who could build up forces in Tunisia the fastest.

British General Anderson was put in charge of troops ashore, now called First Army. He had commanded only a regiment in France, a division at Dunkirk, but it was believed at this time that experienced British officers should be used rather than untried Americans. Anderson with First Army and Montgomery with Eighth Army reported to Alexander. Eisenhower was overall theatre commander. Ike was chosen for his known qualities as a staff officer with tact and energy. Other officers selected by Marshall (such as Patton) had combat experience and would do the fighting. Anderson sent the U.S. First Armored Division from Algiers into Tunisia.

By late November the Germans had assembled the 10th Panzer Division under Nehring in Tunisia and were building up not just to defend but to attack and destroy the Allies in Africa. Hitler could not allow Rommel's army to be trapped, and the only way he could justify sending in more forces was to expect them to win. Thus the folly of fighting in Africa in the first place was compounded by raising the stakes. As a result Hitler sent major forces to Tunisia where a disaster similar to Stalingrad would eventually take place. In November and December, however, the First Armored Division was stopped inside Tunisia just 50 miles from Tunis.

By December 3, a small force of French and U.S. troops occupied Faid Pass only 50 miles from the coast in central Tunisia. In early 1943, First Army in Tunisia was organized with V British Corps in the north, XIX French Corps in the center, and II U.S. Corps in the south. The Germans under von Arnim then had the Fifth Panzer Army of 100,000 men, mostly good German divisions. On

January 18, von Arnim seized the major passes threatening Rommel's rear.

Montgomery was bogged down in Tunisia in early February waiting for supplies, then held up by mud. The G-2 (intelligence staff officer) of Fredendall's II Corps, Colonel Monk Dickson (remember this name, as we shall hear more about him in the Battle of the Bulge) predicted Rommel would attack II Corps, probably at Gafsa. Anderson's G-2 predicted Rommel would attack farther north at Fondouk and so Anderson ordered Fredendell to disperse his armor and his forces at the most likely points of attack, not including Gafsa.

On February 14, von Arnim attacked at Sidi Bou Zid, and the next day Rommel struck at Gafsa. That day Montgomery reached Medenine short of the Mareth Line, where Rommel had built a strong defense. Montgomery took weeks to plan an attack, freeing the Germans to concentrate on First Army. Von Arnim and Rommel attacked on two parallel paths going right through II Corps. Von Arnim took Sbeitla and Fondouk, and Rommel struck 70 miles north west through the Kasserine Pass to Thala and Sbiba. Here a mixed force of British tanks and American artillery brought Rommel to a halt.

It is too bad that Patton was not at this time in command of II Corps. He was probably essential to the landing in Morocco but could have been transferred. He was a senior general, difficult to control, and if Ike (Eisenhower) didn't want him at first, Ike now had no choice. The U.S. casualties at Kasserine were 7,000 men, and on March 4 Patton took over.

On March 6 the Afrika Corps attacked Montgomery at Medinine but was repulsed. Rommel had become ill, and at this time he returned to Germany to recover. Now Patton organized his corps of three divisions for an attack to recover Gafsa. On March 17, II Corps attacked, sent the Italians in front of them flying to the rear, and burst into Gafsa, only 60 miles from the sea. If given permission Patton could have trapped the Afrika Corps still facing Montgomery, but he was ordered to halt and not proceed into the coastal area reserved for Eighth Army.

Patton was disgusted at these orders. They most probably were based on lack of confidence in U.S. forces; Patton was then ordered to attack to the north, parallel to the coast to take Maknassy north of Gafsa.

Certainly Patton's II Corps represented the strength of First Army, and certainly II Corps was located in south Tunisia, not for Monty's flank protection, but to cut the Africa Corps supply line. However, at this stage of the war the British had control over tactics and neither U.S. Army or Patton's capabilities were well known.

On March 22, the First Armored Division took Maknassy then bumped into the Tenth Panzer Division. On March 23, Allen's First Division (The Big Red One) was attacked by elements of the Tenth Panzer with 50 tanks. The attack was stopped by noon with 30 German tanks out of action, but the U.S. lost a lot of artillery and tank destroyers. Patton advised the U.S. Army about overconfidence in the abilities of tank destroyers (self propelled guns). Tenth Panzer was stopped just 2 miles from Allen's command post. The German's attacked again but never reached the American lines. Artillery, particularly air bursts, was very effective.

On March 8, Patton attacked at El Guettar toward Gabes on the coast, hoping to break the enemy lines through which he could send First Armored, but by this time the Germans were well entrenched and the golden opportunity was gone.

Patton complained of lack of air cover over II Corps at this time and in the coming weeks the Allies did eventually gain control of the air. By April 7, Patton was not far from Gabes when Monty broke through. Probably the U.S. pressure in the German rear was a big factor in Monty's ability to break through but the Germans escaped.

Patton was then sent back to plan for the invasion of Sicily on April 12, and II Corps was given to Bradley who reported to Anderson. Patton was used like a relief pitcher, brought in only when needed. For day to day operations, Eisenhower obviously preferred to work with more stable men like Bradley. George S. Patton was a tactical genius and cannot be compared to any of the other U.S. or Allied generals. One night, for example, during the Battle of the Bulge, he woke at 3 A.M. with a premonition that the Germans would attack his exposed flank. He called in his staff, ordered an attack at dawn from the exposed area, and struck a German force just before they could attack. No matter how swiftly Patton moved, he was never caught, always knowing where and when to attack or defend. He was basically unmanageable however, and a continuous problem in his relations with Allies (the British, not the French who he liked in both wars). He regarded the British with contempt. Their caution was foreign to his way of making war. Patton was, however, the mighty sword that cut up the Germans.

On March 27, Montgomery completed a flanking movement around the Mareth Line. The Germans withdrew to Wadi Akarit some 50 miles north. Montgomery broke through there on April 6 and the Germans pulled back to Enfidaville near Tunis. On April 19–21, von Arnim launched a counterattack but was thrown back with heavy losses. By May the German air and sea supplies had been virtually cut off. The British captured Tunis while the Ninth U.S. Division took Bizerte on May 7. The fighting in North Africa ceased on May 11. The Allies had lost 75,000 men but the Axis lost 300,000, including 240,000 prisoners.

The British and French celebrations at capturing Tunis virtually ignored the American contribution. There was much parochialism and considerable resentment by U.S. officers, but Patton would repay this slight at Messina in Sicily.

The Allied victory in North Africa was a huge achievement, as large as Stalingrad, and without this Allied effort the Russian success at Stalingrad might not have been possible. Patton had turned around the U.S. Army's II Corps almost overnight, made them effective in attack or defense, an incredible performance. The overall command decisions made by Army Chief-of-Staff George C. Marshal, placing Eisenhower in overall command and using Patton to lead a fighting army, was not just good luck. Marshall's planning was superb, and the success in North Africa was due not in small part to Eisenhower's managerial ability. Pulling these diverse forces together, making them cooperate, making the overall decisions as to where and when to fight, all these were done by Eisenhower with unbroken success. This was not a war of individuals but one of huge machines managed by large staffs. Marshall put the right men in the right places.

Sicily, July–August 1943

During the campaign in Tunisia, planning continued for the next phase. Where should the next target be? Almost any place on the Mediterranean was possible, but subject to rapid German reinforcements and air power. If Sicily was taken, Italy could be next. Getting troops to Italy from Sicily involved crossing only the two mile wide Straight of Messina from a large land mass where Allied air power could be concentrated. Also, taking Italy out of the war would substantially reduce Axis manpower potential.

The plan for Sicily was to land Montgomery's Eighth Army on the southeast corner of Sicily to take Syracuse which was an excellent seaport, necessary for support of troops ashore. Patton was to lead an American Seventh Army, landing near Palermo on the northwest corner of the island. Palermo was also an excellent port, and the two armies, once ashore, could rush to take Messina on the northeast corner of the island. Once Messina was taken, all Axis forces on the island would be trapped.

In April Montgomery found out about the invasion plan and he objected, stating he could not be involved with such a plan which could only lead to disaster because of the dispersed forces which would not be self supporting. Montgomery was a good general, particularly on defense. On offense Monty was so cautious to avoid a disaster that he delayed on every attack to the point where he would hinder many an effort where a large profit might have been possible had he moved with aggressive speed. Patton's biographer believed that Monty's objection to the Sicily plan was based more on an egotistical concern that Patton would roar out of Palermo and make Montgomery look bad in comparison. To be kind, it could be said that Monty had a sound technical objection as the fundamentals of amphibious operations do involve mutually supporting landings, but we must accept the scheme originally set up by the Allied planners as the proper one. We shall see how important a seaport is to large numbers of troops ashore when we discuss the Allied landings in France.

Monty's success with Eighth Army was his only major achievement, but it placed him high in the esteem of his countrymen and no American general wanted to argue with him for fear of the political fallout. Monty's peculiarities were well known to both British and American officers, and Eisenhower eventually had a showdown with him in France when American prestige was far greater.

Montgomery proposed an alternate plan, soon backed by Alexander and approved by Eisenhower. Patton would land on the beaches at Gela on Monty's left where there was no port. This jeopardized the entire American force, but Patton merely obeyed orders, determined to command no matter how dangerous. Admiral Hewitt said he did not think he could supply Patton's army, but the plan was approved regardless. Eisenhower must have pushed his technical reservations aside to assure Allied unity. His success certainly justifies all his decisions, but they must have been very, very hard to make.

Before dawn on July 10 Patton's 7th Army landed on 69 miles of beaches on the south coast of Sicily. He had the 1st, 3rd and 45th Infantry Divisions, the 2nd Armored, the 82nd Airborne, Darby's Ranger Battalion, and the 9th Infantry Division in reserve, 80,000 men. The initial landings were made by the 1st, 3rd, 45th, and 82nd Divisions. The First Division had been a major discipline problem and Eisenhower wanted to hold them back, but Patton, knowing the fighting quality of the Big Red One, said he had to have them, and his wish was granted, fortunately for the campaign.

Patton was opposed by one Italian brigade right on the beaches, two Italian divisions, and the Herman Goering Division just 25 miles inland. A strong wind scattered the paratroops, many landing in the sea, but the landings went well for a while until Italian light tanks showed up in Gela, which was occupied only by Darby's Rangers with no anti tank weapons. Naval gunfire was directed upon the tanks with excellent effect until the Italians retreated. Conrath's Panzer division was supposed to attack in conjunction with the Italians, but delayed until the next day on Kesselring's orders.

On Sunday morning the Germans attacked the First Division with 60 tanks. All the First Division anti-tank guns had been lost during the landings and the Germans broke through the infantry. Patton came ashore that morning and was in Gela when the German tanks appeared. He found a naval officer and called in naval gunfire. The cruiser Boise was just offshore and immediately started firing with its six inch guns with deadly effect.

Forty more tanks hit the other two regiments of Allen's division and again broke through. The infantry were ordered to take cover from the tanks and prevent German infantry from passing. This was done, then Brigadier General Theodore Roosevelt Jr., Assistant Division Commander, went to the beach, lined up all available artillery and fired at the German tanks at point blank ranges of 400 to 800 yards. Theodore Roosevelt Jr., son of the ex-president, was a fine fighting officer, a credit to his famous father who had commanded the Rough Riders in Cuba during the Spanish-American War. At noon a dozen U.S. tanks moved up, tank killing by infantry began to have an effect, and the situation began to improve.

U.S. air support had been almost non-existent as the Army Air Force was more interested in strategic targets than infantry support. As a result German air made major mischief. This lack of air support was corrected before the D-Day landings in France.

Montgomery's plan was almost another U.S. disaster managed by British generals, but the Big Red One made the difference. It had been a near thing, but once established ashore Patton's army began to move inland.

On Patton's right flank, Eighth Army met almost no resistance and walked into Syracuse on D Day. By July 15, however, Montgomery was held up on Mt. Etna by one German regiment. Montgomery then decided he must move the boundary between his and Patton's forces so that he could use the road west of Mt. Etna. Alexander granted Monty permission without asking Patton. As a result the 45th Division had to be pulled back all the way to the beach, delaying the attack by several days. Now the force of Patton's offensive, instead of moving north to cut off all German forces in the west, was directed northwest toward Palermo, where more Axis forces would be displaced rather than captured. U.S. forces had been attacking, one regiment by day, another regiment passing through them to attack by night. The Axis forces were pelted with artillery day and night, given no time to dig in. Once Montgomery's interference delayed the attack, the Germans had time to bring up reinforcements and set up defenses. Patton's rush to Palermo may have taken his forces further west than necessary, but his army needed the port and should have landed there in the first place.

Patton left Bradley in charge of the push north and set up Keyes with a Provisional Corps consisting of the 3rd 82nd and 2nd Armored Divisions. By July 17, Agrigento was taken and Palermo, 100 miles away, fell on the twenty-second. Patton's advance to Palermo dominated headlines world-wide and was actually done in violation of orders with much criticism that it was done just for publicity. Patton liked his plan because it gave him room to move, would give him the port he needed and opened another road to Messina. It may be that he saw it as an opportunity to avoid the obstacles put upon him by the British plans and to go back to the plan that he and the Allied Staff had drawn up in the beginning. Good generals do what is right sometimes in violation of orders that are not right. It is risky as failure could bring a court martial, but good generals know that they will not fail and success brings promotion. So it was with Patton. This campaign resulted in 50,000 Axis casualties, 44,000 captured.

On July 17, the British attacked Catania, 60 miles from Messina, with a whole division and made just 400 yards. Patton at Palermo was 150 miles from Messina.

As early as July 12, the Germans decided to defend the northeast corner of the island where mountainous terrain was most helpful in defense. German reinforcements were rushed in bringing them up to three full German divisions with more tanks and guns than Rommel ever had in Africa.

By August 2, both Patton and Montgomery were stalled 60 miles from Messina.

The First Division was engaged in tough fighting in front of Troina. Here the Germans even counterattacked. As American casualties mounted progress slowed as there were no replacements. During this campaign Patton replaced both Allen and Roosevelt, the accomplished but unmanageable leaders of the Big Red One. (One can see that compatibility must come before performance in all walks of life.) Troina was pounded by air on the 4th and occupied on the 6th but the Germans pulled back only one mile.

On August 8, Patton landed a reinforced battalion 12 miles behind enemy lines and forced the Germans to pull back rapidly. Inland the First Division took Cesaro. The Third Division made some progress 10 miles in front of Brolo on the tenth. On the eleventh a Third Division battalion landed at Brolo and fought for their lives, but by 10 P.M. two regiments of the Third Division broke through to assist them. In three days Patton had smashed 30 miles through the German defenses. Many of Patton's subordinate officers (including Bradley) resisted the Brolo operation, but it clearly showed Patton's genius when his scheme is compared to those of more ordinary generals who could not have ordered such risky moves and who would have slugged it out yard by yard with the highest possible casualties. Patton quoted Frederick the Great, saying to Truscott (Third Division Commander), "L'audace L'audace, toujours l'audace,"(Audacity, always audacity).

Truscott entered Messina on August 17, a few minutes before a British tank sent by Montgomery to claim the conquest. Churchill and Admiral Cunningham admired Patton's achievements and Eisenhower gave him a DSC (Distinguished Service Cross). The Germans remembered him from Africa, but now the whole world knew who he was and what American armies could do.

Not much has been said of the British accomplishments, but this is an American story. Obviously the British Army and Navy did their share of the work, tied down an equivalent number of Germans, and took their share of casualties. The war was a joint effort with all of the Allies making contributions.

The bulk of the Axis forces did escape from Sicily and the Allies would have to fight them again in Italy. The Naval Historian, Admiral Morison, claimed that Patton would have dashed to Messina and trapped more Axis forces in Sicily if he had landed at Syracuse. Errors in judgment and performance were made in Sicily but the whole affair was a rehearsal for the big show soon to happen in France. It was a victory and represented progress. One huge dividend was the collapse of the Italian government and the replacement of Mussolini with Marshal Badoglio.

Pacific Offensive, 1943

In early 1943 the Allies were on the offensive in the Pacific but only on a limited basis. Supplies and manpower were limited and progress would be slow as the Japanese made major efforts to stem the tide. MacArthur would not advance until late 1943. An amphibious operation against the Japanese in the Aleutians would be made and in the Solomons most of the fighting was in the air and sea until July. The Allies were content to prevent the Japanese from making any more conquests until the Allied war machine in the Pacific was stronger. The advance would be resumed when U.S. forces were strong enough to permit advances with a high probability of success.

Aleutians, May 1943

The Japanese had landed troops in the Aleutians during the battle of Midway, and by 1943 it was decided they should be removed. U.S. submarines sank many a merchant vessel trying to supply the Japanese occupation force. On March 26, a U.S. fleet of one heavy cruiser, one light cruiser, and four destroyers tried to prevent a Japanese supply convoy from reaching the islands and fought a long range battle with two heavy and two light cruisers plus four destroyers. The U.S. shooting was good, but the U.S. heavy cruiser lost power and the Japanese headed for her. Three U.S. destroyers turned and sailed full speed at the Japanese causing them to retreat. Again the courage of U.S. Navy commanders caused a superior Japanese fleet to retire. These were professionals, these U.S. sailors.

In May the U.S. 7th Division landed on Attu and took the island after several weeks of fighting with a fanatical foe. Kiska was retaken in July but the Japanese had left the island.

The Battle of the Bismarck Sea, March, 1943

After the U.S. capture of Buna and Gona on the Papuan Peninsula, the Japanese attempted to reinforce their garrison on New Guinea. On March 3, eight Japanese transports supported by eight destroyers were spotted in the Bismarck Sea on the way to New Guinea. General George C. Kenney had over 300 planes on New Guinea, U.S. and Australian. Kenney had trained his bomber crews to attack at sea level and hit ships with low level attacks involving skip bombing. On March 3, Kenney's fighters took on the Japanese planes over the convoy and simultaneously hit the airfield at Lau to prevent reinforcements. The bombers then struck the convoy, bombs landing on three out of four attempts (unlike Midway where land based aircraft were useless). Seven of eight transports and two destroyers were sunk. Raids continued all day and again on March 4 when two more destroyers were sunk. PT boats came in sinking the last transport and a submarine. Of the 7000 troops, some 3000 to 4000 were lost.

Yamamoto's Last Pass

Once Guadalcanal was secure, in February of 1943, Marines and Army troops moved into the Russell Islands, 30 miles west of Guadalcanal. Yamamoto then launched a furious air campaign over the Solomons and New Guinea. On April 7, 187 planes raided Tulagi, sinking a tanker, corvette, and a destroyer, losing 21 planes. On April 11–12, Jap planes sank two merchant vessels in New Guinea. 174 planes raided Port Moresby but were met with heavy antiaircraft fire and did little damage.

In April U.S. decoders picked up a Japanese radio message announcing Yamamoto's flight schedule for an inspection tour of the islands. Sixteen U.S. Army P-38 Lightnings took off from Henderson Field to intercept him in mid air. Miraculously the Army planes picked up two bombers, shooting down both. The admiral was killed along with some of his staff, and there was no one of equal ability to take his place.

Munda, New Georgia, July 1943

Munda was the airfield used by the Japanese to attack Guadalcanal. It was on the island of New Georgia, about 250 miles west of Guadalcanal in the Solomon Island chain, and in July Halsey sent a task force to occupy New Georgia. The major landings took place on Rendova Island where resistance was light. From there troops were ferried across the strait to New Georgia. It took 34,000 soldiers six weeks to overcome 8,000 Japanese and occupy the Munda air strip by August 5. (The First Marine Division was in Australia, resting and reorganizing. Veterans were being transferred into the Second and new Third Divisions.) The performance of these Army troops wasn't the best according to Admiral Morison. There were too few combat veterans among officers and enlisted men. General Griswold came in to lead the fight and the situation improved.

The Battles of Kula Gulf, Kolombangara, and Vella Gulf

In support of the Munda land battle, a U.S. fleet lost a destroyer to mines the night of July 4, then engaged ten Japanese destroyers the next night, losing a cruiser to torpedoes in Kula Gulf. Two Japanese destroyers were sunk.

On the night of July 12 , a U.S. fleet of three light cruisers and ten destroyers engaged a Japanese fleet of one cruiser, five destroyers, and four destroyer transports off Kolombangara. The Japanese were attempting to ferry troops to New Georgia and were turned back with the loss of a cruiser, but the U.S.fleet chased the Japanese, drew too close and received a barrage of torpedoes which hit all three cruisers. The only U.S. ship lost, however, was a destroyer. Unknown to the Americans, the Japanese torpedo had an effective range of 10,000 yards (six miles).

At Vella Gulf on the night of August 6, Commander Moosbrugger took six U.S. destroyers, surprised a Japanese force of four destroyers and fired torpedoes at 4000 yards, sinking three destroyers. The Navy was learning.

Vella Lavella, August, 1943

After New Georgia the next obvious island objective was Kolombangara, but this island was heavily defended. Nimitz decided to bypass this island and land on the next one in the Solomons chain, Vella Lavella. Over 6,000 army troops were landed on August 15 against light resistance (except from Japanese aircraft). On September 18, the Third Division, New Zealand Army, relieved the U.S. troops, and by October 1 they had trapped 600 Japanese on the island's northwest corner. On the night of October 6, nine Japanese destroyers came down to take off the 600. Three U.S. destroyers intercepted, sinking one Japanese destroyer but losing two U.S. ships. Three U.S. destroyers rushed up to support but could not prevent the relief of the 600. Here again the Japanese Navy had an advantage. Although the Japanese Navy had fought well so far in the war many of their losses were not replaceable. They had lost 40 destroyers by mid 1943 and were running short of these essential ships. Their losses had come from a variety of actions, surface clashes, U.S. land and carrier aircraft, and U.S. submarines. U.S. fleets frequently raided Japanese bases and U.S. submarines roamed everywhere leaving Japan with no safe sea lanes.

The Naval Buildup

1942 was a hard year for the U.S. Navy, depleted of battleships, dangerously low in carriers, low in supplies and repair facilities, and with torpedoes that malfunctioned. The Navy hung on, fighting with what they had until industry could produce the necessary ships and weapons.

At Pearl Harbor the U.S. Navy had had eight battleships on December 7, 1941, *Nevada, Arizona, Tennessee, West Virginia, Maryland, Oklahoma, California,* and *Pennsylvania.* When the Japanese planes attacked, *Oklahoma* took three torpedoes, capsized and sank. *Maryland* took only two bomb hits and stayed afloat. *West Virginia* took six or seven torpedoes and listed to 28 degrees, but was counter flooded (compartments on the undamaged side were flooded) and settled upright on the bottom. *Tennessee* took two bombs and had significant fire damage but also stayed afloat. *Arizona* was destroyed and sank. Her mast remained above the water and is a monument there still. *California* sank but counter flooding prevented her from capsizing and she settled upright. *Nevada* took one torpedo but managed to get under way and was safely beached. *Pennsylvania*, in dry dock, took only one bomb hit.

Three weeks later, *Maryland, Tennessee,* and *Pennsylvania* sailed for the mainland to be repaired. *Maryland* was the first to return, participating in the invasion of Tarawa. *California* was eventually refloated and repaired to return to action. *Nevada* was made seaworthy and sailed to the U.S. for repairs in February, returning to action in 1943. *West Virginia* was also brought up from the bottom, sent back to the U.S. for repairs and returned. Six of the eight stricken battlewagons would return to pay their assassins back with dividends.

Prior to December 7, 1941, the U.S. had five carriers, but four were sunk during 1942. During the winter of '42 and '43, the U.S. had only three carriers left, just two in the Pacific. As the U.S. entered the war, contracts for conversions of cruisers to carriers and for new carriers were let. In May of 1943, the first of these was launched and carriers became available at the rate of one a month. By December of 1943, the U.S. had a two to one advantage over the Japanese in carriers.

Anti-aircraft guns used by the U.S. early in the war were poor, but these were replaced with rapid firing 20 mm and 40 mm guns. Although defense of ships from air attacks was never perfect, a large combat air patrol and innumerable anti-aircraft guns on the larger ships made air attacks on the fleets very expensive. To overcome this the Japanese ultimately relied upon suicide attacks (*kamikaze*).

Early in the war U.S. torpedoes were faulty. Many that were fired went under the targets; others hit squarely without exploding. There were several problems, one with the mechanism controlling torpedo depth and another with the firing pin which would break before detonation upon square hits. The firing pin worked only if the torpedo struck at an angle, a glancing blow. It took a while before these defects became known, and it wasn't until September of 1943 that new U.S. torpedoes became available. One can wonder how many seamen and torpedo plane pilots died firing useless torpedoes.

Bouganville, November 11 1943

From Guadalcanal Halsey's forces moved northwest toward Rabaul on New Britain. This was the main Japanese base in the South Pacific and the source of many a sea and air attack. Bouganville was a step closer, and an airstrip there would permit fighter planes to reach Rabaul. For two weeks General Kenney's planes pounded Rabaul, then on November 1 the Third Marine Division, the 37th Division, U.S. Army, and a brigade of New Zealanders were landed at Empress Augusta Bay in the center of the island's west coast. Most of the Japanese troops were defending the Kahili base on the south coast and a fake landing on an island near Kahili kept them there. Landings were opposed by only 300, but Rabaul based planes tried and failed to interrupt the invasion.

On November 2, a Japanese fleet of two heavy cruisers, two light cruisers, and six destroyers approached Empress Augusta Bay, where it was intercepted by Rear Admiral Merrill with four light cruisers and eight destroyers. Cruisers fought at 16,000 to 20,000 yards, outside of torpedo range, giving the U.S. ships an advantage with their radar. One Japanese light cruiser and one destroyer were sunk. Advantage, U.S.

Ashore, a defensive perimeter was set up to permit construction of an airstrip. On November 7, 475 Japanese attacked the perimeter with the loss of 377 Japanese and 17 Marines. General Hyakutake had 40,000 men on the island but had not learned a thing since Guadalcanal. Later in November and in December the Marines extended their perimeter with heavy fighting before they were relieved. Marines lost 423 dead and 1,418 wounded to 2,000 Japanese known dead and several thousand more estimated dead and wounded.

The Neutralization of Rabaul, November 1943

After the Battle of Empress Augusta Bay, the Japanese brought seven heavy cruisers to Rabaul to finish off the U.S. fleet supposedly hurt in the preceding battle. Halsey sent a task force with two carriers to attack Rabaul on November 5. The seven cruisers were badly damaged and were sent back to Truk for repairs. On November 11, another task force with three carriers hit Rabaul again. Japanese air strength at Rabaul was so depleted with this raid that remaining planes were also removed.

On Thanksgiving Commander Burke (31-knot Burke) with five destroyers attacked a fleet of five Japanese destroyers off New Ireland, sinking two with torpedoes and one with gunfire. The U.S. Navy was rapidly gaining control of the seas around New Britain.

The air and sea attacks on Rabaul made it impossible for the Japanese to resist the American landings at Tarawa later in the month. By December 10, the U.S. had a fighter airstrip, Torokina Airfield on Bouganville, which brought Rabaul into fighter range. From here USMC Major (Pappy) Boyington and his Black Sheep Squadron took off with the new gull wing Vought Corsair fighters for frequent raids on Rabaul. This squadron in one month shot down 59 Japanese planes while losing only two. Major Boyington shot down 28 before being brought down himself and captured.

Tarawa, November 19, 1943

The Navy plan to go straight from Hawaii to Tokyo was instigated late in 1943 with landings planned in the Gilbert and Marshall islands. These islands were over halfway between Hawaii and the Solomons. Possession would shorten supply lines and provide bases for attacks farther west. Tarawa in the Gilbert Island chain was chosen for the next assault and a naval attack force was rapidly assembled.

The Tarawa force was under overall command of Admiral Spruance, who had the Fifth Fleet with battleships, five carriers, new destroyers, and just too much strength for the Japanese fleet to contest. Fifth Amphibious Corps was under Admiral R. Kelly Turner (who had been at Guadalcanal) and ground troops were assigned to Marine General H. M. Smith. The entire force contained

108,000 men including the Second Marine Division and the 27th New York National Guard Division.

The Second Division under General Julian Smith would land with two regiments, the Second Marines under Colonel David Shoup and the Eighth Marines. The critical landing consisted of three battalions under Col Shoup. The other three battalions were in reserve. The Sixth Marines were held back for operations elsewhere.

Tarawa was an atoll of many islands. The Marines were assigned to Betio which had an airstrip. The 27th Division was assigned to Makin, defended by about 600 Japanese.

For a week before the landing planes bombed Betio, defended by 4,500 good troops. On D-Day, November 20, naval guns pounded the islands for two and a half hours before troops were sent ashore. Unfortunately the bombing and shelling were not sufficient to destroy the extensive concrete, log, and sand fortifications. The first three waves went ashore in amtracs, boats with treads, but many of these were damaged.

Subsequent waves, carried in landing craft, had to be discharged at the coral reef which boats could not pass except at high tide. (The landings were delayed and missed the narrow high tide period.) As a result the Marines had to wade ashore in waist high water for a quarter of a mile under intense fire. Casualties were terrible. By 1:30 P.M. only 1,500 men were ashore, pinned down on the beach behind the seawall. Second Division Commander J.C. Smith reported the situation doubtful and called for the reserve battalions.

All day the men on the beach were hit by machine gun fire if they raised their heads above the sea wall. If they crouched on the beach they were hit with mortar fire. Tanks coming ashore had difficulty avoiding the bodies of dead and wounded.

During the first day two of the three reserve battalions had been committed, these taking heavy casualties as they waded in. Gradually small groups worked their way inland, knocking out Japanese defenses with tanks, antitank guns, flame throwers, and satchel charges. By dusk, on the left, Colonel Shoup occupied a command post in an area 600 yards wide, 250 yards inland at the point of deepest penetration, held by the remnants of four battalions. On the extreme right at the end of the island, one battalion held 100 yards of beach, also 200 yards deep. In between were 600 yards of beach with no penetration.

The first day at Betio was horrible. Five thousand Marines had gone ashore, but 1,500 were dead or wounded. Units were fragmented and a counterattack could have been fatal. The Japanese had planned to counterattack but the bombs and shells had knocked out their communications and it wasn't possible to organize the attack.

On November 21, the second day, the sixth battalion came in at dawn, wading and taking heavy casualties, 108 dead, 235 wounded, with only 600 survivors. Then men like Lt. Hawkins crawled inland, tossing grenades, finding, shooting. Artillery, tanks, naval guns, diving aircraft, all began to take out enemy positions. On the right flank Major Ryan's battalion began clearing the tip of the island, coming in on the Japanese flank with tank-infantry teams, and by 4 P.M. Col. Shoup could finally report that his forces were winning in spite of many casualties. Just to be sure, a battalion of the Sixth Marines was landed on the right flank at the western end of the island. Pill boxes were covered with sand by bull-dozers and the inhabitants flushed out. In some works the Japanese committed suicide. Colonel Shoup, who had directed the fight for over twenty-four hours after being wounded, was relieved by General Edson.

On the third day the Sixth Marines drove east and rolled up the Japanese line. The Sixth Marines had been in Belleau Wood and they, like the Fifth, were a fabled regiment. By nightfall the airstrip had been captured. After dark the Japanese did attack, three times in groups of fifty, then a fourth time with 300. Shouting *"Banzai,"* they charged and died. On November 23, the fourth day, the last Japanese pockets were eliminated and Betio had fallen, but 1,000 Marines were dead and 2,300 wounded.

The defenses at Betio were many, strong, self supporting, and in great depth. The conquering of this island by one division of Marines was an incredible achievement, considered impossible by the Japanese. Some hard lessons were learned here, but landing on heavily fortified islands would never be easy. As long as America exists, Americans should pause on occasion to remember the courage of the Marines who fought and won at Tarawa.

MacArthur Advances, 1943

After the capture of Buna and Gona in early 1943, MacArthur had to build up his forces for further advances. The Japanese did the same, and it was not until June 30 that MacArthur made his next move. On that day he occupied the Trobriand Islands off the New Guinea coast and Nassau Bay. The landing at Nassau Bay required a shore to shore hop of 40 miles, leaving MacArthur only 40 miles from the Japanese base at Lau.

In mid August, Allied planes attacked Wewak—destroying 100 planes on the ground.

Paratroops landed at Nadzab on September 5 just 15 miles from Lau. On September 6 Aussie troops landed at Lau. During the fighting for Lau, Aussies from Nassau Bay took Salamaua, and on September 16 Lau fell. The last major town on Huon Gulf, Finschafen, 50 miles from Lau was also captured by an amphibious operation on October 2. MacArthur was then in control of the New Guinea sea coast across from New Britain.

Cape Gloucester, New Britain, December 1943

The Joint Chiefs of Staff had decided to capture islands around New Britain, thereby isolating the huge Japanese base at Rabaul. Rabaul was defended by 100,000 troops, well fortified, and a landing there was probably not feasible. MacArthur did want to occupy the western end of New Britain, however, to interrupt Japanese troop barge movements to New Guinea via the Campier and Vitiaz Straights, and to capture an airfield that would threaten Rabaul. On December 26 the First Marine Division landed at Cape Gloucester, 300 miles from Rabaul.

There were 4,000 Japanese troops at the Cape, but their defenses were inland. No solid defensive positions in the swamps near the beach were practical. As a result the Marines landed, moved inland, and captured the airfield with only light resistance. On December 27, 1000 Japanese attacked in another of their fierce, piecemeal efforts, completely underestimating the size of the force in front of them. The attack failed with 200 dead.

On the twenty-ninth another suicide charge was made by 116 Japanese with few survivors. By years end Cape Gloucester was secure. General Rupertus, First Division Commander, then assigned Assistant Division Commander General Lem Shepherd to attack the Japanese.

General Shepherd's plan was to hold on his left at Target Hill and attack on the right across Suicide Creek to enable the Marines to hit the Japanese flank. The Japanese also had plans, to hold at Suicide Creek and attack at Target Hill. The Marines attacked at Suicide Creek on January 2 and were stopped. Casualties were heavy as the invisible Japanese shot anything that moved. On the morning of January 3, the Japanese attacked Target Hill. Two hundred Japanese fell and in two hours the attack was over. The Marines struggled for two days at Suicide Creek until a road was constructed and tanks rolled up on the 4th. By then the Japanese had pulled back.

On the eighth the Marines attacked the main Japanese defenses further inland on Aogiri Ridge. Fighting was bitter with no progress until Lt. Col. Lew Walt started pushing a 37mm cannon up the hill. He picked up some helpers and they moved up the hill firing canister as they went until they had reached the top.

When the Japanese counterattacked, Walt called in artillery within 50 yards of Marine positions (observers are taught not to call in artillery within 400 yards of friendly positions). The combination of artillery and machine guns was too much for the Japanese who rushed the hill five times before giving up.

In mid January the Marines went for Hill 660, the Japanese strongpoint from which they threatened the airstrip. A force of 120 men with two tanks, two self propelled guns, bull-dozers, and anti-tank guns under Captain Buckley moved around the hill, cutting off the Japanese defenders and preventing reinforcements. A Marine battalion found a spot on the bill where defenses were light and began to climb. The Japanese, some 2000 to 3000, were routed with heavy casualties. As they retreated Buckleys force took down more. One counterattack and the Japanese were through. The airstrip was secure and Rabaul was now threatened by two airstrips, one to the east (Bouganville) and one to the south (Cape Gloucester).

Italy 1943

After the loss of Sicily, the Germans knew that Italy was next. General Kesselring, Commander in the south, could not defend the long coastline within Allied fighter range of Sicily, but gathered ten divisions (Tenth Army) near Naples where mountainous country was excellent for defense. Rommel had eight more divisions (Fourteenth Army) in the north to control the population and react to new amphibious operations.

The Allied Army under Alexander, thirteen divisions, consisted of Montgomery's Eighth Army and an Anglo-American Fifth Army under U.S. General Mark Clark.

Eisenhower went to England with Omar Bradley to work on the plans for the invasion of France. Patton, out of favor for slapping a shell shocked soldier in Sicily, was given no assignment but was being held for a key role in France. (Patton, however, knew nothing of this.)

On September 9, Eighth Army landed at Reggio di Calabria and Taranto, moving easily up the southern end of Italy. Fifth Army landed four divisions at Salerno 50 miles south of Naples. The Germans expected the Salerno landings and met the invaders at the beach. Bitter fighting continued for a week until Eighth Army arrived. On September 16 Kesselring pulled back.

Eighth Army moved to the east side of Italy and Fifth Army stayed on the west side. Allied strategy certainly suggested more amphibious landings to bypass German defenses, but boats were needed for the invasion of France and were not available except for the one urgent future landing at Anzio. Italy was obviously downgraded to a secondary effort. As a result the Allies could only fight a bitter war of frontal attacks against almost equal forces in country ideal for defense. Naples was occupied on October 1 by Fifth Army and Foggia by the British the same day. Fifth Army was held up for three weeks at the Volturno River, then brought to a halt at the Garigliano River on November 15. Eighth Army reached the Sangro by November 8, then was held up for two weeks, finally forcing a crossing on November 20. Eighth Army broke through the Gustav Line in the east, capturing Ortona before halting, exhausted. Fifth Army crossed the Garigliano on January 17, the Rapido on January 20, then were stopped at the Gustav Line where it ran through Monte Cassino. The U.S. 6th Division took heavy losses at the Rapido but the 34th Division managed to cross further upstream.

On January 22, the 3rd U.S. Division and 1st British Division under General Lucas landed at Anzio, north of the Gustav Line, but failed to move inland, and were eventually hit hard by Germans from the Fourteenth Army. Lucas had four divisions and some 350 tanks at Anzio. The Germans had prepared for such a landing, counting on segments of the eight divisions in Fourteenth Army, but these forces were dispersed and arrived at Anzio at different times. If Lucas had moved thirty miles inland he might have cut Routes 6 and 7, the roads the Germans needed for supply of the western end of the Gustav Line. These must have been the invasion objectives, but the Germans moved in forces quickly and the attack floundered short of the objectives.

In a similar situation in Tunisia, Patton was willing to cut Rommel's supply line at Gafsa where Patton would have been open to attack from north and south. Patton had only three divisions and felt he was strong enough. Lucas, with his four divisions, was almost equal to the five divisions that the Germans eventually put in against him. If the Germans evacuated troops from the Gustav Line, Fifth Army could break through and follow them, and this was the sole purpose of Anzio, to allow a breakthrough of the Gustav Line. Lucas was replaced with General Lucian Truscott (who defended Lucas). Many men died, fighting for months, because of the failure at Anzio. Meanwhile, Patton sat idle, a political liability. If Patton had been assigned to Fifth Army, Anzio might have been a different story, but Mark Clark didn't want him.

Actually the Germans had more divisions in Italy than the Allies and had excellent terrain for defense. Italy was a side show for the Allies with no major strategic objective other than to tie down German divisions. As soon as the 1944 Italian campaign began, the Allies were stalled in front of Monte Cassino and at Anzio in a deadly stalemate.

European Air War, 1942–1943

In 1942 the British began the saturation bombing of German cities at night with large plane raids. From March through June the British struck the Renault factory near Paris, also Luebeck, Augsberg, Essen, Cologne, Essen, and Bremen. The latter three cities were each hit by 1,000 planes. Bombing cities did little to hamper German military capabilities and losses were so high (59 over Cologne, 49 over Bremen) that training programs could not keep up. One thousand plane raids were then discontinued. On July 4, the U.S. Army Air Force joined the British for the first time.

In 1943 General Eaker, Commander of the Eighth Air Force (USAAF), recommended daylight raids, which did more damage, against specific war industries.

The U.S. then bombed by day, the British by night. In April and May 15 raids were made on German industry in the Ruhr. On May 23–24, 826 R.A.F. bombers struck Dusseldorf on June 13, 60 B-17s bombed Kiel, out of U.S. fighter protection range, losing 26. The U.S. P-47 Thunderbolt was given additional fuel tanks but even so could only reach western German cities.

On June 23, the Eighth Air Force did major damage to a synthetic rubber plant at Huls.

During June and July the R.A.F. struck targets in the Ruhr. 6037 sorties were made with the loss of 310 planes. (Night bombing losses typically were about 5 percent, much less than daytime losses.)

For ten days in July and August, the R.A.F. and Eighth Air Force struck Hamburg. For four days with 3015 sorties, the R.A.F. lost 87. Two U.S. air raids with 281 planes lost 21, but Hamburg was destroyed with a terrible firestorm resulting in 40,000 dead.

On August 1, 163 B-24s struck the Ploesti oil fields in Rumania but lost 54 planes. Much damage was done but the plane loss was unacceptably high.

On August 17, the Eighth Air Force bombed a ball bearing factory at Schweinfurt and a Messerschmidt factory at Regensburg with 376 planes, losing 60. That same night 596 R.A.F. bombers hit the V Rocket base at Peenemuende doing much damage and losing 38 planes.

On August 23, the R.A.F. lost 57 out of 719 planes in an attack on Berlin. In following nights 127 planes were lost out of 2262. Allied air losses were so high that air force morale was beginning to deteriorate.

On September 6, the U.S. lost 45 planes over Stuttgart. On September 22 the R.A.F. made a diversionary raid on Oldenburg, then struck Hanover after German night fighters had left the area. Only 26 planes were lost of 711 in the raid, an improvement. On October 9, Eighth Air Force struck the Focke Wulf plants at Anklam and Marienburg with excellent results. New longer range P-38 fighters arrived and more fighter protection became available. New B-17s had nose turrets which helped defend against frontal attacks. On October 14, Eighth Air Force raided Schweinfurt again with 291 planes, losing 60. After this disaster daylight bombing was limited to areas where fighters could support the bombers.

The new Fifteenth Air Force (U.S.) on November 2 bombed the Messerschmidt plant at Wiener-Neustadt, losing eleven out of 110 planes.

In the fall of 1943 and the winter of 1944, Berlin was given an almost nightly pounding by the R.A.F., but R.A.F. losses mounted; November 18 losses were 9 of 444, late November losses were 80 of 2,040; December losses 130 of 2,037; 202 planes lost of 3,314 in January; 42 of 891 in February; 72 of 811 in March. Finally, although Berlin was destroyed, these raids were not winning the war and costs were too high.

On January 1, 1944, General Carl Spaatz was put in charge of U.S. strategic air forces in Europe. On January 11, 633 planes from Eighth Air Force bombed fighter factories at Halberstadt, Oscherleben, and Brunswick. Thirty-four of 633 planes were lost, but new long range P-5I Mustangs shot down 60 German fighters, and extensive damage was done to the factories. By late February a plan was devised by General Spaatz to concentrate on German fighter production. In six days U.S. and British planes dropped 15,200 tons of bombs on fighter and ball bearing plants. Although production and shipment of aircraft were hindered the new P51s took a heavy toll on German pilots and planes and this marked the turning point in the air war. Herman Goering, German Air Minister, said that the day he saw P-51s over Berlin he knew the jig was up. As 1944 moved toward spring, air attack targets were revised to support the D Day invasion, but the Allies rapidly gained control of the skies.

The Atlantic Sea War, 1943

As 1943 began, German U-Boats continued to destroy Allied shipping, 200,000 tons in January, 315,000 tons in February, 540,000 tons in March, 300,000 tons in May, and 30,000 in June. The terrible losses in March were caused by the concentration of U-Boats in wolf packs attacking eastbound convoys predominately. Forty-one ships were sunk in the Atlantic in the first ten days of March. From March 15–19, two eastbound convoys lost 21 of 98 ships with only one U-Boat sunk. These losses were crucial, more than ship replacements, and if continued would have made an invasion of France impossible.

Convoy schedules were rearranged and more efficient use of escort vessels planned. More aggressive use of escorts was recommended by British Admiral Horton.

On May 4 Convoy ONS 5 was attacked by 40 U-Boats. Twelve ships were sunk in 36 hours. The seven escorts sank only one U-Boat. Then on May 6 the convoy was reinforced to thirteen escorts. These sank four U-Boats with no further convoy tosses. This was the turning point. Subsequent convoy and submarine losses were as follows:

Convoy	Ships Lost	U-Boats Sunk
HX 237	3	3
SC 129	2	2
ONS 7	I	1
SC 130	0	4

In May, 41 U-Boats were sunk, and by June U-Boats were recalled from the Atlantic! The British had broken the German submarine radio transmission code and enabled the Allies to attack the U-Boat wolf packs. Submarines had to surface frequently to recharge their batteries and this made them visible to aircraft which could then call for an attack. Planes had been scouring the ocean from land bases for some time and eventually enough destroyer/carrier hunter/killer groups were supplied to cover those portions of the Atlantic not covered from land bases. The U-Boats returned but Allied ship losses continued to decline from the levels seen in early 1943.

Russia, 1943

During the attempted relief of Stalingrad in December of 1942 Hoth had been only 16 miles from the German lines at Stalingrad, but the subsequent Soviet offensive pushed the whole southern German front back, recapturing city after city. In January the Germans began to withdraw from the Caucasus. That same month the siege of Leningrad was broken. At Voronezh on the Don, 80,000 Hungarians and Italians were encircled and captured. All along the front the Germans pulled back from exposed salients, and in the south they occupied a shorter line along the Mius River west of Rostov. In February the Soviets occupied Rostov, Krasnograd, Kharkov, Belgorod, and Kursk, pushing 450 miles west of Stalingrad. Hitler was ready to fire von Mannstein, but this crafty general had shortened his lines and pulled out numerous divisions in preparation for a counterattack (which pleased Hitler). In late February von Mannstein's SS Panzer Corps struck Vatutin's right flank at Krasnograd, while XL Panzer Corps attacked in the south against Popov's flank. Vatutin's counterattack was thrown back with heavy loss and the Russians, overextended, short of supplies, pulled back to the Donets. Von Mannstein advanced, retaking Kharkov, Belgorod, and by mid March had pushed the Russians into a salient at Kursk. Spring mud stopped von Mannstein, and both sides beefed up forces for the showdown at Kursk. Hitler delayed until July so that he could bring in his new Panther and Tiger tanks. The Russians meanwhile built three extensive defensive rings in the salient backed by a mobile force of tanks. The Jewish uprising in Warsaw in April, futile as it may have seemed, tied up German forces and may have contributed to the delay at Kursk.

The Germans massed 900,000 men under Model (north of Kursk) and Hoth (south of the city) with 2,500 tanks and mobile guns, but the Russians had 1,300,000 men available with 3000 tanks. On July 5 the Germans attacked and managed shallow penetrations of 6 to 7 miles. In one day Model came to a halt. Then the Russians concentrated against Hoth. At Prokhorovka a huge tank battle involving 1300 tanks and motorized artillery was fought on July 12 and Hoth came to a halt.

A Russian counterattack in Model's rear began, but Hitler had to pull out troops to reinforce his western armies where the Sicilian invasion posed a new threat. German offensives against the Russians were now finished and Germans would continue to retreat on all fronts for the duration of the war.

The Russians recaptured Orel and Belgorod by August 5, Kharkov on August 23, Taganrod (west of Rostov) on August 30, and Chernigov on the Dnieper on September 21. By then the Germans were behind their East Wall along the Dnieper. Several Russian bridgeheads over this river were, however, quickly established against a very thin German line. On September 25 Smolensk and Roslavl were retaken after two years of German occupation. The last of the German Caucasus force was pulled back into the Crimea from Taman by October 9. On October 23, Dnepropetrovsk, and on November 6, Kiev, both on the

Dnieper, were taken. By years end the Russians were 80 miles west of Kiev, 700 miles west of Stalingrad, and only 375 miles from Warsaw in Poland.

Pacific Offensives, 1944

On February 29 MacArthur's First Cavalry Division invaded the Admiralty Islands west of New Britain. The island first occupied was Los Negros; from there Army troops moved into Manus, the largest of the group. The key harbor came under American control by April 3. There had been 4,000 Japanese in the Admiralties, but their attacks were typical (piecemeal). Now Rabaul was threatened from three sides.

In the central Pacific the Combined Chiefs of Staff wished to take Guam, Tinian and Saipan (in the Marianas) in order to provide airfields for the new B-29s (Superfortresses) which could reach Japan from these islands. Also, submarines could be sent into Japanese home waters from the Marianas to attack Japanese merchant shipping. Possession of the Marianas would also isolate Truk, the key Japanese base in the Carolines. Before the Marianas, however, the Marshalls would have to be conquered.

These islands lay northwest of the Gilberts, southeast of the Marianas. The Japanese had been unable to build extensive defenses in the Marshalls because of the unexpected speed of the American advance. Japan planned to make their next line of defense from western New Guinea through the Carolines (Truk) to the Marianas.

The Marshall Islands, 1944

The Marshalls consisted of 36 atolls, some 2,000 islands. Here the Japanese had built airfields on six of the atolls defended by 26,000 troops. Most of these troops were on the eastern atolls so Admiral Nimitz decided to invade a central atoll, Kwajalein. The Fourth Marine Division was assigned the task of taking Roi-Namur and the Seventh Army Division would land on Kwajalein. These islands were defended by 3,500 Japanese on Roi-Namur and by 5,000 on Kwajalein. The invasion fleet under Rear Admiral Mitscher had 6 large carriers, 6 light carriers, new battleships, and much too much power for the Japanese to contest. The islands were pounded by sea and air from January 29 to February 6, eliminating most of the Japanese aircraft. The Marines landed on January 31, took only light casualties and mopped up by the next day. The Seventh Division took four days to clean up Kwajalein after some heavy fighting. Thirty other islands in the atoll were occupied by February 7, leaving few Japanese alive, with only 372 U.S. casualties.

Eniwetok was the next objective, the northernmost of the Marshalls only 1000 miles from the Marianas. Before attempting Eniwetok, however, it was necessary to neutralize Truk. On February 17–18, Admiral Mitscher launched planes from four carriers repeatedly, destroying 275 planes, many on the ground. Dive bombers attacked 50 merchant ships in Truk harbor, destroying 200,000 tons of shipping. Admiral Spruance chased Japanese naval vessels with battleships *Iowa* and *New Jersey*, two cruisers, and four destroyers, sinking one cruiser and one destroyer. A U.S. sub sank another cruiser while carrier planes sank two Japanese destroyers. Truk ceased to be a naval threat to U.S. forces.

Three islands in the Eniwetok Atoll were defended by 3,000 Japanese. The invasion on February 18 by one Marine and one Army regiment was over by the 22nd with only 339 U.S. dead.

New Guinea, 1944

After securing the Admiralties, MacArthur was ready to take the northern coast of New Guinea. In April General Kenney's planes neutralized the Japanese air field at Hollandia. On April 22, MacArthur's forces made amphibious landings near Hollandia and Aitap while Australians moved along the coast. This was a leap of 500 miles, trapping the Japanese 18th Army, increasing Japanese losses to 110,000 men, almost half of the 250,000 men originally available. The area was secured by May third.

On May 17, MacArthur moved again, 140 miles to Wadke, taken in three days against heavy resistance. Biak Island was needed for an air base and was therefore invaded on May 27, but 10,000 defenders held out until June 22. The Japanese Navy made two half-hearted attempts to bring in reinforcements, but finally gave up to concentrate on defense of the Marianas.

The Japanese 18th Army, trapped at Aitape, tried to break out to the west on July 11, but was mowed down. For 20 more days the starving Japanese attacked, then the Allies countered, wiping out the remnants by August 10. Japanese General Adachi later wrote that the history of his army was tragic after losing 10,000 men in the initial assault at Aitape.

On July 30, MacArthur jumped another 200 miles to Sansapor on the Vogelkop Peninsula at the western end of New Guinea. Another 25,000 Japanese were isolated and MacArthur was master of New Guinea, having advanced 1,800 miles in one year and standing only 600 miles from the Philippines.

MacArthur was asked by Washington if he shouldn't clean out the pockets in New Guinea, but MacArthur replied that it wasn't necessary. They posed no offensive threat. New Guinea was, no doubt, MacArthur's greatest achievement. Here he turned back the Japanese and destroyed them. Australian troops played no small part and General Kenney's airmen cleared the skies of Japanese planes, which aided the campaign immeasurably.

While the Navy and Marines struck at Peleliu in the Palaus, east of the Philippines, MacArthur next invaded Morotai in the Hamaheras on September 15. The island was taken with little resistance and now MacArthur was only 300 miles from the Philippines. Of greater significance he had bypassed the Dutch East Indies and the 200,000 Japanese troops there.

June 1944, Saipan and the Battle of the Philippine Sea

The Marianas chain consisted of 15 islands in an arc *425* miles from end to end. Only four were of major size, Guam, Tinian, Saipan, and Rota. After taking the Marshalls the U.S. needed the Marianas to move closer to Japan and isolate Truk. In February carrier planes and submarines attacked and sank 45,000 tons of merchant shipping. Three Marine and two Army divisions, 127,571 troops under Marine General H. M. Smith were to be used with Saipan the first objective. Vice Admiral Richmond Kelly Turner was in charge of the Amphibious Force involving 535 ships. Some of these sailed 2,400 miles from Guadalcanal, some traveled 3,700 miles from Pearl Harbor, and some came from the nearest island, Eniwetok, 1,000 miles away. Turner reported to the Fifth Fleet Commander, Admiral Spruance (the victor at Midway) whose total force was 800 ships.

The Japanese wanted to make the Marianas a part of their next line of defense and had plans for a maximum effort by air and sea. They were, however, unable to reinforce the army to any great extent due to troop ship losses at sea to U.S. submarines. General Saito had 22,700 troops and there were 6700 naval personnel on Saipan but there had not been time to build extensive defenses along the beach.

On June 11, preparation for invasion began with carrier planes raiding air fields in the Marianas while battleships blasted Saipan targets. On June 15, the Second and Fourth Marine divisions landed along four miles of beaches on the south west coast and by evening there were 20,000 men ashore. Artillery and mortar fire were devastating on the boats coming in and on infantry on the beach. Japanese infantry fought on the beach then pulled back to allow artillery fire to come in, causing 2,000 U.S. casualties the first day. The beachhead was pushed inland no more than a mile at the point of deepest penetration. At 3 A.M. on June 16, the Japanese attacked the Second Division flank with a furious charge. Finally stopped by Marines with the aid of tanks and naval gunfire, they withdrew with 700 dead. On D-Day the approach of the Japanese combined fleet was spotted near the Philippines.

The Japanese had lost their best navy pilots at Coral Sea and Midway. These were replaced but the second stringers were lost in the Solomons and over Rabaul. Without air power the Japanese fleet was held back until June of 1944. A third set of pilots were available with two to six months of training (compared to two years for U.S. Navy pilots). Now the Japanese determined to strike first, hit U.S. carriers, then using air and naval forces, deal the U.S. fleet a decisive blow. They had several advantages; their planes had a 100 mile longer range than U.S. planes, and they had land air forces on Guam, Yap, and Rota.

The Japanese expected Spruance to sail southwest to meet them and deployed 25 submarines in two lines north of the Admiralties. The U.S. found out about this, sent a fleet of destroyer escorts, and sank 17 of the subs (not a very promising beginning to the all out decisive battle).

The fleets concentrated, Spruance 180 miles west of Tinian, the Japanese west of the Philippines, sailing east into the Philippine Sea (which gave its name to the upcoming battle). Comparable strengths were:

	U.S.	Japan
Carriers	15	9
Battleships	7	5
Cruisers	21	13
Destroyers	69	28
Aircraft	956	473

Obviously the Japanese were inferior; their only chance was for a mighty first blow like the U.S. first strike at Midway. In late May and early June U.S submarines sank two of Ozawa's tankers and three destroyers before he could get started.

Task Force 58, under Vice Admiral Mitscher, included four task groups around carriers and one composed of Admiral "Chink" Lee's battleships (including several Pearl Harbor survivors). Most of the tactical decisions were made by Mitscher in Task Force 58 (which was known as TF 38 when operating with Halsey's Third Fleet.) Spruance sent one of the task groups up to Chici Jima and Iwo Jima to bomb air fields; this group returned to join the fleet. On June 19, carrier planes engaged Japanese aircraft over Guam and over 30 Japanese planes went down. Planes from U.S. carriers then proceeded to neutralize Guam and Rota, eventually clearing the air of all land based planes.

The Japanese launched four separate raids on the morning of June 19. The first was 69 planes, spotted 150 miles away at 10 A.M. U.S. fighter planes shot down 41; one enemy plane hit *South Dakota* with a bomb, but none got through to the carriers. Only 24 planes returned. The second raid, 130 planes, was also hard hit; 20 planes tried but missed hitting the battleships; six planes broke through to the carriers where they were shot down; 98 planes in all were lost. Submarines then sank two of the Japanese carriers, *Taiko* and *Shokaku* (one of the last two Pearl Harbor carriers still afloat.) The third raid of 47 planes never made contact, but seven were shot down anyway. At 11 A.M. the fourth raid, 82 planes was launched. These missed contact as well, but they were spotted and attacked. Only nine returned to the carriers. On this day, called the Great Marianas Turkey Shoot, Ozawa lost two carriers and 346 planes. The U.S. Navy lost 30 planes and had only one ship hit by a bomb.

At night the U.S. fleet turned west to pursue the Japanese, finally launching 216 planes at 4:20 P.M. on the twentieth, 275 miles from the Japanese! The target was spotted by 6:40 and attacked. Two oilers were sunk along with carrier *Hiyo*. *Zuikaku* was hit and another 65 Japanese planes shot down with a loss of 20 U.S.

planes. Returning U.S. planes came back between 9 and 11 P.M. in the dark, but every U.S. ship turned on their lights! Many a U.S. plane ran out of gas or crashed trying to land.

Total Japanese plane losses were 480; few of their pilots were recovered. U.S. plane losses rose to 130 but only 76 airmen were not recovered. The defeat was a crushing blow to the Japanese, eliminating their ability to attack or defend in the air.

Their surface vessels were now vulnerable if and when they should venture into waters contested by the U.S. Navy. Many a brave young Japanese pilot died in a hopeless cause to defend his government's plans for conquest and empire.

Back on Saipan on June 16 small gains were made; some of the enemy artillery were silenced. That night another counterattack struck the Second Division left flank, this time an infantry regiment and a tank regiment. The tanks were destroyed by bazookas and Marine self propelled artillery. Only 12 tanks survived while another 700 Japanese infantry went down. The Marines suffered another 1500 casualties the second day, but the beachhead was expanded and the Army 27th Division came ashore.

On the third day the island was crossed and the airfield taken. By June 23, six of the island's fourteen mile length had been occupied, but the terrain was getting higher.

Mount Tapotchau was overcome on June 25 as three U.S. divisions attacked abreast with tank-infantry teams.

On June 24–25, U.S. carriers attacked Japanese air bases at Iwo Jima, Guam, and Rota, destroying 95 Japanese planes.

The fighting slowed until July 1 when the U.S. offensive resumed. In the next four days progress accelerated with General Saito and Admiral Nagumo (of Pearl Harbor fame) committing suicide on July 6. On July 7, two or three thousand Japanese (the few still alive) attacked two 27th Division battalions along the west coast, overrunning the soldiers who fought tenaciously. Army artillery and tanks finally stopped the Japanese (including hundreds of walking wounded who joined the attack) but Army casualties were 668. The Japanese were through, however, and the entire island was occupied on the next day. The battle for Saipan was won but the U.S. suffered 14,111 casualties and Tinian and Guam in the Marianas still remained to be invaded. Saipan was a brutal contest with every yard contested.

The Battle for Monte Cassino, 1944

By February 1, the U.S. 34th Division had taken some foothills across the Rapido.

Above them loomed 3,000 foot high Monte Castellone and to their left, dominating the river and Route 6 leading north, Monte Cassino topped by a monastery. By February 4, the 34th, reinforced by the depleted 36th Division, had captured Monte Castellone and turned left along the narrow crest, but by February 10, the two U.S. divisions had suffered 4,200 casualties, 80 percent in some front line battalions. They were so isolated that supply, reinforcement, and evacuation were extremely hazardous. The men were so weak from cold and hunger that some had to be carried down by stretcher when replaced. One U.S. soldier was found three years later, his skeleton leaning against a boulder, his rusty helmet and rifle still with him. The U.S. divisions were replaced with an Indian and a New Zealand Division, two good outfits.

By the third of February, the German Fourteenth Army had arrived near Anzio in strength and attacked the beachhead. By February 16, the Allies in the beachhead had been pushed back to positions six miles from the beach and the forces attacking the Gustav Line were called upon to attack to help relieve pressure at Anzio. The Germans attacked at Anzio again and gained another mile before being stopped. The Germans had the equivalent of five and a half divisions to four Allied but the Allies had air superiority when the weather permitted. On February 18, the U.S. Third and First Armored Divisions attacked the German flank and advanced. The Germans had lost 5,000 men but attacked one more time, losing 2,000 more. The beachhead was finally safe.

At Monte Cassino the Indian Division claimed that they were being shelled by Germans in the monastery. As a result the monastery was leveled by U.S. bombers, unnecessarily, as it was later learned that the Germans had not been using the monastery. The attack on Monte Casino was made by Indians, New Zealanders, and by Poles, but always with no success. The main problem with these assaults was that the defenders equaled the attackers in numerical strength. Finally General Alexander decided to quietly move Eighth Army in from the Adriatic lines to support Fifth Army. Elaborate deceptions were put in place to convince the Germans that another amphibious operation was about to take place north of Rome, and that forces still remained on the Adriatic side of Italy. Risks were enormous but the Germans were completely deceived.

Alexander packed thirteen divisions into a 20 mile front defended by four German divisions. Two German divisions (one armored) were held back to defend against the amphibious attack. Two other German armored divisions were kept near Anzio to guard against an Allied breakthrough there.

From the sea inland the Allies had a U.S. Corps (two divisions, the 85th and 88th), French Corps (over four divisions, 100,000 men), Eighth Army (six divisions including two armored and two Canadian), and a Polish corps (two brigades with a tank brigade).

On May 11, the big offensive jumped off. The Poles took heavy losses near Monte Cassino, the British made no headway up the Liri Valley below Monte Cassino, but the French broke through and turned right to outflank the Germans in the valley. The Americans made no headway at first, but by the thirteenth they, too, had broken through.

When the French occupied the hills overlooking the Liri Valley, the Germans had to withdraw from the Gustav Line. On May 18, the Poles occupied Monte

Cassino, unopposed. The Poles had taken many casualties in their futile attacks on Monte Cassino as had three other Allied divisions. The only consolation is that four German divisions were also hard hit in the fighting. By May 25, the Americans rushing up along the coast linked up with the Anzio forces.

Instead of proceeding to the northeast to cut Route 7, General Mark Clark ordered Fifth Army to move up Highway 6 to Rome. This move was sensational but allowed elements of the German Tenth Army to escape. History has not been kind to General Clark for this decision. Rome was occupied on June 4, but only 20,000 Germans had been captured. Rome was taken finally, four months behind schedule.

The Allies in Italy had 28 divisions to 21 depleted German. If they had continued north they could conceivably have reached the Alps, but it is hard to believe that they would have quickly fought over and through that formidable obstacle. As it was Allied plans for an invasion of southern France pulled major forces out of Italy. The greatest opportunities were in France where Allied forces were to concentrate and drive into the German heartland. The Italian campaign was necessary, however. Before the invasion of France the Allies had to fight somewhere, and Italy was the place.

Stilwell's Chinese Attack in Burma, 1944

In 1942 General "Vinegar" Joe Stilwell was assigned as Chang Kai-shek's military advisor. Chang was the Generalissimo of Nationalist China which had been fighting the Japanese sine 1937. Stilwell went to Burma to command the Chinese army there during the futile British-Chinese defense of that country. Burma was important to China because all the supplies from the Allies had to pass through Burma to get to China. The Burmese railroad went only as far north as Lashio and the road from there to Yunnan Province in China was known as the Burma Road.

Stilwell had tried to convince his own Chinese and the British to stand, fight, and attack in 1942, but the British were unable to do this, and the Chinese under Stilwell seldom complied with his orders. Instead Chang frequently sent orders directly to his generals, bypassing Stilwell, usually ordering defense or retreat. The Chinese war strategy was to avoid combat, thereby preserving their army. Poorly equipped and trained as they were, this is understandable, but was not acceptable to Stilwell, who was responsible for the defense of Burma.

During 1943 a number of Chinese divisions were assembled and trained in India, provided with modern equipment, and by the end of the year, Stilwell had a small modern army in which he (but no one else) had confidence. After the loss of Burma the only way to get supplies into China was to fly them over the Himalayas (over the "hump"). An operation was planned for early 1944 to retake Burma and reopen the Burma Road. It was essential to keep China in the war to prevent the huge Japanese army there from being sent to fight the Allies elsewhere. A strong Japanese offensive in 1943 in China added impetus to the Burma plan, and another offensive in 1944 served to remind both the Chinese and the British of the urgency. In late 1943 American engineers with multi-national labor started building a road from Ledo in India into northwest Burma. The road would advance only if fighting could push the Japanese back.

Japan had only six divisions in Burma, one on the Bay of Bengal, three in the northwest opposite Imphal and Kohima in India, and two in northern Burma. A joint effort by British and Chinese forces in early 1944 was planned. The Chinese forces consisted of X Force, two divisions (later three) near Ledo under Stilwell, and Y Force in Yunnan Province under General Wei Li Huang.

The British were not ready to move in late 1943, and Stilwell decided to attack from Ledo, hoping that success would encourage the British to attack and Chang to release the Yunnan army. Stilwell's army would be unsupported and the operation was risky but Stilwell was paid to fight and that is what he did.

X Force was at the Chindwin River when Stilwell arrived on December 21, 1943. On the twenty-third the Chinese attacked elements of the Japanese 18th Division on both flanks at Yupbang and wiped out the whole force by the twenty-ninth.

Neither Lord Mountbatten (British Theatre Commander) nor Chang Kai-shek would initiate offensive actions, each waiting for the other to do something. Stilwell was in a dangerous position where the Japanese could possibly concentrate six divisions against him. At this time, however, Frank Merrill arrived with an American regiment, Merrill's Marauders, with a tank unit consisting of 87 light and medium tanks under Colonel Rothwell Brown. With these significant reinforcements Stilwell moved forward again, taking Taipha Ga on February 1, 1944.

Maingkwan, 15 miles south in the Hukawng Valley, was the next objective, but the Japanese were reinforced by elements of their 56th Division. Plans called for the Chinese to attack frontally while Merrill and Brown made a wide envelopment move to take Walawbum, eight miles south of Maingkwan. Merrill took off on February 24 taking Walawbum on March 4. One Chinese regiment bypassed Maingkwan ambushing the Japanese retreating from the main attack. The Chinese 22nd Division had beaten two of the best in the Japanese Army.

Soon after this battle Mountbatten flew in to see Stilwell with 16 fighter escorts. Stilwell's entire air support consisted of just four planes.

Meanwhile on the Bay of Bengal the British XV Indian Corps had occupied Maungdaw, Burma, in January. They were attacked by the Japanese 55th Division in February and their supply line was cut. Rather than the usual retreat, the British made a stand with supplies delivered by air until the Japanese attacks tailed off. On March 7, well inland, the Japanese 33rd Division attacked the 17th Indian Division, moving into India until the 17th made a stand at Imphal. On March 14, two Japanese divisions, further north, moved into India threatening Kohima, cutting the road from Imphal to Kohima. At this point the Japanese were close to cutting the supply line to Stilwell and to the air base ferrying supplies to

China. Again the British made a stand and in bitter fighting took the steam out of the Japanese. British General William (Bill) Slim can be given credit for putting backbone into the Empire troops that stopped this offensive. Slim was the one British commander in the area for whom Stilwell had high regard. The Japanese were stopped in April, pushed back in June, and forced out of India in July. This was the last Japanese offensive in Burma.

In spite of British reverses in March, Stilwell determined to keep pushing. His next objective was Jambu Bum in the hills south of the Hukawng Valley, overlooking the Mogaung Valley. Jambu Bum fell on March 19, and the next day the Japanese pulled back from other positions on the flank. By March 31, the Chinese had taken Shaduzup with the help of another envelopment by Merrill's Marauders, now led by Colonel Frank Hunter (Merrill had had a heart attack and was out of action).

The monsoon season starts in May, and Stilwell decided to gamble; go for Myitkyina, 100 miles away. The Marauders, backed by one Chinese regiment, would go over 6,000 foot mountains to sneak into lightly defended Myitkyina while Stilwell's army moved down the Mogaung Valley. Once Hunter had the Myitkyina airstrip, a division of Chinese troops would be flown in. This was a very ambitious and courageous plan but it offered an alternative to fighting down narrow mountain passes. Stilwell acquired another division from Chang who was much impressed with Stilwell's successes. The Marauders started out on April 28, and by May 17 they had the Myitkyina airstrip. A Chinese regiment was then flown in according to plan and attacks on the Japanese in Myitkyina were launched. The Japanese brought in 5,000 or more men while Stilwell had yet to take Kamiang, a good sixty miles away.

The rains came and Stilwell worried over the status of his troops in Myitkyina who were taking heavy losses while he could only inch his way down the Mogaung Valley. Finally, on June 16, Kamiang was taken from the Japanese who suffered more losses. On June 22, the remnants of the Japanese 18th Division were destroyed and by the 27th Stilwell had Mogaung, only thirty miles from Myitkyina. Here he was assisted by the British Chindits, assigned to his command for this campaign. By July 26, the Japanese in Myitkyina were reduced to only 400 men and the town fell on August 4.

Stilwell had moved across Burma to positions on the Irriwaddy River not far from the Chinese border and within striking distance of the Burma Road. He had beaten the Japanese with Chinese troops and set an example for all the other reluctant forces. A U.S. commander for all Chinese armies was considered and Stilwell was recommended for the job. He was given a fourth star putting him in a class with MacArthur, Eisenhower, Arnold and Marshall. Chang Kai-shek, however, did not want the dominating general that Stilwell was, fearing that such a man would become too powerful. Stilwell was therefore recalled back to the United States, sent home, and asked to be silent about Nationalist China. Stilwell's knowledge of the corruption in Chang's government could become harmful to the war effort if it should reach the public, and so he languished for the rest of the war as a non combatant.

U.S. General Chennault, in charge of American Air Forces in China, was a strong advocate of air power and believed that the Japanese in China could be stopped with air power. The disastrous results of the Japanese offensive in China in 1944 not only disproved that concept, but the very air bases being used were overrun by the Japanese. This lesson was surely not remembered by the Johnson Administration during the Vietnam War, when too much was expected of air domination.

The Invasion of France, June, 1944

From the earliest days of 1942 the U.S. and Britain planned to invade Europe as soon as strength would permit. As months went by it became clear that the only practical place to fight in 1942 was in Africa, and the invasion of France would have to wait. Once forces were committed in Africa, Sicily, and Italy, the invasion of France was not possible until 1944. Sufficient landing craft would become available in May of 1944 and the invasion was then scheduled for June.

Stalin had insisted all along that the Allies do something to tie down German forces. Certainly in late 1942, Russia was fighting for survival. The Allies did tie down Axis forces in Africa by direct action, and forced the Germans to keep substantial numbers of divisions all over Europe to counter the threat of an amphibious operation. By mid 1942 Axis forces were located as follows:

Location	Number of Divisions
Finland	6
Russia, north	40
Russia, cental	41
Russia, south	41
Rumania	36
Balkans	21
Italy	26
Norway	12
France, west	38
France	12

In 1942 the Russians faced 164 divisions, Tito (with partisan forces up to 150,000 men) tied up over 20 divisions in Yugoslavia, and the Allies tied down 88 more along Europe's southern and western coast lines. In France, the most likely place for invasion, the Germans had 50 divisions.

By mid 1944 the Russians had 580 divisions but even so could only move the Germans back slowly. The Allies had 31 divisions in the Mediterranean and 39 divisions in England. In Italy the Allies faced equal forces, but in England 39 divisions forced the Germans to deploy 62 divisions from one end of Europe to the other.

Obviously once Allied armies were landed in Europe, there was a possibility of a rapid, huge German concentration against them. To avoid this air raids were conducted for long periods against road and railroad access to the landing beaches. Dummy armies were created, some on paper, some with wood and canvas to make the Germans think the invasion was only a feint, that the real invasion would be elsewhere.

The closest point to England was the Pas de Calais area, and the Germans concentrated there. Any landing point had to be within Allied fighter range and not too many good beaches fit that requirement. The next most likely landing area was Normandy and here the Allies planned to commit their forces.

Five divisions would land along the northern Normandy coast from Caen to Carentan on five beaches. The Germans had three divisions (352nd, 716th, 711th) in this area with three more around Cherbourg, the 21st Panzer Division behind Caen, the 12th SS Panzer 50 miles east of Caen and the Panzer Lehr Division 60 miles southeast of Caen. If all these forces rushed to the beaches the first day, the Allies could be defeated.

From east to west, the landing site labels and the assigned divisions were:

Beach	Divisions
Sword	British 3rd
Juno	Canadian 3rd
Gold	British 50th
Omaha	U.S. 1st, 29th
Utah	U.S. 4th

On the east flank, the British 6th Airborne Division would be landed by glider and parachute. On the west flank, the U.S. 82nd and 101st Airborne Divisions would be landed to prevent the German 91st Division from reaching the beach. Allied naval gunfire and air support would be used to counter the lack of artillery and armor on the first day.

The weather turned bad, and as manageable tides were rare, it was necessary to schedule the invasion on June 6. Surf was high and the weather was considered just barely acceptable that day but the die was cast.

During the night of June 5, the airborne troops landed, but were scattered badly by missed drops, glider crashes, and high winds. The 82nd landed right on top of the German 91st Division. Nevertheless, key objectives were taken and the invasion flanks secured until ground forces could move inland.

At dawn German observers on the Normandy coast saw the English Channel filled with ships as far as they could see in all directions, 700 warships, 2,700 support ships, and 2,500 landing craft, the greatest armada the world had ever seen.

On Sword the British landed without much difficulty and moved inland about seven miles, about three miles shy of the objective, Caen. On Juno and Gold the Canadians and British moved inland about five miles and formed a common front.

On Omaha the German 352nd Division had extensive fortifications overlooking the beach and met the incoming Big Red One with devastating fire. Most of the U.S. tanks were lost in the surf, and the men remained behind a sea wall much of the day. By midday the situation was very much in doubt, but gradually small groups of men led by officers of varying ranks worked around and behind the German positions. By days end 55,000 men were ashore and had moved a few miles inland, but there were 4649 casualties. This was Tarawa all over again but on a larger scale.

On Utah the landings met only light resistance and by nightfall the Allies had 155,000 men ashore in Normandy.

The huge area covered by the invasion surprised and confused the Germans who could not decide what was happening. The 21st Panzer Division did move into Caen and held that town, but the 12th Panzer and Panzer Lehr Divisions were held back for one whole day due to lack of a decision by Hitler's headquarters. Rommel, commander of the German forces had gone to Germany, believing that the weather would prevent an invasion that day. The German 15th Army was held at Pas de Calais in the belief that that was the place for the real invasion. (This decision was made in Germany. If a good description of the armada that had appeared could have been supplied, there could have been little doubt that this was the invasion.)

As the days went by, each opponent rushed in forces as fast as possible. For the Germans, this was not easy as vehicles had to take long circuitous routes to reach the front. By June 12, the Allies managed to link up with adjacent divisions, but their deepest penetration was in the St-Lo, Caumont area, about 20 miles. On both flanks, Caen and Carentan, penetration was less than 10 miles. The country was broken with streams and hedgerows which the Germans used for a stubborn defense. The U.S. objective was the port of Cherbourg, desperately needed to supply the huge forces accumulating. Two temporary harbors at Arromanches and Colleville had been shipped in but these were destroyed by a storm on June 19–22. By this time sixteen German divisions faced twenty Allied divisions.

On June 18, U.S. forces had crossed the Cotentin Peninsula, isolating Cherbourg and three German divisions; Cherbourg was taken on June 27. German generals wanted to retreat, shorten their lines, and pull out their armored divisions for a counterattack, but Hitler wanted to destroy the Allies on the beaches.

The British were unable to make headway in the Caen sector, but they faced seven panzer divisions while U.S. forces were opposed by only one. At this time the Allies had only two armored divisions ashore, British 7th, and U.S. 2nd.

Montgomery was temporarily in charge of troops ashore until Eisenhower could come over from England. The U.S.1st Army under Bradley had two Corps,

VII under Collins, and V under Gerow. The British 2nd Army was commanded by Dempsey. Most of the Allied armor and Patton were still in England.

By June 30, U.S. forces faced south from St. Lo to La Haye-du-Puits. St Lo was taken on July 18. On that day Allied air forces dropped 6,800 tons of bombs on German lines near Caen, followed by an assault with three British armored divisions. The Germans quickly reacted, however, and destroyed 400 British tanks.

By July 25, U.S. forces had torturously moved down the south coast of Normandy to Coutances. On this day 4,000 tons of bombs were dropped on a small sector of the German lines according to Bradley's plan Cobra. At this time the German Army Group B was commanded by von Kluge as Rommel had been wounded by R.A.F. fighters.

On July 25, after the massive bombing, Collins VII Corps advanced two miles and on the next day broke through German lines. Near the west coast Middleton's VIII Corps also advanced with three infantry divisions. On July 27 Bradley called for Patton. Bradley had been promoted over Patton who was Bradley's senior, and Bradley hesitated to bring Patton into action under him. Neither Ike or Bradley were certain they could control the free wheeling Patton, but when the breakthrough occurred, Allied plans called for Patton and a new Third Army.

Patton and the Third Army

Patton should have been in command of U.S. forces in Tunisia from the beginning, and he sat idle all during the period between Sicily and D-Day in France, and this is also unfortunate. If he had been assigned to the Italian campaign at Anzio, Patton most likely would have made the difference between victory and stalemate. But, bringing in Patton at this moment in Normandy was just what the struggling Allies needed.

Patton was given the minor title of Deputy Army Commander and ordered only to supervise the VIII Corps. Patton could have been completely demoralized by the humiliating treatment he had received. His outspoken public comments and his slapping of a shell shocked soldier in Sicily had almost destroyed his career, but he worried about only one thing, that the war would be over before he could fulfill his destiny. Now Patton took his staff to Middleton's CP (Command Post), looked at the disposition of his four infantry divisions and two armored divisions, then looked at the map. The key town, the hub of roads and railroads, was Avranches, forty miles away.

Patton ordered Wood (4th Armored Division Commander) and Grow (6th Armored Commander) to lead the advance. U.S. Army doctrine was to attack with infantry supported by armor, but Patton wanted speed and power. General Wood had been ridden over by a jeep but he was, amazingly enough, still functional.

Patton was eventually slated to take over a Third Army consisting of four corps with thirteen divisions. During the breakout, however, Patton only had VIII Corps, but once he had the authority, Patton's divisions started to move. Bradley's orders to Middleton had been to keep pressure on the Germans. This implied following the German retreat. Patton's concept was something he had practiced in the 1941 maneuvers. Dash around them, past them, cut off their supplies and retreat. Confuse them and force them to run away or surrender. This was the German blitzkrieg concept—something Patton carried with him from World War I.

On July 28, the 4th and 6th Armored moved through the infantry with the 4th taking Coutances. On the twenty-ninth, 6th Armored stopped at the Sienne River halfway to Avranches. Patton drove down to find Grow motionless at the river waiting for his advance force to find a bridge. Patton swore at Grow, waded out into the river, only two feet deep, and ordered Grow to cross (Grow was one of Patton's favorites but Patton demanded speed and warned his generals not to stop on the wrong side of a river).

Patton borrowed 400 trucks from a quartermaster outfit to speed up his advance.

On July 30, 4th Armored dashed past German 7th Army Headquarters and reached Avranches. On the thirty-first, 4th Armored was south of Avranches as 6th Armored closed in on the town.

Bradley ordered VIII Corps to halt at the Selune River but 6th Armored was already across. Patton then ordered Grow and Wood to move into Brittany. VIII Corps had actually been directed to move into Brittany and Patton was not out of compliance but he, many times, ignored orders to halt, always claiming he was past the points designated.

On July 4, German Commander in Chief West, von Runstead, had been asked what to do. His suggestion to sue for peace was not pleasing to Hitler and von Runstead was replaced by a politically acceptable von Kluge who then wore two hats. On July 29, von Kluge reported his left flank gone and the front ripped wide open. Hitler adopted a scheme to cut off Patton's divisions and deluded himself into believing that this would solve all his problems.

On August 1, Patton took over command of Third Army. He picked up XV Corps consisting of the 5th Armored Division and the 83rd and 90th Divisions transferred from VIII Corps. He spoke to his officers telling them to push hard, that this results in more German casualties and fewer American. He told them not to worry about their flanks, that this was a German problem, and there would be a constant advance.

Patton did not worry about his flanks unless he saw a reason, then he moved to counter the threat. His lack of concern was based on knowledge or a sense of knowing where the enemy had the capability of causing damage. There weren't too many enemy forces around capable of hurting an armored division.

On August 1, Patton ordered the 6th Armored and 79th Divisions to take Brest, 200 miles away, bypassing all resistance. The 80th and 4th Armored Divisions were ordered to take Rennes, halfway across Brittany. XV Corps was held back near Avranches to prevent the Germans from cutting the narrow supply route.

After two months the Allies had one million men in France in ten corps, with three more corps ready, against only seven German corps.

By August 4, Patton was looking south and east, visualizing a huge sweep to trap the Germans in Normandy. He moved at a speed far beyond the concept of Allied planners but as he moved east it became obvious to anyone looking at a map that a move behind the Germans was possible. XV Corps was ordered to move to the southeast and his new XX Corps was sent to the south to guard against any German moves from that quarter.

XV Corps, by August 6, was across the Mayenne River, moving east to Le Mans. First Army had taken Vire but the British were still at Caen.

On August 7, the Germans attacked at Mortain, hoping to capture Avranches. Their corps of three weak armored divisions and one infantry division hit VII Corps, the 30th Division primarily. The Germans gained some ground but Bradley scraped up a few divisions and stopped the attack in 24 hours. The defense of Mortain was a brave endeavor by U.S. infantry, many of whom died in position facing the enemy. The Germans tried again on August 11 but were stopped and pushed back by the 2nd Armored Division.

Patton, sensing the need for better information, formed a number of scouting groups, each of 30 men in six jeeps and six armored cars. These groups traveled far in advance of the tanks and gave Patton valuable information about enemy dispositions. (All great generals went to great lengths to find out enemy strength and location, one reason why they became great generals.)

On August 7, Patton learned that Angers, 100 miles south of Avranches was undefended. Walker's XX Corps (one division at this time, the 5th with another, the 35th, soon to join) moved south to take Angers and Nantes on the Loire before the Germans could take these towns. This anchored the southern flank against a German concentration south of the Loire.

On August 8, XV Corps, moving east, took Le Mans, 75 miles from Avranches and began moving north. On August 9, Bradley ordered Patton to move only as far north as Alencon, 30 miles from Le Mans. XV Corps was now moving behind the German Army pointed straight at Alencon, Argentan, Falaise and Caen.

Montgomery launched an attack south from Caen to Falaise on August 8, but the attack was made with just two armored divisions and stalled 12 miles from Falaise on the 9th. On this day Patton was past Bradley's Alencon objective, moving on Argentan. Ike's headquarters (SHAEF, Supreme Headquarters, Allied Expeditionary Force) now planned to encircle the Germans with the Americans taking Argentan from the south, and the British taking Falaise then closing to Argentan from the north. On the twelfth, Haislip's XV Corps (with the French 2nd Armored and the U.S. 5th Armored followed by the 79th and 90th Divisions) took Argentan and sent recon units within two miles of Falaise with no Germans in front of them. The British were still a long way from Falaise and were certainly not going to make Argentan any time soon. Patton asked Bradley, Eisenhower, and Montgomery for permission to take Falaise, close with the British and trap the Germans.

Neither Bradley, Ike, or Montgomery would agree to change plans, and Patton was ordered several times not to bring forces north of Argentan. XV Corps stayed at Argentan while the bulk of nineteen German divisions slipped away. The gap wasn't closed until August 19, and only 50,000 prisoners were taken. If Patton had been allowed to close the gap on the 12th and 13th, it is quite possible that Germany could not have defended her western front and the war might have ended in 1944 without all the agony and casualties that followed. Ike later admitted that an opportunity had been missed. His decision not to change the U.S./British boundary was probably based on British sensitivity. Ike was often forced to alter strategy to avoid offending his Allies, and based on the success of his efforts it is hard to criticize. It had been difficult to plan ahead too precisely as Patton invariably moved faster than anticipated and the British slower. Patton was well aware that the Falaise fiasco would end up in the history books, but it is interesting to see how various accounts downplay the magnitude of the mistake made there.

The Liberation of France

Eisenhower did not publicly announce that Third Army was commanded by Patton until August 12. This was not military secrecy; this was politics. Too much glory for Patton took away from the publicity due to other generals. Certainly there were plenty of good professional soldiers in this army, but Patton dominated the headlines. By August 14 Patton had XII Corps and his complete army. XII Corps moved east from Le Mans to Orleans. Further north, XX Corps moved east to Chartres and still farther north XV Corps moved from Argentan to Dreux. These objectives were taken by August 20, and Third Army was then only 35 miles from Paris. By August 23, Walton Walker (who would command in Korea six years later) and XX Corps were on the Seine. Word came from SHAEF, however, that Patton was to hold and not take Paris (although his army was approaching the Seine both east and west of the city). The French 2nd Armored Division was ordered to enter Paris and claim they were part of 1st Army. The 2nd Armored tankers under General Leclerc, established as a valued and proud part of Third Army told everyone they were Third Army. (British Broadcasting Co. also announced correctly that Paris was liberated by Third Army much to Patton's joy.) The French entered the city on August 25, followed by the 4th Division of 1st Army, shipped 100 miles to make the parade.

The Allied Armies approaching the Seine consisted of U.S. 3rd on the right, U.S. 1st, British 2nd and Canadian 1st. The Canadians turned to attack the port of Le Havre while the British and U.S. First Army raced north to the Somme, sixty miles away.

German resistance now was almost nonexistent and the Allies reached the Somme by August 31. On that day, Patton, moving east, closed in on Verdun on the Meuse. over 100 miles east of Paris, only 60 miles from the German border.

The Allied drive was primarily parallel to the coast. and not, except for Patton. east to Germany. The prime reason for this was the need for ports to supply the growing Allied armies, now 2,000,000 men. At Verdun Patton was 240 miles from Normandy and with few railroads he relied on trucks (The Red Ball Express) to keep him supplied. The German strategy of allowing troops to be cut off and isolated in port cities (there were some 200,000 Germans in this category) now began to pay dividends. The Allies were running out of gasoline. In fact there was only enough to supply one of the four armies and the most critical objectives were the port cities in the British sector. Eisenhower therefore assigned priorities for gasoline, and Patton became the lowest. Third Army now advanced toward Metz with limited forces and met with stiffer resistance. A quick push with strong forces could certainly have broken through the West Wall defenses before they were heavily defended but this was not to be. The British pushed into Belgium and took Antwerp but failed to clear the northern estuary shore line where the Germans prevented use of the approaches to the port.

Von Kluge was called to Berlin for questioning and committed suicide. He was replaced by Model who tried to find some forces to use to stop Patton. German casualties for the period of June–August were 700,000 on the Eastern Front, 500,000 on the Western.

On August 15, French and U.S. forces landed on the Riviera, the French Mediterranean coast, against light resistance. By August 28, Toulon and Marseille were taken. The U.S. 7th Army under General Patch, and the new French Army B under General de Tassigny (all under U.S. General Devers) moved up the Rhone River to Lyons which fell on September 3. Soon afterward these forces moved up to the German border to fall in on Patton's right flank.

A Bridge Too Far

Supreme Headquarters (SHAEF) visualized the advance to be on a broad front. A limited push by only one army was too easy to oppose. To advance on a broad front however demanded huge quantities of supplies, far more than could be supplied from Normandy. Ports, however, only became available as Germans surrendered as follows:

Le Havre	September 12
Brest	September 19
Boulogne	September 22
Calais	September 30
Antwerp	November 26 (first ship arrival)

Once Antwerp was cleared for use, shipping tonnage increased from 10,000 to 19,000 tons per day within one week.

Montgomery, in early September, vehemently pushed for approval of a plan to push north into Holland, partly to clear the port cities in Belgium and Holland, partly to cross the Rhine near Arnhem where the Rhine turns east. Here Montgomery expected light resistance and an end run around the German defenses. Monty obtained Ike's approval, borrowed the U.S. 82nd and 101st Airborne Divisions, added his own First Airborne, and a Polish Parachute Brigade. By September 17, the British were 60 miles from Arnhem when the assault began. The 82nd dropped into Eindhoven, securing bridges over the canals. The 101st landed at Graves and Nijmegen, taking a bridge over the Maas River. The British First Airborne took Arnhem (on the north bank of the Rhine) and the bridge over the Rhine. The British XXX Corps was to strike north to Arnhem before the Germans could react.

Unfortunately, however, the British First Airborne dropped in the midst of two refitting panzer divisions. Lacking tanks and heavy artillery the British paratroopers were in serious trouble, but they set up a defensive perimeter in Arnhem and around the bridge.

XXX Corps moved to Eindhoven by the 18th but there the advance was limited to one road surrounded by water. Nijmegen was reached on September 19 and the Waal River crossed on the twentieth only 20 miles from Arnhem, but then the advance stalled. The Polish Brigade was dropped on the south bank of the Rhine near Arnhem on the twenty-first but was unable to prevent German recapture of the bridge.

By September 26, First Airborne was finished. Only 2,000 escaped across the Rhine, leaving 8,000 captured or casualties.

No additional ports were taken with this exercise and the advance was not directly into Germany but north, almost perpendicular to the road to Berlin. Certainly, Montgomery hoped to snatch some Pattonic glory by liberating Belgium and Holland and by invading Germany, but his plan sacrificed an airborne division in country easily defended by limited forces. Allied Headquarters approved this plan but there must have been some head shaking doubts by Ike's staff who almost certainly gave in to political pressure.

It would have been better to assign the British on the Channel flank to the immediate objective of freeing Antwerp and the other ports. As it was, the U.S. Army was stymied for lack of gasoline, and a quick breakthrough to Germany was forfeited. A plan for multiple thrusts toward Germany would have been a better one with the size of the thrusts based upon the quantity of gasoline available. Patton thought he could do it with Third Army in a single drive and he considered this scheme to be a certainty. Patton felt that he was fighting Germany, the British, and Allied Headquarters.

The Battle of the Bulge

By the end of September, U.S. 9th and 1st Armies were at the German border and Third Army had reached Metz along the Moselle. By this time the Germans had established a good defense along their West Wall. The one month delay for the British sideshow turned a rout into a slugging match. There was bitter fighting by First Army in the Huertgen Forest and at Aachen. Patton was stymied at the fortress of Metz, which was not taken until November 18. By December, from north to south, the British 2nd Army, U.S. 9th, 1st, 3rd, 7th, and French 1st Armies were at the German border. The Canadian 1st Army had been clearing Germans from the Scheldt Estuary in order to free Antwerp. The Allies occupied a line along the Roar, Our, and Saar Rivers all the way to Switzerland. On December 4, Patton broke through the West Wall and crossed the Saar, but these months brought heavy casualties as every advance was against strongly fortified positions.

Allied forces, 70 divisions in all, held a front of 500 miles. Hodges First Army held 120 miles from Aachen to Luxembourg with three corps, VII, V, and VIII. General Middleton's VIII Corps with only four divisions held an 85 mile front in the Ardennes where hilly, wooded terrain was considered a poor place to attack.

During the fall the Germans began to form new divisions to build up a fresh assault army. Many of these had been used to plug holes in the defenses, but Sixth Panzer Army stayed back and slowly grew. At the end of October the Germans decided to launch a surprise attack against the weak VIII Corps front in the Ardennes with the objective, Antwerp. Capture of this port would split the Allies, permit isolation and destruction of some of their forces, and create huge supply problems. It was a desperate gamble, but Germany's last chance to reverse its fortunes. There was a better chance to do something in the west than in the east where the Russians were in complete control.

The Germans accumulated 24 divisions in three armies, 5th Panzer, 6th Panzer, and the 7th. Most of the Allied intelligence officers predicted German collapse as there was an attack attitude everywhere, but there was one G-2 (intelligence officer) in Hodges First Army who did warn of a possible large scale German attack perhaps before Christmas. He was Colonel "Monk" Dickson, the same man who correctly predicted the German attack at Kasserine in Tunisia. Unfortunately Dickson's report also mentioned other possibilities (as was the custom at the time) and was diluted by numerous intelligence reports from other headquarters predicting numerous other events. As the Allies were busy planning attacks, Dickson's lonely warning received little attention.

It wasn't possible to be strong everywhere, and the Battle of the Bulge was made possible when the Allies lost their momentum in September. On the morning of December 16, on the northern flank of VIII Corps, the 14th Cavalry Group covered the gap between VIII Corps and V Corps on their left. The green

106th Division, further south, was in the line only five days and had two regiments forward in the Schnee Eifel.

On their right, covering a distance of 27 miles was the worn out 28th Division. To their right was a combat team of the 9th Armored Division, north of Echternach, and on the VIII Corps south flank, the battered 4th Division stretched south toward Third Army.

The Germans attacked early on December 16 along a 100 mile front, with orders which stressed surprise and speed. Sixth Panzer Army, in the north, pointed towards St. Vith, 8 miles west; Fifth Panzer Army headed for Bastogne, 20 miles west; Seventh Army moved into Luxembourg to guard the southern flank. Plans called for reaching the Meuse River, 60 miles east, in four days.

The Allies did not believe the Germans had the strength to make a strong offensive and made no special provisions for meeting one. There was no way that VIII Corps alone could stop the Germans no matter what defensive measures they took.

Sixth Panzer struck V Corps 2nd and 99th Divisions and the 14th Mechanized Cavalry Group. These units fought and the hard pressed 2nd and 99th Divisions were soon fighting in front, flank, and rear. The commander of the 14th Mechanized Cavalry, however, ordered a withdrawal, opening a large hole which Sixth Panzer poured through, bypassing the 422nd and 423rd Regiments of the 106th Division. (Withdrawal to save a unit in such cases jeopardizes the safety of all neighboring units and is absolutely unacceptable. The 14th Mechanized Cavalry commander was relieved, but the damage was done.) Another breakthrough occurred just south of the 106th Division and by nightfall the two forward regiments were in danger.

Some units of the 28th Division fought, but others, quickly bypassed, pulled back.

By days end the roads to the rear were jammed with retreating U.S. vehicles. A picture of the situation was not immediately clear to Allied officers, but it was soon obvious that a major German offensive was underway on a broad front.

Late on the sixteenth, Ike began the counter moves. Two airborne divisions were transferred to First Army. Two more divisions were ordered over from England; the 7th Armored Division was ordered to assist VIII Corps, and the 10th Armored Division was requested from Patton.

On the seventeenth, the 99th and 2nd Divisions were pushed back, but held the crucial northern shoulder, the 2nd Division performing magnificently. The 422nd and 423rd Regiments were just about cut off. The 106th Division commander could have ordered them to attack to the rear, but did not want to jeopardize the VIII Corps defense without orders. Elements of the 9th Armored Division counterattacked near Echternach. Further south the 424th Regiment of the 106th Division began a fighting withdrawal.

Combat Command B of the 7th Armored Division moved toward St. Vith from the north with orders to support the 106th Division but the roads were so jammed with retreating vehicles that forward movement was delayed, then stopped. Hope for the two regiments in the Schnee Eifel began to fade. The 291st Engineer Combat Battalion held a roadblock near Malmedy. Various other groups stopped, fought, and held up the German advance. In the south, the 4th Division and 9th Armored units were reinforced by elements of the 10th Armored. Fighting doggedly, these forces held the southern shoulder near Echternach.

On the eighteenth the 101st Airborne arrived at Bastogne and the 82nd Airborne reached Werbomont, 25 miles northwest of St. Vith. That same day Patton was called to a meeting with Bradley and asked what Third Army could do. Patton replied that he could attack with three divisions and promised to start the 4th Armored to a jump-off point at Longwy (40 miles from Bastogne) by the night of the 19th Patton also stated that the 80th Division could start for Luxembourg on the 20th and the 26th Division would be alerted. Patton returned to his Command Post and directed his staff to carry out the moves. The next day, the 19th, Ike called for a staff meeting at Allied headquarters. Over the last two weeks, Patton had, on several occasions, considered the possibility of a German attack in the Ardennes and now that the crisis had arrived his plans were already conceived.

Meanwhile, as Allied units were transferred, Ike rearranged army boundaries to suit the changing order of the divisions. The 30th Division arrived at Malmedy, extending the northern defense line to the west, but the Germans were already attacking Spa and other towns 10 miles northwest of Malmedy, only 20 miles from Liege and the Meuse.

At Spa a fight was made by cooks, clerks, MP's, and headquarters personnel and casualties were heavy, but then a hole in the clouds appeared and a U.S. artillery spotter plane called for a strike by P-47s which halted the Germans there. At Stoumont a 30th Division tank battalion attacked the Germans who were then struck by another air strike. U.S. air smashed another Panzer column at Stavelot and the German advance to the north was checked for a distance of 30 miles from the shoulder at Butgenbach. Sixth Panzer however continued to move to the west. (The German attack had been planned to coincide with bad weather in order to minimize U.S. air activity, and weather did aid the offensive for a while.) At the crucial shoulder on this day of trial the Big Red One, the fighting First Division, arrived at Butgenbach to hold the line between the 99th and 30th Divisions.

At St. Vith the 7th Armored dug in, now under attack and unable to move forward, now bolstered by fragments of other units including some from the 9th Armored. A large perimeter was established and many gaps plugged with a hodge podge group of units.

Many who had retreated joined the 7th Armored at St. Vith here to make a stand with some chance of success. Lt Colonel Stone gathered 250 men at Gouvy, then was absorbed by the 7th Armored into Task Force Jones to guard the southern flank. At St. Vith Americans held a vital crossroads, channeling the Sixth Panzer advance into a narrow ten mile channel between St. Vith and Malmedy with only one road not subject to artillery fire.

The 422nd and 423rd Regiments finally received orders to fight to St. Vith in their rear. They had held, counterattacked, and fought well, but now they were surrounded by three German divisions. Their counterattack to the rear went badly as units lost contact with each other and supplies began to run out.

On the nineteenth, at Bradley's headquarters at Verdun, Ike and his staff gathered. Ike asked Patton how long it would take him to attack to the north with six divisions. Patton said his attack would start on the 22nd with three divisions; this date stunned everyone. Ike thought Patton was joking, but Patton explained that his staff had already started working on the plans. Patton was given temporary command of all forces south of the bulge and Montgomery was given temporary command of all forces north of the bulge. This was not a slight to Bradley whose forces were split by the German advance but a practical temporary arrangement.

Monty began by suggesting a pull back in the north to shorten and "tidy up" the lines. The Americans were horrified at the thought of widening the bulge and retreating through swamps on few roads while under pressure. (This wasn't Monty's best idea and it wasn't followed.)

The Germans bypassed St. Vith on both sides and by now were bypassing Bastogne as well, but both of these towns tied up German divisions and blocked their roads.

The 422nd and 423rd attacked Schonberg, attempting to get through to St. Vith, but they were uncoordinated, had no artillery and nothing to fight with but rifles and machine guns, and these ran out of ammunition. On the nineteenth many surrendered; some held out one more day, some for two days, but 8,000 to 9,000 men were lost, most of them captured. They had done well, however, holding up three German divisions. Three more were occupied at St. Vith, three at Bastogne, and eight or ten at the north and south shoulders, leaving few German divisions to mount the attack to the west.

On the twenty-first, VII Corps under General Joe "Lightning" Collins began to move to the tip of the bulge. The 84th Division moved in alongside of the 82nd Airborne to extend the northern line. St. Vith still held out with a narrow supply corridor defended by the 82nd Airborne. On this day the Germans attacked in masses, took heavy casualties but finally broke into the town. The defenders pulled back to a line just west of St. Vith and continued to dominate the roads with artillery.

At Bastogne the 101st, reinforced to 18000 men by a combat command of the 10th Armored, some 9th Armored units, a tank destroyer battalion, and artillery, fought on.

Now the Germans could only move west and hope to outflank the American line to the north.

On the twenty-second, three divisions (60,000 men) of Third Army started their attack to the north (the 4th Armored at Longwy, the 26th further east, and the 80th on the right). Bastogne was 40 miles away and the men of Third Army had driven, walked, and stumbled many miles to get this far. The defenders of Bastogne would not be relieved until Patton got there, but now his divisions had to fight through the German Seventh Army. On this day the Germans asked General McAuliffe, in command of U.S. forces at Bastogne, to surrender. McAuliffe replied with a word that most Americans understand, "Nuts!" but the meaning of the word was not immediately clear to the Germans.

Patton's advance went well. The 4th Armored moved up to Burnon, the 26th moved 16 miles before contacting Germans, but the 80th advanced only 5 miles before meeting resistance.

On December 23, the Germans broke through at St. Vith and orders were given for the defenders and the 82nd to pull back. Twenty-one thousand men had held the Germans for six days, only eight miles from their starting position. The defense of St. Vith was a magnificent feat of arms, and an everlasting credit to all the brave men who fought there.

The defenders of Bastogne had pulled back to tighter perimeters but could not withdraw further without jeopardizing the entire defense. Ammunition was dangerously low, and survival was a question. But the sky cleared enough to permit American planes to fly over Bastogne and to drop 144 tons of supplies. Third Army was heavily engaged as they moved closer, but the defenders of Bastogne did not know when relief would come.

On the twenty-fourth the skies cleared and 5,000 American planes pounded the Germans, but their advance continued west leaving Bastogne far behind. That night, however, the 2nd Armored under Ernie Harmon ambushed the 2nd Panzer, destroying 200 tanks. Some German tanks arrived at Dinant on the Meuse and were hit by tanks from the British 29th Armored Brigade.

On the twenty-fourth Montgomery authorized Collins to withdraw VII Corps, but Collins was "authorized," not ordered, and he was reluctant to lose contact with the British and to leave the Meuse bridges to the Germans. Collins called Harmon and told him in double talk to order Combat Command B to attack but in words foreign to the English.

On Christmas day the 2nd Division attacked the 2nd Panzer at Celles and, with the aid of air power, destroyed the 2nd Panzer. The German advance was stopped short of the Meuse nine days from the initial assault. The issue was resolved between one single U.S. division and one single German division. Many of the German self propelled guns were out of gas and their ammunition was low. It was the last gasp, the final offensive (except for a brief attack on January 1 in Alsace).

On December 26, Patton's 4th Armored broke through to Bastogne and the defenders were saved. It took Third Army seven days to move six divisions 100 miles, 40 miles against stiff resistance, using 133,178 motor vehicles, driving 1,600,000 miles, shifting 62,000 tons of supplies in 120 hours, using 20,000 miles of field wire, issuing hundreds of thousands of new maps, transferring and erecting new field hospitals. Third Army was not just Patton; the staff was superb, and the men were dedicated professionals. Perhaps Sherman's army was the greatest since Caesar, but Third Army might have been the greatest since Alexander.

On into January the Germans fought as they gradually pulled back from the Bulge. They held their flanks and contested every mile. St. Vith was finally recaptured on January 23 as the last traces of the bulge were eliminated.

The U.S. had 76,000 casualties (8,607 dead, 47,139 wounded, 21,144 missing and prisoners) and lost 471 tanks. The Germans lost 100,000 to 120,000 men, 800 tanks, and 1000 planes, about half of everything employed in the attack. Allied plans were certainly disrupted by this affair but German ability to defend was reduced and their final capitulation date may not have been affected. The Battle of the Bulge did illustrate one important military fundamental: the need to keep moving forward aggressively in order to prevent an enemy from having such opportunities. The U.S. soldier was tested in this battle and was not found wanting. For him, this was a great victory.

If the Russians had maintained pressure on the Eastern Front, the Germans would not have been able to collect so many divisions. The Russians did not take the offensive again until January 12, well after the issue was no longer in doubt. Perhaps this was the best that they could do but one feels that they were in no particular hurry to upset their plans. Sixth Panzer Army reappeared on the Eastern Front after being pulled out of the Bulge.

Tinian, July, 1944

After the seizure of Saipan, the U.S. Marines next invaded Tinian, only $3\frac{1}{2}$ miles away in the Marianas. Tinian was only ten miles long, but was needed for the long runways necessary to launch B-29s, the new long range bombers. Already the Japanese Empire shook with the loss of Saipan, which gave the U.S. an island within bomber range of Japan. (After this defeat Premier Tojo resigned in disgrace.)

On the night of July 10, Captain Jim Jones and his Reconnaissance Company were launched in rubber boats from two destroyers, looking for a suitable landing beach on the rocky island. One site near Saipan was found with two small beaches, one 60 yards wide. the other 150. These were too small for a major landing but deemed adequate with a careful plan. The 2nd and 4th Marine Divisions led by Major General Harry Schmidt were to make the invasion. The 2nd would sail to Tinian Town off the island's southern shore. The 4th would land on the northern beaches under cover of naval guns and artillery from Saipan, using the tanks from both divisions. Once the 4th was ashore, the 2nd (used as a decoy) would return and land behind the 4th (a very professional plan, cute and clever).

On July 24, the 2nd Division Marines arrived off the coast of Tinian Town, climbed into landing craft, and headed for the beaches. Japanese infantry rushed to the area and Japanese guns opened up on the U.S. ships and landing craft. While all this was going on the 4th Division poured ashore in the north. The 2nd Division landing craft, however, never touched the beach; instead, they circled and returned to the ships. The Japanese were elated, thinking they had won a victory, but their joy was brief. When they found out about the landings in the north, it was too late to intervene effectively. The 4th Division moved inland about a mile, occupied the key terrain and dug in, waiting for the suicide attacks.

The first attack came at 2 A.M., 600 men at the Marine left flank, then 200 in the center at 2:30, and a final charge on the right at 3:30. The Japanese were slaughtered, losing up to 2,000 men, a quarter of their forces on the island. On the twenty-fifth the 2nd Division landed and it took the Marines only seven days to clean up the island.

Guam, July, 1944

The last major island in the Marianas to be attacked was Guam, captured by the Japanese from the United States in 1941. The island was 32 miles long and defended by 19,000 Japanese. USMC Major General Roy Geiger was to command the Third Marine Division, the First Marine Brigade, and the U.S. Army 77th Division in a landing scheduled for July 21. Landings were planned for both sides of Apra Harbor, with the First Brigade on the south shore and the Third Division on the north shore. The First Brigade beaches were heavily defended and 815 men were lost in the first two days. It took four days for the regiments to make contact, six days to drive one mile inland. The 77th Division came ashore and the First Brigade sidestepped to the left to seal off Orote Peninsula, trapping the Japanese troops there. Some of these tried to escape by water but were blasted by artillery. After dark the Japanese on the peninsula drank Saki, then attacked, screaming, through the swamps. Artillery fire cut them to pieces, 26,000 rounds in two hours. Those who survived the barrage reached Marine positions only to die there.

In the northern beachhead, by July 25, the Third Division held an area one mile deep and five miles wide. This line was thinly manned and on the night of the twenty-fifth, Japanese patrols found a number of gaps. On the left flank a Japanese brigade attacked, but was thrown back. Six more attacks were made, all futile. By 9 a.m. on the twenty-sixth, this assault was over with 950 dead Japanese.

On the left center an under strength Marine company was overrun by a battalion of Japanese. Both neighboring Marine companies held but the Japanese poured into the rear through the narrow gap, taking casualties from both flanks, then from tanks and finally from battalion CP personnel until all were dead. The gap in the Marine line was plugged with a company of engineers and three weapons platoons just prior to another Japanese attack. This assault by Japanese reserves was wiped out.

On the right center a third Japanese attack was made with another battalion. This attack broke through a gap but was stopped by Division Hospital personnel and patients. Another group of MPs, Seabees (Navy construction personnel, also trained to fight), and truck drivers attacked and drove the Japanese back, killing all those who did not commit suicide.

The First Brigade had 431 dead and 1,525 wounded, but they had killed 3,372 Japanese. The Third Division had wiped out 3,500 Japanese and these heavy casualties near the beaches hurt the Japanese chances for effective defense of the island. They fell back allowing the Third and 77th Divisions to link up while the First Brigade cleared the Orote Peninsula. The peninsula was cleared by July 31, and the island secured by August 10, at a cost of 7,800 U.S. casualties. The island was American again after two and a half years of Japanese occupation.

Peleliu, September, 1944

After the Mariana's, the next attack was to be made in the Palau Islands, only 550 miles east of Mindinao in the Philippines. These islands were needed to allow U.S. fleets to navigate and land in the Philippines. Well to the west of Truk, capture of the Palau's would complete the encirclement of that once mighty bastion. The Japanese had some 30,000 to 40,000 men in the Palau's, many of them on the largest island, Babelthuap. Another island, Peleliu, was small, two miles wide and six miles long, but had two excellent airfields. This island was defended by 10,000 to 11,000 men in superbly fortified positions blasted out of coral rock. This island was the primary target for the U.S. invasion and was assigned to the 20,000 men of the First Marine Division.

The island had a coral ridgeline running two miles along the longer north-south axis of the island, not more than 120 feet high, but honeycombed with caves, and here the Japanese placed most of their defenses. The island consisted of white sand and white coral with some sparse vegetation, all contributing to extreme temperatures which ran as high as 115° F.

On September 15, after intensive naval bombardment and air bombing, the First Marine Division landed on the southwestern beaches, three regiments abreast, First Marines on the left, Fifth Marines in the center, and Seventh Marines on the right.

The First Marines received a terrible enfilading fire from a rocky point on their left. There, the Japanese had machine guns and a 47 mm (two inch) gun. Two platoons attacked the point but could not take it. A company attacked and failed. One whole battalion was sent up the point and eventually took it but only 30 men survived and these were hard pressed to hold it.

On the right the Seventh Marines took a pounding as they made their way through barbed wire, mines, and narrow channels covered by artillery. Fortunately the Marine tanks managed to find a way through the mines and the Seventh managed to work their way inland.

In the center the Fifth Marines moved inland to the edge of the airfield, but then a charge by Japanese tanks was made. The Marine tanks arrived at the right place at the right time, and aided by air strikes, demolished the Japanese armor. By nightfall the Fifth and Seventh Marines had crossed the southern end of the island, but the left flank of the First Marines still clung precariously to the rocky point.

On the sixteenth, the Seventh Marines began a push to the southern tip, facing a battalion of first class Japanese infantry in every conceivable kind of fortification. Here PFC (Private First Class) Jackson knocked out twelve pillboxes single handedly with explosives. The southern tip was cleared out within two days.

Also on the sixteenth, the First Marines on the point were reinforced and the beachhead finally secured. The First and Fifth Marines then faced north over the airfield, taking heavy losses from artillery fired from the coral ridge (called the Umerbrogal). That night 350 Japanese attacked the point but were wiped out. On the seventeenth, the First Marines also reached the Umerbrogal. A huge blockhouse was destroyed using naval gunfire from the battleship Mississippi. The First Marines, under Chesty Puller, then fought to the top of Hill 100, taking heavy casualties, and now facing two miles of defenses just as tough. By the twenty-third, the First Marines had 1,749 casualties and were unable to continue. They had, however, killed 4,000 Japanese and destroyed one third of their weapons. They were replaced by the 321st Army Regiment of the 81st Division.

On September 25, the Fifth Marines on the right flank switched to the west coast, drove up the west shore road past the Umerbrogal, fighting off counterattacks, and advancing. On the twenty-seventh, they reached formidable defenses in the north at Hill 200 where artillery fire came in from both flanks. Tanks and Amtracs were used to counter the incoming fire from the right; naval guns and artillery were directed against fire coming from islands on the left. Smoke shells were fired to allow tanks to move up with infantry and an Amtrac flame thrower. On the twenty-eighth, the Fifth Marines landed on the adjoining islands with the aid of very close air support and wiped out the Japanese force there.

On the twenty-seventh, Captain Neal of the 321st formed a task force of 45 men, seven tanks, six Amtracs, and an Amtrac flamethrower. Moving north behind the Fifth Marines, he crossed over to the east road to a point north of the Umerbrogal which was now surrounded.

On the twenty-eighth, the Seventh Marines relieved the 321st and fought until October 4. They used massive air strikes with tons of napalm but took 1,497 casualties. The Fifth Marines took over and fought until the 15th, until they had taken 1,378 casualties. By this time the Japanese pocket had been reduced to 500 men in an area 400 by 600 yards. The Marines were relieved by the 81st Division which finished the job.

Marine casualties were 6,526, with 1,252 dead. Army casualties were 1,393 with 208 dead. The Japanese troops were good and they fought well, no drunken banzai charges, just well planned and effective defense and counterattacks. The performance of the 81st Division on Peleliu was excellent. The achievement of the Marines was outstanding, heroic, and the awful casualties provide agonizing testimony to the quality of their efforts. As the island fighting approached Japan, there were fewer target choices and the Japanese knew where the attacks would be. As a result defenses were tougher and the defenders more numerous, but the Americans kept coming.

The Philippines, Autumn 1944

During the Japanese occupation, Philippine guerrillas formed major units all over the islands, tying up large occupation forces, but at a bloody cost to the guerrillas. As the U.S. invasion grew closer, MacArthur sent them arms and supplies in increasing quantities.

Japan was determined to hold the Philippines. Loss of these islands would put Allied ships and planes in the South China Sea, isolating Japan from all their resources in the East Indies and in Southeast Asia.

On October 19, MacArthur returned to the Philippines, but he brought a few friends, 174,000 men in 700 ships. The Japanese had over 300,000 men in the islands, but they were scattered. Their air bases in the Philippines had been pounded for weeks by Halsey's Third Fleet.

The U.S. Sixth Army under Lt. General Kreuger landed on the beaches of eastern Leyte. (Mindinao was the southern most island, but Leyte was in the middle of the islands and made access to the other islands easier.) The U.S. landings, however, depended on control of the sea, and air superiority with naval aircraft. Siberts X Corps (1st Cavalry and 24th Divisions) landed near San Jose and Hodges XXIV Corps (7th and 96th Divisions) landed near Dulag, dominating an 18 mile stretch of beach. In the next two days U.S. forces secured the beaches and moved inland against light resistance.

The Japanese in the Philippines were commanded by General Yamashita, the conqueror of Malaya and Singapore, and he expected to beat MacArthur. Before the crucial land battle, the Japanese had to try to control the seas, and they gathered the remaining might of their navy to make a do or die attempt.

The Battle of Leyte Gulf, October 1944

The bulk of the Japanese fleet was in Singapore, but their aircraft carriers were in Japanese waters and it was not possible to concentrate in time to attack the U.S. landing forces. The Japanese were too weak, particularly in naval aircraft and carriers to attack Halsey's Third Fleet and MacArthur's Seventh Fleet (Admiral Kincaid), therefore it was decided to use the Japanese carriers (Admiral Ozawa) to lure Halsey north, away from Leyte, then strike at Kincaid and the Amphibious Fleet by nighttime approaches. The Central Group under Admiral Kurita would come through San Bernardino Strait, north of Leyte and Samar, with 5 battleships, 12 cruisers, and 15 destroyers. The Southern Group under Admiral Nishimura would come through Surigao Strait, south of Leyte, with two battleships, one cruiser and four destroyers, but would be followed by Admiral Shima from Japan with three more cruisers and four destroyers. Ozawa had four carriers, two carrier battleships, three cruisers, and nine destroyers, but only 116 planes. The total strength was 4 carriers, 2 carrier battleships, 7 battleships, 19 cruisers, 33 destroyers, and about 300 to 700 planes, mostly land based.

Kincaid's 7th Fleet had 6 old battleships (including 5 survivors of Pearl Harbor), 16 escort carriers, 8 cruisers, many destroyers, and numerous smaller vessels. Halsey had 16 carriers, 6 new battleships, 15 cruisers, and 58 destroyers. Halsey, not under MacArthur's command, was ordered to support MacArthur, to destroy enemy naval and air forces threatening the invasion, but given a primary task, if given an opportunity, to destroy a major portion of the enemy fleet. U.S. naval forces combined had 32 carriers, 12 battleships, 23 cruisers, over 100 destroyers and destroyer escorts, with 1,000 to 1,400 planes. The Japanese had little chance, but they had to take it. If they could approach undetected, if Halsey could be lured away, if land based aircraft could minimize U.S. air activity, just maybe the U.S. fleet could he punished, chased away, isolating the land forces which then, perhaps, could be beaten by Yamashita with air superiority. Loss of the Philippines would ultimately deprive Japan of access to Southeast Asia and the supplies necessary for survival. All possible means had to be utilized, even if it meant losing the fleet.

Kurita's Central Force was spotted by U.S. submarines *Darter* and *Dace* on October 23. These vessels torpedoed three cruisers, sinking two (including Kurita's flagship) and forcing the third to retire, escorted by two destroyers. Kurita kept coming, however.

On October 24 at 7:46 A.M. one of Halsey's planes picked up Kurita's fleet in the Sibuyan Sea and Third Fleet moved to concentrate off Samar. At 8:20 A.M. Nishimura was spotted. No search to the north was made and Ozawa's fleet was not yet discovered. Ozawa's planes and land based aircraft hit the U.S. fleet at 9:30. Two raids were intercepted as U.S. planes shot down 58 with no losses, but at 9:38 an enemy dive bomber hit carrier *Princeton* and she sank later, damaging the cruiser *Burmingham* when she blew up.

At 10:25 A.M. U.S. planes struck Kurita. Cruiser *Myoko* was hit and forced to return to base. Battleship *Musashi* was hit but kept her speed. At noon U.S. planes attacked again with *Musashi* taking two bombs, two torpedoes and dropping out of formation. At 1:30 a third raid crippled *Musashi* and hit battleship *Yamato*. A fourth attack hurt *Yamato* again and damaged battleship *Nagato*. At 3 P.M. a fifth attack finished off *Musashi*, and at 3:30 Kurita veered to the west. U.S. planes reported Kurita retreating to the west. Halsey wanted to know where the Japanese carriers were, and at 2 P.M. he sent search planes north where they located Ozawa at 4:40 P.M. Halsey headed north (leaving San Bernardino Strait uncovered) with his whole fleet to strike Ozawa, believing that *Kurita* was still sailing for home. Kurita however, at 5:14 P.M., reversed course to reenter San Bernardino Strait, this time undetected.

Kincaid, believing that Halsey left ships to guard San Bernardino Strait, sent his big ships to Suragao Strait to wait for Nishimura and Shima (20 miles behind). Kincaid's commander, Oldendorf, posted PT boats deep into the strait, then destroyers further back, then a line of cruisers, and finally a line of battleships. A night battle loomed as Nishimura sailed on in column.

At 11:30 P.M. 39 PT boats attacked but caused only alarm. At 3 A.M. two columns of U.S. destroyers flanked the Japanese column, launching torpedoes. Nishimura's flagship, the battleship *Yamashiro*, was hit, one destroyer sunk, two others put out of action. An hour later *Yamashiro* sank. One Japanese battleship, one cruiser, and one destroyer remained. Then the U.S. cruisers and the Pearl Harbor battleships commenced firing simultaneously. The Japanese battleship *Fuso* and cruiser *Mogami* were hit and set on fire. *Fuso* sank but *Mogami* floated helplessly, burning beyond control. Only one destroyer escaped.

Shima, totally ignorant of Nishimura's fate, sailed into the strait, observing only one Japanese destroyer going home. Then, one cruiser took a PT boat torpedo, and Shima's flagship collided with burning *Mogami*. That did it for Shima, and he turned around, obviously preferring to be an unemployed civilian than a dead admiral.

As October 25 dawned, 50 transports and amphibious ships lay at anchor in Leyle Gulf. Meanwhile, Ozawa sailed south toward Luzon with only 30 planes left from the previous day's combat. At 7:12 A.M. Halsey's planes attacked, returning again and again all morning. By days end Ozawa lost four carriers, one cruiser, and two destroyers. He did, however, succeed in luring Halsey from San Bernardino Strait.

Early that day, 16 Seventh Fleet escort carriers sailed leisurely off Samar with destroyers and destroyer escorts. Patrol planes and ground support planes were launched and all hands relaxed. Then a search plane spotted Kurita's fleet only 20 miles away and coming fast. The escort carriers pointed east into the wind, launching all planes (armed mostly with anti personnel bombs). Kincaid's battleships started north, but were low on armor piercing shells. Halsey was notified, but he was far away.

One destroyer attacked the Japanese fleet, launching torpedoes, but was badly damaged. Two more destroyers attacked, firing shells, torpedoes, and making smoke. One destroyer survived but two went down. Four U.S. destroyer escorts attacked, two managing to survive, but Kurita now chased the small carriers, heading for Leyte Gulf.

Japanese shells began to hit the small carriers, one carrier taking five hits, another fifteen, but *Gambier Bay* took one on the flight deck, lost power, and was sunk by the Japanese cruisers. Many shells passed right through the small carriers without exploding. Carrier planes struck back, shooting down 100 Japanese planes, strafing and bombing the Japanese ships. Destroyer and carrier five inch guns scored many hits; destroyer and aircraft torpedoes also scored. Kurita's fleet was now spread all over the ocean at varying speeds, one wounded cruiser at 16 knots, two others badly damaged. Many ships had been hit during days of pounding. Without Nishimura and air superiority, Kurita had no hope of beating Halsey. Further, he expected Halsey's fleet to cut him off from his route home, and so, at the moment of a huge opportunity, he turned around. Admiral Sprague, commander of the escort carriers, claimed his task force was saved by torpedo attacks, smoke screens, and major assistance from God himself.

As Kurita made his torturous way home, part of Halsey's fleet, Task Group 38.1, back from a resupply mission, launched a massive air strike, continuing with many other aircraft to pound Kurita for two days (October 25 and 26), sinking four more cruisers and six destroyers. Japanese losses in the disastrous battle were 4 carriers, 3 battleships, 8 cruisers, 12 destroyers, up to 10,000 men, and hundreds of planes. U.S. losses were 2,800 men, several hundred planes, one light carrier, two escort carriers, two destroyers, and two destroyer escorts. The Japanese navy was destroyed, no longer a force to be reckoned with.

MacArthur blamed the miscommunication between Halsey and Kincaid, resulting in the vacating of San Barnardino Strait, on lack of a single overall command. Actually. MacArthur himself could have acted in this capacity but for the fact that his flagship, cruiser *Nashville*, was used in the Surigao Strait and Kincaid didn't want his boss to be at risk, so MacArthur went ashore, out of touch with the Navy. The final result, the sweeping of the air and sea of Japanese, was so fortunate that little blame could be cast on any of the U.S. commanders. The attack by destroyers and destroyer escorts was as brave as any other effort in U.S. Navy history.

The Conquest of Leyte

The Japanese determined, in spite of their naval disaster, to try to hold Leyte, key to defense of the Philippines. Their air forces were replenished, and U.S. air forces, suffering from the loss of escort carrier planes, could not dominate the skies. 50,000 more Japanese troops were sent in and a strong defense, the Yamashita Line, was built across the narrow neck of Leyte.

MacArthur brought in two more divisions, the 11th Airborne and the 32nd. The Japanese mounted frequent counterattacks, and weather helped to slow down the American advance. By December the Japanese stood firmly in front of MacArthur, but on December 6 the U.S. 77th Division arrived, was loaded on to ships, and landed at Ormoc, behind the Yamashita Line. MacArthur attacked the Japanese from front and rear, making contact with the 77th Division on December

11. The Japanese were cut into two segments, both isolated from their supply routes. It was all over by December 26, and MacArthur had done it again. 80,557 Japanese were dead, only 798 captured. U.S. losses were 3,320 dead, 12,000 wounded. The Japanese 16th Division, responsible for the Bataan Death March, was wiped out with no survivors. This campaign was outstanding but was certainly made possible by control of the sea and air, the key to the early Japanese successes.

Russia, 1944

After mid 1943, the Russian offensive continued with blows, first here, then there, in order to keep the Germans off balance, to prevent their concentration at any one point. As 1944 began, the German generals asked for permission to withdraw from salients in the Ukraine and at Leningrad in order to shorten the lines to be defended, but Hitler refused. The mad dictator could not accept the thought of defeat or retreat, and sacrificed his armies, leaving them thinned out in huge salients all over Russia. Even at Stalingrad, as the end drew near, he had proposed sending "a battalion" of new tanks to relieve the town when he could have ordered Paulus to fight out towards Hoth's relief force, only 30 miles away.

On December 24, 1943, the Russians attacked at Kiev, opening a 40 mile gap and roaring west 150 miles in a month, reaching Lutsk on the Styr, near the Polish border, only 200 miles from Warsaw. On January 5, 1944, the Russians attacked in the south along a huge front from Kiev toward Nikopol, west of the Dnieper.

On January 14, the Russians attacked near Leningrad. Here, the Germans had fifty divisions, but only one was armored as all the German armor had been shifted to the south. By March 1 the Germans were pushed back to their Panther Line on the Estonian border. Leningrad was relieved on January 29, after a legendary siege of 900 days involving enormous civilian hardships (including even cannibalism).

In the Ukraine the whole German front was pushed back about 50 miles by March 1, clearing the Dnieper of Germans. After a brief pause, the attack resumed, this time pushing swiftly through the Germans, 25 miles in two days in some places, trapping the First Panzer Army. By April 10, Odessa was taken and the German 17th Army isolated in the Crimea. The Hungarian and Rumanian borders were reached in places. Hube's First Panzer Army managed to break out but in April the Russians entered the Crimea at Kerch and Perekop. The 17th Army, 25,000 men, surrendered by May 12.

In June the Russians attacked everywhere from the Arctic to the Black Sea. In many places pockets of Germans were surrounded, killed, and captured. On June 22, a complete German corps of the Third Panzer Army was destroyed at Vitebsk. By June 28, the whole army was shattered. Much of Ninth Army was surrounded at Bobriusk and Fourth Army was cut off at Minsk, 57,000 men surrendering there on July 4. Army Group Center (Riga to Warsaw) had lost 28 divisions and was no longer effective. German Army Group North Ukraine lost 25,000 dead and 17,000 captured at Brody by July 13. On July 20, the Russians were near Warsaw at the Polish border; on August 1, they were near Riga in Latvia (close to isolating two armies in Estonia).

On August 1, the Poles in Warsaw revolted, but the Germans put up strong resistance to the Russians east of the city. The Russians went on the defensive in this sector and made no further moves to liberate the city. The Germans proceeded to wipe out the Poles in the city, a result probably not unpopular with the Russians, as the Poles resisting were mainly anti-communist. Earlier in the war the Russians massacred 4,500 Polish officers at Katyn for the same reason.

In the Baltic States Estonia was occupied in September. By October 14 the Russians reached the Baltic at Memel, trapping part of German Army Group North on the Courtland Peninsula near Riga. At the Nieman River on the East Prussian border, the Germans finally stabilized the northern front.

In Rumania the Russians, who had made no major moves since entering the country in the spring, took the offensive in August, moving quickly to take Bucharest and the Ploesti oil fields by the end of the month. Rumanian divisions surrendered rapidly, some joining the Russians. The Germans soon had 20 divisions trapped near the Dniester. Here, the Sixth German Army and part of the Eighth were destroyed.

On August 25, Finland sued for peace. In September Bulgaria deserted Germany, joining the Russians. On October 4, British troops landed on the Greek Peloponnese west coast, moving east. The Germans evacuated Corinth on October 8 and Athens on the twelfth. A Greek communist uprising erupted on December 3, but the British managed a feeble truce by February.

In September the Russians moved north from Bucharest towards Hungary, then south into Bulgaria and west to Yugoslavia along the Danube. Greece was left to the British and Greeks to liberate (fortunately for Greece). On September 5, the Germans and Hungarians counterattacked the Rumanians in the southern Carpathians, but a week later the Russians put in a tank army and pushed the Axis forces north to Targu Mures, reaching the Hungarian border by the twenty-fourth.

The Russians moving west along the Danube reached Yugoslavia, crossing the Morava River south of Belgrade by October 12. By this time remaining German forces in Greece and lower Yugoslavia moving north were in danger of being cut off. The Russians took Belgrade on October 20, but the Germans kept the roads from the south open halting the Russian attack temporarily.

By years end the Russians cleared Hungary, except for Budapest where one Hungarian and four German divisions were trapped. From East Prussia, along the Vistula in Poland, and south to Budapest, the Russians had cleared vast territories of Germans and now began to concentrate for the last push from the Vistula to Warsaw and Berlin. The German Army had suffered huge losses in 1944, but their defensive responsibilities and front lines on the eastern front were substantially reduced. With Russians near the German eastern border and the

Allies on the western, the end for Germany was definitely in sight.

Italy, Summer and Autumn, 1944

After the fall of Rome the Germans planned to make their stand in the Apennine Mountains (the Gothic Line) but they needed time to prepare defenses. By mid June they stabilized their defense at the Albert Line, 80 miles north of Rome, and by mid July, they made another stand on the Arno River, 75 miles further north. Here the Allies stalled while troops were transferred to the southern France invasion force. Veteran U.S. divisions were replaced by a Brazilian division and one all black U.S. division, the 92nd, commanded by Ned Almond (who was to command X Corps in Korea six years later).

On August 25, Alexander launched a U.S. Fifth Army attack on the west side of Italy where the Germans were strongest, then he threw the British Eighth Army in on the Adriatic Coast. Eighth Army broke through the German defenses and across the Foggia River. By September 2, the Canadians broke through the Gothic Line and across the Conca River. Kesselring brought forces over from the west coast to stabilize this front for a time.

On September 12, the Fifth Army attacked in the mountain passes in central Italy, making some progress initially, advancing ten miles by the end of October, still 10 miles from Bologna and the vital German supply road, Route 9. U.S. casualties exceeded replacements and the Fifth Army advance was halted. On December 26, the Germans struck the U.S. 92nd Division, and many black units turned and ran. The gap was plugged by the 8th Indian Division. Almond was to follow up his disastrous WW II experience with an even less glorious Korean War career.

Meanwhile the Eighth Army (British, Canadians, Poles, and Greeks) crossed river after river (Marecchis, Rubicon, Savio, Cesano, Ronco, Rabbi, and Lamone) by December, stopping on the south bank of the Senio. Casualties and weather brought the Italian campaign to a halt by winter. The Allies had moved only 180 miles since taking Rome in early June and occupied a line from Ravenna to Massa, still 25 miles from the Po River and 70 miles from Venice.

The Russian Advance, 1945

In the fall of 1944, the Russians maintained pressure on the entire German line from East Prussia to Hungary to prevent the Germans from concentrating. Meanwhile the Russians concentrated in the center along the Vistula in Poland. The Germans knew this and informed Hitler, recommending the transfer of troops from the cut-off peninsula in Latvia and from Norway. Hitler showed no interest in these recommendations, as he was obsessed with relieving the trapped Germans in Budapest. Hitler therefore ordered the transfer of a Panzer Corps from the center to Budapest. The German attack on Budapest jumped off on January 7 and was thrown back within five days.

The Allies were in trouble in the Bulge and requested the Russians to do something. Finally, on January 12, Konev attacked across the Vistula 100 miles south of Warsaw, roaring twelve miles through Fourth Panzer Army. The next day on the Baltic Front Third Panzer Army was attacked and pushed back. On the fourteenth, Zhukov attacked north and south of Warsaw. The same day Rokossovsky crossed the Narew, moving north 50 miles in five days behind the German Fourth and Third Panzer Armies. Here, also, Hitler had transferred a Panzer Corps to the south. On the sixteenth, the Germans began to evacuate Warsaw. By the nineteenth, the Russians were up to 100 miles west of the Vistula.

The Oder River runs northwest inside Germany some 30 to 60 miles inside the border, and by the end of January, the Russians occupied the east bank as far north as Frankfurt, just 60 miles from Berlin. By February 10, 27 German divisions were cut off in East Prussia, where Hitler refused to allow a retreat. The German Army in front of Berlin was put under Chief of Police Heinrich Himmler, as Hitler no longer trusted any of his generals to obey his orders. On February 13, Budapest fell to the Russians and the Germans there were destroyed.

Refugees poured into Germany from the east where the Russians raped, robbed, and slaughtered in revenge for German atrocities. Eight thousand refugees drowned when the *Wilhelm Gustloff* was torpedoed by a Russian sub. The U.S. bombed Berlin, Magdeburg, and Dresden (February 13) in support of the Russians. Dresden was destroyed along with 50,000 people, including many refugees.

On February 15, Zhukov, at the Oder, was attacked from the north and forced to divert his efforts in that direction. By the end of March the whole Baltic coast from Danzig to the Oder was cleared of Germans.

In mid February the Russians started an offensive in the south from Budapest towards Vienna. This was no doubt politically motivated to give the Russians control of Austria. Vienna fell on April 13. The Russians controlled the Baltic States, Rumania, Hungary, Poland, Bulgaria, Yugoslavia, and half of Austria and Czechoslovakia.

In Yugoslavia the Germans attacked into Hungary but were stopped and thrown back within ten days.

On April 16, the Russians began their offensive across the Oder. Zhukov and Rokossovsky made little headway but Konev broke through fifty miles south of Frankfurt. By April 25, the whole Oder front was smashed and Berlin encircled by Konev and Zhukov.

The Russians advanced in Czechoslovakia taking Brno by April 26. On April 30, Hitler committed suicide, but the Germans in Berlin fought on until May 2, when the city was surrendered. The capture of Berlin cost the Russians 300,000 casualties since crossing the Oder. In two weeks they took 480,000 German prisoners. German casualties in this period are unknown.

The official German surrender occurred on May 7, and on May 9 the Russians took Prague. The Germans in Czechoslovakia surrendered on May 11 and the Germans in Yugoslavia surrendered to Marshal Tito on May 14. The Russians occupied almost all of Czechoslovakia and Austria before meeting U.S. forces. The Allies had not agreed on preset boundaries in Europe, as the military situation was too unpredictable. Eisenhower held up advancing U.S. forces which could have taken Berlin, Vienna, and Prague, for reasons which will be given later.

Italy, 1945

By the end of 1944, the Allies had stalled in the Apennines and along the Senio River because of heavy casualties. All available troops had gone to France to stabilize the Bulge front in Belgium. There was no worthwhile strategic objective in Italy and no reason for purposeless casualties. Alexander, however, had been ordered to keep pressure on the Germans in Italy to prevent them from reinforcing other fronts or taking up defensive positions in the Alps. It wasn't until April that Alexander was ready, however. The weather most probably was a factor in setting the date for the renewed offensive.

On April 9, the British attacked on the right, breaking through for a distance of ten miles by the eighteenth. Mark Clark's Fifth Army attacked on the fourteenth but was delayed by bad weather. By April 21, his forces had moved forward ten miles and out of the Apennines. Poles from Eighth Army moved up Route 9 and took Bologna on April 21. Resistance by the sixteen German divisions crumbled and their retreat was almost impossible since Allied Air had destroyed railroads and bridges. By the end of April, the British were past Venice to the Piave River. Fifth Army took Genoa, Milan, and Verona. Mussolini was captured by partisans, murdered with his mistress, and hung by his heels in Milan. The Germans surrendered in Italy on April 29. On May 2, the British met Tito's Yugoslav forces at Trieste. On May 6, Fifth Army met the U.S. Seventh Army in the Brenner Pass.

The Western Front, 1945

By mid January 1945, the Allies on the western front had the Bulge situation under control and formed for assaults on the West Wall which ran along the Rohr, Our, and Saar Rivers from 10 miles west of the Rhine in the north to 75 miles west at Saarbruecken before running southeast to the Rhine at Karlsruhe. Simultaneous assaults were to be made by (from north to south) the 1st Canadian, 2nd British, 9th U.S., 1st U.S., 3rd U.S., 7th U.S., and 1st French Armies. Eisenhower chose a general assault to prevent German concentration at any single point should a limited push be made. This strategy was questioned by the British and by Patton, each favoring a concentrated attack by themselves.

The British protest to the broad front strategy was at the highest level. Chief of Staff Field Marshal Brooke and Montgomery both predicted another failure (like the Bulge), questioning Eisenhower's judgment and ability, demanding that Montgomery be given control of all U.S. forces. Actually the British contributed heavily to the Bulge setback by not capturing the Antwerp bridges, not freeing the port, limiting the receipt of supplies, and holding up all the U.S. Armies for want of gasoline. Montgomery even stated that U.S. forces should fall back while the British advanced. He was a major irritant to Eisenhower and the U.S. Army leadership.

U.S. Army Chief of Staff George Marshall would not agree to give command of 50 U.S. divisions to the British who had only 15, but Ike appeared to compromise by giving Monty Simpson's 9th Army (this was due primarily to Ike's plan to encircle the Ruhr) and a certain priority in attack strategy. To support Ike, Patton and Bradley advised that under the circumstances they simply could not serve under Montgomery. Ike issued an outline with objectives: the clearing of all German forces west of the Rhine and north of the Moselle. Ike's outline satisfied the British but he gave Bradley back his First Army which had been split between Montgomery and Patton during the Bulge.

Ike's actual orders were for First and Third Armies to push to the Rhine. Once at the Rhine the U.S. 9th and 1st Armies were to encircle the Ruhr. This was the U.S. plan, not just Ike's. Ike had a staff and the plan was prepared by them. The British protest against this plan had some merit. They, in the north, were closest to Berlin. But should Berlin be the only objective? How about Vienna, Prague, etc? If the Germans still had 50 divisions and only the British advanced, they would soon meet substantial resistance. On the other hand, if the Germans were so weak that they could not stop a single thrust, how would they stop a multiple thrust? The British protests were not logical and not consistent with Churchill's desire to liberate as much of Europe as possible.

But what about Patton and Third Army? Were they to be forgotten? Their position in rugged country (75 miles from the Rhine) did not look favorable to strategic planners, but Patton was not a man to sit still. In January Bradley did authorize Patton to attack and Patton happily made plans to do what he did best.

Patton, on January 29, had thirteen divisions facing the German West Wall. VIII Corps attacked, crossing the Our River with two divisions. An attack toward Bitburg was planned for February 4, but Bradley's chief of staff told Patton permission to attack was refused by SHAEF. The British influence on the Combined Chiefs of Staff was probably behind this.

Montgomery then told Ike he was planning to leave several divisions on his flank to wait for the Germans, then jump on them like vicious rabbits. This statement amused Patton.

Bradley, however, told Patton he could attack until the tenth, providing that casualties and ammunition consumption were not excessive. Patton and Bradley planned a two pronged attack toward Prim and Bitburg. Thus began the Eifel campaign. Patton wanted to get through the West Wall and take Trier and he managed to get his 10th Armored Division back for this purpose on February 15. On the twenty-first, while the entire front sat idle, Third Army's front was on fire.

The 90th Division took six towns. The 11th Armored Division widened the breech in the West Wall and took Roscheid. The 6th Armored took four villages east of the Our. (All this activity was in the VIII Corps Sector.)

In XII Corps the 80th Division enveloped and destroyed German positions in the West Wall between the Our and Gay Rivers, taking three towns. The 10th Division of XX Corps drove to its final position in the Saar Moselle triangle, taking five towns, then driving northeast to Saarburg. The 94th Division cleared the area between Orscholz and Saarburg east to the Saar River, all this in one day.

Bradley agreed to allow Patton to proceed east, and even though SHAEF did not order this advance, their situation map must have shown Patton's progress. Again Patton's advance gave the U.S. Army the opportunity to take advantage of his forward positions to plan a more aggressive plan of attack. Certainly Ike knew and quietly approved of Patton's moves.

By February 25, Patton cleared the Saar-Moselle triangle, then ordered the 10 Armored to take Trier. (This division was loaned to Patton only to help clear the triangle and Patton was close to disobeying orders.) He was given 48 more hours to use the division, so he attacked Trier through minefields and pillboxes, supported by the 94th and 76th Divisions. Tenth Armored took the town by March 1 and was through the West Wall. Patton then moved to the Rhine north of Koblenz, trapping 11 German divisions in a pocket between U.S. 1st and 3rd Armies.

On March 9, Patton's XII Corps took a bridge over the Moselle. Ike and Bradley immediately gave Patton authority to cross and occupy the Palatinate, behind the Germans in the West Wall between Third and Seventh Armies. That night the bridge was blown but Patton ordered the campaign to proceed in spite of the loss. XII Corps put up three bridges and roared across before SHAEF found out there was no bridge. On the eighteenth Patton, having lost the 10th Armored was given the 12th Armored. XII Corps, led by the 4th Armored, rushed into the Palatinate. XX Corps broke through the West Wall to link up with XII Corps, trapping the remnants of 10 enemy divisions. The Germans, now completely broken, tried to set up defenses west of Mainz and Mannheim, but failed. All the German escape routes across the Rhine were cut except for one at Speyer. Here German fugitives attempted to cross hounded by two armored divisions and the XIX Tactical Air Command. Koblenz fell on March 18 and two German armies were destroyed with 80,000 prisoners. All the Allied armies were on the Rhine by this time, but Patton was as close to Berlin as any of the others. He, without direct orders, had moved 75 miles east through the West Wall in difficult terrain, destroyed two armies, allowing few Germans to escape across the Rhine, and had broken his front wide open. The Seventh Army Commander, General Patch, congratulated Patton for surrounding three armies, two German, one American.

The British attacked on January 16 to clear a salient at Roermond, west of the West Wall. This took ten days. The French attacked at Colmar and with the U.S.7th Army closed up to the Rhine south of Karlsruhe (This was not a critical sector. The terrain across the Rhine was formidable.) On January 28 the U.S. 1st Army attacked the West Wall. The Germans opened the gates of the Roer Dams, flooding the valleys and stalling the 9th U.S. Army advance until February 8. From Nijmegen, the Canadians attacked southeast into the Reichswald Hills to clear the west bank of the Rhine, but were slowed by stiff resistance. By February 21, 7th Army was attacking north along the west bank of the Rhine.

On February 23, 9th Army crossed the Roer, drove east to the Rhine at Duesseldorf by March 2, then moved north to meet the Canadians on March 3. On March 7, the 9th Armored Division reached the Rhine at Remagen and captured the bridge intact. By March 10, the British were at the Rhine at Wesel.

These were days of heavy fighting, but once through the West Wall the Allies quickly closed to the Rhine at so many points that the Germans were unable to use the river as a major defensive barrier.

U.S. First Army attacked southeast from their Remagen bridgehead. On the night on March 22, Patton crossed the Rhine at Oppenheim, and on the next night he crossed again at Mainz. The British crossed at Wesel on March 24, and the following night Patton crossed in two more places, Boppard and St Goer. By the end of March, the Allies were across in ten places. Patton, by March 25, was across the Main River and moving so fast the Germans could not form in front of him. The British staged a huge theatrical show for their crossing of the Rhine at Wesel. By the time they crossed however on March 24, both 1st and 3rd U.S. Armies had already crossed and made the British show seem ridiculous. British politics played an enormous part in the conduct of the war, and Eisenhower was forced to recognize this. Alterations in strategy and tactics were made as Ike felt compelled to make adjustments to keep the British Empire in the fight.

When First Army crossed the Rhine on March 7, Bradley was told to commit no more than four divisions as the crossing was not part of the plan. The plan was to wait for the British to cross seventeen days later. The British ignored the American crossings in their exuberant announcements of being the first to cross.

At this time Churchill bombarded Eisenhower with requests to move as far east as fast as possible, particularly to take Berlin. Ike's orders from Marshall, however, were to concentrate on military goals. Ike did not want to risk any military setbacks or any confrontations with the Russians and was not (most unfortunately) primarily interested in occupying real estate. He therefore advised Stalin that his drive into Germany would be toward Dresden, well south of Berlin. Stalin gleefully lied, agreeing to meet the U.S. forces at Dresden, then lied again by stating that his offensive would be launched in mid May. (It was actually done in mid April.) Stalin was pulling out all stops in his efforts to overrun as many countries as possible. Roosevelt should have intervened at this point to direct the military toward political objectives, but he was probably too sick to do what a president had to do at that time.

By March 28, the U.S. 1st and 3rd Armies encircled a German corps at Giessen.

By April 1, U.S. 1st and 9th Armies had encircled the Ruhr, trapping Model's Army Group B. German resistance was just about non existent at this point and the U.S. Armies began to roll. On April 4, Patton captured Kassel, 180 miles from Berlin. On April 10, U.S. 9th Army (84th Division) was in Hanover, 150 miles from Berlin. By April 11 the 2nd Armored Division reached the Elbe at Magdeburg, 70 miles from Berlin. The following day the 2nd Armored and 63rd Divisions crossed the Elbe and asked permission to attack Berlin (The Russians were still at the Oder, 50 miles east of Berlin, would not start their offensive until April 16, and would not reach the city until April 21!). Eisenhower ordered Simpson not to advance further. By April 13 Patton had crossed the Mulde River about 100 miles from Prague, the capital of Czechoslovakia, where he was ordered to stop.

On March 27 Marshall, himself, recommended that Eisenhower change his direction of attack toward southern Germany, where the U.S. believed that the Germans had a Nazi National Redoubt south of the Danube. This turned out to be a myth perpetuated by the Germans but accepted by the Americans as a real possibility. U.S. policy was to destroy the German Army and was carried out far too long after the German Army in front of the Americans was shattered.

On April 16, Patton was ordered south into Austria. The British were ordered north to Kiel and Denmark. Patton believed he could liberate Prague and much of Czechoslovakia as the Russians were held up in the eastern end of the country; however, as ordered, on April 22 Patton attacked to the south, crossing the Inn River on May 2, reaching Linz in Austria by May 4. Finally, on May 5, Patton was ordered back into Czechoslovakia. XX Corps moved into Czechoslovakia with two divisions, heading for Prague. On the fifth an OSS unit drove into Prague where they were welcomed as liberators. Patton, still 60 miles away at Pilsen, was told to stop as Eisenhower had agreed with the Russians not to liberate Prague. Czechoslovakia, which could have been saved, was left for the Russians.

Patton and Third Army had, during the campaign in Europe, occupied fronts from 75 to 200 miles wide. Starting on August 1, 1944, with 92,000 men, Patton commanded 438,000 by war's end. His casualties were 160,692; 72,104 dead, 86,277 wounded, 18,957 missing. His opponents suffered 47,500 dead, 115,700 wounded, 1,280,688 prisoners, for a total of 1,443,888. Patton stated that, had he been permitted to go all out, the war would have ended sooner. When one looks at his achievements, the rapid movement across France and the rapid movement of the U.S. Army across Germany, one has to wonder, how the U.S. supplied these forces, so many men, moving so quickly. It has been said that only U.S. and German armies were capable of the continuous rapid attack. It wasn't until 1991 that such rapid movements were seen again in warfare (Iraq).

A Look Back

It is hard to imagine the defeat of the German war machine without the huge Red Army, the Russians. Hitler had mobilized all of Europe and a landing on the continent against his total force was inconceivable. The Russian victory is remarkable in many ways, considering their huge early losses and the quick occupation of so many of their industrial cities. After forty-four years of confrontation with communism, it is painful to say, but perhaps the world should be thankful for a strong Soviet Union at that time, without which Hitler might have been unstoppable.

We can also be thankful that Hitler did not occupy England. With a little more effort he could have finished off the R.A.F. and then invaded. With England occupied he could have concentrated all his might on Russia. The two front war was too much for Germany. The courage and fortitude of Winston Churchill and the English people was a key factor in the eventual victory.

Admiral Halsey said that no man is great but there are major challenges which some men overcome. Well, perhaps so, but we can all praise our gods for Winston Churchill and Franklin Roosevelt. Both had been Secretary of the Navy and miraculously were available when needed in their country's greatest challenge. Winston, a brilliant man, was a tower of strength.

After 1942 the Germans were generally on the defensive, but the key to their defeat was control of the air. Many brave airmen, English, Polish, American, Canadian, and Russian, perished fighting the Luftwaffe. In 1943 Allied bomber losses over Germany were tragically high, but then the long range fighter became available, the P-51 Mustang, with a Rolls-Royce engine and spare gas tanks. By the time of D-Day in mid 1944, the Allies controlled the skies.

On land in Europe, the overall success is a huge credit to General Eisenhower, who was rewarded with the American Presidency as a result of his enormous popularity. However, during the campaigns in Africa, Sicily, and France, situations arose which, under different circumstances, might have changed the course of the war. Time after time, the British interfered with Ike's plans. In Tunisia, Patton could have cut off Rommel at Gafsa. In Sicily, Montgomery forced Patton to land on the beach at Gela, instead of at Palermo. From Palermo, with a port behind him, Patton might have been able to dash to Messina before the German buildup. At Falaise in France, Patton could have trapped the German Army but Eisenhower stopped him to wait for the British who could not close the trap.

In September of 1944, Eisenhower gave all his gasoline to the British to move north towards Arnhem around the north end of the West Wall. This route had one single road, much water, and was easily stopped by the Germans. U.S. planners hoped the British would at least capture a port or two, but this was not accomplished. Far better would have been a plan to supply Patton in his drive to the Rhine, while asking the British to concentrate on taking the port of Antwerp.

With Antwerp captured in September, Patton and supporting 1st and 9th Armies could have driven to the Rhine. Holding up Patton for just a few weeks allowed the Germans to man the formidable fortifications of Metz and set up a strong defense in front of Third Army and to man the West Wall. The Germans were totally disorganized in their retreat from France and should have been pursued with all possible means. Trapping the Germans west of the Rhine did eventually prevent a strong defense inside Germany. A rapid drive to the Rhine would have prevented the Bulge affair and could have resulted in the occupation of all of Germany, Austria, and Czechoslovakia. These countries could have been saved from Russian occupation but many others were, including Greece, Yugoslavia, Italy, France, Holland, Belgium, Norway, Denmark, and West Germany. Austria was split into two zones but was given its freedom a few years later. Only Poland, Hungary, Bulgaria, Rumania, Czechoslovakia, East Germany, and the Baltic states fell to the Russians. Many lives could have been saved with a quicker decision but the victory, if not the best that could have been obtained, was not far from it.

Burma, 1945

In late 1944 the Japanese had seven divisions facing the Chinese and British. The 1st and 6th Chinese Armies were south of Myitkyina and Force Y was near Lungling on the Burma Road. The British had eight or nine divisions, the 36th in north Burma, the rest along the India-Burma border. On November 1, Y force took Lungling, and on December 15, the Chinese 1st Army had taken Bhamo 100 miles to the east.

The British under General William Slim attacked on December 3 with three divisions, moving east across the Chindwin toward Mandalay on the Irriwady. The 36th Division took Indaw on December 16, and by mid January the British had advanced up to 150 miles, establishing two bridgeheads over the Irriwady, 40 to 70 miles north of Mandalay.

On January 27, the Ledo and Burma Roads were connected by the Chinese. Stilwell was gone, but his troops finished the job he had trained them to do.

By mid February the British had two more bridgeheads over the Irriwady southwest of Mandalay; moving inland, they took Meiktila on March 3. The Japanese cut the road behind the British at Meiktila and attacked the 17th Indian Division, causing some difficulty.

On March 7, the Chinese took Lashio and Mandalay was almost surrounded. The 19th Indian Division, moving from the north, and the 2nd British Division, coming from the west, took Mandalay by March 20. On March 28, the Japanese 33rd Army withdrew to Pyawbwe, south of Meiktila. On April 6, the 17th Indian Division occupied positions south of Honda's 33rd Army, trapping two divisions which were mostly destroyed.

Japanese defenses were in disarray by mid April as the British raced to the south, taking Toungoo on April 23, isolating the Japanese 15th Army in the mountains of eastern Burma. On April 29, Pegu was occupied 50 miles north of Rangoon. On May 1–2, parachute and amphibious landings were made south of Rangoon, and the city fell on May 3. By August 4, all fighting ceased. Few Japanese escaped from Burma. The British under Slim had waged a brilliant campaign, erasing the stigma of 1942. War is easier when the enemy is outnumbered and you have control of the air and sea.

The Philippines, 1945

After the conquest of Leyte, MacArthur planned the big one, the invasion of Luzon where he had been defeated three years earlier. MacArthur concentrated some of his forces on northern Leyte, threatening to land on southern Luzon. As a result the Japanese concentrated there as anticipated. The main landings were planned for northern Luzon, at Lingayen Gulf where the Japanese themselves had landed. When the Japanese shifted forces to the north, MacArthur planned another landing in the south. (Montgomery had objected to separated landings in Sicily but obviously multiple landings were accepted military tactics, providing they were made in sufficient strength.) MacArthur took some risk sailing to the north of Luzon in the presence of land based aircraft, but this time MacArthur had land based air forces to neutralize Japanese air strength. (On Leyte, he had had to depend on naval aircraft.)

On December 15, 1944, the U.S. 24th Division landed on Mindoro, occupying the island closest to Luzon and building airfields. On January 9, MacArthur put two corps ashore at Lingayen Gulf, four divisions (6th, 37th, 40th, and 43rd), I Corps on the left flank (east), and XIV Corps on the right. Twenty-five hundred landing craft were used to put the troops ashore against light resistance on an extended beachhead twelve miles wide. Japanese *kamikaze* attacks hit a number of ships but could not interfere with the landings. A few Japanese planes approached the beaches but were quickly shot down by U.S. fighters.

The Japanese on Luzon were 250,000 strong but could not stand and fight U.S. armor and infantry in open country exposed to overpowering air support. As a result the Japanese occupied the more mountainous terrain. I Corps was assigned to hold the Japanese in the northeastern hills, guarding MacArthur's left flank and supply line while XIV Corps drove south in the central plains. In twelve days XIV Corps was at Tarlac, halfway to Manila.

The Japanese brought forces up from the south, but they could not form solid defenses against the drive from the north. At San Manuel the Japanese counterattacked with tanks and infantry but were destroyed by the 161st Regiment. By January 29, XIV Corps was at Clark Field less than fifty miles from Manila.

Seventy of MacArthur's transports were taken to carry supplies and munitions to the Russians at Vladivostok to support their future efforts against Japan. These supplies were not used against the Japanese but did end up in Korea where they were used against U.S. forces during the Korean War.

On January 29, MacArthur put XI Corps ashore north of Bataan to shorten his supply line, to outflank the Japanese, and to prevent their retirement into Bataan. On the thirty-first, the 1st Cavalry Division was brought ashore to envelope the Japanese right flank. That same day the 11th Airborne and 24th Divisions landed at Batangas south of Manila. By February 5 XI Corps had sealed off Bataan. On February 4, the 1st Cavalry and 37th Divisions from XIV Corps entered the northern outskirts of Manila while the 11th Airborne entered from the south. Motorized columns were sent to concentration camps where many were liberated before the Japanese could kill them.

By February 10, I Corps had crossed Luzon, isolating the Japanese in the north. On February 15, XI Corps attacked in Bataan, occupying the peninsula in seven days. XI Corps dropped a parachute regiment on Corregidor on February 16, shortly followed by an amphibious landing. Six thousand Japanese fought hard and it took twelve days to overcome them.

By mid February the Japanese casualties were estimated at 124,000, almost all dead. MacArthur's casualties were 8,000 dead and 17,000 wounded. These figures testify to the magnitude of the fighting and also to the efficiency of MacArthur's campaign. Manila was pacified by March 3, but the city was in ruins and 100,000 Filipinos were dead (no matter what this figure included, it is terrible, but it may include casualties outside Manila and over a wider time span than it took to capture the city). Regardless, the Japanese butchery in the Philippines, like the brutality of the Germans, is hard to believe of a "civilized" Twentieth Century nation—although this century has seen horror far greater than any century, ever, in the entire history of man.

After the fall of Manila, I Corps moved into the Cagayan Valley in the north. XI Corps attacked in the Sierra Madre hills east of Manila, and XIV Corps moved into southern Luzon. Southern Luzon was cleared by May 23, and by this day the 25th Division broke through in the Cagayan Valley. Remnants of the Japanese Army were surrounded in the hills, and by June 28, MacArthur reported the island liberated.

The rest of the Philippines were liberated by X Corps, six divisions. The Australians retook Borneo against light resistance. The rest of the Dutch East Indies and indeed all of Japanese occupied Southeast Asia was isolated from Japan. The Chinese coast was only a few hundred miles from the Philippines and all shipping from Japan south was subject to submarine and air attack. Indeed, after occupation of the Philippines, few supplies from the south reached Japan and few military supplies reached Japanese forces. This was a major factor in the weak resistance put up by the Japanese in Burma, Borneo, and many other islands in 1945.

In the Philippines the Japanese had had 23 divisions, 450,000 men, most of whom died. The U.S. had 17 divisions. MacArthur had destroyed or isolated two Japanese armies in the Philippines, three in New Guinea, and three in the Borneo, Celebes area, some millions of troops.

Iwo Jima, February, 1945

Once MacArthur was ashore in the Philippines, the next step closer to Japan was Iwo Jima, halfway between the Mariana's and Japan, 760 miles from Tokyo. B-29s, bombing Japan from Saipan needed a closer base for fighter cover and from which to recover damaged bombers. Large B-29 losses occurred during the raids over Japan from Japanese fighters, and fighter protection was necessary. Additionally Iwo could be used for air attacks on Okinawa, the next objective. There was no question that Iwo had to be taken and the Japanese knew it. They had 21,000 men, 149 artillery pieces, 69 anti-tank guns, 484 mortars, 1228 machine guns, 200 rocket launchers, 61 flame throwers, and 30 dug-in tanks. These were all protected in invisible caves (1,500 total) or dug-in pillboxes. Tarawa's pillboxes had been above ground and Peleliu's caves numbered only 500. This island would be the worst yet seen.

To take Iwo, 72 days of air bombardment and three days of naval shelling were used to soften defenses. In spite of all this most of the Japanese defenses remained intact.

Three Marine divisions would be used, 60,000 men. The Fifth Division would hit the eastern coast beaches on the southern portion of the island with the Fourth Division on their right. The Third Division was in reserve. General Harry Schmidt commanded. (By this time, the Marine Corps consisted of six divisions, 200,000 men. Each new division was sprinkled with veterans of other tested divisions.)

The landing beaches extended from the forward slopes of Mount Suribachi at the southern tip to the middle of the island where the land rose steeply to the north. The whole island was a volcanic rock, 4,000 yards wide in the north, only 1,000 yards wide in the south across Mt. Suribachi, and 8,000 yards long. In the flat area in the center the island was covered with volcanic ash or sand.

Japanese defenses were everywhere, but strongest and deepest in the north where there were two major defense lines. On February 19, at 9 A.M., the Fourth and Fifth Divisions landed all their assault battalions in one hour. Moving quickly inland they penetrated some 300 to 400 yards before the Japanese opened up. The defenders, however, had waited too long; if they had commenced firing upon the first wave, when men and boats were concentrated on the beach, casualties could have been catastrophic. Casualties would be terrible anyway, but that one hour allowed the two divisions to disperse. During the next two hours very few boats, amtracs, tanks, or equipment could be brought in. The beaches were a shambles. On the left the Fifth Division fought forward pillbox by pillbox, crossing the island and cutting off the Japanese on Mt. Suribachi.

On the right the Fourth Division took 35 percent casualties in one regiment, but penetrated inland to Airfield Number One, and took the high ground on the right flank from which devastating gunfire poured onto the beaches. The first day cost the Marines 2,420 casualties, with 600 dead. A beachhead 4,000 yards wide and 1,000 yards deep on the left, 400 yards deep on the right, had been achieved.

The next day, February 20, the 28th Marines under Colonel Harry Liversedge turned south to attack Mt. Suribachi which looked down on everything, and from which heavy artillery fire poured out incessantly. In one day, however, the 28th Marines gained only 200 yards, taking heavy casualties. On the twenty-first, with the aid of close air support, tanks, flame throwers, and naval gunfire, the 28th cleared out all the defenses up to the base of Mt. Suribachi. On the twenty-second the volcano was completely surrounded, and on the next day the Marines went right up to the top. They had broken through in the south. The 2nd Battalion commander formed a 40 man patrol, gave them a U.S. flag, and told them, if they reached the top, to hold the position. They reached the top with no resistance and at 10:30 A.M. raised the flag, which was 28" wide and 54" long. The Japanese then sprang from their caves but were quickly shot down. By 2:30 the volcano was secure.

Down below, no one could see the flag, so another marine took a flag from a ship on the beach and brought it up to the top. This time a photographer followed and took the picture, still famous, of the raising of the 56 by 96 inch flag. Now marines all over the island could see the flag and know they were winning. Just at this time, General Holland M. (Howling Mad) Smith, overall commander of the Amphibious Force, and Secretary of the Navy, James Forrestal, stepped ashore. As Forrestal looked up at the flag, he said that flag flying on Mount Suribachi guarantees the survival of the Marine Corps for 500 more years. (December 1945, President Truman would try to incorporate the Marine Corps into the Army but failed, fortunately.)

Meanwhile, the battle for the northern half of the island continued. Here, men crawled forward. Artillery spotters, if they survived, called in fire on each strongpoint. One officer crawled forward to direct fire for two days from the same spot in the hills. The Airfield Number One was taken on the twentieth, but by the twenty-third progress through the first defensive belt was limited, a little deeper on the coast lines. The 21st Marines from the Third Division were thrown into battle on the twenty-first and ordered to charge on the twenty-third. Charge they did, and they broke through, passing many obstacles, followed by tanks, taking Airfield Number Two. The rest of the Third Division came in, poured through the gap and into the hills overlooking the airfield. It wasn't until the twenty-seventh that the first belt was completely cut.

The Fifth Division, on the left, struggled for Hill 362, while the Fourth Division on the right fought in tightly defended hills called "The Meatgrinder." Here the Japanese used dug-in tanks, only turrets showing. The Fourth Division fought in this area until March 3 before it was taken for good. By this day the Fourth Division had 6,591 casualties, 30 percent. The Third Division in the center, meanwhile, had moved north to take Airfield Number Three, only 2,000 yards from the northern coast, but they faced defensive belt number two. On the left Fifth Division fought on Hill 362 until it fell on March 1.

On March 7, an hour and a half before dawn, the Ninth Marines tried to outflank the defensive belt number two by attacking east to Hill 331 and 362-C without any preparatory shelling (which usually warned the Japanese and allowed them to take cover). The Japanese in the first line on Hill 331 were caught asleep. Fighting was terrible but the hill was taken by nightfall. Hill 362-C fell soon afterward. Resistance began to crumble as Japanese began to commit suicide. One group of 784 men launched a *banzai* attack and were slaughtered. On the ninth a patrol reached the northern coast; it had taken 18 days to get there.

The Fourth Division finished cleanup in the east coast area and returned to Hawaii minus 9,098 men—1,806 dead. In three major battles the division had lost 17,722 men. The Fifth Division moved onto Kitano Point to eliminate the last strongholds on March 18. On the night of March 25, 300 survivors slipped out and attacked an Army Air Corps group, killing many, then ran into the Fifth Marine Pioneer Battalion, who finished them off. Iwo was now quiet, but there were 5,885 dead and 17,272 wounded marines. There were also 738 dead and wounded Navy corpsmen and doctors. Admiral Nimitz said that on Iwo Jima "uncommon valor was a common virtue." Such a phrase can only hint at the tenacity and courage of the marines who fought at Iwo.

Okinawa, 1945

While the battle for Iwo Jima raged, U.S. aircraft bombed Japanese air bases on Okinawa and Kyushu, the southernmost of the islands of Japan. Okinawa was the largest of the Ryukyu's, only 400 miles from Japan, the last stepping stone before the invasion of Japan itself. The island is mountainous, about sixty miles long, with widths varying from five to fifteen miles with a ten mile long peninsula (Motobu Peninsula) in the northwest.

For defense of the island, the Japanese had about 100,000 men, of whom 20,000 were native Okinawan conscripts. Okinawans were a very placid, peace loving race of farmers and those enlisted by the Japanese were disdainfully called the "Bimbo Butai" (Poor Detachment), and thus the word "bimbo" which is now common slang in the English language. The forces were not considered adequate for defense of the entire island and were concentrated mostly in the southern hills. There was almost no air force for defense, but the Japanese had prepared a large striking force of second rate planes with hastily trained young pilots for suicide attacks on the U.S. Navy.

This method of warfare, suicide attacks by aircraft, involving a pilot crashing his bomb laden plane on an American ship, was referred to as *kamikaze* (divine wind). Four hundred years ago a divine wind had destroyed a Mongol fleet as it was underway to invade Japan and the Japanese hoped their suicide attacks would destroy the U.S. Navy off Okinawa.

The U.S. approached Okinawa with a huge armada, 1,300 ships, 548,000 men of all services, and 183,000 soldiers and marines. 24th Corps under General Hodges consisted of four divisions (7th, 27th, 77th, and 96th). The Marine Third Corps under General Geiger included the 1st, 2nd, and 6th Divisions. Three of the Army divisions had been trained in amphibious operations by the Marines. In World War I, the British landing at Gallipoli in Turkey had been unsuccessful, and amphibious warfare was considered a bad risk by most military people. The Marine Corps (a unit of the U.S. Navy), however, had prepared for amphibious assaults prior to World War II in anticipation of the type of fighting that actually became a necessity. Working closely with the Navy, all marines were trained in ship to shore attacks.

The landings were planned for south-western beaches at Hagushi. The Marines on the left would attack across the island, then face to the north. The 24th Corps, on the right would also cross the island, then turn to the south. The Marines brought in replacement battalions and numbered 85,246 (normally a Marine division numbered about 20,000 men). The Army's four divisions numbered 88,515 soldiers.

On April 1 the men went ashore against light resistance. The Bimbo Butai had been expected to fight on the beach, but they fled soon after the naval bombardment began. Two Marine and two Army divisions were landed on a beachhead eight miles wide. The other Marine division (the 2nd) faked a landing off the southern beaches which were heavily fortified. By nightfall 50,000 men with tanks were ashore, and had pushed inland three to four miles. The next day, the island was crossed, and after clearing operations the Marines turned north. The 24th Corps turned south but by April 4 they were meeting increasingly stiff resistance.

On April 6, the *kamikaze's* attacked. First came Japanese fighters, which drew off the U.S. carrier air patrol (CAP). Then came 200 *kamikaze* planes, roaring in for five hours, hitting the first ships they saw, destroyers in the radar picket screen, then the maze of ships in Hagushi Anchorage. Two U.S. destroyers, two ammunition ships, and one LST (Landing Ship, Tank) were sunk; nine destroyers, four destroyer escorts, and five mine vessels were damaged. Elsewhere a carrier and two destroyers were damaged. 135 Japanese planes were shot down, but it was a brutal day for the Navy.

Also on April 6 the Japanese managed to accumulate enough fuel to power one battleship (the 72,000 ton *Yamato*, with 18 inch guns, the most powerful ship afloat), one cruiser, and eight destroyers on a one way trip to Okinawa for a suicide attack on the U.S. Navy. This group was spotted by a U.S. submarine and aircraft, then attacked by 380 U.S. planes on the seventh. In three separate attacks by dive bombers and torpedo planes, the whole Japanese fleet was sunk, the last of the Japanese Navy.

The Sixth Marine Division was given the assignment of attacking to the north. By April 8 they had reached the entrance to the Motobu Peninsula. Here some 2,000 Japanese had dug in on Mount Yaetake. By April 13, the Marines were near the crest, but small groups of Japanese armed with machine guns were everywhere. Artillery and naval gunfire were employed to help wipe out these nests, but it wasn't until April 20 that the Motobu Peninsula and the northern two thirds of the island were secured.

In the south 24th Corps came up against the outer works of the Japanese defenses on April 8. With two divisions in line, the 7th and 96th, 24th Corps was stopped completely by April 11. During the nights of April 12 and 13, the Japanese counterattacked. Both attacks were thrown back with heavy Japanese losses, 1,574 men.

On April 12, another massed *kamikaze* attack was made on U.S. shipping. On April 16, the 77th Division landed on Ie Shima Island off the coast of the Motobu Peninsula, running into a hornet's nest. In four days the soldiers killed 4,706 Japanese while losing 258 dead and 879 wounded. Among the dead was Ernie Pyle, probably the most famous and respected of the war correspondents.

On April 19, General Hodge attacked on a five mile front with three divisions, supported by 21 warships, 650 Marine and Navy planes, and 27 battalions of artillery (3 battalions per division was normal). In one day the 27th Division lost 22 of its 60 tanks. In twelve days only two miles were gained. The Japanese, well dug in, were almost immune to conventional shelling and bombing. Tanks could not reach many of the defenses and the job fell to the infantry.

During the first week of May, two battered Army divisions were pulled out and the fresh divisions from the north brought in. From left (east) to right (west) U.S. forces then consisted of the 24th Corps (7th and 77th Divisions) and the Marine Third Corps (1st and 6th Divisions). Before the U.S. could regain the initiative, the Japanese struck. On the night of May 3, *kamikazes* sank a destroyer and an LSM (Landing Ship, Medium) damaging three other small vessels with the loss of 36 planes. Then the Japanese tried amphibious night landings on both coasts. On the west coast, instead of landing behind Marine lines, they came ashore right at the flank outposts, and were destroyed with the loss of 500 men. On the other coast, the Navy spotted them, bringing in gunfire from ship and shore to wipe out another 400. At dawn on the fourth, the main attack came against the Army. One Japanese division was to punch through and a second division was to pour through the breech then turn left behind the Marines. As they attacked the soldiers, a terrible barrage of shells and bombs from aircraft, artillery and naval guns pulverized them. That same day, the Marines attacked, gaining a half mile in two days. By the night of May 5, the Japanese attack was finished with losses of 6,227 men. The Army lost 714, the Marines 649.

On May 4, *kamikazes* came again, sinking two destroyers and two LSMs. They damaged a carrier, a cruiser, two destroyers, a mine sweeper and an LCS, but lost 95 planes. On May 10, 50 *kamikazes* attacked two destroyers. The ships shot down over 20 and Marine pilots picked off 19, but each destroyer took four hits. The ships were towed to repair yards on islands south of Okinawa.

Rain and mud delayed progress for awhile, but on May 11, U.S. forces launched a full scale attack all along the line. The 6th Marine Division rushed men to the top of "Sugar Loaf" hill time and again, only to be attacked from the reverse slope and thrown off. On the seventeenth, the 29th Marine Regiment worked around the side of the hill, finally taking Sugar Loaf with the help of tanks on the 18th.

The 1st Division took three days to capture Dakeshi and another week to fight through Wana Draw, fighting uphill against flanking high ground with the aid of tanks and mechanized flame throwers. On the twenty-third, the 6th Division took Naha, outflanking the Japanese Yonabaru-Shuri-Naha Line. That night *kamikazes* sank two ships and damaged eight while losing 150 planes.

The Japanese tried to pull back to a last stand position in the Kiyamu Peninsula but they were spotted and shattered by aircraft, naval vessels, and artillery, leaving 500 to 800 more dead and much damaged equipment. Marines from the 1st Division then occupied Shuri Castle, the key to the whole central position. The Marine advance had opened up the side door and they took the Castle even though it was in the Army zone. There was some wrangling over this, but possession of the key terrain was too significant to justify a protest over improper procedures. (This incident contrasts with the reluctance of Eisenhower to allow Patton to take Falaise in the British zone in France, allowing the Germans to escape the Falaise pocket.) The flag first raised over Shuri Castle was the Stars and Bars (the Confederate Civil War flag).

The final offensive was slated for June 4. Twenty-fourth corps had three divisions and on their right the 1st Marine Division was reinforced with a regiment from the 2nd Division (8th Marines). The 6th Marine Division was pulled out of line to make an amphibious landing on the Oroku Peninsula, jutting out from southeastern Okinawa. On the peninsula in nine days of bitter fighting, 5000 Japanese died, but 6th Division casualties were 1608. By this time the 1st Division had broken through to the south coast and 24th Corps, fighting over the Yaeju-Yuza peaks, was also near the coast. On June 18 Generals Ushijima and Cho committed *hara-kiri*. Ara Point was taken by June 21, and a few mopping-up operations in the south and north were required, but the battle was over.

Japanese losses were 90,000 dead, 10,000 captured. U.S. casualties were 49,151.

The Marines had 2,938 dead, 13,708 wounded; the Army had 4,675 dead 18,099 wounded. At sea, the Navy lost 4,907 dead with 4,824 wounded. After six months of aerial combat, the Japanese lost 7,800 planes to 763 American, and their air power was gone. At sea the Japanese lost *Yamato* and 15 other ships, but the U.S. Navy suffered 36 ships sunk, 368 damaged. Even so the U.S. Navy was still strong, but the Japanese Navy was finished.

Okinawa was a brutal battle, involving every U.S. service. Casualties were awful, and gave the U.S. reason to suspect the price for occupying the Japanese home islands would be a bloody one. Almost every Japanese soldier fought to the death as he was expected to give his life for his Emperor. Over half the casualties on Okinawa and more then half the fighting men were U.S. Army. By wars end there were many fine Army divisions in the Pacific. The Pacific battles won by Marines had drawn much publicity but the Army record in the Pacific was also outstanding. The Marine achievements in the Pacific were incredible, however, and added to the glorious tradition and pride of the Corps and everyone who ever served in it. There would be no more combat amphibious landings. The Marines had finished their job. There is a poem, popular in World War 11, which bears repeating:

And when he gets to Heaven,
To Saint Peter he will tell,
"One more marine reporting, Sir;
I've served my time in Hell!"

MacArthur was planning the invasion of Japan when the atomic bombs were dropped, August 7 on Hiroshima, and August 9 on Nagasaki. One hundred thousand died instantly at Nagasaki. Japan sued for peace on August 10. Russia declared war on Japan on August 9, not to help the U.S., but to grab as much land as possible. The U.S. had asked the Russians to assist in the war against Japan, but the atom bomb eliminated the need for their assistance, and as it turned out it was a huge mistake, allowing Russian occupation of Manchuria and North Korea, resulting eventually in another war five years later in Korea.

The Aftermath

World War II, undertaken against the awesome powers of Japan, Italy, and Germany, brought out the best in the American people. With superb leadership from President Roosevelt, Army Chief of Staff George Marshall, Chief of Naval Operations Ernest King, and all their staffs, an army and navy were formed and trained from very little. Production of weapons was planned and initiated before the war and as these weapons appeared in the battlefields, the United States military force became formidable, something this world may never see again. The people at home, including many women, worked in the war industries, and the results of this enormous effort are history.

Many of the men who served in these victorious services are still with us and take pride in their accomplishments with them forever. Every citizen should recall what they did and thank the Almighty that such men were there when they were needed.

In 1946 Winston Churchill praised the creation of a huge American army from a force of only several hundred thousand men. He had witnessed the training of the U.S. Army and the rapid formation of divisions into corps and armies which, when thrown into battle, would ultimately be successful in each war theatre. This achievement, he felt, was one of the great accomplishments in military history.

Beyond this Churchill wondered where the U.S. found all the officers and staffs necessary to lead these vast forces over much of the earth in an effort above any other ever seen in war. These praises, although directed at the U.S. Army apply equally to all the American services. The generation of men and women who won this war have been called the greatest generation and they were, but when future challenges to this nation arise other Americans will rise to the occasion.

In World War II the forces of Fascism were crushed and the United States emerged as the world's dominant power. The atom bomb and our economic strength made this so. There would be five years before the Russians developed an atomic bomb and the U.S. would have to pick up arms again.

World War II occurred because Germany was suffering and the German people found a pied piper to lead them to prosperity: the madman, Hitler. It occurred also because in the Pacific a militant Japan was determined to obtain two things that she did not have, land and natural resources. As Germany rearmed, the French and English refused to acknowledge the threat and to take up arms again. Their peoples, sick of war and death, wanted peace and the French and English politicians reflected the wishes of their peoples. Churchill, out of power in England, was a solitary voice warning the world about Hitler. No one listened, but when they were in trouble, the English people put him back in power to lead them out of their dilemma.

The people in the United States, concerned with their domestic problems, the Depression, were little concerned about Hitler and paid little attention to the aggressions and atrocities of the Japanese in China.

Somehow the United States managed to stop the Japanese with toothpicks and baling wire and the courage of a few brave pilots at Midway, a few courageous sailors in the Solomons, and a small force of well trained Marines. Small contingents of Australians did the job in New Guinea under the brilliant guidance of MacArthur. In North Africa George Patton took the beaten Americans at Kasserine Pass and turned them around almost overnight. Americans took their weapons and went out to face the most formidable armed forces the world had ever seen. To read about their accomplishments is to admire them, but to read about their struggles and casualties also brings up the question, "Why didn't we see it coming and prepare sooner?" The U.S. just was not prepared for any of its conflicts up to and including World War II. Maybe the U.S. had learned; maybe the U.S. would be ready for the next war. Let's take a look at the Korean War, just five years later.

Chapter VII
The Korean War, 1950–1953

Communism Threatens the World Balance of Power, 1945–1950

With the close of World War II, the age of emperors, kings, dictators, and Fascists came to an end. But on the eastern bank of the Elbe River in Germany, the huge Soviet Army sat, cutting off all access to the eastern European nations. The Russians had agreed to self determination for these countries, but it soon became obvious that their future was to be determined by Russia. By March 6, 1946, Churchill made his famous speech in which he stated that "an iron curtain has descended across the Continent." This was the start of Communist expansion into many nations, no longer by direct invasion, but by instigation and support of revolutionary movements (if the revolution was or claimed to be by communists). Continued Russian support was obtained only if the leaders of the revolution followed Russian policy guidelines. Thus one communist country, like cancer, became a threat to spread communist revolutions to its neighbors.

In 1947, President Truman said that the U.S. would assist those nations whose freedom was threatened by internal subversion by a militant minority or by direct interference from other nations. Support was given to Greece where a civil war against communists did break out. The communists were eventually defeated.

Concerned about economic chaos in Europe where communist revolts were a threat, the Marshall Plan for economic aid was developed. In Japan, MacArthur governed, encouraging democracy and capital based economics. Europe and Japan began to recover and the fear of communism in these places faded.

In 1948, a communist uprising began in Malaya where the British fought for twelve years to finally win. In Indo-China, a communist, Ho Chi Minh, who sought an independent Vietnam, began to fight the French. In the Philippines the Huks rose up again, with communist support, and this fight lasted from 1946 to 1957. In China Mao Tse-tung led a communist civil war against Chang Kai-shek and the Nationalist government. Chang was given some financial aid by the U.S. but no direct assistance. Americans close to China, like General Joe Stilwell, clearly spelled out the rotten, corrupt nature of the existing government. The only good thing about Nationalist China was its sympathy for the western world and the fact that it wasn't communist. The communists won by October 1949, and the Nationalists retreated to Formosa, which was renamed Taiwan. MacArthur stated that the effects of this would last for centuries. The immediate impact would be felt within a year and MacArthur would have to deal with it. He might have softened his prediction to say "decades" rather then centuries.

In 1949, however, Russia and China had common interests in expansion and made a sudden shift in the world balance of power. The masses of China combined with the proven armament capabilities of the Soviet Union became a dangerous and formidable threat. To make this shift more dramatic and serious, in late August of 1949, the U.S. detected atmospheric radioactivity which had to come from a Russian atomic explosion.

After World War II, President Truman, comfortable with his atomic bomb superiority, allowed the entire U.S. defensive establishment to deteriorate to a dangerously ineffective level. He was obsessed with cutting military costs to help balance his budget, and appointed a Secretary of Defense, Louis Johnson, to do the work. Johnson did so with excessive energy and, along with Truman, must be held responsible for the sad state of our armed forces at the time of the Korean War.

In 1950 the Army had 10 divisions, all but the 82nd Airborne under strength and not combat ready. The Army had about 600,000 men, 360,000 in the U.S. and other miscellaneous places, 110,000 in the Far East, and 100,000 in Europe. In Japan MacArthur had most of his old Eighth Army, four divisions (1st Cavalry, 7th, 24th, and 25th Divisions) under Patton's former XX Corps Commander, Walton Walker.

MacArthur's chief of staff was Ned Almond, who had commanded the ill fated all black 92nd Division in Italy. Almond was a brilliant, extremely energetic man, highly regarded in the Army in spite of his war-time failure.

At the end of World War II the U.S. 24th Corps from Okinawa was sent to Korea to meet the Russians at the 38th Parallel, north of Seoul. This occupation force was continuously reduced until 1950 when only 500 advisors were left. In the meantime the Republic of Korea (ROK) Army was enlarged to 100,000 men. These troops had been fairly well trained but were poorly led and were not armed with aircraft, tanks, or much artillery. (The U.S. was afraid they would invade North Korea.) When the Russians pulled out of North Korea, they left an army of 135,000 men, well equipped with planes, tanks, artillery, and a good nucleus with combat experience in the Chinese Civil War.

The United States had no plans for fighting Asian masses on the continent of Asia, feeling that this was a most undesirable place to fight a war. To make matters worse Secretary of State Dean Acheson and Senator Tom Connally both made public statements excluding Korea from our sphere of interest. To counter such invitations to potential aggressors, MacArthur told the President of South Korea, Syngman Rhee, in 1948, that if South Korea were attacked, he

(MacArthur) would defend it. In this MacArthur was exceeding his authority. In 1949 Korea was removed from his sphere of responsibility. The Truman Administration had done well in resisting world wide communist threats except in the Far East where it had lost China and now gave the North Koreans and their Russian and Chinese backers reason to believe they could take South Korea without U.S. opposition.

North Korea Invades South Korea, June 25, 1950

The ROK Army had four divisions in position near the 38th Parallel, with the 1st, 7th, and 6th guarding the most likely invasion routes in the low lying hills on the western side of the peninsula and the 8th Division in the mountains on the east coast. The 2nd Division was in reserve. Many of the battalions in the front line divisions were not actually in the front lines on June 25, nor were their commanding officers all at the front.

Early on Sunday morning, June 25, the North Korean People's Army (NKPA) attacked. Two divisions, each led by forty good Russian T34 tanks struck the ROK 7th Division. In the 1st Division sector, a regiment of NKPA's took a train into Kaesong behind one ROK regiment. The other two regiments formed back on the Imjin River. Further east two NKPA divisions struck the 6th Division. This division had two full strength regiments on line with artillery support and did some damage.

The 7th Division soon collapsed leaving the 1st and 6th Division flanks exposed.

Both of these divisions also fell back. The 8th Division was overwhelmed also and within three days all four divisions were in retreat.

When the news of the invasion reached Washington, there was initially a belief that the ROKs would hold. There was also much concern that the attack was a feint, and the main effort would be in Europe after the U.S. committed forces in Korea. Army Chief of Staff J. Lawton Collins (of First Army, VII Corps, WW II fame) and his assistant, Matt Ridgeway, commander of WW II paratroop divisions urged immediate partial mobilization. A meeting was held with Truman, Acheson, Chairman of the Joint Chiefs Omar Bradley, and the Joint Chiefs—fourteen men in all. All agreed the attack was an outrage, testing American resolve. Not to respond would be to invite similar aggressions all over the world. Stalin had in the years 1945-1950 caused the U.S. much agony. There was no interest in Korea but the U.S. had to draw a line, and this was the place.

Macarthur was asked to go see what was going on. MacArthur sent General Church instead, who, upon arrival in Korea soon saw the ROK Army in a disorganized retreat. Church organized a stand on the Han River south of Seoul during the night of the 27th. During the next morning he advised MacArthur who arrived the next day. MacArthur ordered an aerial attack on North Korean airfields (without the authority to do so). MacArthur also observed that American ground forces would be required to stabilize the situation and so advised Washington. His recommendations arrived in Washington at midnight on June 29. The next morning Truman approved the use of U.S. forces, and personally gave MacArthur permission to use all the forces at his disposal. Truman also suggested the use of Nationalist Chinese troops, but fortunately the Joint Chiefs did not heed this idea (this surely would have brought in the Communist Chinese long before they actually did jump in). Truman then tried to minimize the conflict by labeling it a "police action." This definition represented his approach to the war and was the direct cause of much of the trouble soon to develop.

MacArthur's staff made plans immediately for the transfer of two divisions to Korea, the 24th to move up on the western (left) side and the 25th to move up on the right. Immediate success was expected and an amphibious landing at Inchon by the 1st Cavalry Division was planned. The 24th Division, commanded by General William Dean (the only division commander with combat experience) was beefed up to 16000 men by transfer from the other divisions. Four hundred fifty men were all that could be flown to Korea; the rest of Dean's division would have to go by ship.

The Ordeal of the 24th Division

On July 1, the first contingent reached Pusan by air, two rifle companies with ten 2.36 inch bazookas and two heavy weapons platoons. Of four 75 mm recoilless rifles and four 4.2 inch mortars, only half could be flown with the heavy weapons men. The infantry were joined by one artillery battery (six 105 mm howitzers) with only six armor piercing rounds per gun. On July 3, this pitiful little group of 540 men moved north to Taejon where General Dean soon arrived to plan a defense, relieving Church. Dean sent the first arrivals under Lt. Colonel Smith, called Task Force Smith to a position north of Osan, on the Seoul-Pusan highway. On July 5, at 7:30 A.M. an NKPA column came down the road led by 8 T34 tanks, followed by 25 others, leading a column six miles long, one armored regiment and one infantry division.

At a range of 1700 yards, the U.S. artillery fired high explosives at the tanks with no effect. At 700 yards, the recoilless rifles fired, again with no results. At 15 yards bazookas were fired and the shells could not stop the tanks. T34 tank armor was too thick for these weapons and the agony of Smith's men must have been great. Four tanks were eventually knocked out with armor piercing shells and the bazookas, but the rest of the tanks went right through Task Force Smith.

At 11:30 A.M. the NKPA infantry attacked. The Americans fought until 2:30, but by then they were almost surrounded. Smith gave the order to withdraw, but the men panicked and ran, leaving most of their weapons. Smith should have ordered an attack by platoons or companies to selected terrain features in the rear, but such moves could only be accomplished by well trained, disciplined, veteran troops, which these were not. Smith lost 185 men and the rude setback was very bad for troop morale.

A battalion of the 34th Regiment was sent forward to fight a delaying action at Pyongtaek, but was soon ordered to withdraw. These troops, seeing the columns of NKPA, threw down their weapons and ran. As the 34th Regiment tried to concentrate at Chonan, every withdrawal from forward positions produced the same results, and the men that gathered at Chonan were a pathetic mob. General Dean, who had ordered resistance on a line through Pyongtaek was furious when he found out about the withdrawals. Dean ordered a battalion counterattack at Chonan, and this effort ran into an ambush, then another bugout. Three able officers tried to stem the retreat; one, personally attacking a tank with a bazooka, was cut in half by an 85mm shell from the tank; another died and another was captured, badly wounded. Finally General Walker arrived to confer with Dean and they agreed to set up the 24th Division in a defense south of the Kum River near Taejon. Delaying fights had been very disappointing, but even so, by July 8, the NKPA were only at Chonan, halfway between Seoul and Taejon. Their speed south had been slowed. The mere presence of U.S. forces must have caused them to pause, patrol, and regroup. As poor as it was, Dean's delaying tactics were accomplishing something.

On July 8, Dean wrote to MacArthur explaining the quality of the NKPA and the poor quality of U.S. equipment, asking especially for the 3.5 inch bazooka, armor piercing artillery, 90mm anti-tank guns, and tanks with 90mm guns. Dean also stated that a two battalion regiment was not effective, that the full three battalions were required as well as three full regiments per division.

On July 10 at Chonui, Dean sent out another battalion to fight another delaying action. Major Jenson led this battalion in a counterattack with three tanks, but the tank guns had no recoil oil and blew up. Jenson took some ground and found six dead Americans, hands tied, shot in the head, execution style. These men fought for three hours, then ran. U.S. planes came in, bombing and strafing the U.S. troops. (There were no air spotters with U.S. infantry at this time.)

That same day U.S. aircraft found an NKPA column, knocking out 38 tanks, 124 vehicles, and killing a large number of enemy troops. This was a huge victory, badly needed.

On July 11, Jensen's battalion was encircled and hard hit at Chochiwon, losing over 300 men. Brad Smith's battalion came next but fought well, withdrawing one company at a time. The Army was learning how to fight. This regiment, the 21st, had done well, unlike the 34th which, so far, had been unable to resemble a military unit.

After one week the U. S. had lost some 3,000 men in a performance quite comparable to Bull Run in the Civil War.

Between July 2 and 10, MacArthur advised Washington that a real war was at hand, requesting his four divisions be brought up to strength, requesting four more divisions including Marines and three tank battalions. He wanted Marines to make his Inchon landing. He was granted most of the units needed in his four divisions, plus the 2nd Division, the tanks, and the artillery. At this time the U.S. should have gone into a war preparation mode, initiating the draft and calling up the National Guard, but, gambling that the limited forces just mentioned could defeat the NKPA, the Joint Chiefs of Staff did not press Truman for such drastic action. Omar Bradley, Chairman of the Joint Chiefs of Staff (JCS) must bear some responsibility for this.

Truman did approve of the moves made to reinforce MacArthur, but the eight division request (which was not unreasonable) would not be met. Large forces were needed to cover the width of the Korean peninsula adequately. This was a war on the Asian mainland and the forces potentially available to the enemy, including Chinese, were unlimited.

Collins and Vandenburg (Air Chief of Staff) went to Japan to see MacArthur. Collins explained to MacArthur that all the forces he requested would not be forthcoming; then, MacArthur knew he was going to have to fight with limited forces, again. From this moment on the tension between MacArthur and Truman would grow. After Collins returned to Washington, the Army National Guard and Reserves were called up as were the Marine Reserves. The entire First Marine Division would go to Korea with the 5th Marines going early. (The 5th Marines of Belleau Wood and Guadalcanal renown had a glorious history, but their achievements in Korea would equal any of their past triumphs.)

Taejon, July, 1950

Forming on the Kum River, Dean brought up his 19th Regiment, putting the 21st in reserve. On the left, he set up the battered 34th. At about this time the 25th Division was landing in Pusan, moving up to the central front. The ROKs were holding in the mountains in the east. The 1st Cavalry Division was scheduled to come ashore on the 18th to reinforce the western front (a landing at Inchon was being postponed until Eighth Army could stabilize their defense). On July 14, the NKPA attacked the 34th which had only two companies in line. The NKPA went right through one company (the other held) wiping out much of a field artillery battalion behind the lines. That night the 34th pulled back. The 19th Regiment held on for a while but straggled back on the sixteenth. Dean now gathered his forces around Taejon while the NKPA regrouped. On the eighteenth Walker urged Dean to hold Taejon for two more days while the 1st Cavalry Division came ashore, and so Dean held on. The NKPA attacked on the 19th and managed to get around the flanks of many of Dean's defenses which were not continuous. NKPA poured into rear artillery, medical, and command units. On the twentieth, the infantry around Taejon disintegrated. Beauchamp, 34th Commander, ordered counterattacks with limited forces which accomplished little. Dean and Beauchamp grabbed bazooka teams and went tank hunting (a strange occupation for senior commanders, probably indicating excessive stress and frustration, similar to the actions of Vendome at Oudenarde in 1708.)

On the twenty-first, Dean ordered a withdrawal from Taejon, but it was too late for an orderly retreat as most of the roads out were blocked. Dean ended up in the hills on foot and was captured 36 days later. He was awarded a Medal of Honor for his heroic efforts but later stated that he wasn't proud of his achievements. His had been the sacrificial division with the job of buying time and his piecemeal but frequent counterattacks and stands were the proper approach. The effort was chaotic but few would have had the stamina or courage to stand and fight as long as he had.

MacArthur, at this time, could see the full extent of his dilemma and ordered all new troops, the 2nd Division and the 5th Marines, to Pusan. Inchon would have to wait a little longer.

The Pusan Perimeter

It was 65 miles from Taejon to Taegu and 55 miles from Taegu to Pusan. Taegu was about as far east as Eighth Army could afford to retreat, but Walker had to set up some kind of stable defense. When the 25th Division arrived at Pusan between July 10 and 12, it was directed north of Taegu to back up the ROKs holding precariously north of that town. The 25th Division had three regiments, the 24th (all black and held in poor regard), the 27th, and 35th, both of which had been robbed to supply the 24th Division. The 27th "Wolf-hound" Regiment was commanded by Mike Michaelis, one of the most able officers in the U.S. Army, recently given the 27th. The Wolfhounds, containing a large number of proud, dedicated Hawaiians, were a fine regiment right from the start, as shall be seen.

The 27th landed on July 10 at Pusan and sent one battalion north of Taegu and one battalion to Pohang on the coast. The ROKs north of these positions were holding, however, and the 27th had ten days to dig in. The 24th landed on July 13 and moved north of Kumchon on the left of the 27th. On the nineteenth the NKPA, pushing the ROKs back, captured Yechon. The 3rd Battalion of the 24th was ordered to retake the town. This black battalion attacked in good form and recaptured Yechon. A flanking movement by the NKPA was spotted by a black engineering officer, Charles Bussey, who grabbed some troops and two machine guns which he manned to good effect. Bussey was wounded but killed 258 NKPA. He was recommended for a Congressional Medal (which he deserved) but received only a Silver Star. The 24th, at this point, looked very good. On July 20, the 35th arrived and the entire division was shifted left of the ROKs on a line running northeast from Kumchon to Hamchang.

On July 18, the 1st Cavalry Division came ashore, the 8th, 5th, and 7th Regiments. The 8th Cavalry's two battalions were sent out to block roads from

Taejon to Taegu, but the roads were seven miles apart. The NKPA attacked the two battalions on July 23 and one held, but the other was encircled and cut off. The 5th Cavalry came up but the encircled battalion had to extricate themselves, which they did, but with loss. By the twenty-fifth, three of the four 1st Cavalry battalions had been thrown back. The 7th Cavalry landed, sent one battalion into battle and it too was dispersed. The U.S. Army, thrown in piecemeal in widely separated locations was taking a beating. By the twenty-sixth, the 1st Cavalry Division had formed a defensive line, thin, but with the units in contact. On July 24, four NKPA divisions struck the 25th Division. Michaelis had his 1st Battalion on the line which beat off one attack, withdrew during the night, leaving the positions under the guns of the 2nd Battalion stationed on the next ridgeline. The NKPA attacked the vacated positions the next day and were decimated by the 2nd Battalion. Michaelis pulled back the 2nd Battalion before it was surrounded in a brilliant action.

The 35th Regiment held but ROKs and the 24th Regiment collapsed leaving the northern defenses in poor shape, but the NKPA pulled out two divisions for an offense in the south and failed to take advantage of the situation.

The 24th Division, held in reserve while rebuilt, was put back into the line at this time to meet the new threat in the south. The 29th Regiment, refilled with green replacements, was moved to Chinju to hold the NKPA and suffered 618 casualties.

On July 28 Walker pulled back to Hwanggan, Kumchon, and Sangju. MacArthur ordered Walker to stand, no more retreats, and Walker advised his army accordingly.

When the 24th Division was pushed back to Masan on the southern flank, Walker replaced it with the 25th Division. By the end of July, Eighth Army was pushed into a box about 100 miles from north to south and 50 miles from east to west, the "Pusan Perimeter." The U.S. had broken the NKPA radio code and now knew where the enemy would attack but the U.S. lines were very thin.

By August 1, U.S. losses were 6,000; 2,300 dead or missing; 2,700 wounded; 1,000 captured, most in the 24th Division. Eighth Army had 30,000 U.S. troops already ashore with 40,000 ROKs. Unknown however was the fact that the NKPA had suffered 70,000 casualties and had only 70,000 effectives. Eighth Army was dispersed however and the NKPA retained the initiative. They had ten divisions and poured in green replacements for their casualties. Then, in early August, the U.S. 2nd Division, U.S. 5th Regiment, and the 5th Marine Brigade (reinforced Fifth Marine Regiment) arrived. From this moment on Pusan was safe, but the nature of the fighting didn't change.

From south to north, Eighth Army units in the line were, 5th Regiment, 25th Division, 24th Division, 1st Cavalry Division, and ROKs in the north. The 5th Marines were in reserve in the south and the 2nd Division would replace the beat-up 24th Division.

Before the 24th pulled out of the line near Masan, Michaelis was ordered to launch a counterattack with a battalion of his 27th, the 19th Regiment, and some of the new Sherman tanks. This force took the two main roads leading west, but the 19th ran into trouble. This outfit, with many green replacements from Okinawa, fell back in confusion. On the south road, the 1/27 (First Battalion, 27th Regiment) struck the flank of the NKPA attacking the 19th and punished them severely. The Wolfhounds had to fight their way back and fought off a counterattack the next day at the Regimental CP, killing 600 NKPA. The Wolfhounds had done it again.

On August 7, another attack by the 5th and 35th Regiments took off on the same two roads near Masan. The 5th Marines further south would outflank the NKPA and turn north. The 24th Regiment was in reserve between the two roads. The 35th advanced to its objective, fighting off NKPA attacks, but a major attack struck the 24th, causing a whole battalion to bug out.

The 5th Regiment first took the wrong road, then sent one battalion ahead to link up with the 35th. The other two battalions were ambushed along the way on August 12, and the regiment was in trouble.

The Fifth Marines (a whole brigade under General Eddie Craig) consisted of 6,500 men, three infantry battalions, one artillery battalion from the 11th Marines (eighteen 105mm howitzers) and a tank battalion with Pershing's (90mm guns). Each Marine squad had three Browning automatic rifles. Each company had a platoon of 60mm mortars and light machine guns. Each battalion had a heavy weapons company of 81mm mortars and heavy machine guns. They had 3.5 inch bazookas, and each front line battalion had artillery, air, and Navy spotters. The Marines had their own aircraft and could bring down a torrent of fire and steel on anyone they confronted. Many officers and non commissioned officers (NCOs) were World War II veterans.

By August 9, the Marines were on the move, and by the eleventh they had advanced fifteen miles to Sachon, behind the NKPA. Meanwhile 300 of the Army 5th Regiment artillery men were being wiped out. A battalion of the 24th Regiment was ordered to come to the rescue but these blacks turned and ran, killing or wounding three of their officers who tried to stop them. The Marines were ordered to attack to the rear and support the 5th Regiment. Their progress was supervised by Colonel Murray from a helicopter. The NKPA melted away in front of the Marines and the entire force returned to their lines without further damage. Marine planes from carriers, however, caught an NKPA motorized regiment on the road and smashed most of the vehicles, causing heavy casualties. The Fifth Marines then joined the Wolfhounds as Army reserves, used to stop breakthroughs wherever they occurred.

With early failures of regimental and division commanders, numerous replacements and promotions of successful combat proven officers took place. The choice of one good regimental commander could upgrade the whole regiment just as Patton's appointment to command the U.S. II Corps in Tunisia had transformed the whole corps. In a small organization like the Marine Corps, all the top commanders were combat proven.

On August 6, the NKPA 4th Division punched right through the weak and thin defense of the 24th Division along the Naktong River. The 9th Regiment of the 2nd Division came up to help but made little progress. By August 10, the NKPA were threatening Yongsan 8 miles east of the Naktong. Two battalions of Wolfhounds were sent up from the south with another 2nd Division battalion from the north, and the three battalions broke through to Yongsan. Meanwhile the remnants of the 24th Division remained at their defenses facing the Naktong. Attempts to dislodge the NKPA east of the Naktong were, however, unsuccessful. Walker then cancelled the southern offensive and brought up the 5th Marines who attacked on August 17 in conjunction with the seven army battalions already there. The Marine attack included their tanks, artillery, and aircraft and the NKPA 4th Division was slaughtered, with remnants fleeing back across the Naktong.

About this time three army tank battalions arrived with 200 tanks, new Pattons, Shermans, and Pershings.

On August 9, the NKPA attacked the 5th Cavalry at Taegu and were pulverized. A counterattack by the 1/7, Clainos' Clouters, wiped out the remnants. A few days later the 10th NKPA Division attacked the 7th Cavalry and were stopped, then smashed by Clainos' 1st Battalion. On August 14, the NKPA 3rd Division struck a battalion of the 5th Cavalry and caught the men asleep, taking a key hill. A counterattack failed but another counterattack following a massive air attack regained the hill. Twenty-six more Americans were found executed on the hill. In these actions the First Cavalry Division had punished two NKPA divisions.

On the right of the First Cavalry, the ROK First Division was attacked by three NKPA divisions (20,000 men). The ROKs fought well but the North Koreans managed to advance to Tabu, just fifteen miles north of Taegu by August 15. On the coast two NKPA divisions outflanked the ROK Third Division, isolating the ROKs and capturing Pohang.

Walker sent the Wolfhounds up to support the ROK First Division and the Wolfhounds dug in. Night after night the NKPA attacked and every night they were smashed. This area became known as the "Bowling Alley." The NKPA 13th Division lost 4000 men. Just to the east segments of the NKPA First Division ran into the U.S. 23rd Regiment and were stopped. The 23rd counterattacked and destroyed an NKPA regiment. The two army regiments probably caused 10,000 enemy casualties.

On the coast the ROK Third Division was removed by sea, was joined by the Capital Division, and then attacked, recovering Pohang and killing 3800 North Koreans.

By this time Walker had 122,000 combat troops, half American, backed by 24,000 service troops with 500 tanks and 360 artillery pieces. Eighth Army was constantly being reorganized as more and more combat proven officers were brought in to command the weaker units. Gradually, for example, the 24th Division was transformed from one of the worst to one of the best divisions.

Planning for Inchon

A landing at Inchon near Seoul behind enemy lines had been MacArthur's intention since the very beginning. Now it was decided the entire First Marine Division and the U.S. Army Seventh Division would make the landings. Nobody but MacArthur liked the site chosen (Inchon), however. It had fortifications, limited high tide periods, was too close to Seoul which was bound to be heavily defended, had a narrow access channel, etc., etc. MacArthur liked Inchon because it was close to the enemy supply line which he expected to quickly sever, and so he fought for his plan, and he won.

Army Chief-of-Staff Collins thought that a Marine General should direct the landings (and he was quite correct) but MacArthur appointed his own Chief-of-Staff, Ned Almond, to command the new X Corps. This decision shocked and offended Collins who feared that Almond would not cooperate with Walker.

MacArthur liked him and probably appointed him just to get the Inchon plans set up to suit MacArthur. Considering the opposition to the landing plans, the appointment is understandable, but led to many future problems.

MacArthur received permission to land at Inchon finally, but the JCS ordered him to develop alternate plans for another site in case the landings did not go well, and to submit these plans to the JCS for approval. MacArthur did not develop alternate plans and did not submit his plans until one week before Inchon.

MacArthur's Message to the VFW

MacArthur's appointment of Almond was done without consulting his boss, Joe Collins. MacArthur now began to ignore his responsibilities to his superiors. He was particularly disgusted with Truman for the deplorable state of the armed forces, for the poor foreign policy which had encouraged the North Koreans and their supporters (China and Russia), and MacArthur must have been under great stress trying (again) to stop a well armed army with inadequate forces. Additionally, MacArthur had not received the divisions he had requested for which he blamed Truman and the JCS. MacArthur had reason to be contemptuous of those in Washington, but, when the VFW asked him for a "message" to be read at their annual convention, MacArthur sent them a bomb. He accused the administration of appeasement for reluctance to defend Formosa for fear of offending mainland China. Instead, he said Orientals respect purposeful and forceful leadership.

This was just part of the message but it was extremely critical of the Administration and violated his instructions to clear any statement involving foreign policy with his superiors. Every word was true but the message was extremely hostile toward China and it was not a good time to enrage China. Truman wanted to fire MacArthur then and there, but with Inchon coming up, the firing was postponed for another time. MacArthur seemed determined to bring Truman down, and in this he was ultimately successful, but he sacrificed himself in the process. The next war (Vietnam) also involved an administration adrift, needing a public protest from the military or someone else in high position, but there would be none.

Pusan, the Last NKPA Attacks, September 1950

The NKPA knew that a landing would take place in their rear and made one last ditch effort to push the Americans at Pusan into the sea. Instead of a massed attack to achieve a breakthrough, they attacked everywhere on September 1, four divisions in the southwest, three divisions near Taegu, and four divisions in the north, 98,000 men. The U.S. had broken the NKPA code and knew the attack was coming. Walker placed the 2nd and 25th Divisions and the 5th Regiment in the southwest backed by the Fifth Marines. The 2nd Division, however, at the Naktong Bulge, had two under strength regiments with only two battalions each.

At Taegu, the First Cavalry Division was spread over a wide front. A new battalion commander here was Harold K. Johnson (who would be Chief-of-Staff during the Vietnamese War). In the north four ROK divisions held the line. The U.S. 24th Division, rebuilding behind Taegu, was available as a reserve.

When the NKPA attacked in the south, they went right through the black 24th Regiment of the 25th Division. (The segregated units consisting of blacks had few experienced enlisted men or officers and no past record of achievement which installs pride in a unit. The poor experience with segregated units in the U..S. Army in World War II and Korea caused the Army to desegregate and this problem went away. There have been some outstanding black units, in the Revolution, in the Civil War, and in WW II—the famous Red Tails, pilots trained in Tuskegee for example.) The 35th Regiment, next in line, held, killing 3,000 NKPA, but some ROKs gave way and the 35th was surrounded. The 5th Infantry and one battalion of the Wolfhounds closed the hole in the 24th sector. Then, two battalions of the Wolfhounds broke through to the 35th killing another 2,000 enemy. Two NKPA divisions were destroyed in these actions.

At the Naktong bulge, two divisions of NKPA split the two weak regiments of the 2nd Division. One of the regiments was in attack positions and poorly placed to resist an assault. Walker now had another gap to plug and he sent in the Fifth Marines. In they came with tanks, artillery, and air strikes, and they smashed the NKPA again. In two days the Marines wiped out an NKPA division, causing an estimated 5,000 casualties.

At Taegu a British Brigade (called the Commonwealth Brigade) arrived and was placed in reserve behind the First Cavalry. Here the 7th Cavalry attacked the NKPA but were thrown hack. The North Koreans counterattacked the 7th and went right through. On September 5, Walker pulled the Cavalry Division back into new defensive positions, just eight miles west of Taegu where they were able to hold with the help of the ROK First Division.

In the north two of four ROK divisions were pushed back but the 24th Division filled the gaps and stabilized the defense. The NKPA had caused over 18,000 Eighth Army casualties, but had lost the usefulness of six divisions. From Washington it seemed unlikely that Eighth Army could go on the offensive but the poor state of the North Koreans was not immediately evident.

Inchon, September 15, 1950

On September 15, the 5th Marines overpowered defenses on the island of Wolmi and landed at Inchon. They were joined by the 1st Marines, and with light casualties there were 13,000 men ashore the first day. The 7th Marines and a regiment of Korean Marines (called KMCs) also landed. (The KMCs would turn out to be first class troops, as reliable as a regular Marine regiment and, of course, backed by the same firepower). The 1st Marine Division would move inland, cross the Han River, and take Seoul. The U.S. Army 7th Division would land behind the Marines and take up blocking positions south of Seoul on the Seoul-Pusan road. NKPA forces retreating from the south would be blocked by the Seventh Division.

On September 20, the 5th Marines crossed the Han River and approached Seoul from the west. The 1st Marines were held up on the south bank of the Han, south of Seoul by increasing NKPA resistance. The 7th Division progress to the south was also slowed by enemy resistance, but by September 21 there were 50,000 troops ashore and Inchon was a success despite all the fears of everyone except MacArthur. He had the courage of his convictions and once again he had demonstrated the genius that separated him from the rest.

Final Victory Over the North Korean Army

On September 16, Walker's Eighth Army went on the offensive. He had 150,000 combat and 75,000 service troops to about 70,000 NKPA. The North Koreans however were well dug in on key terrain. In the south the 25th made no headway until the NKPA suddenly pulled out on the nineteenth. The 2nd Division made progress, crossing the Naktong on the eighteenth. At Taegu however the 1st Cavalry and 24th Divisions could not crack enemy defenses. From the nineteenth to the twenty-first progress improved, and finally late in September the NKPA in the south were in full retreat, pursued westward by the Americans and northward up the east side of Korea by the ROKs.

General Almond wanted Seoul taken by the twenty-fifth as he had promised MacArthur. When the Marines did not honor that promise, Almond took an ROK and a 7th Division regiment to attack Seoul from the east, much to the displeasure and dismay of Marine General O.P. Smith. The specter of Army/Marine casualties by friendly fire in a crowded city loomed ominously. In addition the 7th Division blocking position in the south was weakened and soon in trouble when attacked by an NKPA armored division on September 24.

On the twenty-fourth, the 1st Marines crossed the Han to link up with the 5th Marines. The 7th Marines were now ashore and the 1st Marine Division was united for the assault on Seoul. On the twenty-fifth, the Army and ROK regiments entered Seoul, allowing Almond to claim that the city was liberated. It took three more days of bitter house to house fighting before Seoul was secure.

At Suwon south of Seoul the Seventh Division troops were reinforced by armor and troops coming ashore and a counter attack on September 26 by U.S. tanks and infantry stabilized the situation. On September 27, a tank/infantry task force from the 1st Cavalry Division met the 7th Division roadblock at Osan where Brad Smith had first met the NKPA on July 5. The NKPA army was not destroyed, however; they suffered losses and desertions in their retreat but some 30,000 to 40,000 probably escaped. They fought some rear guard actions but they retreated just as fast or faster than the Americans could advance.

The Invasion of North Korea

The United States had to make a decision: stop at the 38th Parallel or keep going to occupy all of Korea. Unifying Korea was very appealing to Truman, MacArthur, the JCS, almost everybody. Whenever discussions about Chinese intervention were raised, there were self serving statements about the Chinese lack of armor, artillery and air power, or, the time for intervention has passed. Some of the experts in the State Department warned however that China would not take an American (or UN) invasion of North Korea lightly. Actually Communist China could not accept a hostile capitalist army on their border, and this position is (today) not hard to understand. Starting in mid October 180,000 Chinese troops entered Korea and were in place by the end of the month. Apparently the UN Army crossing of the 38th Parallel was the event resulting in the decision to intervene.

North Korea was mountainous with the major hills running up the center of the peninsula. The peninsula is only about 150 miles wide at Wonsan, but expands to about 400 miles at the Chinese border. As a result UN forces were split with Walker's Eighth Army on the west coast and Almond's X Corps on the east coast. Eighth Army included four U.S. divisions (1st Cavalry, 2nd, 24th, and 25th), three ROK divisions (1st, 6th, and 8th), a Commonwealth Brigade, a Turkish Brigade, and other smaller UN forces. X Corps included the 1st Marine, U.S. 7th, ROK 3rd, and ROK Capital Divisions, 83,000 men, 50,000 Americans. The U.S. Third Division was on its way from Japan to beef up X Corps.

On the west coast the Commonwealth Brigade led the way north but ran into strong NKPA resistance at Chongju on October 25. The brigade was replaced by the 24th Division and they ran into strong defenses further inland, 18 miles from the Yalu River on Oct. 29. Here two Chinese prisoners were taken. On October 31 a strong force of 5,000 North Koreans was encountered. Further inland the ROK 1st Division met a Chinese (CCF, Communist Chinese Forces) army of 30,000 men and fell back but held. Prisoners were taken and confirmed as Chinese regulars. At the right flank of Eighth Army the ROK 6th Division raced to the Yalu on many small roads, then ran into another CCF army, collapsed and ran, leaving the inland flank wide open. On the left (inland) flank of X Corps the ROK 3rd Division struck a Chinese army near the Chosin Reservoir, ran and reformed south of the reservoir, but took 16 CCF prisoners.

All this data was passed back to MacArthur's G-2 (Intelligence Officer), Charles Willoughby, who organized it to show MacArthur that there was no credible evidence of the CCF presence in force. Many forward elements of the armies had been thrown back by large forces, many of which were found to include Chinese troops, but Willoughby probably wanted to be optimistic. After all, the Chinese could be volunteers. Willoughby was not alone in his rosy analysis. Walker's G-2, possibly to be politically in line, also downplayed the CCF intervention. MacArthur probably assumed that his forces could handle the Chinese if they were actually in North Korea in formal units in large numbers. As a result MacArthur ordered the army to continue north! As elements of the UN Army moved towards the Yalu they were dispersed with many isolated units and many an exposed flank. In late October however the advance met little resistance, but many a commander moved into trackless mountains with an ominous feeling of danger.

The First Chinese Offensive

Walker anticipated trouble and began to move his regiments up to obtain divisional integrity but the Chinese masses attacked at Unsan on November 1, going through a ROK regiment and two battalions of the Eighth Cavalry regiment. A third battalion of the Eighth Cavalry was isolated and surrounded. The rest of the division was too far to the rear to help and 800 men fought in little circles with no hope for relief. 600 men died or were captured much like the Seventh Cavalry at Little Big Horn, 75 years earlier. Eighth Army pulled back to the Chongchon River and the Chinese kept coming. On the Chongchon the

Commonwealth Brigade performed well. The 24th Division was hard pressed but held. On the right flank at Kunu the ROKs were in trouble, but two U.S. regiments rushed up and stopped the CCF on November 4. By November 6 the CCF offensive against Eighth Army mysteriously ceased.

In X Corps Almond, who had personally seen Chinese prisoners, ordered his two ROK and his 7th Divisions to the Yalu at top speed. One regiment of the First Marine Division was ordered to the Chosin Reservoir, then to the Yalu on the left of the 7th Division. General Oliver P. Smith, Marine Division Commander, foresaw 30,000 Chinese falling on one Marine regiment. As it was only one Chinese division attacked the 7th Marines for three bloody days. The Marines fought with massed artillery and close air support, causing up to 7000 CCF casualties while losing only 314 men.

Two regiments of the 7th Division followed Almond's orders, pushing rapidly inland into the formidable mountains. But as in the Eighth Army sector the CCF pulled back. It may have been that this first Chinese offensive was designed to warn the UN Army to stay away from China. If so the message was not received. Back in Tokyo no acknowledgement was yet made of massive CCF forces. Willoughby upped his estimate of the number of Chinese forces from 16,500 to 34,000. (By this time there were 300,000 Chinese in Korea.) The orders were, still, to press on. MacArthur believed the CCF would be slaughtered if they intervened, but his optimism was expressed in Tokyo, far from the fighting.

The Home by Christmas Offensive

When the 3rd Division arrived at Wonsan, it relieved the First and Fifth Marines who had been mopping up in the coastal area. The Marines moved inland to close the gap with the Seventh Marines who had reached Hagaru on the Chosin Reservoir by November 15. At this time General Smith complained to the Commandant of the Marine Corps about Almond's dispersion of forces in a huge area of northeast Korea. MacArthur's G-3 advised Almond to close with Eighth Army but Almond did not immediately comply. MacArthur therefore personally ordered Almond to close up, with only minimum forces going to the Yalu. Almond however sent two of the three Seventh Division regiments to the Yalu. He then ordered the Marine Division to attack west from the Chosin Reservoir on November 27. This order was given to try to close the gap between X Corps and Eighth Army, but it sent the Marines into terrible country far from any supporting units. Some Seventh Division units were ordered to gather on the east shore of the Chosin Reservoir on the Marine right flank but these units were dispersed.

The weather in this part of Korea was Siberian, down to 30° below zero.

On November 25, the 7th Marines were at Yudam west of the reservoir; the

5th Marines were east of the reservoir, and the 1st Marines (under Chesty Puller of WW II fame) had one battalion in each of three towns on the road to the coast (Hagaru, Koto, and Chinhung). There were 120,000 CCF troops in the Chosin Reservoir vicinity, far more than then supposed.

Eighth Army, now 118,000 men in eight divisions and two brigades, planned to attack on November 24. The three ROK divisions on Walker's right flank were, however, poorly armed and in poor shape generally, but there were orders to attack, and orders are orders. Unknown at the time enemy strength in the area was over 200,000 men. Before the offensive began MacArthur toured the front, then publicly announced the offensive, apparently still unaware of the masses of CCF in Korea.

The Second Chinese Offensive

The offensive went well for two days, but at 8 P.M. on the night of November 25, the Chinese attacked. Human waves poured out of the hills with flares, bugles, shouts, and massive gunfire. In the 24th Regiment of the 25th Division, three of nine companies were surrounded. In the 9th Regiment of the 2nd Division, one battalion was overrun, another battalion gave way except for a valiant stand by one company, and only one battalion was left intact. The 38th Regiment, 2nd Division was directly in the path of the CCF onrush. Four companies were hard hit and two others isolated forward were wiped out while trying to rejoin the regiment. The 23rd Regiment 2nd Division, in reserve, fought off all attacks and reinforced with tanks was able to hold. The 61st Artillery Battalion was overrun but managed to recapture half of their 18 howitzers. The 38th tried to form, defending north and east as the ROKs to the east had either been overrun or bugged out.

On November 28, the 2nd Division was ordered to pull back to Kunu and managed to do so with the magnificent rear guard efforts of 2/9 and 1/23 (2nd Battalion, 9th Regiment, and 1st Battalion, 23rd Regiment). Walker also ordered the 24th Division on the left flank to pull back and join the 1st Cavalry Division at Sunchon south of Kunu.

While Eighth Army was being hammered, X Corps was being ordered to attack on November 27 by General Almond. These were General MacArthur's orders and Almond followed them to the letter.

As a result the Fifth and Seventh Marines attacked on the morning of the twenty-seventh at Yudam, on the west shore of the Chosin Reservoir, 14 miles from Hagaru at the south shore. The Marines gained a mile but took heavy casualties.

The 7th Division began to gather forces on the east shore of the reservoir. These forces, called Task Force MacLean, using the name of their commanding officer, had two battalions, Faith's 1/32 and the 3/31, a tank company, eight antiaircraft vehicles, two artillery batteries, and a heavy mortar company, 3,200 men in all. Faith's 1/32 was the northern most force with the 3/31 several miles south. Still further south at Hudong were the tanks and the AA vehicles. Hudong was four miles north of Hagaru and the Marines there.

On the night of November 27, the Chinese attacked around the reservoir. Two divisions hit the Marines but they held. South and west of the Marines, a battalion of the Third Division was surrounded but held also, fortunately as they tied up CCF that might otherwise have closed in behind the Marines. Faith's perimeter was hit hard but held with the help of Marine aircraft, although a scouting platoon was wiped out and the 1/32 took heavy casualties. The 3/31 battalion was surrounded, losing one whole medical company and taking heavy casualties. 16 tanks that tried to relieve 3/31 from Hudong were ambushed, then retreated losing four tanks. By this time both infantry battalions were cut off, but a clear picture was not immediately available. On the twenty-eighth Almond helicoptered into Faith's perimeter and again ordered an attack. That same day in Tokyo, MacArthur acknowledge the presence of 200,000 Chinese and declared that his forces would go on the defensive. MacArthur was however reluctant to withdraw X Corps as he believed it posed a threat to the flank of the CCF attacking Eighth Army.

On November 28 President Truman held a meeting of the National Security Council and finally agreed to a massive military buildup to meet the threat of Communist aggression, not just in Korea but worldwide. The United States was now at war with China. The limitations on the U.S. armed forces would force the United States to fight off the armed masses of Asia with seven American and six to eight unreliable ROK divisions. The decision by Bradley and Collins not to press Truman earlier for mobilization now came back to haunt them.

The Eighth Army Retreat

General Walker ordered Eighth Army to retreat, to reform at Pyongyang with 2nd Division holding the rear at Kunu. Second Division did hold but two regiments were badly depleted and by the 29th the division had to fall back. Unfortunately the road to the rear was occupied in force by the CCF for a distance of six miles. There was another road but the division commander thought he could punch through on the road for which his plans had been made. During the retreat however organized efforts fell apart and the road to the rear became one of wrecked and stalled vehicles, dead and dying men, chaos, terror, and agony. Casualties are estimated at 3,000 but some got through with the help of air strikes.

The Commonwealth Brigade, ordered to attack from the south, did not help. The 23rd Regiment holding the rear managed to escape south on the other road. In this CCF offensive, Second Division lost 4,940 men. The division commander and other officers were eventually replaced.

The Chinese that had routed the ROKs on Eighth Army's eastern flank came down to Sunchon south of Kunu but here they met the First Cavalry Division on November 29. The Chinese were stopped and a major threat to all of Eighth Army avoided, but the fighting was typically brutal.

General Walker gathered the remnants of his army at Pyongyang, three U.S. divisions (1st Cavalry, 24th and 25th) and one ROK. He had four effective divisions out of eight before the CCF offensive. He was in poor condition to defend anything and ordered a retreat all the way to South Korea.

The X Corps Retreat From The Chosin Reservoir

In the X Corps sector on November 28, General O.P. Smith ordered the 5th Marines to hold Yudam (these were his veterans, the pros from Pusan), while the 7th Marines attacked south toward Hagaru. Almond was advised of these plans and wasn't pleased but did not object. The 1st Marines were ordered to reinforce the battalion at Hagaru which had to be held at all costs. On the twenty-ninth, 900 British, U.S. Army, and Marine personnel were ordered to attack toward Hagaru from Koto, 11 miles south. 300 men were lost, 300 turned back, and only 300 broke through to Hagaru.

On the twenty-ninth, Task Force MacLean moved south to join up with the surrounded 3/31 and managed to fight their way into the perimeter. U.S. tanks from Hudong four miles away tried again to reach the 3/31 perimeter but failed. Lt. Colonel MacLean was killed and replaced by Lt. Colonel Faith. Faith could not retreat without orders and prepared to fight where he was.

After receiving strong suggestions from the Join Chiefs of Staff that he pull back and consolidate, MacArthur ordered Almond to withdraw to the coast. Finally, on November 30, Faith was ordered to fight his way south to Hagaru. Unfortunately the Army forces at Hudong only four miles away pulled out to be replaced by Chinese. Faith's force was now hopelessly trapped. Faith organized attacks to the south and gained some three miles but he was killed and all other senior officers killed, wounded, or captured. All order was lost and some 600 stragglers were able to walk over the frozen reservoir to Hagaru. Marines from Hagaru did manage to recover 300 to 400 wounded. Of the 2,500 Americans east of the Chosin Reservoir, about 1000 were lost in an episode not unlike the 2nd Division ordeal at Kunu. Faith was awarded a Congressional Medal of Honor posthumously and it was well deserved as he had been magnificent. The epic of Task Force MacLean/Faith was tragic but tied up CCF forces on the Marine eastern flank and helped save the Fifth and Seventh Marines, who managed to reach Hagaru.

General Smith had 10,000 men at Hagaru and the Chinese could not penetrate the perimeter. Reinforcements and supplies were flown in and 4,300 wounded evacuated. Almond flew in and suggested the Marines fly out but Smith refused to sacrifice a rear guard. Almond was in tears as he tried to give medals to Marine officers. On December 6, Smith sent the 7th Marines and an Army brigade in an attack down the Hagaru-Koto road while the 5th Marines held the rear. The soldiers and marines gained just two and a half miles the first day against heavy resistance. Smith ordered the attack to continue at night and the attack succeeded, as Koto was reached on the morning of the seventh. The rest of the Hagaru forces followed in one long line.

The plans now were for all of X Corps to head for Hungnam on the east coast to set up a defensive perimeter. ROKs and the two 7th Division regiments at the Yalu managed to get back without much difficulty. Third Division which held positions around Hamhung was ordered to send forces part way to Koto (to Chinhung) to close the distance between the Marines and friendly forces. X Corps (those elements that could be saved) would be shipped to Pusan and points south where they could join Eighth Army in defensive positions somewhere in South Korea.

By December 7, Third Division was in Chinhung in force. The Marine battalion there moved up to attack toward Funchilin Pass where a bridge had been blown and where the Chinese were entrenched. On December 8, the Seventh Marines and the Army Provisional Regiment attacked south from Koto toward the pass, five or six miles away in a heavy snow storm. On the ninth, the sun was out and so were Navy and Marine aircraft. The Chinese at Funchilin Pass were hit from the sky and by land from north and south.

The pass was cleared and a large gully bridge installed by 3:30 P.M. (bridge sections were dropped into Koto by air and trucked to the pass by army engineers). All night and all day on the tenth, the 15,000 Marines and soldiers from Koto crossed the bridge and passed into U.S. lines. O.P. Smith had brought his division out in one piece, a tremendous achievement which earned every member of the division a Presidential Unit Citation; however, the entire campaign cost the Marines 10, 500 casualties (over half were non-battle, mostly frostbite, and many of these were eventually able to return).

The Chinese are believed to have lost 70,000 men in the fighting around the Chosin Reservoir, perhaps as many as 30,000 from frostbite. This no doubt explains why the CCF did not strike the retreating American forces harder. There were numerous attacks on the column as it meandered from Hagaru and on the Hungnam perimeter, but all were successfully beaten off. When O. P. Smith was questioned at Hagaru about a Marine retreat, O. P. said, "We're not retreating! We're just advancing in a different direction."

Ridgeway Assumes Command

As the UN Army regrouped in South Korea, General Walker was killed in a vehicular accident on December 23. Matt Ridgeway, the commander of paratroops in World War II, was appointed commander, arriving in Tokyo at midnight on December 25. MacArthur gave him total control and responsibility for conduct of the fighting in Korea, and this was good news for Ridgeway. He landed at Taegu on the afternoon of the 26th and took control of a beaten army. American casualties in North Korea had been 60,000 and ROK casualties were perhaps as high as 300,000. Ridgeway did have 350,000 men, about half of them ROKs. The situation was desperate as MacArthur and the Joint Chiefs were not sure that South Korea could be defended. There were no more U.S. divisions that could be spared from world wide responsibilities and a pullout was discussed. Truman was opposed to this which would have exposed our friends to a massacre. It was decided in Washington that a pullout would be made only if necessary, and an attempt at holding on would be made. Fortunately a very good soldier was now in charge in Korea and he was determined, not just to hold on, but to attack, and he put life back into the whole army.

From west to east the UN Army took positions along Line B (starting at the Imjin River north of Seoul) as follows: 25th, ROK 1st/6th, 24th, ROK 2nd/5th/7th/8th and 9th, and in the east, the ROK 3rd and Capital Divisions. The U.S. 2nd and 1st Cavalry were in reserve.

The 1st Marine Division was refitting after its ordeal at frozen Chosin. X Corps was ordered to set up headquarters at Wonju in central Korea, south of Line B, where a second line of defense, Line D was to be established. Ridgeway then began a thorough reorganization, replacing inept generals with combat proven men. The purge affected corps, division, and even regimental commanders.

The Third Chinese Offensive

On New Year's Eve, the CCF attacked again all across Korea, hitting the ROKs, bypassing the Americans. Many of the newly formed ROK regiments and divisions turned and ran, some actually fighting for a while, others offering little resistance. Ridgeway was forced to abandon Seoul and occupy Line D just south of Wonju. On January 2, the 2nd U.S. Division launched an attack north of Wonju. As Ridgeway retreated the Third and Seventh Divisions moved up to Line D. The Marine Division was south of Line B in a position to support ROKs on the east coast. Ridgeway now moved to correct a major problem. Rapid retreats left his forces without contact with the enemy. To win in battle knowledge of the enemy's location and strength is essential. Local tank-infantry attacks were organized, one by the Wolfhound Regiment on January 7 and another by an infantry battalion from the Third Division.

Ridgeway waited on Line D for the Chinese onslaught, expected at any time, probably in central Korea near Wonju where the enemy were concentrating. The refurbished 2nd Division was placed there with the 7th Division and the 187th Airborne Regiment on their right. On January 10, the NKPA did attack at Wonju where they were met by the 2nd Division and the French battalion. All attacks were repelled and hordes of North Koreans were caught in the open where they were blasted by air strikes and artillery fire. Enemy casualties at Wonju were terrific and the Second Division had their revenge for Kunu. After this attack the enemy offensive ceased and there was a lull over the battlefield. Ridgeway then decided to launch a local attack around the 27th Regiment (the Wolfhounds) already forward on Line D.

Ridgeway Takes the Offensive

Six thousand men, 150 tanks, and 3 artillery battalions moved out toward Osan on January 15. Contact was made with the CCF and the offensive halted. Ridgeway took a mobile command post right up to the front lines and ordered the attacking troops to form a solid defensive front, anticipating a counterattack. But there was no counterattack and now it occurred to the Americans that the CCF might be a little reluctant to attack American forces in relatively open country. Morale started to lift as confidence returned.

On January 21, Ridgeway delivered a message to his troops. Some of the more significant statements can be summarized as follows: This is a war between Western civilization, where the rule of law and human rights are valued, and the forces of Communism, where citizens are enslaved, prisoners are shot, and the people live in oppressed existence without a God. All this explains why the war was not just for the survival of the free people of South Korea but also for the very existence and freedom of our own nations.

On January 22, Ridgeway ordered another reconnaissance in force by battalions from the Third and First Cavalry Divisions with tanks. Advancing beyond Osan this probe showed that the CCF on Ridgeway's left flank were not keeping contact nor pressing for attack. These limited offensives gave a number of units experience in the kind of attack Ridgeway expected and as a result I and IX Corps were ordered to advance on January 25. The 8th cavalry Regiment ran into some trouble but was assisted by the 7th Cavalry. The Turkish Brigade took a hill with a bayonet charge which gave Ridgeway the idea to order fixed bayonets for all infantry. Eighth Army was by this time organized into two Corps, I and IX. On January 29, the I and IX Corps made contact with the CCF defenses. A CCF attack on the Greek battalion was fought off in a valiant stand; the UN Allies were performing well.

Ridgeway also ordered X Corps to patrol north toward Chipyong, northwest of Wonju where his intelligence indicated the CCF were massing. The patrol finally found the CCF at Chipyong but here they were ambushed and surrounded until rescued by a company from the 2nd Division. A U.S. battalion from the 23rd Regiment (2nd Division) and the French battalion were sent into the Chipyong vicinity to guard the 24th Division right flank. These two battalions were hit hard by a Chinese division, held on, but came close to running out of ammunition. Just before dark a squadron of Marine air support planes came in and slaughtered the

Chinese with bombs, rockets, and machine guns. The Chinese retreated and the two UN battalions counterattacked, achieving a major victory.

Chinese casualties may have been 4,000, one whole division put out of action. Ridgeway flew into the perimeter to give Colonel Freeman and Colonel Monclar (a fearless, legendary French officer) Presidential Unit Citations.

Early in February Ridgeway ordered I Corps (on the left flank) and IX Corps (further inland) to advance toward the Han River which had flooded and formed a formidable barrier. The hills south of the Han were heavily defended and it took some intense fighting to push the Chinese back. The Han was reached by mid February in some places, but the Chinese still remained in strong positions south of the river. This offensive against the Chinese marked the first time that the UN Army had been able to fight effectively against the CCF, particularly on the offensive. There were two reasons for the turnabout; the first was the terrible dispositions of UN forces in North Korea which made defense very difficult. This time Ridgeway kept his divisions in mutually supporting positions. The second reason was the new leadership structure with Ridgeway in overall command. This offensive raised morale sky high, endowed confidence, and marked the achievement of a new level of efficiency. At this time MacArthur ordered Ridgeway to continue to advance across the Han. Ridgeway made plans for this but kept his two corps south of the river for the time being. MacArthur wanted to crush the Chinese, and he insisted on aggressive advances, yet in messages to Washington he warned of catastrophe if all out war wasn't waged. He sought more forces and a larger war than anyone in Washington or among the Allies, but in this he had no support. MacArthur had had a brilliant career but in the war against the CCF his forces were unable to achieve his goals.

Meanwhile on February 5, X Corps sent two ROK divisions into an attack north of Wonju, even north of Chipyong. These divisions were backed by considerable American artillery and some infantry but advanced beyond any support from left or right and rushed right into the strength of the CCF.

Attacking the CCF with ROK troops would seem risky but it must have been hoped that American artillery support would assure success. However the affair would become another disaster. Ridgeway would ultimately order an investigation of this offensive but would not be able to build a case against Almond. He remained as a MacArthur protégé.

The Fourth Chinese Offensive

The X Corps offensive was aimed at Hongchon, east of Seoul in central Korea, which Almond tried to encircle with his two ROK divisions. Ridgeway's Intelligence Officer issued a report early in February predicting a massive CCF attack toward Wonju with twelve divisions on February 15, yet Almond continued his attack. Then on February 11, the CCF hit the ROK 5th Division flank. Almond turned them to face east, then brought up the ROK Third Division to form towards the north with more American artillery in support. Three battalions (one of them Dutch) of the U.S. 38th Regiment were sent forward to three different areas. The CCF then struck the ROK 8th Division which was soon surrounded. Eight hundred ROKs were killed or captured, only 3,000 escaping. The American artillery units were also cut off but they combined with the 1st Battalion, 38th Infantry, to try to fight their way back at 3 A.M. on February 12. They broke through to the 3/38 perimeter by dawn but two companies of infantry were decimated and many a truck driver killed. A battery of big 155 mm howitzers was also lost. The Dutch battalion was at Hoengsong further south and the combined 1/38 and 3/38 tried to fight through to save the artillery battalion (still consisting of 17 of 18 105 mm howitzers). An armor-infantry team from Hoengsong reached the desperate men and managed to get them back to Hoengsong where the Dutch held their positions firmly, but on the way back most of the artillery and 120 trucks were lost.

The battered remnants made their way back to Wonju followed by a badly depleted Dutch battalion. In this latest gauntlet, U.S. and Dutch casualties were 1,769.

The remnants of the 3rd and 5th ROK Divisions collapsed and were swept away. More Americans were trapped. These followed bulldozers, which plowed new roads to the southeast, finally arriving at Wonju with light casualties.

X Corps survivors gathered at Wonju on February 13, 11 infantry battalions (7 U.S., I Dutch, and 3 ROK), with one tank and five artillery battalions. This force was commanded by George Stewart, the assistant commander of the 2nd Division. Stewart ordered all artillery units (100 guns) to zero in on key numbered points so that observers could call for any or all guns on any one point instantaneously without adjustments which take time.

On the morning of the fourteenth, four CCF divisions attacked in large masses over open terrain, and wherever they massed 100 guns pulverized them. For three hours they kept coming and by noon the remnants of the four CCF divisions retreated, leaving 5,000 dead, certainly 10,000 or more wounded. This was known as the "Wonju Turkey Shoot," a huge victory, but the crisis was not yet over.

Colonel Freeman's 23rd Regiment at Chipyong was now cut off. Ridgeway did not want to widen the CCF breakthrough, and ordered Freeman to hold Chipyong and promised reinforcements. Freeman had 4 battalions, a Ranger company, 14 tanks, 10 AA vehicles, and 24 artillery pieces.

On the night of February 13, some 18,000 Chinese attacked at Chipyong. This first attack was thrown back and a later attack also. A third attack was repulsed when the French fixed bayonets and charged.

The Commonwealth Brigade was assigned to reinforce Chipyong but couldn't get through. The 5th Cavalry Regiment, commanded by Marcel Crombez, also assigned to reinforce Chipyong, had to cross the Han River and was obviously not going to arrive quickly. Freeman was attacked again on the night of February 14 and his perimeter was penetrated. All day on the fifteenth, the 23rd Infantry struggled for survival, running low on ammunition. That day, however, Army, Navy, and Marine planes came over to support Freeman. They forced the CCF to take cover while cargo planes dropped supplies. Freeman was given new life.

Crombez attacked on February 15 but was not able to make much progress and he was still six miles from Chipyong. He decided to send his 23 tanks on ahead with infantry support and selected L Company (160 men) of Edgar Treacy's 3rd Battalion. Treacy insisted that the mission was a death sentence for his men but Crombez said that if fire became too close or too intense, the tanks would stop to help the infantry. Treacy and Crombez had a long history of bitter dispute and this task was part of it. Treacy insisted on going with his men and he did although ordered not to. The first time the Chinese fire became intense, the men dropped off the tanks and fought. Then, without warning, the tanks took off leaving 30 men behind. Further up the road the Chinese fire became hot again. The tanks stopped, infantry jumped off and there was another fight. The tanks took off, again leaving 60 men behind. Treacy was wounded and stayed with the stranded men. Most of the infantry still on the tanks were eventually wounded, but the tanks reached Chipyong just as the defenders were counterattacking. The arrival of so much armor while the defenders were counterattacking was too much for the Chinese and they retreated. Chipyong was saved.

Crombez had done his job but he had deserted his men, paying dearly for the eventual success. Treacy was recommended for a Congressional Medal, but Crombez cancelled the request. Ridgeway gave Crombez a Distinguished Service Cross. Treacy was captured, survived his wounds, but died in captivity, where he gave his food to his men. Crombez had to transfer every officer in Treacy's Third Battalion to erase the memory of this sad affair.

When Ridgeway attacked the Chinese flank along the Han River on February 16, the Chinese were gone. Their whole army had retreated and broken all contact. Ridgeway had not only stopped the CCF, he had beaten them. The Chinese general, Lin Piao, was relieved of his command. Ridgeway's performance in Korea is one of the most remarkable in the history of U.S. arms.

Advance to the 38th Parallel

After the I Corps advance to the Han River, Ridgeway planned an advance east of the Han by IX and X Corps to catch up to I Corps, called Operation Killer. The Marines, now in IX Corps, were ordered to attack north from Wonju with IX Corps on the left and X Corps on the right. I Corps on the Han was ordered to stay put, but feint at crossing the Han to keep the CCF in place. The attack commenced on February 21 with eight divisions, 100,000 men.

For this offensive the Marines were without their own air support as their air wing had been absorbed into the Far Eastern Air Force under General Partridge who believed that close air support did not pay dividends. The enemy armies at this time were estimated at 500,000 men. Ridgeway had 500,000 men also, but 150,000 were support personnel and 120,000 were ROKs.

For three days IX and X Corps crawled north over rugged hills in the east, in melting snow, rain, and bottomless mud. Enemy resistance was sporadic, and on the twenty-fourth the Marines reached Hoengson, 8 miles north of Wonju.

On February 25, Ridgeway ordered I Corps to join the offensive. This full scale attack was called Operation Ripper with objectives Seoul and the 38th Parallel. No one in the JCS or elsewhere in Washington could agree on public statements regarding a recrossing of the 38th Parallel or on the orders to be given. Ridgeway himself stated that the terrain at the 38th Parallel was poor for defense and recommended crossing the 38th but moving only as far north as necessary to obtain good defensive positions. MacArthur stated that he did not believe in stopping or in trying to defend static positions, but he offered no solution other than all out war with Communist China. Logic required UN forces to stop somewhere in the narrow waist of Korea and Ridgeway's suggestions were accepted. No other orders to Ridgeway were ever given other than to advise the JCS in advance before crossing the parallel.

Operation Ripper

The 25th Division in I Corps was given the task of crossing the Han, taking the high ground east of Seoul, between the city and the Pukhan River. This was a risky assignment, but was to be disguised with feints, an amphibious landing at Chinnampo and a fake Han crossing by the ROK 1st Division. Operation Ripper began on March 7.

Three battalions of the 25th Division crossed the Han in boats followed by tanks able to ford the shallow river. Foot bridges were put down and more battalions followed. High ground was taken, but a counterattack that night by the Chinese drove one battalion off the heights. Pontoon bridges were constructed; the heights were retaken the next day, and the whole division was across.

Before Operation Killer, MacArthur delivered his usual speech in Korea, denouncing Truman's policies but claiming credit for the offensive. Before Operation Ripper, Ridgeway told in advance of his planned offensive, praising MacArthur only for giving Ridgeway freedom to act.

On March 7, the Marines moved north of Hoengson and reached the valley where the Dutch and 2nd Division troops had been ambushed. One marine put up a sign:

MASSACRE VALLEY
SCENE OF HARRY S. TRUMAN'S POLICE ACTION
NICE GOING HARRY

Bodies were everywhere as were the wrecked vehicles. The press found out about the disaster for the first time.

The advance continued on a 50 mile front with 150,000 men. By March 10, the 25th Division had taken the high ground east of Seoul where they threatened access roads into the city. On March 14, the Marines took Hongchon, and on the fifteenth a ROK patrol walked into a deserted Seoul, raising the ROK flag. This attack by Ridgeway's forces freed Seoul without agonizing house to house fighting, and was a brilliant stroke.

The words "Killer" and "Ripper" were too aggressive for the public, so the offensive was renamed Operation Courageous.

On March 20, MacArthur received a letter from the JCS instructing him to plan to stop somewhere near the 38th Parallel. Finally MacArthur knew that all of his recommendations for waging war against China were being ignored. Stopping and trying to talk truce was, to him, appeasement, a sign of weakness, leading to endless conflict, and constant risk (of a massed CCF attack at a time and place of their choosing). Furious, he wrote another letter to Joe Martin, Minority Leader in the House of Representatives, again recommending strong measures against China and use of Nationalist troops on the Chinese mainland. (This would be his final barb.)

Ridgeway's next objective was Line Kansas—the Imjin River running northeast, then a line east to the south shore of the Hwachon Reservoir and to Yangyang on the Sea of Japan. This line was 20 miles north of the Parallel at the Reservoir. JCS approval was required before crossing the Parallel, but on March 23, MacArthur authorized Ridgeway to cross it.

An attack was planned for two armored spearheads from I Corps to attack north to Munsan. The 187th Airborne was ordered to parachute into the town and (it was hoped) trap some NKPA. The mission was successful but few NKPA were taken.

On March 28, I Corps pincers had closed at the Imjin River but the enemy escaped. On the thirty-first, 3rd Division tanks crossed the 38th Parallel as Eighth Army approached the parallel at almost every point. By April 9, the whole army was at Line Kansas. The last objective in central Korea, Inje, was taken on that day.

On April 11, I Corps attacked from Line Kansas northeast toward Chorwon in the Iron Triangle (a triangle of towns where CCF assembled prior to launching offensives). Occupation of the Iron Triangle had been added to the final objective to reduce the CCF attack potential.

Prisoners taken told of a planned CCF offensive on April 22. New estimates put CCF strength at 570,000 men, 19 armies, far above previous estimates. The I Corps advance to Chorwon, however, continued, opposed on occasions, and the rest of the front grew quiet. In IX Corps, by April 21, the Marines were north of the Hwachon Reservoir with the ROK 6th Division on their left.

On April 22, U.S. planes raiding airfields in North Korea met large formations of Russian MIG-15s from Manchuria in "MIG Alley." The forces of the world were facing each other in Korea and here the Cold War was on fire.

On April 11, MacArthur learned he had been fired to be replaced with Ridgeway. The Eighth Army was given to James Van Fleet who had been a corps commander in Europe and the advisor to the Greeks in their successful civil war against the communists. He was chosen by the generals in Washington and presented to a rather concerned Ridgeway. The timing was terrible as a huge Chinese offensive was expected within a few days. Van Fleet took over on April 14 as Ridgeway debated over the extent of his participation with Eighth Army.

Truman versus MacArthur

Prior to the Korean War, Truman and his Secretary of Defense, Louis A. Johnson, in a cost cutting frenzy, had devastated the armed forces. Omar Bradley was Chairman of the Joint Chiefs of Staff and Joe Collins was Army Chief of Staff. Bradley and Collins approved the budgets, but approval must have been very hard to give.

After the Russian atomic bomb test and the victory of Mao Tsetung's communists, Dean Acheson, Secretary of State, proposed a major rearmament in National Security Council Policy Paper NSC-68, and on March 22, 1950, a meeting was held with the Departments of State and Defense. Louis Johnson went to the meeting, blew his top at the thought of State telling Defense what to do, and stormed out of the room. Truman eventually decided not to spend the money on rearmament, and so the Korean War caught the United States totally unprepared for any kind of fight other than atomic war.

When the North Koreans invaded South Korea, MacArthur recommended committing U.S. troops. This decision has been criticized because of their poor state of readiness, but here he did what he had to do. Truman, however, wanted to downplay the conflict and approved a reporter's reference to it as a "police action." These words would remind American troops throughout the trials to come of the Administration's level of support.

In July, MacArthur, realizing the strength of the NKPA, asked for men and equipment to fill out his four divisions plus four more divisions and a Marine division.

Joe Collins went to Tokyo to see MacArthur and explained that forces would be sent but those requested by MacArthur were not available. At this time MacArthur knew he would not receive the forces he believed he needed for a successful campaign. Less than an all out effort was never understandable or acceptable to MacArthur.

There can be no doubt that Truman was responsible for the terrible condition of the armed forces, much of the early trials, and most of the early casualties. MacArthur stood up like the patriot he was and fought Truman on foreign policy and military strategy from the beginning in June, 1950, to the moment he was fired in April, 1951.

If Truman had had some of the statesmanship of his predecessor, Franklin D. Roosevelt, he would have spoken to the country and advised that communist armies have spilled over their borders and that they would be thrown back by a United Nations Army. He should have stated right in the beginning that we did not covet the land of the communist country, North Korea, but insisted on the existence of a free South Korea. Then he should have followed up his words with the mobilization that enlightened men like Ridgeway believed necessary. This was war with a good communist army backed up by all the might and perhaps even the manpower of Communist China and/or the Soviet Union. To do less than a maximum effort was to sacrifice American lives in a struggle too large for the minimal forces originally sent.

A successful stand against the NKPA was accomplished only by use of poor quality ROK divisions. When the Chinese intervened, these divisions became unreliable, deserting their positions and causing many American troops to be cut off and slaughtered. Adequate U.S. forces would have prevented these disasters but unfortunately these were not available to the U.S. Army in 1950. It was bad in Korea but new horrors would occur again in Vietnam.

History can not forgive Almond for the losses suffered by his forces or MacArthur for the disasters in North Korea. MacArthur was responsible for U.S. military policy in Korea, but he was in Japan. He believed that he was in control of events in Korea, but he was too far away and out of touch.

MacArthur used every argument he had over the months to force Truman to build up the military strength in Korea, even predicting disaster almost to the day he was fired. He was right about the inadequate force but kept insisting on an all out war against China. In this, he had no supporters in the Administration and Joint Chiefs of Staff. The subjugation of China was a task too huge to even contemplate, and almost certainly would have involved Russia and World War III. MacArthur was right; there is no substitute for victory, but victory with unconditional surrender was not possible. The defeat of China's army and the successful recovery of South Korea was a victory, all that was needed, all that was possible. It was achieved with minimal forces and is a tribute to Ridgeway, but was a terrible gamble in which American troops were the pawns, many of whom were sacrificed due to inadequate American response.

Time after time MacArthur issued statements critical of Truman and his policies. Truman issued a Presidential Directive requiring State Department clearance of all statements on military policy. MacArthur deliberately ignored this, too, determined to get his way or get fired trying.

On March 20, 1951, MacArthur answered a letter from House Minority Leader, Joe Martin, saying he agreed with those proposing use of Nationalist Chinese forces and the use of maximum counterforce against China, saying it was a war against communism that we had to win and, "There is no substitute for victory."

At about this time, MacArthur also answered a JCS cable advising of a UN peace initiative to be made before crossing the 38th Parallel and asking for

MacArthur's recommendations for the safety of Eighth Army. MacArthur replied he needed fewer restrictions on use of air, naval, and ground forces as our numerical inferiority made it difficult to occupy North Korea.

The March 20 letter to Joe Martin did it; it was the straw that broke the camel's back. Truman could no longer sue for peace with MacArthur in command of the war theatre. Martin read MacArthur's letter in the House on April 5, and Truman immediately called a meeting of all involved parties, asking what should be done. The JCS finally, reluctantly, after days of deliberation, concluded that MacArthur must be dismissed because he was not sympathetic to limiting the war to Korea, had failed to comply with Truman's Presidential Directive, and jeopardized civilian control over the military. In a meeting on April 9, these views were given to Truman. Van Fleet would replace Ridgeway who would replace MacArthur. The official notice was to be given by the Army Secretary, Frank Pace, but there was a leak and MacArthur heard it on the radio before he received official word.

Everyone involved regretted the act, sorry to be in a position of having to relieve one of our great soldiers, but it had been a major conflict between Truman and MacArthur and could no longer be tolerated. The fight MacArthur made over U.S. policy was not repeated by the Army in Vietnam as no general wanted to disobey orders.

MacArthur's arguments had one major flaw. He was adamant in his demands for all out war against China. The use of Nationalist troops on the mainland would lead to endless war. His insistence on recovering all of North Korea was a demand for a victory beyond his means. Recovery of South Korea should have been victory enough. If he had had adequate forces, the quick absorption of North Korea might have been achieved without Chinese intervention. Would the Chinese have attacked a 500,000 man U.S. army?

History will properly glorify him for what he has done for us, and should not blacken his record because of his troubles in Korea. He did beat the NKPA while Ridgeway completed the job against the Chinese, and he did bring Truman down. Truman lost the 1952 election to Eisenhower.

The Fifth Chinese Offensive

On April 21, Van Fleet launched the final I Corps advance to Chorwon and the IX Corps attack above the Hwachon Reservoir. A CCF attack was expected and fall back positions selected. The enemy resisted only at times but continued to withdraw. On the twenty-first, the CCF set numerous brushfires, filling the air with smoke, no doubt to cover troop movements from aerial observation.

The Marines moved into the town of Hwachon but lost contact with the ROK 6th Division in mountainous terrain, leaving a one mile gap. The ROKs were ordered to close the gap but it was too late. From west to east, Eighth Army had the following forces at the front: ROKs, British Brigade, 3rd Division, 25th

Division, 24th Division, ROK 6th Division, 1st Marine Division, 2nd Division, ROKs, 7th Division, and ROKs on the right (eastern) flank.

At 10 P.M. on the 22nd nine CCF armies, 27 divisions, 250,000 men, attacked across a 40 mile front in huge swarms accompanied by horns, bugles, and flares. The main attacks were in the west (six armies) and central (three armies) regions. I Corps was on Line Kansas at the Imjin River. In this sector the CCF hit the British Brigade, stretched out over a 9 mile front, isolating the battalions, surrounding a Belgian battalion. The British held however and took a heavy toll of Chinese.

To the right of the British, the 65th Regiment of the 3rd Division was also struck and two battalions forced back several miles.

Further east the Turkish Brigade was isolated into battalions but these disintegrated, the Turks retreating without much of a fight, leaving a large gap in the front. On their right one regiment of the 25th Division was attacked but held. Here massed artillery caused heavy CCF casualties.

In the IX Corps sector the ROK 6th Division turned and ran leaving a 10 mile gap to the left of the Marines. Behind the ROKs however, the 92nd Field Artillery Battalion formed a defensive perimeter and waited. They were joined on their southern flank by the First Marines and on the northern flank by the Seventh Marines as the Marine Division pulled back to Line Kansas.

In the X Corps sector NKPA troops attacked the ROK 5th and 7th Divisions which were on the move at the time.

Several of the ROK regiments gave way but X Corps held and moved back to Line Kansas, tying in with IX Corps.

On the first day the major crises were the predicament of the British Brigade and the need to hold Kapyong, a key road center behind the ROK 6th Division.

One U.S. and one British battalion managed to extricate the Belgian battalion but on the left of the British line, the Gloucester battalion was exposed due to a three mile withdrawal by the ROK 1st Division. A counterattack by a ROK battalion supported by 22 U.S. tanks temporarily restored the line to the left of the Gloucesters. A Filipino battalion was sent to rescue the Gloucesters but turned back due to a misunderstanding. Two 3rd Division battalions were also ordered to join the Filipinos but a massive attack on the ROK 1st Division forced the ROKs back one mile and the three battalions sent to rescue the Gloucesters were diverted to the ROK 1st Division sector. Four British battalions held their ground, throwing back every assault, inflicting enormous casualties on the CCF, but their own losses mounted and their situation became precarious.

One regiment of the 3rd Division was partially overrun as was one regiment of the 25th Division. By the morning of April 25, I Corps was no longer able to hold Line Kansas, and orders were given to withdraw. Three of the British battalions were able to fight their way through, but the Gloucester Battalion was cut off and surrounded. A pitiful rescue force of 4 tanks was sent but was not able to help. Three of the four Gloucester companies tried to fight their way out to the south, but were all killed or captured. One company moved north, then west, then south, and met an ROK rescue force with 15 tanks. Only 50 of the 800 Gloucesters escaped.

In the IX Corps Sector, the gap in the line caused by the ROK 6th Division collapse was plugged on the right by the 92nd Field Artillery Battalion supported by Marines. The only other obstacle to CCF moves to the south was the Commonwealth Brigade at Kapyong, where Australian and Canadian battalions were dug in.

The Australians were hit hard but held with the aid of U.S. tanks. The Canadians were also attacked, but drove the CCF back with the aid of New Zealand and U.S. artillery.

The 5th Cavalry Regiment arrived on the 24th to reinforce the Brigade, but Kapyong was safe.

The Chinese attacked the 92nd FA Battalion but these artillerymen were dug in and waiting and they pulverized the Chinese that attacked them. Marine tanks arrived and the 92nd perimeter was secured. The IX Corps front was stabilized by April 25.

Van Fleet pulled back I Corps to prepared positions on Line Lincoln north of Seoul. The withdrawal was orderly except for the rearguard units. The 7th Regiment of the 3rd Division held the rear in one sector and managed to disengage with some courageous and vicious fighting. The 5th Regiment of the 24th Division was not so fortunate as the road to the rear was cut by the Chinese. In a fighting withdrawal, there was another gauntlet, and 800 men were lost along with 13 howitzers, 60 vehicles, and 7 tanks.

By the twenty-ninth, Eighth Army had pulled back about 35 miles into Line Lincoln where defenses were formidable (in the western sector). Van Fleet hoped the CCF would continue to attack but after a few local attacks their spring offensive was over. The Chinese had lost 70,000 men to 7,000 for Eighth Army. The retreat had been planned, but was still a retreat with all the problems of retrograde movements. The defensive lines had been thinly manned and could not be held against the kind of massive, damn the casualties attacks by the Chinese. Heavy weapons, armor and artillery took a huge toll on the attackers but could not cover every yard of the front. The U.S. was pleased with the results, as they proved Eighth Army capable of withstanding the worst the Chinese could deliver. This, certainly, was progress. However, with all the agonies of the units overrun, cut off, surrounded, and ambushed, it is hard to call the battle a victory. Usually a retreat is considered a defeat. It was a magnificent achievement by Eighth Army which was now a fine, veteran, well led force. This was Ridgeway's Army.

The Last Chinese Offensive

Van Fleet expected another Chinese offensive in the Seoul or western area. He then began to beef up his defenses in the center where (like the Fifth Offensive) a breakthrough would threaten Seoul. He therefore brought the 7th Division from the east (X Corps) to join IX Corps. The Marines were reassigned to X Corps. They were now led by General Thomas, who had replaced O. P. Smith. General Smith returned to the U.S., where he would be renowned as the man who had saved the 1st Division at the Chosin Reservoir. The transfer of the 7th Division, however, left the eastern section of the front defended only by ROKs. An attack in the east through mountainous terrain was not considered likely.

On May 4, Van Fleet ordered each division to establish a line of outposts in front of the main defenses. These served as a warning in the event of attack, but those men manning outposts were themselves in some danger, although some of the outposts were of battalion size. A vigorous series of patrols from these outposts were made to try to maintain contact with the Chinese, but the CCF had again pulled back.

On May 7, the ROKs began an offensive in the east and moved forward in most sectors against light resistance. Patrols found no CCF anywhere, and on May 12 Van Fleet planned to resume the offensive. The Third Division was kept in reserve behind Seoul where Van Fleet expected the next Chinese offensive. Soon, however, there were obvious signs of a massive CCF buildup. Thousands of CCF vehicles were spotted by U.S. aircraft. New CCF armies were reported massing in the Iron Triangle in central Korea. Five CCF armies, 150,000 men were reported in the Hwachon Reservoir area in eastern Korea. These were too far east to menace Seoul and presented a threat to X Corps.

From left to right, X Corps (still under Ned Almond) consisted of the 1st Marine Division, 2nd Division, ROK 5th, and ROK 7th Divisions in a line running northeast to Inje in hills 2,000 feet high. East of the ROK 7th, the line was manned by ROK 3rd, 9th, and Capitol Divisions. Van Fleet ordered a halt to the offensive and Eighth Army began to dig in. Masses of CCF were seen moving toward the 2nd Division. The CCF actually massed two armies north of the 2nd Division and three (nine divisions) opposite the ROK 5th and 7th Divisions. Three NKPA corps were poised to strike the ROK 3rd and 9th Divisions.

On the night of May 16, 175,000 men swept down on X Corps. Most of the ROK regiments in the 5th, 7th, 9th, and 3rd Divisions folded within a few hours, running to the rear minus much of their equipment. Second Division was exposed on the north and east and was in danger, but fought hard, held on, and caused enormous CCF casualties.

Almond and Van Fleet conferred and agreed to use the 3rd Division, the only Eighth Army Reserve, to stop the breakthrough. Almond planned to put whole regiments in separate places on key roads. The enemy would have to stop and destroy the regiments before pushing on, but a U.S. regiment could hold off a large force of Chinese and buy valuable time. Van Fleet was determined to hold his positions if at all possible. Retreat is inevitably costly and is held in low regard by American commanders.

Almond was forced to move the 2nd Division back about ten miles to Hangye. Some units had to fight to get back and there were losses, some 500 men (believed mostly captured) and many vehicles. The First Marine Division bent its line back to tie in with the 2nd Division. Units of the Third Division arrived and took positions to the east of the 2nd Division. There was still a gap between the 3rd Division and the Capital Division on the coast. The enemy were much surprised to run into the 3rd Division this far east. By May 20 the X Corps front had stabilized and the last major Chinese offensive ran out of steam. Almond then asked for the 187th Airborne Regiment (in IX Corps reserve) to launch an offensive to cut the supply lines of the enemy east and south of Third Division.

Van Fleet and Ridgeway agreed, as a major CCF attack in the west was no longer expected. Van Fleet and Ridgeway then planned a general offensive across the entire front.

On May 20, I and IX Corps started moving north again, but slowly, in rugged terrain and bad weather. X Corps attacked on May 23. The Third Division attacked to the northeast and the 187th (attached to the 2nd Division) would attack further north to seal off all the enemy that had broken through the ROKs. The 187th was counted on to reach the coast at Kansong. Two of the four ROK divisions were reformed and X Corps moved strongly northeast, but not in time to trap Chinese and NKPA in significant numbers.

As Eighth Army moved north Chinese troops began to defect or surrender in large numbers. Many were sick and under nourished, and their morale was very low.

Almond and Van Fleet wanted another amphibious landing and an all out offensive but Ridgeway called a halt to X Corps attacks before their forces were spread out all over North Korea. After this last CCF offensive, Van Fleet believed the Chinese had been smashed, having suffered another 70,000 casualties in this last offensive (to 4,000 U.S. and 5,000 other UN casualties). The Chinese were hurt but they could always find more men. Ridgeway, on May 30, informed the JCS that final objectives would soon be reached and that it was a good time to pursue a diplomatic solution.

The patchwork UN Army had stopped and defeated the armies of North Korea and Communist China. The U.S. Divisions (1st Cavalry, 2nd, 3rd, 7th, 24th, 25th, and 1st Marine), a mere seven divisions, with other supporting U.S. and UN units, and a poor ROK army, had won, incredibly, miraculously, against the massed armies of Asia; however, the killing wasn't over and the memory of the days of horror and anguish could never be erased.

The Last UN Offensives, 1951

From June until the end of offensives in October, the Eighth Army advance was intermittent as the only objective was to reach good defensive positions. On June 3, the offensive commenced with two objectives, the formerly held positions in the Iron Triangle, and the "Punchbowl" in eastern Korea. The Punchbowl was ten miles north of Marine lines and presented excellent defensive positions. The word "Punchbowl" was used by the Marines to describe a volcanic crater several miles wide and perhaps five to ten miles long (north to south). I and IX Corps advanced slowly over one strongly defended hill after another in bad weather. All thoughts of a vanquished enemy faded. Once the offense slowed, the Chinese and North Koreans dug into the hills, constructing positions that were unaffected by air strikes or artillery. Once a fluid war of mobility was lost, the advance became very very costly. By June 10, the First Marine Division, flanked by two ROK divisions was stalled short of the Punchbowl.

On June 11, the Korean Marine Regiment (KMCs) launched a night attack on the enemy line south of the Punchbowl, caught the NKPA asleep, and destroyed them. The Marines were then able to reoccupy Line Kansas overlooking the Punchbowl from the south.

During the summer most of the Marine veterans of the first year of fighting were replaced as officers generally served ten months and enlisted men 12 months. On July 15, Almond was replaced by General Byers in command of X Corps.

The Marines were replaced by the 2nd Division which was ordered to advance to the hills north of the Punchbowl. These hills, 3,000 feet in elevation, were formidable and strongly fortified, and soon received the names Bloody Ridge and Heartbreak Ridge. The Marines were returned to the right (east) of the 2nd Division on August 23 and attacked along the eastern side of the Punchbowl. Six hundred men fell just taking one hill. By the end of August the Marines and 2nd Division were on the hills north of the Punchbowl and there the advance was cancelled. Some 6,400 casualties had occurred over 10 miles of rugged hills.

The Marines made one more attack on a range of mountains running up to 3,500 feet with a wide valley in front, very good defensive positions. During this attack in early fall the Marines did make some progress but casualties were high and the attack was called off.

On October 3, I Corps attacked, advancing six miles in 16 days at the cost of 4,000 men, most in the 1st Cavalry Division. Then I Corps was ordered to halt and dig in. The casualties in the August to October period were terrible and the Allies wanted an end to the ghastly war.

From 1951 to the end of the war in July 1953, fighting occurred at times at various places. The casualty figures indicate the combat to have been far less than in 1950/51 but still significant. There were outpost and patrol actions and an occasional frontal assault with some vicious fights.

The Truce Talks

Discussions with the Russians in June, 1951, regarding peace, finally resulted in a radio message from Peking on June 25, discussing the possibility of peace. Soon afterward the Russians suggested a meeting of the opposing forces on the battlefield. On June 30, a U.S. statement was delivered by Ridgeway by radio proposing a meeting on a hospital ship. On July 1, the Communists replied, suggesting the place be Kaesong (behind enemy lines). Junior delegates met on July 8 and senior delegates on July 10. The UN team was headed by Ridgeway's naval commander, Turner Joy. The main topic was location of the truce line. UN Secretary General Trygve Lie and U.S. Secretary of State Dean Acheson had both carelessly stated the truce line should be at or near the 38th Parallel, but the JCS and Ridgeway had planned for months to occupy (and were already into) good positions north of the parallel and southwest along the Imjin River, south of the parallel. The Communists accused the negotiators of bad faith and the talks stalled until the enemy walked out on August 23, not to resume until late October.

On October 25, truce talks continued at Panmumjon, east of Kaesong within sight of UN lines, a truly neutral site (actually in no mans land between the lines). A final agreement on the truce line was made on November 27. Military actions continued but on a limited scale.

The next two issues were the armistice and exchange of POWs. When the UN refused to force unwilling Communist prisoners to return, the Communist negotiators walked out again on April 28, 1952. Talks resumed but there were no major agreements. In 1953 the U.S. had a new president, Dwight Eisenhower, who added new impetus. Joe Stalin died on March 5, 1953, and the new Russian leader, Georgi Malenkov also added fresh prospects. On March 28, the Communists agreed to an exchange of sick and wounded prisoners. Still there was no final agreement. On May 13, the Far East Air Force bombed North Korean dams to flood the rice paddies. The Chinese retaliated on May 25 with an offensive that overran some ROK positions, but talks continued. When President Rhee of South Korea balked, the Chinese struck again on June 26. The final agreements were reached at Panmumjon at 10 A.M. on July 27 and the guns fell silent. The war was over.

U.S. casualties were 54,000 dead, 103,000 wounded, 3,600 prisoners. After June of 1951, U.S. casualties were 12,000 dead, 51,000 wounded. 945 British prisoners, many of them Gloucesters, were recovered. Over 12,000 UN prisoners, many of them ROKs, were returned. Over 75000 (only 5000 were Chinese) Communist prisoners were returned.

Total enemy casualties were estimated at 900,000 Chinese and 500,000 NKPA.

There were 17,000 UN casualties (non U.S. and ROK) and a Pentagon estimate of 850,000 ROK casualties but this figure has to be wild as ROK troops would run away and be reorganized later. Civilian casualties had been high also and the whole peninsula of Korea had been ravaged from one end to the other.

What We Learned in Korea

The Korean War was an agony for the Americans who fought there, much more so than should have been. The men of the 24th Division, thrown in piecemeal to stop the NKPA, were sacrificed. The battles in the Pusan perimeter were brutal with a thin line of Americans trying to set up a defense.

In North Korea, 600 men of the Eighth Cavalry died at Unsan fighting to the last man. The First Marine Division had to fight its way to the coast after being isolated west of the Chosin Reservoir with the loss of 10,500 men. One thousand men of Task Force MacLean perished, trapped east of the Reservoir. The 2nd Division, holding the Eighth Army rear ran a gauntlet at Kunu, losing 3,000 men. At Hoengson (Massacre Valley), the Dutch and 38th Regiment were cut off and chopped up trying to get back, losing 1760 men. 90 men of the 5th Cavalry, riding on tanks, were deserted by Crombez in the attempt to relieve Chipyong. The 5th Regiment, another rear guard, lost 800 men when cut off on Line Kansas. The 2nd Division lost 500 men when cut off near Hangye. Countless units were overrun, surrounded, or survived only after vicious fights. The story of the first year of the Korean War is full of tragic incidents such as the above, all involving the death of many a fine U.S. soldier or marine.

The perimeter at Pusan was saved time and again by two magnificent regiments.

The 27th, the famous Wolfhounds, fought like devils with matchless skill. The 5th Marines arrived with tanks, artillery, and their own air support. These veteran troops lifted American spirits with huge victories not unlike Belleau Wood or Guadalcanal from whence their reputation sprang. The Marine Corp maintains combat efficiency between wars, an achievement the army has had difficulty doing (until Vietnam and more recently, Iraq). Harry Truman's attempt to abolish the Corps was a serious blunder.

Truman must be held responsible for the weak foreign policy in the Far Eastern Area which encouraged the North Koreans to attack. His worst mistake however was the miserly budget which destroyed the army and resulted in much of the misery described above. Truman's failure to build up the forces in Korea as required by MacArthur and as recommended by his Secretary of State brought down upon him the wrath of MacArthur, which was publicly demonstrated throughout his involvement in the war.

Truman was called courageous for deciding to fight to stop the North Koreans. He did only what had to be done, what everyone around him advised. MacArthur has been criticized for recommending the use of poor U.S troops. Again, he did what he had to do to stop what might have been the first of many

Communist efforts at expansion. MacArthur asked for eight divisions to meet the NKPA but did not get them. Only Eisenhower and Ridgeway were astute enough to urge immediate mobilization at the start of the war. Dean Acheson, Truman's Secretary of State, had urged massive military measures even before the war to counter the dangerous increase in Communist power, but Truman did not react until the Chinese intervened. Truman wanted to consider the war as a "Police Action" and sent Americans to fight with inadequate forces. If the draft had been incorporated immediately upon outbreak of the war, the necessary forces could have been supplied, at least in time to oppose the Chinese.

In November, when the Chinese attacked, the seven U.S. divisions were not enough. ROK troops were used but many of their divisions were unreliable. A 500,000 man U.S. army was required. Few thought the U.S. forces adequate to deal with the Chinese. MacArthur insisted until he was fired that his forces were inadequate and that the effort against China was also not sufficient. He was right. There is no substitute for victory. The two frustrating years of truce talks indicate the problems of dealing with an enemy who has not been beaten.

MacArthur clashed with Truman to an extreme, making it difficult for those under and above him to manage effectively. He was right about needing a maximum effort but wrong in his insistence on an all out war with China. Bradley said we did not want a war with China on mainland Asia particularly at this time. We did not want to crush China-too much land, too many people, costing us too much. We did want to recover South Korea, and that should have been the definition of victory. Once thrown out of North Korea, and after being involved in war with Chinese armies, it was foolish to think of going back to the Yalu, there to try to defend 450 miles of terrible terrain, when a narrow 150 mile defensive barrier was available in several locations near or north of the 38th Parallel.

The U.S. gambled with forces which were sufficient to stop the NKPA but not the Chinese. Truman was lucky that he did not have a disaster in Korea. MacArthur's unfortunate rush into North Korea and Almond's dispersion of his X Corps forces were costly decisions. The advance into North Korea should have been orderly with units in contact with each other and divisions intact. The rush to the Yalu occurred even after considerable evidence of Chinese intervention. The Communists were beaten however; the U.S./UN Army was victorious, but at high cost and due in no small measure to the skill of Ridgeway and the dedication of the American fighting man, officer and enlisted.

Korea provided one huge lesson, the need to maintain adequate armed forces. U.S. possession of the atomic bomb had led to a belief that no other force was required, but with an atomic stalemate, conventional aggression became a real threat. The U.S. started to build up during the Korean War and had well trained and well equipped forces for the next crisis—Vietnam.

Chapter VIII
Vietnam, 1965–1975

The Crisis

After World War II, French Indo-China was returned to France. Indo-China consisted of Laos, Cambodia, and the larger, more populated Vietnam. During World War II the Vietnamese resisted Japanese occupation led by a communist, Ho Chi Minh. When Ho realized that Vietnam would be returned to France after WW II, he gathered his guerrillas together in a force called the Viet Minh, and began to fight the French. The French held their own until 1954, but in May of that year a French army of 16,000 men was surrounded at Dien Bien Phu. The Viet Minh had artillery and managed to neutralize the French airstrip, overrun French outer works, and shrink the perimeter, making air supply impossible. Reinforcements could not get through by land and the trapped army was forced to surrender. Only 3,000 men from this army ever came back. In the summer of 1954 Groupement Mobile 100 was trapped in the Central Highlands near An Khe. The French fought through numerous road blocks on Route 19, trying to get to the coast, but failed. The last survivors were massacred at Chu Dreh Pass. France was through fighting and peace talks were initiated in Geneva. In the Geneva Accords of 1954, Laos and Cambodia were given freedom under neutral governments. Vietnam was split into a communist north and a non-communist south with provisions for nationwide elections in two years.

A 10 kilometer wide demilitarized zone (DMZ) was created between the two sections of Vietnam, north of the city of Quang Tri. North Vietnam was led by Ho Chi Minh, and the south by Ngo Dinh Diem, a Catholic. South Vietnam was composed of many nationalities, many religions, several parties, and a number of sects. Diem managed eventually to offend most of the various groups until he was killed in a coup in 1963. For the next two years there were numerous coups and coup attempts until one of the generals emerged as a fairly steady premier, Nguyen Van Thieu, in June, 1965.

Soon after the Geneva Accords, communist unrest began in South Vietnam. Political cadres had been left there and in 1959 southern ex-patriots were sent from north to south to create a guerrilla organization in rural villages and hamlets. By 1960 this organization (controlled from the north and called the National Liberation Front) was rapidly gaining influence by persuasion, abduction, and murder. Primary victims were village leaders, government officials, or teachers and in 1964 alone there were 1,795 murders and 9,554 abductions. Murders increased each year and by 1969 6,000 people were killed. The Vietnamese communist insurgents became known as the Viet Cong (VC) and were called VC long after many in their ranks were North Vietnamese regulars (NVA).

In 1961 the VC began operating in small military units by capturing and temporarily occupying Phuoc Vinh, the capital of Phuoc Long Province (north of Saigon on the Cambodian border) where they decapitated the province chief. President Kennedy reacted by increasing the number of U.S. military advisers to the Army of the Republic of South Vietnam (ARVN). Some of these were Special Forces (Green Berets) whose exploits would become legendary. As VC activity increased the ARVN was expanded and the U.S. sent more advisers, reaching 16,000 in number by the end of 1963. The U.S. wished to avoid the concept of invasion by foreign troops by enabling the South Vietnamese to do the fighting and pacification of their own country.

Communism had already spread from Russia to Eastern Europe, China, North Korea, Cuba, and North Vietnam. Communist domination of more and more of the world's nations threatened the world balance of power which involved not just military power but economic influence and the well being of all free people. There was a domino effect, and like cancer communism had to be stopped at the source. The expansion into South Korea had been turned back but in South Vietnam the U.S. would be tested again. Failure to react would open the flood gates and encourage communist uprisings everywhere.

In early 1964 the ARVN had 192,000 men in nine divisions, one airborne brigade, one marine brigade, and four ranger battalions. They also had 181,000 men in Popular Forces (hamlet defense) and in Regional Forces (general province defense) with another 18,000 in 25 Special Forces outposts along the borders. They had 190 old aircraft but the U.S. provided 140 new planes and 248 new helicopters. In general the ARVN lacked combat proven officers and non-commissioned officers, and an outstanding performance could not be expected.

In June of 1964, General William Westmoreland assumed command of the Military Assistance Command in South Vietnam (MACV) reporting to Admiral U.S. Grant Sharp, Pacific Theatre Commander. General Earle (Bus) Wheeler was Chairman of the Joint Chiefs of Staff and General Maxwell Taylor became Ambassador. President Kennedy had been assassinated and Lyndon Johnson was President with Robert S. McNamara as Secretary of Defense. In August North Vietnamese patrol boats attacked two U.S. destroyers in the Gulf of Tonkin. The destroyers were not damaged and the Navy retaliated, but President Johnson used the incident to obtain Congressional authority to take certain military actions against North Vietnam. This was the start of a series of decisions related to the direct use of U.S. forces.

When General Westmoreland assumed command he had to contend with a guerrilla war and to develop a strategy for it. He planned to pacify the countryside outward from key cities into an ever expanding zone, starting with military activities-clearing the enemy from an area, securing the area with outposts and patrols, searching for enemy bases and destroying the enemy and their bases. (Search and destroy was a term much used by the media often suggesting needless killing of civilians.) Once the VC were cleared from an area the South Vietnamese government was expected to send in people for government and defense to complete the act of pacification. South Vietnamese efforts at pacification however were slow and inefficient by personnel who were inexperienced, corrupt, or inept. These plans had some success originally, more later when U.S. troops became involved, and more still after the 1968 Tet Offensive. There was never a time, however, when some guerrilla activity would not occur. In addition to military problems there was continuous civilian unrest with riots, protests, and coups. All this seemed to indicate a lack of progress to the American public.

Westmoreland never had the freedom to make decisions that would be considered normal for a military commander as many were made in Washington. U.S. combat units were originally prohibited from engaging in combat; targets for bombing were selected in Washington, etc, etc. Reasons for such control included diplomatic, political, and military concepts obtained from bureaucrats unfamiliar with the principles of war.

In late 1964 VC terrorist activities grew considerably. A U.S. bomber was shot at while landing, then exploded and set off numerous bomb explosions at the Bien Hoa airport north of Saigon. On November 1, the VC shelled the airport with mortars, killing six men, destroying five B-57 bombers and causing heavy damage. Several days later a snack bar shack was blown up at Tan Son Nhut Airport, wounding 18 Americans. On Christmas Eve, the Brink Hotel was blown up, killing two and wounding over 100, including 66 Americans. In January of 1965, the bodies of four American soldiers were found, weighted and drowned off the coast.

Bob Hope stopped in Vietnam to entertain U.S. troops as he had so many times before in Korea and during World War II. The Brink Hotel blast had been designed to get Bob and his troupe.

In late 1964 Westmoreland visited the U.S. for his father's funeral. Asked to talk to the Joint Chiefs of Staff (JCS), he found that Washington was considering new military measures against North Vietnam. Neither the President or Secretary of Defense asked to see him to obtain first hand information.

As the VC grew stronger, they began to control larger areas of the countryside.

The ARVN had been performing reasonably well in the early years, but in 1964 in Binh Dinh Province (a mid-coastal region), the ARVN placed small units in many hamlets, rather than keeping their military units intact. In November two VC regiments came into the province and wiped out the small units one at a time, there being no nearby ARVN unit large enough to counter the VC attacks. After this incident it was clearly understood that military units had to be kept intact to counter the big VC attacks. By the fall of 1964 there were 230,000 ARVN and 270,000 Regional and Popular forces personnel. The VC were estimated at 170,000 men, all free to strike anywhere and at any time they chose. Of these, some 12,000 were North Vietnamese.

For every VC or NVA success, there were many enemy attacks that were repelled and communist losses were high, but they kept coming. Their primitive weapons were replaced with modern Soviet weapons, and their firepower increased accordingly.

On December 27, in Phuoc Tuy Province, near Saigon, two VC regiments captured Binh Gia hamlet. A South Vietnamese ranger battalion came up and was hard hit. An ARVN marine battalion arrived, and the VC pulled back, but the fight went on until January 1. The VC withdrew but both ARVN units were decimated. ARVN losses were mounting rapidly and the situation seemed grim. Since October NVA soldiers had been sent to South Vietnam and it was later learned that the first NVA regiment arrived in the Central Highlands in December of 1964.

Westmoreland had advised McNamara in May of 1964 that the war would be long and difficult and would require infinite patience by the American people. A program to inform the public was recommended but the Johnson Administration was into the Great Society Program, both guns and butter, and like the Truman Administration during the Korean War, was committed to a policy of downplaying the war.

MACV tried in vain to obtain permission for use of U.S. aircraft against the VC and was denied until February of 1965. The first mission was against a reported VC regiment in Phuoc Tuy Province and the next was on February 24 when an ARVN ranger battalion was trapped on Route 19 near An Khe where Groupement Mobile 100 had been ambushed 10 years earlier. Helicopters finally evacuated the ARVN.

At the end of 1964 U.S. personnel in Vietnam had increased to 23,000. By this time Washington had developed a plan for bombing North Vietnam with gradual escalation, believing that at some point the North Vietnamese might pull out. Such pie-in-the-sky plans had little appeal to General Westmoreland. There was in Washington a fear that a major escalation would trigger a Russian or Chinese response. At this time, however, bombing was about the only additional move the U.S. could make.

On February 7, 1965 the VC attacked the U.S. Advisory Compound at Pleiku City, killing five Americans and destroying five aircraft. Air raids against targets in North Viet Nam were soon launched in reprisal. On February 10, the VC blew up an enlisted men's hotel in Qui Nhon, on the coast, killing 23 and wounding 21. On March 30, the U.S. Embassy was bombed, killing two Americans and wounding 54. More air raids were ordered under the code name Rolling Thunder, two to four air raids a week south of the 19th Parallel in North Vietnam. In May a pause was ordered to give the North Vietnamese time to think about a treaty. Limitations and pauses served only one purpose: to indicate U.S. weakness and lack of resolve. Johnson was surrounded by liberals (Johnson later regretted not cleaning house when he was suddenly named President), and the restrictions imposed upon the military were based upon politics and undue fear of WW III in various proportions. The missing ingredient was the military requirement which was sacrificed. The civilians in Washington all adopted the same attitude of low level military effort. In psychology terms this is called, "Group Think."

By March of 1965 the situation in Vietnam was bad, continuous loss of real estate with the VC closing in on major cities. Westmoreland predicted that in six months the ARVN would control only district and province capitals. Frequent reports of ARVN defeats came in and it was obvious, even to a concerned stateside observer, that South Vietnam would fall unless something drastic was done. There was nothing else to do but send in U.S. troops.

A Strategy for Winning

In March of 1965, this writer (a USMC 1st Lt. during the Korean War) followed news reports and neither saw nor heard mention of a strategy to win in Vietnam. U.S. troops were definitely required, but if sent there had to be a strategy for achieving a "victory." A victory such as occupation of North Vietnam and destruction of the NVA was not possible without the huge risk of all out war with communist China. We had suffered through one war against China and that was enough. A letter was composed by me in March of 1965 with a strategy for "victory" and this letter was sent to Senator Case, Congressman Widnall, and to the Bergen Evening Record. The letter stated the following:

The situation in South Vietnam has now deteriorated to the point where U.S. troops will be required. We cannot invade North Vietnam without risk of another war with China, but the next best strategy must be pursued. The overall objective has to be the sealing off of the land approaches to South Vietnam by setting up a 150 mile long defensive barrier from the South China Sea through the DMZ across South Vietnam, across Laos to the Mekong River on the Thailand border. The coast of South Vietnam has to be patrolled and the Cambodian coast as well as Communist supplies are shipped to Cambodia and from there to South Vietnam. By sealing off all approaches to South Vietnam, the VC would receive few replacements and few supplies. Once this task is completed the war in South Vietnam will wind down. U.S. forces in the land barrier can eventually be replaced with ARVN troops and a free South Vietnam can exist as South Korea exists today (there are still U.S. forces in South Korea). Anything less will create an endless war so long as the U.S. and North Vietnam wish to send in people.

This was the message sent out in March of 1965. Senator Case's staff replied with a form letter, "I don't believe the President has told us all the facts about the bombing of the Qui Nhon Barracks." Congressman Widnall's office was even more efficient, "I sympathize with your views." The Record sent my three page letter back and asked me to drastically shorten it. The war went on, and on, and on.

The successful sealing off of South Vietnam and elimination of the VC threat to South Vietnamese security should have been the definition of "victory" and a military strategy for accomplishing this objective should have been set in place with the necessary troops sent in as fast as possible to strike with maximum power in minimum time, thereby reducing total war casualties. Ho Chi Minh had been fighting for almost 25 years already and certainly was willing to fight forever if necessary. He was definitely not sensitive to casualties and would never admit he could not win.

The endless war referred to has been described by Westmoreland as a "war of attrition," and is the most inhuman kind of war. Any government that has a choice and chooses to fight a war of attrition is brutal, dangerous, and unacceptable. A prolonged war would inevitably wear thin on the American people and is a strategy for losing.

No one wanted to send in U.S. troops but all the ex-presidents and generals agreed that it was necessary. The strategy for winning described above was well known to military men (If it was obvious to a mere 1st Lt. it was certainly obvious to the generals.) A large force would have been needed (There were over 500,000 men in the UN Army in Korea in 1951 defending a barrier 150 miles long.) Unknown to me until Westmoreland's book (*A Soldier Reports*) was published, the U.S. Army Chief of Staff made a similar recommendation to President Johnson.

The U.S. Strategy Recommended

In early March 1965, President Johnson called in Army Chief of Staff Harold K. Johnson and ordered General Johnson to go to Vietnam and find out what we needed to do. General Johnson arrived in Saigon on March 5 and talked to Westmoreland, who advised that VC were concentrating in I Corps (the northern military district), and were planning an offensive in the Central Highlands to cut the country in half. The 325th NVA Regiment was known to be in the highlands since December and two NVA battalions had been met by ARVN units near Dak To. The rainy season in May and June was the probable date of the enemy attacks and it would not be possible to increase ARVN forces by then. Westmoreland told General Johnson that U.S. forces would be required.

As additionalU.S. forces were most likely to be committed, Westmoreland had earlier advised Washington that he would require engineer and logistics units to provide support facilities before substantial forces were sent. General Johnson went back to Washington and recommended use of a UN Army in the DMZ to prevent enemy reinforcements and resupply.

Westmoreland has stated that the barrier would also extend across the

Laotian panhandle. President Johnson was also told that 500,000 men would be required and that the war would last five years. The President did not at this time follow the Army's recommendations for UN forces, additional U.S. troops, or logistical and engineering units.

President Johnson, like Truman during the Korean War, and like Lincoln early in the Civil War, tried to minimize our efforts for political purposes, and ignored the advice of his professional soldiers. The Army now had no choice but to do what they could with the forces and strategy made available to them. The missing ingredient in the General Johnson/President Johnson meeting was the contribution of Secretary of Defense McNamara. He should have talked earlier to General Johnson, developed a winning strategy, and strongly advised the President and State Department of the necessary course. When President Johnson ignored General Johnson's recommendations, a winning strategy was forfeited. Every escalation, every strategy adopted instead, was merely doing the best that could be done under the crippling restrictions of a misguided Administration. Secretary McNamara chose a convenient strategy of trying to convince the North Vietnamese that they could not win.

U.S. Forces in Vietnam, 1965

Without presidential approval of the forces needed to decide the issue in Vietnam, limited American military efforts were made to resolve local problems and steady the situation in Vietnam with the hope that the enemy would give up. For the entire war, however, the huge land approaches to South Vietnam were never closed off and the North Vietnamese had free access to reinforce and resupply forces in the south whenever and wherever they wished. Westmoreland never gave up on plans to close off the DMZ and the Ho Chi Minh Trail in Laos, and that story will be told.

The first U.S. Infantry forces brought ashore were two U.S. Marine battalions to guard the big air base at Danang. They stormed ashore on March 8 in a typical Marine assault to be welcomed on the beach by South Vietnamese girls and officials and some U.S. Army advisors. Marines were used in the north where they could be supplied by the Navy without being dependant on supply roads from the south. In addition Marine divisions are large and heavily armed, and would be most useful in defense in the north. Lighter, more mobile Army units would be used over the vast areas to the south. The President gave the Marines permission to conduct operations only as far as 50 miles from their base.

On April 20, the U.S. decided to send 13 U.S. battalions and 4 other battalions from South Korea and Australia, raising outside forces to about 90,000 men. At about this time the President also approved the dispatch of engineer and logistics troops. Westmoreland thought about sending some infantry to the DMZ but first local fires had to be extinguished. Units started coming in May and Westmoreland was given permission to use them in "counterinsurgency combat."

His strategy for this limited force was to secure bases, initially along the coast, later further inland; commence offensive operations and deep patrols; operate as a reserve to ARVN and conduct long range offensives. The Johnson Administration refused to acknowledge that Americans were given combat missions, preferring to say that Westmoreland could support ARVN units when required, a very unfortunate, deceptive approach leading to gross mistrust by the press and later the public.

Early in May the first major U.S. infantry unit, the 173rd Airborne Brigade, began to arrive. That month a VC regiment attacked Song Be, the capital of Phuoc Long Province, near the Cambodian border, north of Saigon. An ARVN regiment arrived to hold the town. In late May a VC regiment ambushed an ARVN battalion at Ba Gia in Quang Ngai Province near the coast in I Corps Zone. A relief ARVN battalion was also hit hard.

In the Central Highlands a Special Forces camp at Duc Co was surrounded for two months and several district headquarters towns were abandoned by the South Vietnamese.

On June 10, two VC regiments overran a Special Forces camp at Dong Xoai in Phuoc Long Province; Three ARVN battalions responded and all three suffered heavy casualties; the VC withdrew on the twelfth.

Special Forces soldiers performed prodigious feats during many of these battles. By this time one NVA division was known to be in South Vietnam and two more were believed present. The communists were into the last stage of guerrilla activity, big unit offensives (timed to conquer before substantial U.S. forces arrived).

On June 18, Westmoreland obtained a B-52 high level bombing raid on a VC base in War Zone D, north of Saigon with excellent results.

The situation in Vietnam was deteriorating rapidly and it was obvious to Westmoreland that 17 battalions would not stem the tide. In June he stated that more troops were needed just to stabilize Vietnam, and the forces requested plus those already committed added up to 44 battalions. Westmoreland also stated that a step-up in aggression by North Vietnam could increase troop requirements and that mobilization would be necessary.

The U.S. 7th Fleet was already patrolling the coast of South Vietnam aided by South Vietnamese and some new U.S. Coast Guard craft.

On June 27, Westmoreland gathered the U.S. 173rd Airborne Brigade (2 battalions), one Australian battalion (these good troops were well trained in small unit operations), and five ARVN battalions for a venture into War Zone D where the VC had settled in comfortably. The enemy evacuated after some fighting but left behind supplies and extensive underground facilities which were destroyed.

In July Secretary McNamara talked to Westmoreland about future troop needs asking how many were needed to convince the enemy that they couldn't win. There were 175,000 men planned already and Westmoreland advised that with another 100,000 he could improve from a stabilization situation to the beginning of a "win phase." This force would have amounted to 71 battalions but

McNamara told Westmoreland to ask for more if he needed them.

On July 28, the President said that the 1st Air Cavalry Division (Airmobile) would go to Vietnam increasing our forces to 125,000 men. He said more forces would be sent, but again he was minimizing the effort needed.

The first big fight involving U.S. troops occurred near Chu Lai in August. Elements of the 3rd Marine Division had already been in Vietnam and another regiment was landing when a VC regiment was detected on Bantangan Peninsula. General Lew Walt (hero of Bouganville) sealed off the peninsula with one battalion moved by helicopter and landed a second battalion on the beach, killing 700 VC in a classic hammer and anvil maneuver.

Westmoreland, by late summer, still had only three Army brigades, including the 1st Brigade, 101st Airborne Division. The 1st Cavalry Division landed in September and was established at An Khe on Route 19 in the Central Highlands, about 50 miles inland. An airbase was also being constructed at Pleiku, another 50 miles further inland. This was the area where the French had been destroyed 11 years earlier. This was also the area where the VC and NVA were concentrating, and Westmoreland's move demonstrated his confidence in his troops. These were not occupation soldiers but well trained, well armed professionals.

The first big fight by the U.S. Army occurred near An Khe on September 18. when the 1st Brigade, 101st Division, spotted the 95th Battalion, 2nd VC Regiment. Some units of A and C Companies, 2nd Battalion, 502nd Regiment, were landed right in the middle of the VC with little available artillery or air support. Many of the officers were hit in the first few minutes and NCOs had to direct the action. By mid afternoon air support was available and by morning the VC were gone, minus 257 men. The 101st lost 13 dead and 40 wounded, but the affair had not been pretty.

Three NVA regiments, 6,000 men, concentrated near Pleiku and in late October one regiment surrounded the Special Forces camp at Plei Me. This was beaten off by the ARVN but Westmoreland ordered the 1st Cavalry to find the NVA. They were eventually located in the Ia Drang Valley near the Cambodian border. The 1st Battalion of the 7th Cavalry Regiment (Custer's old regiment) was lifted into the valley by helicopter and landed right on top of two NVA regiments in wild country. From November 14 to 19 the 1st Battalion under Lt Colonel Harry Moore fought off incessant attacks, aided by the rest of the regiment and daily B-52 strikes. The NVA retreated into Cambodia, leaving 1300 dead in one month of combat.

Enemy casualties are mentioned here knowing the questions raised by the press during the war. In Korea, U.S. units would guess enemy casualties, but in Vietnam U.S. totals were verified by North Vietnamese General Giap in 1969 who told an Italian correspondent he had had 500,000 men killed. Artillery and air power kill many that are never counted (or ever seen again); sick and wounded men die and all these are not included in on the scene body counts either.

By the end of 1965 Westmoreland had 184,000 U.S. troops including three divisions, the 3rd Marine, 1st Cavalry, and the 1st Division (the Big Red One) which arrived in the fall. He also had three Army brigades, a Marine regiment, a South Korean division, a South Korean brigade, and an Australian battalion, for a total of 45 battalions. (Only 2 of 5 personnel were infantry, the rest were support (tank, artillery, etc). At least one third of the infantry were occupied in the defense of base areas which grew into huge installations.

Combat and Buildup, 1966

Army divisions had been reorganized into pentomic divisions in the 1950s with five independent battle groups, each with five companies for battle in the nuclear age. For the kind of flexibility needed to fight in Vietnam, the division was reorganized into battalion and brigades. Westmoreland revised the battalion from three to four companies.

A brigade could consist of up to five battalions, but a division would consist of two or three battalions per brigade and three brigades per division (a brigade thus resembled the standard regiment).

The 1st Air Cavalry Division was trained and equipped to move for great distances by helicopter in minimum time. When operating in a region where VC were expected, the division would send out a Blue Platoon. These units would scan an area and if a strong enemy unit was contacted, they would call for reinforcements from their parent units, located within striking distance. The First Cavalry Division was extremely effective and gave Westmoreland the means of bringing major forces quickly into any threatened area.

Other divisions learned to search with groups, company size or smaller, then concentrate once contact was made. Concentration by standard routes (roads or paths) was dangerous as the enemy anticipated relief forces and set up ambushes. Approach to the area by helicopter was also hazardous unless landed some distance away, and the safest way to move in was overland.

Americans were committed to attack tactics and these were costly when the attack had to be made over open fields. It was standard procedure to approach the enemy using tree, bush, or grass cover, locate them, then crush them with air strikes or artillery before closing in. Fighting in the jungle on a man to man basis gave the U.S. troops little advantage. The enemy would often be very close, too close to call in artillery or air strikes. In such cases U.S. forces could either call in support fire at risk or slip back some distance then call in artillery and air strikes. If the enemy had time to build extensive defenses there was no alternative to the costly conventional infantry assault. Such previously prepared defenses could be impervious to conventional air strikes or artillery. Any defense, however, could be destroyed by high level B-52 bombing raids which were almost surgical in their delivery and at times would eliminate entire enemy units.

In February of 1966, Westmoreland met with Admiral Sharp in Honolulu. At the same time President Johnson came in to meet with President Thieu and extended his agenda to meet Westmoreland (for the first time). McNamara and Secretary of State Dean Rusk were there also. Westmoreland had been told by McNamara to ask for troops if he needed them so Westmoreland advised of the NVA buildup and asked for 79 U.S. and 23 UN battalions, to achieve a force of 429,000 men in 1966. Now aware that the administration would at least supply enough troops to win, Westmoreland was thinking ahead with the correct strategy, hoping that present restrictions would eventually be removed, and that the U.S. would be permitted to do what was necessary. President Johnson advised Westmoreland he hoped he didn't get a "MacArthur" from him. General Westmoreland, according to Nixon, was a professional soldier who performed by the book, but the temptation must have been there, to announce to the world that the Administration was badly bungling the management of the war effort. President Johnson asked Westmoreland how long the war would last, but the General could only say a few years. Any answer was only a guess. Who could say when or if the NVA would quit? The question might have been asked, "How long will the U.S. stay the course?" Westmoreland warned that the victor will be the one that fights hardest and perseveres longest.

In early 1966 the VC had temporarily quieted down after their 1965 setbacks. The U.S. 25th Division had arrived and was stationed northwest of Saigon in the "Parrot's Beak" section where the Cambodian border was only 30 miles from Saigon. As U.S. forces were not permitted to fight outside of South Vietnam, the enemy had safe base camps just across the border.

During 1966 the U.S. 4th Division, the Marine 1st and the South Korean 9th Division, and the 196th Light Brigade would all arrive. The 4th Division was sent to the Highlands, the 1st Cavalry to Binh Dinh Province, the South Koreans to coastal bases Qui Nhon and Cam Ranh Bay, and the Marines to northern bases Phu Bai, Chu Lai, and Danang. The northern provinces were covered by the ARVN.

In early 1966 combat would be close to major cities where the VC were concentrated. NVA troops gathered along the western borders.

In January the Marines started the Combined Action Program (CAP) at Phu Bai where small Marine units patrolled and assisted in local hamlet defense. Four Marine battalions combined with the 1st Cavalry Division in Operation Double Eagle against the 325th NVA Division in the southern region of Zone I.

Also in January, the 1st Brigade, 101st Division, a Korean brigade, and an ARVN regiment searched for an NVA regiment near Qui Nhon while guarding the local rice harvest. In March the 25th Division cleared Route 14 in the Highlands. In Operation White Wing, the 1st Cavalry Division chased a VC regiment in the rugged Do Xa Hills overlooking the rice growing coastal plains. In one operation, the 1st Cavalry, with South Korean and ARVN troops, managed to surround one enemy force, killing more than 2000. By late fall the rice growing plains were free of enemy control, although remnants of their regiments remained in the Do Xa.

In February two battalions of the 1st Brigade, 101st Division searched for the 95th NVA regiment near Tuy Hoa. C Company of the 2nd Battalion ran into the VC in fortified positions in a little village called My Canh. The 1st Battalion, 327th Regiment, brought in a Tiger Platoon on the VC flank and attacked the rear with B Company, but both forces crossed open fields, losing 26 killed and 28 wounded. Sixth-six NVA were killed and the NVA withdrew but U.S. losses were high.

On March 4, B Company, 1/327, caught three NVA companies on the march at My Phu and attacked doing much damage, but A Company moved up over dry rice paddies and lost 13 killed, 40 wounded. Major Hackworth blocked the enemy retreat with two companies and the Tiger Platoon, then called in artillery. Some of the NVA escaped but 118 dead were left behind. The Screaming Eagles of the 101St Airborne learned fast and soon became an elite force. Major Hackworth was one of several outstanding army officers.

In February the Marines went into the Que Son Valley, occupied by two NVA and VC regiments. In this operation and a repeat, 2389 enemy were killed. In March a combined Marine and ARVN force relieved An Hoa, killing 1029 enemy. At this time, most of the 1st Marine Division were at Quang Tin and Quang Ngai while one third of the division defended Chu Lai base and vicinity. The 3rd Marine Division operated around Danang and Phu Bai.

Twenty to twenty-five miles northwest of Saigon, troops from the Big Red One, from the 173rd Airborne Brigade, and the Australian battalion, cleared out the Michelin Rubber Plantation, the Boi Loi Woods, and Ho Bo Woods, where the 5th VC Division had been located.

A battalion of the U.S. 1st Division, guarding road building engineers, was attacked by a thousand VC. The soldiers killed 122 enemy before they withdrew.

One U.S. company was surrounded by a VC battalion and 48 Americans were killed before reinforcements arrived. Although VC losses were double ours, this was a nasty event.

During the entire war major UN units were never beaten. Some took high losses and a number of small units lost heavily in ambushes or assaults. However, the necessity for repeated fights on the same ground with the same enemy units, resupplied and reinforced from protected sanctuaries in Laos and Cambodia, was due entirely to the tragic strategic decisions made in Washington.

In March the NVA overran and captured the Special Forces outpost deep in the A Shau Valley. This valley came under enemy control and was a dagger aimed at the northern city of Hue.

In late May, four companies of the 141st NVA Regiment were located at Bu Gia Mop near the Cambodian border at the division between Zones II and III. (There were four zones for the ARVN, I in the north, II in the highlands, III near

Saigon, and IV in the Mekong Delta, south of Saigon.) The 1st Brigade, 101st Division, with Recondo, Montagnard (mountain people), and 1st Cavalry units, encircled the four companies and destroyed them, killing 400. Six other NVA companies were spotted, but these escaped into Cambodia. General Larsen (from MACV Headquarters) came up to see this situation first hand.

In June two brigades of the U.S. 1st Division and an ARVN division moved up Route 13 from Saigon into Binh Long Province near the Cambodian border. The 9th VC Division resisted on numerous occasions over a six week period but took heavy losses from U.S. armor, air, and artillery.

On June 3, the 1st Brigade, 101st Division, was called upon to relieve the Special Forces camp on Tou Marong mountain, surrounded by the 24th NVA Regiment. An ARVN battalion came to Tou Marong by road and was ambushed, losing 23 men. 1/327 under Major Hackworth moved overland and successfully relieved the camp without meeting the NVA or taking casualties. The brigade then hit the trails, looking for NVA. The 1/327 artillery battery was attacked at night by an NVA battalion, but firing point blank at charging NVA, the artillerymen, with some infantry support, fought off the attack successfully. Hackworth set up five blocking positions while blasting NVA positions with mortar, artillery, and air, including "Puff the Magic Dragon" (a C-47 transport type plane equipped with gatling guns that could kill anything above ground in areas taken under fire, named after a song of that era). The 1/327 then fanned out in 10 groups, looking for NVA. On June 7, contact was made and there was another fight. On June 9, the battalion was called upon to relieve C Company of 2/502, also from the 101st Division.

C Company had run into strong NVA defenses, was stopped, then surrounded. C2/502 was led by Captain William Carpenter, formerly the "Lonesome End" of Army football fame. The enemy were so close that Carpenter called for an air strike on his own position and got it, but the aircraft called had napalm. C Company survived with only 12 men burned and only one seriously. Enemy casualties from the air strike were believed to be light.

A Company of 1/327 fought their way into Carpenter's position, losing 6 killed and 23 wounded in the process. C Company had 6 killed and 25 wounded. Carpenter was lionized by the press, but A Company was not mentioned.

The 1st Brigade then combined and moved forward. On June 17, a 1st Cavalry gunship came in, firing by mistake on U.S. positions, killing one and wounding 21. B-52s were called in and these were on target, killing 200 NVA. After three weeks of fighting, 1/327 marched back to base, having lost 27 dead and 129 wounded, but killing 276 NVA and assisting in the destruction of numerous enemy units. The battalion had done well and marched into camp with flags flying and a band playing.

During the summer an NVA division appeared again in the Central Highlands.

Westmoreland sent the 3rd Brigade (25th Division), the 1st Brigade (101st

Division), and the 1st Cavalry Division. These units combed the jungle covered hills, eventually killing 2000 enemy. In October, the 1st Cavalry returned to kill another 1000. Enemy plans to capture the Central Highlands were to no avail.

In August the 196th Light Brigade arrived and was sent into War Zone C near the Cambodian border, northwest of Saigon. In this area, the 9th VC Division (returning after its beating by the Big Red One) and an NVA regiment attacked a Special Forces camp and ambushed a relieving CIDG (Civilian Irregular Defense Group) company.

Westmoreland sent in the 1st Division, the 173rd Brigade, and brigades from the 4th and the 25th Divisions. The Big Red One came in with bulldozers, air strikes, artillery, and B-52s turning the jungle into a desert. This operation, called Attleboro, involved 22,000 U.S. troops and drove the enemy back into Cambodia, leaving 1100 dead. The U.S. lost 155 dead, 741 wounded.

As early as mid 1965, Westmoreland had proof that the VC were using bases in Cambodia and receiving supplies from Communist China through the Cambodian port of Sihanoukville. By mid 1966, there was also proof that the North Vietnamese had a complex system of roads and paths from North Vietnam to Laos, into Cambodia and from there to South Vietnam, the Ho Chi Minh Trail. Special Forces patrols from border camps and air raids caused the NVA some problems on the Trail, but never stopped the flow of men and supplies.

Westmoreland recommended counter measures against Cambodia, which were supported by the Joint Chiefs then rejected by the State Department. State wanted to confine the war to South Vietnam and tried to bring Prince Sihanouk to our side, even sending Jackie Kennedy to visit the temples at Angkor Wat in Cambodia in 1967. Members of the press visited Cambodia but were allowed to see nothing, and even the CIA refused to admit the enemy use of Cambodia.

General Larsen went to Washington and one day spoke to the press, telling about the enemy disappearance to the west after the battles along the border. When asked if this meant they had crossed into Cambodia, the General said there was no other possible conclusion. The reporters then asked Defense Secretary McNamara about this, and he said there was no proof. When the press told Larsen of this, the General smiled and apologized. All the politicians in Washington were marching to the same tune. All the Army could do was obey orders and turn to face the enemy in very unpleasant circumstances. Westmoreland was not even allowed to mention the enemy use of Cambodian bases until 1970.

In 1965 the U.S. and South Vietnamese navies began to patrol the South Vietnamese coast where 70 percent of enemy supplies were shipped. By the end of 1966, this means of supply was almost eliminated. River boats patrolled inland waterways, supported when needed by aircraft, thereby interfering with VC food shipments and other activities.

In the fall of 1966 President Johnson met with other heads of state in Manila. Westmoreland was invited but not consulted before a statement was issued stating that our forces would withdraw from South Vietnam not later than six months after the enemy withdrew to the north. If ever a weak signal to the NVA was needed, here it was. North Vietnam needed a military victory before negotiating. Only in this way could they obtain their goal, control of South Vietnam.

At about this time Westmoreland told President Johnson (who visited South Vietnam) that no commander had ever had finer troops.

McNamara visited Saigon again and asked Westmoreland about future troop needs. The general wanted to ask for the troops he needed to go into Cambodia and Laos but as President Johnson's policy was still to confine the war to South Vietnam, there would only be a public outcry if he asked for a huge increase. Westmoreland tried to use restraint, but advised that the NVA had sent in 60,000 men during the year, increasing enemy strength to 282,000 men. These estimates were the combined efforts of a large number of intelligence officers, and certainly included numerous assumptions, but to ignore them would have been dangerous. Westmoreland had 384,000 men by the end of 1966 and asked for a 30 percent increase.

The North Vietnamese began, in the summer of 1966, to send troops across the DMZ into the northern provinces of South Vietnam. Westmoreland sent more troops to relieve the Marines defending the northern airbases, freeing some of them (3rd Division) for action along the DMZ. Westmoreland was also anxious to maintain the Special Forces outpost and airstrip at Khe Sanh near the DMZ and the Laotian border. From here he hoped eventually to move into Laos to cut the Ho Chi Minh Trail. Again, Westmoreland pushed for an international force along the DMZ; again, it was rejected in Washington.

Ten miles south of the DMZ and seven miles west of Dong Ha on Route 9, the Marines ran into the NVA in late July. Using six Marine and five ARVN battalions in Operation Hastings, the Marines threw the enemy back, killing 900. Nearer the coast, more NVA were detected and the Marines attacked with seven battalions and three ARVN battalions, killing another 1000.

Westmoreland planned a series of strong points along the DMZ at key points where there was high ground, Gio Linh, Con Thien, Camp Carroll, Cam Lo, Dong Ha. at the Rock Pile, and at Khe Sanh.

These defenses were designed to channel enemy infiltrators into areas where they could be spotted by patrols and punished by air strikes, artillery, and mobile forces. A scheme preferred by Westmoreland would have been a continuous defensive line running through Laos but he had neither the troops or permission to go into Laos. The strong points, however, were a good start on what might eventually become a defensive line. By mid September, the strong point construction was under way.

In heavy fighting at Con Thien and Gio Linh in late 1966, the Marines, in Operation Prairie 1, killed 1397 NVA.

Achievements in 1966

1966 was the year the U.S. built up their strength in Vietnam, and in the process pushed the VC back from cities and the rich rice growing areas. U.S. bases were set up and supply networks established. The VC and NVA had tested U.S. forces and found them determined. Strong points were established along the DMZ forcing the enemy to bring supplies and reinforcements down from North Vietnam through Laos much further west.

As 1967 began, the U.S. was able to operate all along the coast and certain distances inland. (At this time no U.S. forces were sent into Zone IV, the Mekong Delta, where the VC were strong but not an immediate threat.) Forays to the Cambodian border were made but the ground wasn't held. The North Vietnamese, safe and secure in Laos and Cambodia, were free to enter western Vietnam and move east until American or Vietnamese forces were encountered. Some of the VC units had been punished but any losses could easily be replaced by North Vietnamese.

The South Vietnamese government stabilized and the country no longer appeared to be collapsing. Although the U.S. forces had won battles and made progress, much of the country's remote areas remained under control of or accessible to the VC and North Vietnamese.

Ominously, however, one and three-quarter years had passed since the decision to send U.S. forces. News and TV coverage showed the unhappy effects of war on the populace, showed every agony of U.S. soldiers, and seldom showed the impact on the enemy. Each reporter, anxious to present a story, took what was convenient, even if it was a lone VC rocket dropped near Saigon. One rocket did not affect the military situation but it had an impact on the Americans at home. Newsmen and every citizen could begin to wonder why we were fighting the same enemy units in the same territories time and again. No newsmen would disclose, and perhaps none understood, the total scope of the crippling restrictions imposed upon the services by the administration in Washington.

1967

During 1967, the American buildup continued, bringing in the 9th Division, the 11th and 198th Brigades, a regiment of the 5th Marine Division, and the other two brigades of the 101st airborne Division, increasing U.S. strength by 100,000 men. In April, Ellsworth Bunker became Ambassador to South Vietnam and the aggressive, abrasive Robert Komer was appointed Director of Pacification, reporting to General Westmoreland, with the task of pushing the South Vietnamese to move on the program.

The objective of pacification was revised from pushing out from cities to expanding where the enemy was weakest, hoping thereby to isolate strongly held enemy country.

In January Westmoreland launched Operation Cedar Falls, sending the 1st and 25th Divisions, the 173rd Airborne Brigade, and the 11th Armored Cavalry Regiment into 60 square miles of woods north of Saigon, called the Iron Triangle, a major VC base area. Fighting was scattered with 700 VC killed, 700 captured, and vast stocks of supplies destroyed. The woods were leveled with plows, then burned.

In February the same units moved into War Zone C northwest of Saigon, again, in Operation Junction City, near Cambodia. Troops sealed off three sides of the area and armored/mechanized forces moved in from the fourth. 3000 enemy were killed and only 282 U.S. and ARVN troops were lost, but the forest was too vast to be plowed under.

In Operation Fairfax the 199th U.S. Brigade and the ARVN 5th Rangers formed hundreds of night ambushes around Saigon with squad sized units and numerous other operations, killing 1000 VC and providing a great deal of night fireworks for observers in Saigon. The operation improved security in Saigon but ended up with Americans doing most of the fighting. Westmoreland decided against such integrated operations in the future, preferring to let ARVN units fight in whole units with the goal of making them capable of their own defense. (Westmoreland had been responsible for buildup of the ARVN from the day he took over MACV.) The fireworks also tended to show American TV watchers how active the VC were, even in the Saigon area, lending strength to civilian protestors who claimed there was no progress in the war effort.

Early in 1967 the NVA came out of the Do Xa Hills again into coastal Binh Dinh Province. The First Cavalry fought for the province in small or large actions throughout the year. The enemy were forced to break up into small units and lost 3000 men.

In two provinces north of Binh Dinh (Quang Ngai and Quang Tin), a similar situation existed. The 2nd ARVN Division and 1st Marine Division tried to control coastal areas, but VC remained strong and NVA kept coming out of hills further inland. In Operations Union I and II, the Marines killed 2250 enemy.

A U.S. battalion was sent into Long An Province, not in the Delta, but in the swamps south of Saigon for the first time. This improved operations against the VC in the area. When the 9th Division arrived, one brigade was sent to My Tho in the Delta in Dinh Tuong Province; one brigade went to "Bear Cat" east of Saigon, and the other brigade was attached to the Navy, operating from Dong Tam on armored troop carrier boats with armored gun boats in the Riverine Force. Five major assaults were made and over 1000 VC killed, making some areas of the Delta accessible.

In the north, on March 20, the North Vietnamese commenced heavy artillery fire from the DMZ on Marine strong points Con Thien and Gio Linh, attacking a Marine supply convoy near Gio Linh and a Marine company sized patrol near Cam Lo. Westmoreland decided to build up along the DMZ and moved the First Marine Division up from Chu Lai to Danang on April 20. To replace the Marines at Chu Lai, Westmoreland set up Task Force Oregon from miscellaneous units, which were eventually called the Americal Division.

At Khe Sanh, in the northwest corner of South Vietnam, the Marines had only one company. A base was established on a plateau, and from there the Marines patrolled the surrounding hills and jungle. On April 24, contact was made with a company of NVA. An NVA regiment was moving in to attack the base. Two battalions of the Third Marines were helicoptered in to attack enemy occupied Hills 861, 881 South, and 881 North. After heavy air strikes and vicious fights, the Marines took the hills (861 is 861 meters, almost 3000 feet high) by May 5. On May 4, the Special Forces Camp at Lang Vei was attacked, but the Montagnards and Green Berets defended successfully. The Marines killed 639 NVA and Khe Sanh fell quiet for awhile.

The North Vietnamese concentrated on shelling Marine outposts along the DMZ and planned to attack. On July 2–3, 51 Marines were killed, 200 wounded or missing in ground action. Sixty-five NVA were killed and 150 more on July 6. In September, two NVA battalions attacked Con Thien. Forty-four Marines were killed in this fight. Every available U.S. weapon was employed along the DMZ including B-52 strikes for 49 days, and by the first week in October, the NVA gave up, minus another 2,000 men.

Westmoreland finally obtained permission to shoot into the DMZ and even to launch patrols up to the DMZ midpoint (the Ben Hai River).

The base at Khe Sanh was of great value in U.S. plans as it was near the Laotian border and the Ho Chi Minh Trail which ran through Tchepone, 12 miles inside Laos.

Westmoreland planned to move the First Cavalry Division there, invade Laos, cut the Ho Chi Minh Trail, and launch an amphibious hook behind the NVA on the eastern flank, north of the DMZ. He had plans, but he could not get approval from Washington, yet he hoped the administration would reconsider.

Westmoreland was invited to Washington in November. By this time, the press and Congress were extremely critical of the war effort. Senator Fullbright, Chairman of the Senate Foreign Relations Committee, was one of many doves, totally opposed to the war. In October, 35,000 people demonstrated outside the Pentagon. On November 20, Westmoreland heard from the President that Secretary McNamara was stepping down to be replaced by lawyer Clark Clifford, who President Johnson felt was a man who would help the war effort (in this the President was to be bitterly disappointed). At this time, President Johnson asked General Westmoreland what the troops would think if their president did not run for reelection, mentioning concern for his health. Westmoreland thought the troops would understand, but Johnson's decision not to run could easily be interpreted by North Vietnam to be an indication of a weakening of U.S. resolve. A formal announcement would not be made until March 31, 1968.

During this visit Westmoreland advised the press that the war was in Phase Three, with U.S. forces trying to destroy the enemy, while building up the ARVN. Phase Four would be the phasing out of American units. Without being allowed to follow the strategy recommended by General Johnson, Westmoreland had to have a strategy for saving South Vietnam and withdrawing U.S. forces. It gave hope, and it might have worked. He estimated that phasing down could start in two years (which it did). Washington was quick to adopt this strategy, and when Nixon became president, the name "Vietnamization" was applied to it.

On October 27, an NVA regiment attacked the CP (command post) of an ARVN battalion at Song Be in Phuoc Long Province near the Cambodian border. The ARVN punished the enemy with heavy losses (134 to 13 kill ratio) and threw them back.

On October 29, a VC regiment attacked Loc Ninh in Binh Long Province, also near Cambodia, a town defended by three CIDG (Civilian Irregular Defense Group) companies, a Regional Forces company, and a Popular Forces platoon. Two ARVN companies rushed in and the VC were driven out. Two days later, the attack was repeated and again repulsed. A brigade of the U.S. 1st Division came in, scoured the surrounding rubber plantations and after 11 days the VC were gone minus 852 dead to 50 South Vietnamese and U.S. killed.

A few miles south of Loc Ninh a U.S. 1st Division battalion was ambushed, killing the commander, Lt. Colonel Terry de la Mesa Allen, Jr., whose father had led the Big Red One in WW II. Also killed was Major Don Holleder, an All-American end at West Point in 1954. The VC lost 103 dead in this fight but the U.S. toll was heavy, 55 dead, 66 wounded.

There was a CIDG-Special Forces Camp at Dak To in Kontum Province in a valley surrounded by mountains as high as 6000 feet. A huge force of NVA, five regiments, moved into the area in late October. In early November, three ARVN battalions and two U.S. 4th Division battalions were sent in to occupy the hills around the camp. Heavy fighting resulted and the 173rd Airborne Brigade was sent in. The NVA were plastered with artillery, air strikes, and B-52s. On November 17, a battalion of the 173rd attacked Hill 875, but was stopped, taking heavy casualties. The battalion was replaced but the press reported them "trapped." It took five days to take the hill. A U.S. company on the hill was assaulted several times until the NVA ceased, leaving 100 dead. Before the battle was over, sixteen ARVN and U.S. battalions were used with 73 ARVN and 289 U.S. dead to 1400 NVA. The affair was an NVA disaster.

These border battles raised questions as to NVA strategy as there was little they could accomplish. It became apparent that the NVA wished to draw major U.S. units away from the cities, to demolish a U.S. unit, hurt the ARVN, and prepare for a major offensive effort throughout Vietnam. This picture became clear to MACV and the ARVN with the study of events, captured prisoners, and enemy documents. A major enemy buildup was observed around Khe Sanh and heavy enemy truck traffic on the Ho Chi Minh Trail (highway would be more appropriate) was detected.

Accomplishments, 1967

The year had dealt major blows to the VC and NVA. Although many U.S. units were tied down defending coastal bases, cities, and food growing regions, most of the major fighting occurred on South Vietnam's borders. Press reports and TV coverage during the year focused on U.S., ARVN, and civilian casualties, and on a continued high level of fighting, indicating a lack of real accomplishment. The picture of despair shown on TV was however inconsistent with the location of the battles along the DMZ and Cambodian borders, much further inland than in 1966.

The enemy tried hard to accomplish something and achieved only terrible losses, loss of real estate, and utter frustration. He began to look for a new strategy for 1968. The Johnson Administration strategy, based on limiting the war to the boundaries of South Vietnam, however, allowed the enemy free access to South Vietnam over 1500 miles of land borders. General Johnson's recommendation to seal off the land access was not accepted, and as a result, many of the ARVN and U.S. units were tied up in defensive positions. The whole 1st Marine Division was in defense around coastal U.S. bases and the 1st Cavalry Division plus some 50,000 South Koreans were also tied down along the coast, defending rice growing lands, towns, and bases.

I spoke to a Marine lieutenant, just back from Vietnam at this time, and asked if he could see any progress. He stated that he was patrolling the same areas for his entire tour of duty.

Only brief mention is made of the air war, but U.S. air strikes on enemy installations in North and South Vietnam were applied to a maximum during 1967 and U.S. plane losses up to the end of '67 were high—670 planes! These losses were partly due to the limited routes of attack in North Vietnam permitted by Washington and to the advantages given the NVA antiaircraft defense. Such incredible restrictions were a factor in affecting even Congressional hawks and resulting in their withdrawal of support for the war.

The war progressed too slowly because of the restrictions imposed on the military, the gradual buildup, and the limitation of the U.S. forces to South Vietnam while the enemy used Laos, Cambodia, and North Vietnam as safe sanctuaries. If General Johnson or General Westmoreland raised his voice in protest as did MacArthur he would have been fired. The country should appreciate the skilled service that these two fine soldiers gave, and only regret that they were not allowed to conduct the war according to sound military principles.

Secretary McNamara must be held responsible for not presenting the necessary strategy in strong enough terms to the State Department and the President. McNamara, former top man at Ford Motor Company, later head of the World Bank, an extremely capable executive, had a disastrous impact on the Vietnamese War. His early strategy, of convincing the enemy they could not win, had failed.

1968 was the crucial year, when progress needed to be accomplished to quiet the uproar and dissent within the U.S. A key figure in this would be incoming Secretary of Defense, Clark Clifford. He had the opportunity to correct the U.S. strategy. Johnson might have listened; he did care; he wanted to win, and depended on Clifford to find a way.

In 1967 U.S. forces increased to 486,000 men. During the year, Westmoreland's staff developed three plans for going into Laos to cut the NVA supply line. One involved the capture of the central Bolovens Plateau in the Laotian panhandle by the 1st Cavalry, a westward drive from Khe Sanh by the Third Marine Division and drives northwest from the Central Highlands and A Shau Valley by the U.S. 4th and an ARVN division. The other plans used different forces, anticipating Administration restrictions. Westmoreland was convinced that these plans were workable, would have stopped the North Vietnamese from sending supplies and reinforcements through Laos, and would have resulted in a stable situation permitting the withdrawal of U.S. forces. Westmoreland, knowing President Johnson's determination not to broaden the war, and knowing of his plans to step down, could only hope that some new element would cause the Administration to see the light.

1968, The Tet Offensive

Desperate to win something, the North Vietnamese hoped to lure U.S. forces to the borders, inflict some damaging blows there, but concentrate on South Vietnamese towns for maximum impact on the people of South Vietnam, who the North Vietnamese hoped would revolt and join them. A general offensive throughout South Vietnam was therefore scheduled for the big holiday season, Tet, which begins on January 29, and lasts for a week. The North Vietnamese announced a cease fire during the holidays and the U.S. responded by nicely halting the bombing of North Vietnam.

While the enemy concentrated for this offensive, MACV planned to kick off operation York, movements to the Laotian border in the four northern provinces, occupying the A Shau Valley (where the NVA were building a road) and setting up for an offensive into Laos. Preparations for this offensive were coordinated with plans to meet the expected enemy offensive and major forces were retained not too far inland for this reason.

On January 15, North Vietnamese were spotted crossing over from Cambodia. The 4th Division hit them with artillery and air strikes, reducing two regiments to one battalion by the start of Tet.

The fireworks started at 12:35 A.M. on January 30 with the following:

- six mortar shells fired at the Vietnamese Navy Training Center in Nha Trang;
- mortars and rockets fired into Ban Me Thuot followed by an

attack by two battalions;
- Tan Canh attacked by one battalion;
- Kontum City assaulted by three battalions;
- Nha Trang struck by one battalion;
- Hoi An attacked;
- A VC company attacked the Vietnamese I Corps Headquarters;
- Two VC battalions invaded Qui Nhon, occupying the radio station;
- Pleiku attacked.

These attacks were launched by mistake one day early and warned the ARVN and MACV that more would follow the next day. Preparations were made and as expected on January 31, all hell broke loose in or near Saigon:

- 15 sappers attacked the U.S. Embassy;
- 12 VC attacked Vietnamese Navy Headquarters;
- VC attacked the government radio station;
- a VC battalion was trapped in a cemetery;
- two VC battalions occupied ARVN Armored Headquarters;
- VC occupied the Phu Tho Race Track;
- three VC battalions attacked Tan San Nhut Airport;
- VC attacked the compound of the Joint General Staff;

Many of these attacks were over in a matter of hours. The VC attacking the U.S. Embassy killed some of the guards but never occupied the building and were killed by morning. ARVN troops cleaned out most of the infiltrators with U.S. help. Saigon was quiet within six days.

In the rest of the country the NVA and VC sent 84,000 men into Saigon, Quang Tri, Hue, Danang, Nha Trang, Qui Nhon, Kontum City, Ban Me Thuot, Dalat, Phan Thiet, My Tho, Can Tho, and Ban Tre in strength. Overall they attacked 36 of 44 provincial capitals, five of six autonomous cities, 64 of 242 district capitals, and 50 hamlets. In most cases militia and ARVN troops pushed the enemy out in hours or in two to three days. Many U.S. troops were also involved, some because they were at the point attacked, others because they were sent to help the ARVN. Heavy fighting lasted some days longer in Kontum City, Ban Me Thuot, Phan Thiet, Can Tho, Ben Tre, and Saigon. By February 11 it was over except for the fighting in Hue. In this city, the enemy had direct access through the A Shan Valley and sent the equivalent of two divisions into the city. An ARVN division and three Marine battalions responded but the enemy had occupied the ancient Citadel and raised a VC flag. Twenty-five days later, the ARVN pulled the flag down. When Hue was retaken, 2,800 South Vietnamese civilians were found massacred along with some ARVN officers and U.S. reporters, a good indication of what might be expected by a North Vietnamese victory in the war.

In the entire Tet Offensive, 37,000 enemy were killed and the VC would never be the same. U.S. troops killed were 1001, ARVN and Allied dead, 2082. This was the greatest victory of the war for the U.S. and South Vietnamese, however, the impact on the people of the United States was devastating. Continuous press and TV reports of Armageddon convinced the American people that nothing had been accomplished in the war and that Vietnam was a totally futile endeavor. Officials in the Administration were of the same view. The news reports of this affair were extremely negative, and if written by the enemy could not have been more effective. Thus the North Vietnamese achieved the success they had sought, not in Vietnam where they expected it, but in the United States.

The Battle for Khe Sanh

In late 1967 and early 1968, the North Vietnamese began a buildup of forces around Khe Sanh which ultimately reached 15,000 to 20,000 men. If the NVA were to score a Dien Bien Phu type of victory against the U.S., Khe Sanh was the most likely place, close to their supply sources, far from ours. MACV was well aware of the enemy buildup and well aware of the risk but Khe Sanh had to be retained if ever a move into Laos was to be made. Unlike the French, the U.S. had the power to reinforce Khe Sanh by air or even by road, if necessary, and no Dien Bien Phu was really possible, but that did not prevent President Johnson from worrying about it.

Marine General Cushman put the 26th Marine Regiment and a battalion of the 9th Marines into Khe Sanh with tanks, artillery, and vehicles armed with 106mm recoilless rifles. Defenses were built on the Khe Sanh combat base and on surrounding Hills 558, 950, 861, and 881 South. Westmoreland added a CIDG company and an ARVN ranger battalion, bringing total forces to 6,000 men. One hundred seventy-five (175) millimeter guns from fourteen miles away were within range and unlimited U.S. air power was available.

The enemy accumulated seven divisions in the northern provinces and Westmoreland had to bring up units to reinforce the two Marine divisions. The Americal Division, two brigades of the 1st Cavalry Division, one brigade of the 101st, and the Korean Marine Brigade were shifted into the area.

The fighting began on January 21 with heavy shelling of Marine positions, and an attack on an outpost. On February 5 NVA attacked Hill 861 A, penetrating Marine defenses. After vicious hand to hand fighting, Marine positions were restored. On February 7, the NVA overran the Lang Vei Special Forces Camp, 9 miles west of Khe Sanh, using 10 tanks. At Lang Vei, ten of 24 U.S. advisors were killed. 14 got out but of these, 11 were wounded. Of 900 Montagnard defenders, only 60 reached Khe Sanh. One Marine outpost was overrun on February 8, but the post was retaken by tank infantry teams.

The North Vietnamese kept pressure on Marine positions on the hills around Khe Sanh, but accomplished nothing. On one hill, the Marines raised an American flag every morning accompanied by the correct bugle call. Helicopters brought in supplies. On the night of February 29, the NVA attacked ARVN positions three times, but failed each time. No other major ground attack on the combat base was made.

From mid February to early April tactical aircraft attacked on an average of one plane every five minutes, dropping 35,000 tons of bombs. B-52s dropped 75,000 tons of bombs. Marine and Army artillery fired nearly 1500 rounds a day. When the enemy moved in closer, artillery followed. Even B-52s could strike within 1000 yards of friendly lines. Electronic sensors were dropped into the enemy occupied jungle from aircraft at night, undetected. When the NVA massed for infantry attacks, these sensors located them, then artillery and air strikes were dropped upon them. Local tribesmen told of hundreds of enemy bodies stacked alongside trails.

On April 1, Westmoreland launched Operation Pegasus, using ARVN and 1st Cavalry troops to reestablish ground contact with Khe Sanh. Marines moving out from Khe Sahn met ARVN troops coming up Route 9 on April 6. By then the NVA were gone. The North Vietnamese lost 10,000 to 15,000 men at Khe Sanh. The U.S. lost 205. It was a crushing defeat for the NVA.

There was a C-130 cargo plane wrecked on the airstrip at Khe Sanh, shown on TV and in newspapers repeatedly. Stateside citizens could easily get the impression that air supply to Khe Sanh might not be feasible. In this way, a reporter anxious to produce a story, contributed to the undermining of American public support for the war.

To continue holding Khe Sanh, a decision was required from Washington. Did the MACV have the approval for a drive into Laos to cut enemy supply lines? They did not; therefore there was no point in staying there. Khe Sanh was evacuated on June 23 and a new base established, Camp Vandegrift, farther from the borders and NVA artillery. The pullout from Khe Sanh was an ominous sign that the U.S. was pulling out and that no further attempt to cut the enemy supply lines was going to be made.

Westmoreland launched another operation, Operation Delaware, to clear out the A Shau Valley. ARVN troops and 1st Cavalry helicopters were used with such success that Westmoreland decided to equip the 101st Airborne Division with helicopters for airmobile operations.

On March 31, President Johnson ordered a halt to the bombing of North Vietnam above the 20th Parallel to encourage peace seeking efforts. On April 1 Clifford took over as Defense Secretary. On May 3 the North Vietnamese agreed to truce talks. In May the Marines attacked the 320th NVA Division at Dong Ha near the DMZ.

The enemy had planned a new series of attacks in May, but with far less force than at Tet. The U.S. personnel called the offensive a Mini-Tet. The NVA attacked a Special Forces Camp at Kham Duc in Quang Tin Province. The attack was repulsed but Westmoreland saw little need for the camp and evacuated it. In the Central Highlands, an enemy concentration was attacked by the 4th Division 173rd Airborne Brigade, and B-52s, before the NVA could attack anything. In

Saigon small groups tried to enter the city and some succeeded, setting fires or fighting until wiped out. One VC force of almost battalion size tried to enter the city but was destroyed by the ARVN and U.S. troops. Enemy mortars and rockets were fired into the city, all this for the benefit of American TV. The enemy were by now pretty much aware of the impact they were having on the U.S. population.

On May 31, Operation Toan Thang commenced with 79 battalions searching for VC around Saigon. The bombing of North Vietnam resumed as the enemy showed little inclination to negotiate.

Westmoreland was promoted to Army Chief of Staff taking over in July of 1968. His long tour in Vietnam had been as tedious and difficult as that of any U.S. commander with the exception of George Washington. He had performed with skill and a steady determination that impressed the President, General Wheeler, and the Defense Secretaries. General Creighton Abrams was recommended by Westmoreland as the new commander of MACV and Abrams was given the assignment, taking over in June.

On October 31 all bombing of North Vietnam was cancelled to encourage peace negotiations.

Meanwhile U.S. forces searched for the enemy. Marines combed the hills around Khe Sanh until February of 1969, killing 3921 NVA. It is estimated that the Marines killed some 13,353 enemy in 1968.

By 1969 U.S. forces were at 536,000 men; the ARVN at 427,000; and Regional/Popular forces at 393,000, a massive horde. The forces needed to win were at hand but the American will was not.

Strategy Reconsiderations, 1968

General Wheeler went to Saigon on February 23, 1968, to discuss strategy with Westmoreland prior to discussions with the new Secretary of Defense, Clifford. The two men anticipated a renewed effort and perhaps removal of some of the crippling restrictions imposed by the Administration in view of enemy losses and an aggressive new Secretary.

As there were only three divisions left in the U.S. and communist inspired incidents from Korea to Berlin, there was a strong feeling that more troops should be called up and strategic goals were reconsidered:

- finish the elimination of enemy base areas in South Vietnam;
- extend the bombing of North Vietnam to include Hanoi port;
- send ground forces into Laos to cut the Ho Chi Mihn Trail;
- raid enemy sanctuaries in Laos and Cambodia;
- make amphibious moves north of the DMZ;

There isn't much doubt that these operations, if carried out, would have defeated North Vietnamese efforts to take South Vietnam.

The additional force decided upon was 200,000 men. It was not felt that all had to be sent to Vietnam but should be available so that more troops could be called upon if needed.

Wheeler, Westmoreland, Admiral Sharp, and Ambassador Bunker all called for a revision to the Administration policy of forbidding U.S. troops to enter Laos and Cambodia. Admiral Sharp felt that a decision was required immediately to proceed with maximum power and to follow the correct strategy or face the fact that the war would drag on indefinitely.

General Wheeler, in requesting more troops, distorted the need into a sense of urgency and had a negative effect on the civilians in Washington. Secretary of Defense McNamara had already come up with a new strategy, De-escalation. Westmoreland felt that McNamara's defeatist attitude had been due to the influence of those around him in Washington. His soldiers, Generals Johnson, Wheeler, and Westmoreland never changed their views on what was required, but their views were never allowed to be disclosed to Congress, the press, or the public.

McNamara, in his tour of duty, at least talked to Westmoreland. Clifford, when he took over never did talk to Westmoreland while the latter commanded MACV. Clifford quickly showed himself to be a pessimist and a pacifist. He leaned toward negotiations at any cost with one requirement, release of prisoners, followed by a pullout of U.S. personnel. In later years, Clifford said on a TV series on Vietnam, that "when he took office, there was no strategy," inferring that the military were incompetent. In so speaking, he exposed himself, as it had been his responsibility as Defense Secretary to come up with an acceptable strategy.

And so it was that President Johnson, who needed sound advice, had two Defense Secretaries who failed him.

On March 24, General Wheeler met again with General Westmoreland in the Philippines and advised that the President did not have the necessary support to change the strategy. Leading Senators Fullbright, Al Gore, Frank Church, Bob Kennedy, and George McGovern were fighting the President. Former war supporters Dick Russel and John Stennis pulled back and took a position for no increased effort. President Johnson, at this time, felt he had to hold the present war efforts because, if he increased them, he feared the public and Congress would demand a sudden pullout (leaving our friends in South Vietnam to be murdered).

The bombing halts, called to encourage negotiations at the peace conference in Paris, accomplished nothing for four years. Why should the North Vietnamese make concessions when the Americans were talking about pulling out? All the North Vietnamese had to do was wait, then take it all.

The Nixon Administration Strategy

When Nixon won the election in 1968 (defeating Johnson's vice president, Hubert Humphrey), he appointed Henry Kissenger, a Harvard history professor, to be Chairman of the National Security Council.

Melvin Laird was appointed Secretary of Defense. General Westmoreland was Army Chief of Staff and the ingredients were finally in place for making the required changes in strategy. President Johnson would make decisions only after a consensus of his advisors. Nixon would listen to recommendations, then he would decide.

Kissinger studied all the options. He heard Westmoreland's strategy. Every option from the most drastic to the most cautious were listed and considered. The only strategy that showed any promise was a major escalation; resume the bombing of North Vietnam, mine Haiphong Harbor, threaten to invade North Vietnam, and pursue Communist forces into Laos and Cambodia. Closing the Ho Chi Minh Trail in Laos was a key as Eisenhower had explained to President Kennedy. Nixon said that failure to do so was the reason for failure of President Johnson's efforts.

Nixon, after hearing the choices, decided that it was too late to do what had to be done, that he could not govern if he increased military efforts. The protests and public uproar had undermined Congressional support and the call for withdrawals was too strong. Protestors gathered in huge mobs and anarchy was possible. The only feasible strategy now was withdrawal, or so it seemed at the time.

This policy was given the pleasant name, "Vietnamization." Although U.S. forces would be withdrawn, Nixon said that he would not abandon the people of South Vietnam. Vietnamization would be combined with diplomatic efforts toward China and Russia in order to isolate them from North Vietnam to some degree. In addition Nixon planned to pursue Pacification while conducting peace talks and withdrawing U.S. forces. Nixon's strategy called for a complete withdrawal and with these words it seemed that the U.S. government was pulling out with brave words not backed by the necessary actions. Without a residual force of U.S. support troops, particularly air forces, there would be considerable doubt about South Vietnam's ability to survive. Westmoreland stated that Melvin Laird seemed interested only in the quickest schedule of withdrawal of U.S. forces he could get. Westmoreland, in his book, said after retirement in 1972 that he assumed support for South Vietnam, including air support, would be provided.

1969

As 1969 began, combat in Vietnam did not produce the major battles seen previously. The VC had been badly depleted in the Tet Offensive, and the NVA had been severely hurt as well. U.S. divisions continued to patrol and sweep vast areas, but the fighting was on a smaller scale. Sweeps were conducted into the Michelin Plantation and coastal Quang Nam Province. The Marines were still active in the Khe Sanh area, and from January 22 to March 19, they launched another operation called Dewey Canyon in the Da Krang Valley in Quang Tri Province, killing 1,617 NVA.

In early 1969 the North Vietnamese and the VC concentrated on actions that would produce U.S. casualties and the result was an average of 380 U.S. dead and 500 ARVN dead per week in February. As part of this effort, the enemy fired mortars and rockets with some ground attacks at 115 bases and towns. Nixon retaliated by secretly ordering bombing of enemy sanctuaries in Cambodia.

In April Secretary Laird asked MACV to prepare a withdrawal plan. Within two months the first withdrawal would be announced.

In May the 187th Airborne Brigade (101st Division) conducted an operation in the A Shau Valley, isolating an enemy force on Ap Bia Mountain, a high peak often reaching above the clouds, only one mile from Laos. B-52 strikes and artillery were used and three infantry assaults made before the hill was taken only to be abandoned two days later. This hill was called "Hamburger Hill" by the press, suggesting senseless slaughter. In fact it was the final act of throwing the enemy out of the critical A Shau Valley. Senator Ted Kennedy called this battle purposeless, sending American troops to their death merely to claim a victory. Actually the battle killed 597 NVA with a loss of only 50 Americans.

In March an ugly incident occurred at a little village called My Lai. A platoon of the Americal Division led by Lt. Calley massacred 347 people, all non combatants, mostly women and children. Such conduct on the part of American forces is not permissible, and the Lieutenant and other officers were court-martialed. In Vietnam women and children did aid the enemy, sometimes firing on U.S. troops themselves. Soldiers, seeing their friends killed by fire from "peaceful" hamlets become enraged and this incident was certainly not the only one of its kind. War is hell; no doubt about it. It becomes glorious only from great distances. In this vicious war butchery and unbelievable savagery were common on both sides, but Americans could seldom sink to the depths of barbarism employed by the enemy. Hamburger Hill and My Lai, however, just added more fuel to the antiwar fire.

Peace talks were going nowhere, and finally on June 5 Nixon ordered the resumption of air raids on North Vietnam.

On August 10, another sweep into the A Shau Valley was conducted. On August 11, the enemy launched 179 hit-and-run attacks to give U.S. protestors more ammunition.

If there had ever been any doubt about U.S. resolve, Nixon ended it on June 8 when he announced a U.S. planned withdrawal of 25,000 men. On September 16, he announced another 35,000 man withdrawal, and on December 15, another 50,000. The 9th Marines left Vietnam in July, the 3rd Marines in October, and by November 30, the entire 3rd Marine Division was gone, leaving the DMZ and northwest Quang Tri Province. The withdrawal plan allowed for expansion of the

ARVN responsibilities but inevitably large land areas ended up undefended. By years end U.S. forces were down to 474,000 men.

On September 4, Ho Chi Minh died, perhaps with the knowledge that he was going to win. Certainly he sent a few million others to the grave before he joined them. There was no change in North Vietnamese policies.

On November 3, Nixon made a major policy speech warning of a massacre if the U.S. pulled out of Vietnam prematurely and warning of major Communist aggressions around the world if we faltered in Vietnam. He addressed this speech to the "great silent majority" and received a tremendous response (50,000 favorable telegrams) indicating far more support than he had expected. By 1970 Nixon grew more confident and began to try to do some of the things he would (and should) have done in 1969 if he had thought the country was with him. Any aggressive move he subsequently made was received by the military with surprise and appreciation. They had been accustomed to hopeless, senseless restraint, and were pleased to see that someone finally understood what needed to be done, but alas, it was too late.

1970

In 1968 Prince Sihanouk of Cambodia told a U.S. official that Cambodia had no objections to U.S. attacks upon the VC or NVA in the eastern, uninhabited regions of Cambodia. This resentment of the communist presence in Cambodia was not enough to satisfy the right wing element, and the Prince was overthrown on March 18, 1970, in a coup led by General Lon Nol. The Communist positions in Cambodia were threatened and their supplies from the port of Sihanoukville were cut off. On March 27, the NVA sent fresh troops south into Cambodia, enlisting local Cambodians who were called Khmer Rouge. Lon Nol had few good troops and asked for U.S. help on April 14. The NVA and their Cambodians moved within 20 miles of the capital, Phnom Penh.

A Communist takeover of Cambodia would have made defense of South Vietnam utterly impossible and posed a new threat to U.S. forces and the ARVN. Nixon therefore gave MACV permission to go into Cambodia. ARVN troops went in on April 14 and a joint force of ARVN and U.S. troops crossed the border on April 29. U.S. forces included the 1st Cavalry Division and the 11th Armored Regiment. The invasion reached Mimot by May 3 and Snoul by May 5. Huge amounts of war supplies were captured and some 10,000 enemy killed. On May 9, a naval blockade of the Cambodian coast was finally put into place. The pressure on Phnom Penh was relieved, the NVA were pushed back, and VC activity in the Mekong Delta was greatly reduced (the natural result of cutting off all supply routes). At this time, the only means of supplying communist forces in South Vietnam and Cambodia was down the long, slender, vulnerable Ho Chi Minh Trail. This umbilical cord could have been severed at this point in the war, but a major ally jumped in to assist the North Vietnamese, just when they faced defeat, the U.S. Congress.

On April 11, the Church/Cooper amendment was proposed. The amendment, if passed, would limit the allocation of funds for any U.S. ground operations outside South Vietnam. Congress used this proposed amendment to pressure Nixon into pulling out of Cambodia and forced him to agree to do so by June 30. U.S. troops never penetrated Cambodia by more than 21 miles. Supplies and assistance were sent to Lon Nol, who tried to quickly build up an army. He did succeed in holding key towns and the Cambodian front did stabilize. Before the Cambodian invasion, U.S. casualties were 93 a week, and afterward, casualties dropped to 52 per week.

The Cambodian invasion triggered a tremendous response in the United States. On May 9, 100,000 protestors marched in Washington. At Kent State, a mob burned down the ROTC building. National Guard troops were sent to the college and when the mob turned on a platoon of inexperienced guardsmen, someone panicked (surely the mob must have resembled a swarm of Zulus to the young guardsmen) and opened fire, killing two protestors and two bystanders.

On April 1, three thousand NVA attacked the Special Forces Camp at Dak Seang, defended by 400 Montagnards. On April 10, the ARVN arrived and the attack was beaten back.

By July U.S. forces were down to 404,000 and another 40,000 went home in October. By year's end U.S. forces in Vietnam were 335,800.

During the year General Abrams issued the MACV plan called CRIMP (Consolidated Improvement and Modernization Program) which provided for supplies of equipment and munitions, maintenance, and air support for the ARVN following the American withdrawal. This plan called for a residual support force of Americans should the NVA remain inside South Vietnam, or for the necessary advisors should the NVA leave. This plan was the Army's conscientious attempt at saving Vietnam and it was South Vietnam's last hope. The plan, however, was never_implemented and those responsible signed the death warrant for all our friends in Indochina. The U.S. Army,however, served with honor and left South Vietnam with honor.

In spite of the withdrawals, the crescendo of unrest in the U.S. grew dramatically in the fall of 1969 and the spring of 1970. In this period there were 1,800 demonstrations; 2,500 arrests; 247 cases of arson; 462 injuries; 8 deaths; and 40,000 bomb explosions, attempts, or threats, causing $21,000,000,000 of damage and killing another 43.

College campuses were a hotbed of revolt where the war was painted as immoral and U.S. servicemen were treated with contempt. The support Nixon thought he had was not only silent, it was invisible.

On December 29, the Department of Defense appropriation bill was amended by Congress to prohibit the use of U.S. funds for military operations in Laos and Thailand. On December 31, the Gulf of Tonkin Resolution was repealed. The correct military strategy, originally ignored, was now forbidden.

Pacification efforts made little headway until late 1968. With the loss of many local VC, pacification moved rapidly forward in 1969. President Thieu, in

June, drafted all men between ages 18 and 50. All men under 38 went into the armed forces; those older went into the People's Self Defense Force, which soon numbered 1,500,000 men. This, combined with land reform, local rule, new schools, etc, began winning over the people. The ARVN received modern weapons and by February of 1970, even most of the territorial forces had them. The encouraging news about South Vietnamese progress aided and abetted those advocating U.S. disengagement.

1971

On February 8, Nixon gave approval for a South Vietnamese invasion of Laos to cut the Ho Chi Minh Trail at Tchepone. Twenty-two ARVN battalions went in unaccompanied by U.S. troops who were now prohibited from crossing the border.

Twenty-two battalions, the equivalent of just over two divisions, weren't enough; the troops weren't as good as U.S. units and U.S. air support was not as good as it should have been. The ARVN were in retreat by mid March and all units were pulled out by March 25. It was a weak attempt at doing what should have been done by the Marines and 1st Cavalry in 1968 after the success at Khe Sanh. President Johnson had had the forces but didn't know what to do. Nixon knew what to do, but protests and Congress prevented him from doing it.

On April 7, it was announced that 100,000 more U.S. troops would be withdrawn. By July 26, all the Marines had gone home. The 1st Marine Division paraded at Camp Pendleton, California, properly honored by their own. As usual, the Marines had done well, but at a price: 12,936 dead; 88,594 wounded from 1962 to 1972. These casualties tell the story of the intensity of the fighting in many a small battle that no history will ever acknowledge. When asked to hold back the Red tide, they responded and did it. When told to go home, they did, to be ready for the next crisis.

In the United States on April 24, 500,000 protestors converged on Washington and another 150,000 gathered in San Francisco. By this time it was obvious that Nixon no longer had much support for any efforts to save South Vietnam.

In Cambodia the South Vietnamese had kept forces inside the country but never more than 50 miles across the border. These were defeated in 1971 and left Cambodia. The Cambodians began to fall back.

In South Vietnam the enemy launched no offensives in 1971, and there was very little U.S. combat. The North Vietnamese were probably happy to see the U.S. pulling out and did not want to disrupt the process. On November 12, a withdrawal of another 45,000 troops was announced. By year's end only 133,200 U.S. personnel were in Vietnam.

Pacification efforts, strong for three years, had resulted in the achievement of securing 70 percent of the hamlets and 80 percent of the population. As of

1972 the war was simply North Vietnam against South Vietnam and guerrilla activities were a minor concern. This was a situation that the U.S. had wanted as formal warfare was something we could deal with, unlike guerrilla war that caused most of our firepower to be less effective. Unfortunately the U.S. could not stay long enough to enjoy the fruits of its labors.

1972

On March 30, 1972, North Vietnam invaded South Vietnam. Three divisions with 200 tanks crossed the DMZ. Other forces moved down Route 9 from Laos toward Hue. NVA forces gathered to invade the Central Highlands and to attack from Cambodia. The NVA could have waited for the U.S. to leave but may have been concerned by the rapid mobilization of the ARVN and regional forces and decided to strike before it was too late.

On April 2, the ARVN 3rd Division took a beating near the DMZ and fell back before superior forces. On April 5, three NVA divisions moved into Binh Long Province, 75 miles north of Saigon, surrounding An Loc by April 13. In the Central Highlands the ARVN 22nd Division collapsed but the 23rd Division held west of Kontum. In the north Quang Tri City was taken by the NVA by May 1. Nixon responded with maximum air and naval reactions, mining Haiphong Harbor, bombing throughout North Vietnam, doing everything possible to interfere with the shipment of enemy war material. He spoke to the nation on May 8, explaining the failure, so far, of negotiations and the need to save South Vietnam. The uproar from the war opponents was deafening, but Nixon stayed the course.

Nixon had already been to Peking and the Chinese printed his May 8 speech (which condemned the North Vietnamese invasion) in their newspapers. Nixon was on target with his belief that China and Vietnam never trusted each other and there was an opening. Most of North Vietnam's support came from the Soviet Union, however, and Nixon was scheduled to go there on May 22. These efforts to detach North Vietnam's supporters may have encouraged peace negotiations.

By May 4, the ARVN had stabilized the northern front. U.S. tanks were rushed to Vietnam to replace losses and U.S. airpower pounded the enemy in North and South Vietnam. No ships could enter Haiphong and enemy attempts to bring in supplies by rail were unsuccessful. The residual U.S. force needed by South Vietnam used its muscle and by June the ARVN was on the offensive.

At An Loc the defenders held on until the town was relieved on June 12. By August the entire province of Binh Long was clear of enemy. On June 28 three ARVN divisions attacked six NVA divisions on the northern front and on September 16, Quang Tri City was retaken. The NVA had attacked with 14 divisions and regiments equivalent to nine other divisions. Seventy-five percent of their tanks had been destroyed. Some battalions were down to 50 men and many of their troops were only 16 or 17 years old. It is estimated that they lost

100,000 men. The NVA remained, however, in much of Quang Tri Province and in the Central Highlands. As a test of Vietnamization, the NVA invasion of 1972 showed that it was a workable concept (providing that U.S. support was available). U.S. air power tipped the scales where ground fighting bogged down. Finally, on October 26, 1972, the North Vietnamese said they were willing to discard many of their previous demands and seriously discuss a cease fire. This fact they made public, and Kissinger was forced to follow with a public statement that "Peace is at hand." Nixon was not happy with the preliminary disclosure as it put pressure on the U.S. negotiators to come up with agreements and risked forcing them to make concessions.

Hanoi then began to renege on the various conditions and on December 13, the U.S. broke off the talks, resuming bombing again on December 14. The talks resumed on January 8 and the peace treaty was signed on January 27.

During the year U.S. personnel were reduced to 69,000 by May 1, 49,000 by July 1; and on August 12 only 43,500 remained. These were support personnel, mostly airmen. By December 1 there were only 27,000 U.S. personnel in Vietnam.

NVA defeats in 1972 brought them to the peace table. The ARVN offensive might have gained momentum and recovered all of South Vietnam. The NVA needed time to rebuild and at this time a cease-fire was to their advantage.

General Westmoreland retired in June of 1972 from his post as chief of staff, to be replaced by Abrams. General Weyand took over as Commander of MACV.

The Peace Treaty

The agreement signed called for a cease-fire in place, an American withdrawal, and an exchange of prisoners. It prohibited the U.S. or North Vietnam from sending in more troops. It limited supplies to those for replacement only, and established an international agency to supervise the cease-fire.

The agreement was not pleasing to President Thieu, as it left NVA troops in strategic places inside South Vietnam. It satisfied the U.S. as all personnel were already withdrawn or soon to be and provisions for recovering our POWs were established.

North Vietnam was required to respect the DMZ and the neutrality of Laos and Cambodia. If the North Vietnamese complied, they would not be able to maintain troops inside South Vietnam. They solved this problem by denying that their troops were in South Vietnam and then ignored the Laos and Cambodia restriction. Nixon claims he expected the NVA to violate the truce conditions and stated that U.S. retaliatory measures would be taken if he could get the Congress to approve. He promised Thieu that the U.S. would support South Vietnam and retaliate against major NVA violations.

On January 2, 1973, the House Democrats took a poll and voted 154 to 75 for cutting off all funds for U.S. military operations in Indochina, as soon as U.S. troops were withdrawn and prisoners returned. The Senate Democrats took a similar poll and voted 36 to 12 for the fund cutoff. This was a message to Nixon: Get our prisoners back and get out.

Nixon said the Peace Agreement wasn't perfect and it was not our finest hour.

Those were understatements. Not only would there be no residual U.S. support force, but no Congressional support for any U.S. military aid, and the enemy was left inside South Vietnam with only his word that he would respect the neutrality of Laos and Cambodia.

The North Vietnamese reluctance to leave South Vietnam was a clear indication of their intention to resume the invasion at a later date. The Peace Agreement did give the U.S. a chance to get out without the appearance of a disgraceful pullout. And so, U.S. forces left South Vietnam with 46,397 combat dead and 10,340 non-combat dead, not beaten, just withdrawn by higher authority.

The End in Indochina

In January of 1973, President Johnson died at the age of 64. Both Nixon and Westmoreland said that he was a good man, brave, and well intentioned.

During the peace talks, and even after the signing, the NVA launched numerous attacks in South Vietnam, taking 400 hamlets. Most of these were recovered by the ARVN, but, obviously, there was no peace. Two helicopters used by the International Commission on Control and Supervision were shot down over Quang Tri Province in April. The NVA moved in troops and equipment down the Ho Chi Minh Trail and across the DMZ.

By January 1973, Communist forces in Cambodia had been given massive aid, and they closed in on Phnom Penh. Lon Nol had 200,000 troops, but they were dispersed and not very effective. Nixon retaliated using the only option left to him by Congress, the bombing of Khmer Rouge positions. In May a Communist offensive was stopped with the aid of U.S. air power. Efforts at negotiating a peace involving China were made and there were possibilities.

In Laos the Communists launched an offensive, but in mid February, Nixon assisted neutral government forces with air strikes and also stopped removing mines from North Vietnamese waters. On February 21, 1973, a cease-fire was accepted.

Nixon did not react to Communist violations in South Vietnam because he wanted to get the POWs back (the return was scheduled for March 27), and so he waited. Congress was now threatening to cut off funds for the bombing in Cambodia and finally forced Nixon to sign a law on June 30, forbidding the use of funds for direct or indirect combat activities over Cambodia, Laos, North Vietnam, and South Vietnam or off the shores of these countries. This took away the last tool that Nixon could use to enforce the peace agreement.

Not satisfied with this, Congress overrode Nixon's veto to pass the War Powers Act on November 7, 1973. This act required the President to consult with Congress before intervening with our forces in an armed conflict. By this time, Hanoi was almost certain of the fact that there would be no U.S. response even if they invaded South Vietnam again.

To add to Nixon's difficulties, after April of 1973, the Watergate scandal began to undermine his influence and absorb his attentions He resigned on August 9, 1974 to be replaced by Gerry Ford.

In October of 1973, North Vietnam resumed activities in South Vietnam. Vast road networks were built, antiaircraft defenses set up, and a massive buildup of manpower and arms took place.

Congress had appropriated $2.27 billion to South Vietnam in 1973, and although MACV reported that a minimum of $1.45 billion was required to support South Vietnam, Congress cut this to $1.01 billion for 1974 and to $500 million in 1975. The message from Congress was clear, "Sayonara, adios, goodbye South Vietnam."

While the North Vietnamese prepared for all out war in South Vietnam, they continued to advance in Cambodia. By January 15, 1974, they were within artillery range of Phnom Penh, and by April 5, had taken numerous posts around the city.

Russia and China had been willing to reduce support to North Vietnam in 1972, but when the U.S. ceased supporting South Vietnam, the communist giants could see that their aid was not in vain, and resumed their assistance to North Vietnam. Huge shipments of Soviet weapons were supplied to the North Vietnamese who now faced a much weakened ARVN. Finally, on December 13, 1974, the NVA attacked in Phuoc Long Province, 50 miles north of Saigon. Two NVA divisions overcame two battalions of Regional Forces and took the province capital on January 1, 1975. This was a test to see if the U.S. would respond. President Ford was powerless to do anything, and the North Vietnamese could then see that the door to South Vietnam was wide open.

The ARVN by this time was in bad shape, short of ammunition, fuel, spare parts, and just about everything needed to fight. Trucks, tanks, and planes sat idle because of lack of gasoline or spare parts. Lacking planes and vehicles, the South Vietnamese could not move large bodies of troops quickly. The army had only 50 percent of what it needed, could operate only half its vehicles, and had only 33 percent of necessary spare parts. 4000 vehicles and aircraft were out of operation as a result. Firepower was 33 percent of what it had been in 1972. President Ford asked for more money for South Vietnam and Cambodia, but Congress voted no in the House on March 12 and in the Senate on March 13.

On March 10 three NVA divisions attacked Ban Me Thuot, the capital of Darlac Province in the Central Highlands, opposed by a regiment of ARVN and a regiment of Regional Forces. The South Vietnamese fought but were overcome in 24 hours. They were unable to respond with major forces quickly enough to do any good.

President Thieu decided to withdraw from the north and Central Highlands and to concentrate above Saigon. He ordered two divisions from Pleiku and Kontum City to withdraw to the coast, reconcentrate, and retake Ban Me Thuot. The troops could not use highways already cut by NVA and took a back road jammed with civilian refugees and minus a key bridge, where half of them were cut off. NVA attacked the retreating column and, of 18 battalions, only three reached the coast on March 25.

In the north the ARVN's best divisions held until ordered to withdraw to coastal enclaves Hue and Danang on March 18. By then it was too late to get them further south.

On March 19 a major NVA attack across the DMZ quickly overran Quang Tri Province, and as the ARVN tried to withdraw, the divisions melted away as soldiers decided to go home and escort their families to safety. The northern front disappeared. Hue fell on March 25, Danang on March 30. Panic reigned in the cities as thousands tried to find boats or other transportation south.

Few organized units could be concentrated near Saigon, but on April 9, the ARVN put up a noble fight at Xuan Loc.

On April 10 President Ford again asked for funds for South Vietnam. The only funds considered were to evacuate Americans, but the request for funds was not acted upon.

At Xuan Loc, 1,200 NVA were dead, but the defenders finally retreated on April 15, leaving Saigon almost defenseless. On April 21, President Thieu resigned; on April 30, the NVA entered Saigon.

In Cambodia Lon Nol fled the country on April 1, and Phnom Penh fell to the Communists on April 17, two weeks before Saigon. By August 23, the Communists were in power in Laos.

Could the U.S. Have Saved South Vietnam?

If the strategy recommended by General Johnson in 1965 had been followed, there is no doubt that South Vietnam would have existed today as a free nation as does South Korea. With the flawed approach followed by President Johnson, a stable condition could have been achieved, if the U.S. stayed the course.

Without venturing into Laos, it was probable that the NVA would eventually crash through the South Vietnamese unless extensive perseverance was shown by the U.S. and South Vietnam over a long period. The proper strategy was certain, but all the others involved risk and uncertainty and were not good military solutions to the problem.

Without going into Laos, a stable situation might have been possible if the U.S. could have retained support personnel and air forces in Vietnam. A U.S. army recommendation for this residual force was made but never implemented by the Nixon Administration. Perhaps, with the civilian unrest in the country, the residual force was not feasible; however. a total pullout exposed our friends and allies in Laos, Cambodia, and South Vietnam to a probable Communist slaughter. A similar decision had to be made in Korea where the U.S. refused to pull out so long as a stable defense was possible. It may have been that the people and some members of Congress wanted to end the loss of servicemen in Vietnam, and this may sound noble, but the sacrifice of our allies should never have been permitted. Once the U.S. went in, we had an obligation to our allies, and it was also extremely important to show friends and enemies alike our strength of purpose.

A total pullout was apparently the chosen solution in the Johnson and Nixon Administrations. Regardless of public opinion, no government official should have condoned or approved such a procedure. A clear conscience would have required a stand on this issue and even resignation before giving in. Congressional pressure on Nixon was relentless and every Congressman that forced him to abandon our friends is directly responsible for the horror that followed. We could try to blame the war protestors, but without enlightened information or leadership from the government, the general public can not be expected to know the complex issues in such matters.

It is incredible that no one in the Johnson Administration or Congress could see the way to go and bring this to the attention of the public or the government. Congressmen, instead of being leaders to guide the people, were followers, watching the opinion polls.

Vietnam was the lowest point in U.S. history, a national disgrace, and it followed a huge effort by U.S. forces who suffered 55,000 dead. It ranks with the English firing of Marlborough and their withdrawal from the Allied Army in the War of the Spanish Succession. Of that affair, Louis XIV said the removal of Marlborough by the English government had satisfied all his desires. So it could have been said by General Giap, "The U.S. Congress has done all for us we desire."

It is convenient to blame the press, but reporters are reporters. During the Iraqi War, the press were not given too much access to trouble spots or to controversial issues and war being what it is, this procedure is correct. If the press had known of our naval losses off Guadalcanal, the nation might not have had the courage to carry on during World War II.

The Johnson Administration could have won the war and must bear the responsibility for the results. Nixon wrote that Johnson had a limited time to make the correct moves. By 1968 or 1969, it was probably too late to change strategy without internal upheaval.

The Peace Treaty was a farce, but all that we could get once our forces were withdrawn. Talking unfortunately does not win wars.

It should be mentioned that Truman ordered MacArthur to clear all policy statements with the Administration during the Korean War. Similarly, Secretary Laird ordered his Chief of Staff, Westmoreland, not to talk to Kissinger after their first meeting.

What Westmoreland was allowed to say to the Administration or to

Congress was certainly limited as well. Westmoreland was definitely not allowed to insist on an international force for the DMZ into Laos as this position conflicted with the President's policies. In this manner the Army was effectively muted, a byproduct of the war between MacArthur and Truman followed by the firing of one of our great soldiers. If all contact with Congress was only via Laird, it is possible that no Congressman knew what the proper strategy in Vietnam was. If so, we can be frightened by the ability of Congress to make critical military decisions.

Could people or Congressmen argue that saving South Vietnam did not matter (to us) or that U.S. interests would not be seriously affected? Events between 1975 and 1980 would answer that question.

No Substitute for Victory, 1975–1980

When the Khmer Rouge took over in Cambodia, the new Premier was Pol Pot; his communist regime forced four million people (two-thirds of the country's people) to leave the cities to fend for themselves or starve in the countryside. Many were imprisoned if they were educated or of foreign descent. Two to three million people died or were executed. The movie, "The Killing Fields," is about this tragedy. Much later, travelers around the country would see countless pyramids of human skulls designed to encourage loyalty to the new regime. This is one of the worst slaughters of all time, not far behind Russian starvation of farmers after the Bolshevik Revolution or Hitler's Holocaust.

In South Vietnam another 500,000 are believed to have died. This figure includes the losses of boat people who drowned trying to leave. All this was brought about by the failure of U.S. policy.

While the U.S. fought in South Vietnam, good things happened. In Indonesia, the communists were thrown out. Cambodia came over to our side and Chinese and Russian leaders showed an inclination to talk to us. After the loss of Indochina, however, the domino theory became reality as country after country fell to communist uprisings, either instigated or supported by the Soviet Union or one of their communist satellites. Communist takeovers occurred as follows:

South Vietnam	1975
Laos	1975
Cambodia	1975
Mozambique	1976
Angola	1976
Ethiopia	1977
South Yemen	1978
Nicaragua	1979
Afghanistan	1979

Many of these countries, small as they were, were in strategic locations and presented new threats to areas of the world important to the United States. These revolutions represented a shift in the world balance of power, but the U. S. under Presidents Ford and Carter was paralyzed by the failure in Vietnam.

With Afghanistan under communist control and a Russian colony in South Yemen, there was a new risk of interference with a major source of the world's and U.S. oil supplies. In Afghanistan the Russians were only 300 plus miles from the Persian Gulf.

This author spoke to a member of the British Parliament (from Inverness) and a former MP (from London) in 1979 about the Russians in Afghanistan. The MP from Inverness ventured the opinion that the Russians had attempted more than they could handle. (England, worried about Russian expansion to the south in the last century, went into Afghanistan twice, losing an army of 17,000, including civilians, in 1842, losing 1,100 men of a force of 2,500 near Kandahar in 1880, and that same year, having another army surrounded in Kabul.) The MP from Inverness was right, but in 1979, no one could know that.

The Tide Turns, 1980–1990

In 1980, Ronald Reagan, the former governor of California, became president.

Reagan, determined to build up the American armed forces beyond any power level the Russians could match, figured that they would go broke before we did. Every new and novel military weapon was criticized by Congressmen, frequently, as expensive boondoggles, unworkable, and unnecessary, but development continued.

When Cuba sent troops into the island of Grenada, Reagan sent in U.S. forces to clean out the place and restore rule to rightful government. A communist rebellion in El Salvador was resisted with massive U.S. assistance to the government. El Salvador communist forces were supplied from Nicaragua and Reagan allowed a force of Contras to be created to fight the communist government there.

When Vietnam invaded Cambodia, China intervened, now acting as the policeman in that part of the world. Initiated by Nixon, the U.S. made overtures to China, and the old friendship began to return, slowly, cautiously. Everywhere communism reared its ugly head, the U.S. opposed it, and the world stabilized.

In Afghanistan, Iran, China, and Pakistan assisted anti-communist forces who controlled the mountains while the Russians and the communist government controlled the cities. The U.S. began to send arms and supplies to Afghanistan, including the new shoulder fired antiaircraft missile, the "Stinger." Russian plane losses in Afghanistan rose rapidly.

During the Reagan Administration, 1980–1988, the U.S. and our NATO allies developed new weapons and vastly increased power. Of most concern to the Russians was the antimissile system (Star Wars) which, if successful, would have rendered Russia's offensive missile arsenal useless.

The Soviet Union's economy began to crumble in the eighties, burdened with the rot of its system, the continuous drain of all its satellite nations in East Europe and around the world, plus the expense of huge military forces and the additional development costs of new weapons systems to match the U.S. In the mid eighties, the U.S. almost went bankrupt (according to Dave Stockman, Reagan's former budget director), but the Japanese bailed us out. We made it through, but the Soviet Union did not. The Soviets under Premier Gorbachev finally, in the late eighties, made friendly noises towards the U.S. Gorbachev came to Governor's Island in New York to meet Reagan, and announced a new relationship, *Glasnost* (openness). Suddenly, in 1989, the Russians pulled out of Afghanistan, a most significant retreat, marking the start of the decline of international communism, the first retreat since the Russian Revolution. Internal pressures were reduced to give Russian citizens more freedom. Self government in Eastern Europe was permitted and even republics in the Soviet Union were partially freed from the Russian yoke. A Communist Party coup was defeated by the failure of Russian soldiers to fire on civilians and Boris Yeltsin assumed power in Russia.

Democracy may evolve in Eastern Europe and may not occur for decades in Russia, where communists still run the country, but the Cold War is over, and the U.S. won. No one shouts for joy, but history will say that the emergence of democracy as the dominant form of government in 1989 is the greatest moment in the history of man.

The brave fights put up by U.S. soldiers, sailors, marines, and airmen during the Cold War have been a major contribution to the winning of this forty-four-year-long struggle. We held the line in Vietnam until 1975, 30 years after WW II, just long enough (to win the Cold War, not to save South Vietnam). If there had been no military resistance, the Russians and other communist nations would have overrun vast areas of the world and drastically curbed our economic status.

The American fighting men, from the Continentals to the modern armored soldiers, have done it over a period of two hundred plus years, creating a democracy, beating all opponents, fighting off all threats, and emerging supreme. No war was in vain and American valor has never wavered.

Chapter IX

The War Against Iraq, 1990-1991

The loss of Vietnam had reflected on U.S. armed forces, unfairly, and created a fear and doubt in the press and among most Congressmen and government officials about the proper use of military force, not to mention the doubts among our enemies about our will and resolve.

In 1988 George Bush became President, with Dick Cheney as Secretary of Defense, and Colin Powell as Chairman of the Joint Chiefs of Staff. These men, skilled at foreign policy and the proper use of the armed forces, were the right men in the right place at the right time, because in the summer of 1990, Iraq invaded and occupied all of oil rich Kuwait. Bush's team, using Reagan developed forces and weapons, corrected the situation so expeditiously as to prove to the entire globe that the U.S. military were supreme, superb, and totally dominant.

From August 3, 1990, to January 15, 1991, President Bush organized a 38 nation coalition for the purpose of forming an international army in Arabia. The forces gathered there consisted of 2,500 planes; 700,000 troops (including 90,000 Marines and 450,000 U.S. Army personnel); and 200 ships. Forces ashore were under the command of General Norman Schwarzkopf, son of the former head of the New Jersey State Police.

Some of the weapons employed, many in combat for the first time, included the following:

- The Stealth fighter bomber, made of graphite, not detectable by enemy radar, was used to knock out enemy radar.
- The B-52 Stratofortress made bombing runs from high altitude to knock out Iraqi tanks and artillery.
- The A10 Warthog, designed to support troops, fired antitank missiles.
- Navy F/Al8 Hornets, Air Force F111 Aardvarks, and Marine Harriers all were used to support ground forces with missiles and laser guided smart bombs.
- Air Force F 16 Falcons and F 15 Eagles, and Navy F 14 Tomcats swept the skies of enemy planes.

- Army Apache and Marine Sea Cobra helicopters, firing rockets, cannon, and missiles, were used to knock out enemy tanks.
- Army M1A1 Abrams tanks were equipped with gas turbine engines, 120mm cannon, computer controlled firing systems that work in the dark, and a turret that remains level while the tank body pitches and rolls.
- Marine M60 tanks had reactive armor that explodes when hit and deflects the blast.

Facing the Allies was an Iraqi Army, experienced after an 8 year war with Iran, with 509,000 regulars, 500,000 militia, over 5,000 tanks 3,000 pieces of artillery, and 700 planes. Most of the tanks were Russian T-62s but some were modern T-72s.

The Iraqi Army had poured into Kuwait in July 1990, perhaps without an adequate diplomatic warning of the U.S. reaction to such a move. Kuwait was soon occupied and its borders and beaches fortified. The U.S., worried about loss of Arabia, and about Iraqi control of the world's oil and energy supply, sent in a few thousand Marines and airborne troops immediately as a trip wire force, to warn the Iraqis that we would fight for Arabia, that Vietnam was history, and the U.S. was back, armed, and ready. (The first U.S. troops sent to Arabia referred to themselves as a "speed bump.")

U.S. air transport brought in division after division. U.S., British, and French troops from NATO's European Army came in. Arabian divisions were joined by Egyptian, Arab, and other troops from around the world. The Allied Army, built up over a five month period to January 15, 1991, faced the Iraqi Army across the Kuwait border.

Diplomatic attempts at convincing Iraq President Saddam Hussein to evacuate Kuwait failed, and finally, President Bush knew he would have to fight.

From the southeast coast of Kuwait to the west and north along the Kuwait border, Allied forces formed up in the following order:

- Arabians,
- 1st and 2nd Marine Divisions with the Tiger Brigade of the 2nd Armored Division,
- Pan Arabs,
- Egyptians,
- British 1st Armored Division,
- 1st Cavalry Division
- 1st Division (The Big Red One)
- 3rd Armored Division
- 1st Armored Division,
- 24th Mechanized Division,
- 101st Airborne Division,
- 82nd Airborne Division, and
- French 6th Armored Division.

This armchair strategist saw the Iraqi vulnerability with many of their divisions committed along the Kuwait/Arabia border where they could be cut off by an amphibious landing near Kuwait City or an armored thrust near the junction of Kuwait, Arabia, and Iraq. This was, of course, obvious to the Iraqis as well, as they posted their best divisions, the Republican Guard, in southern Iraq where they could strike the flank of an amphibious or mechanized spearhead into Kuwait. What I could not know, nor could the Iraqis, was the tremendous supply capabilities of the U.S. Army.

Starting on January 17, 1991, Allied air forces attacked Iraq and Iraqi forces. Stealth fighter-bombers knocked out Iraqi radar stations. Bridges, communication centers, communication links, and other targets were hit by fighter bombers from Arabia, Turkey, and U.S. carriers in the Persian Gulf, and by Navy Tomahawk cruise missiles.

B-52s from England and Diego Garcia struck Iraqi forces with carpet bombing raids. Iraqi tanks and artillery, dug into the sand were pounded, day after day. Iraqi planes were destroyed, some in the air, some on the ground, and some escaped into Iran. Finally the enemy strength was reduced enough to justify a ground attack which began on February 23.

In Washington strategy had been discussed in the Administration and in Congress. One Congressman, trying to repeat the mistakes of Vietnam, spoke of limiting the war to Kuwait. President Bush, obviously aware of the reasons for failure in Vietnam, said he would not ask Americans to fight with one hand tied behind their backs And so it was that the President and Secretary of Defense and the Army Chief of Staff all agreed to give General Schwarzkopf freedom to move and fight without crippling restrictions.

Schwarzkopf formed a 7th Corps (1st and 3rd Armored Divisions and 2nd Armored Cavalry Regiment) and an 18th corps (82nd and 101st Airborne Divisions). Then, with no enemy aircraft to observe, 250,000 troops were moved into Arabia, up to 100 miles west of Kuwait. These forces included 7th Corps, 18th Corps, the French and British armored divisions, the 24th Division, and the 1st Division. Special Forces moved deep into Iraq to reconnoiter, and by the end of the day on February 23, all was ready.

On February 24, at 4 A.M., the Marines and the Tiger Brigade attacked, broke through, and began to round up huge numbers of captured Iraqis. To their right, the Saudi's broke through also, moving up the coast. These attacks kept Iraqi eyes on the Kuwait front.

Deep inside Arabia, the French, on the extreme left, moved into Iraq to guard the Allied left flank. To their right, 18th Corps pushed into Iraq to set up huge forward supply bases for the armored divisions and to cut off any Iraqi escape to the west. To their right, the 24th Division pushed toward the Tigris-Euphrates Valley to block escape to the north.

Then, the powerful 7th Corps crossed the border, moving north to come in on the rear of the Republican Guard Divisions. To their right, the British and 1st U.S.

Divisions covered the gap between 7th Corps and the Allies in Kuwait. The attacks made across the Arabia/Iraq border were unopposed as Schwarzkopf swept around the entire Iraqi Army in one swift, devastating maneuver.

On the twenty-fourth and twenty-fifth, Saudis and Marines rumbled toward Kuwait City. Seventh Corps turned east, coming in behind the Republican Guard in a huge flanking movement over hundreds of miles of barren desert, made possible only by an extraordinary supply system. Thirty-six thousand troops and 800 tanks of 7th Corps approached the Iraqi Hammurabi Division, 800 tanks and 10,000 troops. The big tank battle began on Tuesday, February 26, with Army helicopters, planes and tanks knocking out Iraqi tanks with ease. The Iraqis were defenseless as Allied aircraft struck from above and M1A1 tanks with superior target finding systems destroyed Iraqi tanks in the dark and dust before the enemy gunners could even see a target.

The U.S. gas turbine driven tanks, reputed to be unsuited for desert warfare, were awesome. The Hammurabi Division was wiped out, leaving only one Republican Guard armored division and 60,000 men, less than half the Guard's original strength.

By the twenty-seventh, the Marines and Tiger Brigade had taken the Kuwait International Airport and blocked exits from the city. Iraqi tanks that contested their advance were destroyed by aircraft, helicopters, tanks, and TOW missiles. That day, Saudi and Pan Arab forces entered Kuwait City, an honor given to them to emphasize the international nature of the forces against Hussein.

By February 28, the Iraqis were beaten and President Bush ordered the advance to stop. Iraqi casualties were probably already 100,000 and no more slaughter seemed necessary. Their army was trapped and at the mercy of Allied forces.

The U.S. did not completely destroy the Iraqi Army. Some of their forces had to be retained as Iraq remains a bulwark against Iranian expansion into the Middle East. Enough damage was done to prevent Iraq from further offensive adventures. An advance into Baghdad to capture Hussein was never intended, to avoid offending our Arab allies who would not be pleased if the U.S. set up a puppet government. Hussein was undesirable, but his replacement would probably be no better.

Allied casualties were about 370 dead. The U.S. lost 210 dead and missing, with 330 wounded. The whole affair demonstrated the overwhelming power of American and NATO arms, and this power, certainly known to the Soviets, must have had a substantial effect on their attitude toward the West. The Russians may have come to the conclusion, "If you can't beat them, join them."

The superior behavior of all of the new American weapons justified all of Ronald Reagan's efforts to build this mighty army. Everything worked and the Iraq-Kuwait War was the proving ground. Of great significance, the Bush-Cheney-Powell-Schwarzkopf team showed the happy results that can occur in war when superior American power is properly managed. This flawless job by these gentlemen is a stark contrast to the Vietnam disaster managed by President

Johnson, McNamara, and Clifford. President Bush lost the 1992 election in a sour economy, but he should not have been surprised. The British rejected Winston Churchill after he brought them victory in World War II and for the same reason.

In 1991 the victorious U.S. troops came home and 8,000 marched up Broadway, the Canyon of Heroes, in New York City, to a thunderous welcome. Americans in that audience washed away all the unpleasant memories of Vietnam and cheered these seasoned professionals, Army, Navy, Marine, Air Force, and Allies. They wore battle dress but carried their regimental colors and they represented Stirling's Maryland and Delaware Continentals, Wayne's Pennsylvanians, The Iron Brigade, the 20th Maine, the Fifth Marines, the Rainbow Division, Third Army, Eighth Air Force, Torpedo 3, 6, and 8 at Midway, Halsey's South Pacific Fleet, the Wolfhounds, the 1st Air Cavalry, and every veteran who ever fought for this country. The Cold War was over and this was the victory celebration. Now, Americans can look inward and straighten out their internal affairs, but U.S. armed forces must never again be allowed to decay as they have so many times before. Those who do not know history are doomed to repeat its mistakes.

Bibliography

The British

Churchill, Winston S. *Marlborough, His Life and Times.* Books One and Two. London: Harrap, 1933.

Fraser, Antonia. *Cromwell, Our Chief of Men*. London: Granada, 1975.

Miller, Charles. *Khyber.* London: Macdonald & Janes, 1977.

Weller, Jac. *Wellington in the Peninsula*. Philadelphia: Curtis, 1962.

The Revolution

Alden, John R. *George Washington*. New York: Dell, 1987.

Scheer, George F. & Rankin, Hugh F. *Rebels and Redcoats*. New York: Da Capo, 1957.

The Civil War

Catton, Bruce, *Grant Moves South*. Boston: Little & Brown, 1960.

Davis, Burke, *To Appomattox*. New York: Rinehart, 1959.

Luvaas, Jay, and Harold W. Nelson, *The U.S. Army War College Guide to the Battle of Gettysburg,* New York: Harper & Row, 1986.

Pratt, Fletcher. *A Short History of the Civil War.* New York: Pocket Books, 1952.

Trudeau, Noah Andre. *Bloody Roads South.* New York: Ballantine, 1990.

World War I

Baldwin, Hanson W. *World War I*, New York: Grove, 1962.

Farago, Ladislas, *General George S. Patton, Ordeal and Triumph*, New York: Obolensky, 1963.

Fleming, D. F. *The Origins and Legacies of World War I*. Greenwich, Connecticut: Fawcett, 1968.

MacArthur, General Douglas, *Reminiscences*, New York: McGraw Hill, 1964.

Marshall, General S.L.A., *The American Heritage History of World War I*. New York: Bonanza, 1982.

Simpson, Colin, and Phillip Knightley. *The Secret Lives of Lawrence of Arabia*, New York: Bantam, 1971.

Tribune, New York, "Program, Parade of the 27th Division," March 25, 1919.

World War II

Baldwin, Hanson W. *Battles Lost and Won*. New York: Harper & Row, 1966.

Bradley, General Omar N. *A Soldier's Story*. New York: Holt, 1951.

Carell, Paul, *Hitler Moves East*, Boston: Little & Brown, 1964.

Churchill, Winston S. *The Hinge of Fate*, New York: Bantam, 1962.

Eisenhower, General Dwight D. *Crusade in Europe*, New York: Doubleday, 1948.

Farago, Ladislas. *General George S. Patton, Ordeal and Triumph*. New York: Obolensky, 1963.

Hoyt, Edwin P. *The Battle of the Coral Sea*. New York: Jove, 1984.

Leckie, Robert. *The United States Marines Against Japan*. New York: Bonanza, 1962.

Lopez, Donald S. *Into the Teeth of the Tiger*. New York: Bantam,1986.

Lord, Walter. *Incredible Victory*. New York: Pocket Books, 1 968.

MacArthur, General Douglas. *Reminiscences* New York: McGraw Hill, 1964.

Majdalany. Fred. *The Battle of Cassino*. Frogmore: Mayflower, 1975.

Merrill, James M. *Biography of Admiral William F. Halsey*. New York: Crowell, 1976.

Messenger, Charles. *World War Two*. London: Bloomsburg, 1989.

Morison, Admiral Samuel Eliot. *The Two Ocean War*. New York: Ballantine, 1972.

Pyle, Ernie. *Brave Men*. New York: Holt, 1944.

Stilwell, General Joseph W. *The Stilwell Papers*, New York: Sloane, 1948.

Thomas, Hugh. *The Spanish Civil War*, Harper & Row, 1961.

Vader, John. *Pacific Hawk*. New York: Ballantine, 1970.

Korea

Blair, Clay. *The Forgotten War* New York: Doubleday, 1989.

Hackworth, Colonel David H. *About Face*. New York: Simon & Schuster, 1989.

MacArthur, General Douglas, *Reminiscences*. New York: McGraw Hill, 1964.

U.S. News & World Report. "The Forgotten War." Washington, D.C., June 25.1990.

Vietnam and After

Bergen Evening Record, "Whipping the Deficit," July 10, 1991.

Brenan, Matthew. *Brennan's War*. New York: Pocket Books, 1986.

Caputo, Philip. *A Rumor of War*. New York: Holt, 1977.

Crown Publishers. *The Vietnam War*. New York, 1979.

Hackworth, Colonel David H. *About Face*. New York: Simon & Schuster 1979.

Herr, Michael. *Dispatches*. London: Pan, 1978.

Marshall, General S.L.A. *Battles In The Monsoon*. New York: Morrow, 1967.

New York Times, "The Pentagon Papers," New York: Bantam, 1971.

Nixon, Richard M. *The Real War*. New York: Warner, 1981.

Nixon, Richard M. *No More Vietnams*. New York: Avon, 1985.
Reagan, Ronald. *An American Life*. New York: Simon & Schuster, 1990.
Westmoreland , General William C. *A Soldier Reports*. New York: Doubleday.

Iraq
Bergen Evening Record. "Biggest Tank Battle." February, 28, 1991.
Bergen Evening Record, "Operation Desert Storm," March 6, 1991.
Newsweek, "The Allies Fire Power."
Newsweek, "Arms and the Men."
Newsweek. "A Textbook Victory." March 11, 1991.

Personal notes were also taken during several television reports on Operation Desert Storm.

Acknowledgement

The chapter on Iraq was written during the war using newspapers, magazines, and television reports to enable the addition of this story. Reliable sources were used for the other chapters, and in a long search for correct conclusions television reports were used to upgrade the material; however, there is no certainty that all of the sources are totally accurate. Furthermore, this work includes numerous expressions of my own opinion of major events and, as fact and opinion cannot be completely separated this book should not be used as a reference or a source for further historical research.